RETHINKING
MODERN JUDAISM

CHICAGO STUDIES IN THE HISTORY OF JUDAISM

A series edited by

WILLIAM SCOTT GREEN

Arnold M. Eisen

RETHINKING MODERN JUDAISM

—◦» «◦—

Ritual,
Commandment,
Community

THE UNIVERSITY OF CHICAGO PRESS
Chicago & London

ARNOLD M. EISEN is chair of and professor in the Department of
Religious Studies at Stanford University. He is the author of *The
Chosen People in America: A Study in Jewish Religious Ideology* (1983),
Galut: Modern Jewish Reflection on Homelessness and Homecoming (1986),
and *Taking Hold of Torah: Jewish Commitment and Community
in America* (1997).

The University of Chicago Press, Chicago 60637
The University of Chicago Press, Ltd., London
© 1998 by The University of Chicago
All rights reserved. Published 1998
Printed in the United States of America
07 06 05 04 03 02 01 00 99 98   1 2 3 4 5

ISBN: 0-226-19528-7 (cloth)

Library of Congress Cataloging-in-Publication Data

Eisen, Arnold M., 1951–
  Rethinking modern Judaism : ritual, commandment, community / Arnold
M. Eisen.
      p.   cm.—(Chicago studies in the history of Judaism)
  Includes bibliographical references and index.
  ISBN 0-226-19528-7 (alk. paper)
  1. Judaism—History—Modern period, 1750– 2. Commandments
(Judaism)—History of doctrines. I. Title. II. Series.
BM195.E37 1998
296'.09'03—dc21   97-41695
                                                                              CIP

⊗ The paper used in this publication meets the minimum requirements of
the American National Standard for Information Sciences—Permanence of
Paper for Printed Library Materials, ANSI Z39.48-1992.

Frontispiece: *La Liberté des cultes*. Musée Carnavalet, Paris. © Photothèque
des Musées de la Ville de Paris. Photo: Olivier Habouzet.

For my teachers

The impetus to this study came on the first day of Sukkot about seven years ago, when I stood in a synagogue in Philadelphia staring at a procession of men, women, and children working its way slowly around the sanctuary. They were holding the three green "species" of the *lulav* (palm, myrtle, and willow branches) as well the bright yellow *etrog* (citron). Many carried prayer books, from which they chanted in singsong repetition a plea for divine salvation that prominently featured the invocation of Israel's ancestors. I could not help but wonder, despite my familiarity with the rituals of the holiday, what on earth these people were doing and why they were doing it. A few moments later, no less incredulous than before, I had joined the march. And several months later, I set to work on the research that eventually resulted in this book, in the hope of better understanding what I had been doing that day and before, and have done on many days since, in the company of many other contemporary religious adherents no less self-conscious than I and often more observant.

I am grateful to my teachers R. J. Zwi Werblowsky, Bryan Wilson, Van Harvey, and Philip Rieff for memorable conversations that have had their impact on this project, direct and indirect, as well as to the Stanford University students who have also taught me much over the past few years during my courses "Modern Jewish Thought," "Theories of Religious Ritual," and "Modernization and Secularization"—most particularly, my graduate students Avi Bernstein-Nahar, Greg Kaplan, and Ken Koltun-Fromm. My colleagues at Stanford—particularly, Bernard Faure, Talya Fishman, P. J. Ivanhoe, Brent Sockness, and Lee Yearley—have knowingly and unknowingly contributed a great deal to my thinking about ritual. Bliss Carnochan,

David Ellenson, Paula Hyman, Adriane Leveen, Steven Lukes, Joseph Reimer, Michael and Ilana Silber, Michael Stanislawski, Ellen Umansky, and Steven Zipperstein have been generous with their reading time, their encouragement, and their unstinting criticism. I am thankful to all for all.

The questioners and commentators at presentations of earlier drafts of the book's various chapters have also left their mark. My thanks go to participants at the Thursday lunch talks at the Stanford Humanities Center; the Jewish Studies Colloquium at Columbia University; the Religious Studies Colloquium at Stanford; the Jewish Studies Lecture Series at Yale; the conference "Religion and the Authority of the Past," sponsored by the Center for the Humanities at the University of Michigan; and the Bilgray Lecture at the University of Arizona.

The writing of the book got under way during my year as a fellow at the Stanford Humanities Center and benefited immensely from the conversations which the Center made possible. My thanks to then-director Wanda Corn and her staff for a year I shall never forget.

Portions of this book were published in earlier versions and appear here with gratefully acknowledged permission. Parts of the Introduction and Chapters 1–3 draw from "Rethinking Jewish Modernity," *Jewish Social Studies* 1, no. 1 (fall 1994): 1–21, and "Gentile Theory, Jewish Practice: Ritual, Commandment, and the Modern Body Politic," *Graven Images* 2 (1995): 91–110. Parts of Chapters 3 and 5 draw from "Divine Legislation as 'Ceremonial Script': Mendelssohn on the Commandments," *AJS Review* 15, no. 2 (fall 1990): 239–67. Parts of Chapter 7 draw from "The Search for Authority in Twentieth-Century Judaism," in *Religion and the Authority of the Past,* ed. Tobin Siebers (Ann Arbor: The University of Michigan Press, 1993), 222–52. Parts of Chapter 8 draw from "American Judaism: Changing Patterns in Denominational Self-Definition," in *Studies in Contemporary Jewry,* volume 8, *A New Jewry? America since the Second World War,* ed. Peter Y. Medding (New York: Institute of Contemporary Jewry and Oxford University Press, 1992), 22–28, and "Constructing the Usable Past: The Idea of 'Tradition' in Twentieth-Century Judaism," in *The Uses of Tradition: Jewish Continuity in the Modern Era,* ed. Jack Wertheimer (New York: Jewish Theological Seminary of America, 1992), 429–61.

Finally, I would like to thank my editor at the University of Chicago Press, Alan Thomas, for unusual insight, patience, and all-around good sense; the editor of the Chicago Studies in the History of Judaism series, Bill Green, for his early support and unwavering enthusiasm for the project; Chicago's anonymous peer reviewers, who gave excellent and detailed advice above and beyond the call of duty; Mary Caraway, for an extraordinary job of manuscript editing; my wife, Ace, who lost a lot of sleep as I tossed and turned and rethought Jewish ritual's rethinking over and over again; and, last but not least, my children, who suffered through more dinner conversations on the subject than they or I would care to recall.

I have dedicated this book to my teachers from college through graduate school, in recognition of the fact that this book was in the making long before that Sukkot morning in Philadelphia and came to be because they convinced me that the work I had chosen was worth doing and that I could do it well.

RETHINKING
MODERN JUDAISM

Introduction

Most scholars of Judaism in the modern period, myself included, understand their subject to be the massive transformation of Jewish religious belief and practice that has occurred over the past two hundred years or so, a change that came in the wake of the awesome double shock that first convulsed the Jews of western and central Europe at the end of the eighteenth century and has since gone on to affect the lives of all Jews everywhere. The first shock, *Emancipation,* meant the opening of doors long closed to Jews, the reality or promise of political and economic opportunities of which earlier generations could not even dream, and the pursuit of new and multiple options by individuals suddenly cut loose from the integral communities which had long anchored Jews and constrained them. *Enlightenment,* the second shock, was no less overwhelming. It entailed a new language on the lips, a new set of furniture for the mind, and a radical questioning of truths long held to be self-evident.

Both developments proceeded unevenly over the years and across the map. Their results even now remain too complex for description in simple terms of revolution. Yet the transformations of Jews and Judaism which Emancipation and Enlightenment initiated were unquestionably so thoroughgoing as to define an epoch in Jewish history. They continue to perplex Jewish communities and shape Jewish religious options today.

I begin with this brief statement of the reigning model of modern Judaism because I accept that model by and large and because my aim in this book is to refine the paradigm by calling several of its principal elements into question. We are now concluding the second century of Judaism's wrestle with Emancipation and Enlightenment and entering on the third. That would be reason enough to prompt a reconsideration of the modern ground traversed by Jews thus far. A rethinking is all the more urgent, I believe, because the scholarly view of European and American Jewish history has changed dramatically in recent decades, as has public reflection on the place of minorities in increasingly multicultural nation-states and, indeed, the conception and valuation of modernity itself. There is ample reason to challenge our collective sense of what modern Judaism has been and, accordingly, our related sense of what it is and can be.

1. REVISING THE REIGNING MODEL OF MODERN JUDAISM

I want, in particular, to reconsider four assumptions of the received approach that have too often been treated as axiomatic: the priority of belief over practice; the characterization and valuation of modernity; the conception of ritual in terms of liberal Protestant notions of the sacred; and restriction of the notion of mitzvah (commandment) to Jewish behavior considered as deriving directly or indirectly from divine revelation at Sinai.

The Practice of Emancipation

The first, and most important, point I will argue is that our effort to comprehend the religious experience of modern Jews should concentrate far more on *practice* than on *belief*. In the reading I will offer, Jews did not go through the simple three-stage process that in all too many accounts of our subject constitutes the master-story of modern Judaism. That narrative has Jews (1) adopting Enlightenment notions, whether learned in new schools or absorbed from the zeitgeist; (2) casting off traditional belief in God and revelation as a result of their new and rational worldview; and then (3) quite naturally or even inevitably rejecting or, at the very least, modifying the performance of inherited commandments. In this view, belief (the word is often used interchangeably with "faith") comes first. Practice "reflects" or "follows" or "enacts" belief. I propose, rather, that Jews for the most part navigated their way through modernity's unfamiliar terrain much as we do today: via *eclectic patterns of observance* and *varied, often individual, sets of meanings* discovered in those patterns or associated with them. Each half of the interacting pair of observance and meaning is tied to the other but is not, in its specifics, determined by it. Our definition of practice must be broad enough to include the distinctive range of activities and associated beliefs undertaken by Jewish actors in response to the set of imperatives which they defined as Judaism.

Let me emphasize, so as not to be misunderstood, that the role of changing belief has been pronounced in the lives of modern Jews: it will figure crucially in this study. I am by training a student of modern Jewish religious thought and take its claims very seriously. What Jews have *done* in the realm of faith, as in every other arena, has of course been inseparable from what they have *believed*. There shall be no reduction of faith to society or politics here—a move far too common in the scholarly literature on modern religion—and no repetition of the old "myth versus ritual" arguments over which came first and which deserves primacy. However, in the story of modern Jews that I want to tell, abstract matters like God and revelation have almost always remained inchoate and of decidedly secondary importance to the decisions that Jews have made about observance of communal commandments. There has certainly been no one-to-one correspondence between observances and beliefs. Nor can beliefs be understood apart from their intimate and varying connection to ritual enactments or abrogations that, in turn, have been tied to immediate and often pressing concerns involving politics, gender, and family relations.

In a word, the role of *Enlightenment* per se—intellectual and ideological upheaval—has not been as predominant among Jews (and, I suspect, others too) in their negotiation of modernity as we might think. But *Emancipation*—by which I mean the assumption of new sorts of selfhood by Jews in a radically altered social and economic order—has, in contrast, been decisive. This has been the case even among Orthodox and ultra-Orthodox Jews who claim utter continuity both with the beliefs and with the observances of "the past." Furthermore, this generalization holds not only for American, western European, and central European Jews, who will be our primary focus here, but also for the various east European and Levant Jewries (the vast majority of the world's Jewish population in the nineteenth century), whose societal conditions and self-understandings differed markedly from those in the West—in large part because the granting of political Emancipation in their cases lagged far behind the introduction, through Jewish and Gentile agency, of Enlightenment (or, at least, of some of its elements).

To some degree, of course, the primacy of Emancipation over Enlightenment is a function of the fact that the vast majority of European Jews were not intellectuals. They experienced no direct confrontation in their own minds between Enlightenment ideas of history, science, society, and self—collectively known, in much scholarship and Jewish thought, as "modernity"—and the variety of Jewish ideas and institutions which were soon given specious coherence and uniformity through their labeling, positively or pejoratively, as "the tradition." I take this point as obvious. The gap between "elite" and "folk" is by now a truism in the scholarly study of Jews as of all other groups. It seems a given that, as Max Weber put it, "virtuosos" should not be confused with the majority of adherents, or professionals with laity, even if we should also not exaggerate the differences between them. "The empirical fact, important for us, that men are differently qualified in a religious way stands at the beginning of the history of religion."[1] We shall assume it no less in approaching the history of modern Jews, men and women alike.

But we need not invoke the "masses," who for decades remained untutored in modern notions, to make our case for the primacy of practice. Even the Jews who attended Enlightenment schools and universities in increasing numbers as the nineteenth century advanced, who read Enlightenment books and journals, and who participated in Reform or modern Orthodox or Historical School congregations were with few exceptions never forced to decide in any rigorous way what they did or did not believe about ultimate matters of faith. Every practice they observed, every regimen of conduct they maintained, permitted many and various interpretations and was compatible with any number of theological claims. Lighting Sabbath candles, separating meat from milk, avoiding bread on Passover, and the thousand other ritual possibilities available to Jews all allowed for the expression of a variety of meanings—whether to one's self, to fellow Jews, or to Gentiles. This was no small advantage, as we will see.

Indeed, the emphasis by Jewish actors on practice rather than belief provided space for a still more precious and perhaps indispensable strategy for dealing with modernity's uncharted territory: avoidance of questions of "ultimate meaning" altogether. This latitude—along with the nature of the reinterpretations afforded Jewish ritual in the modern period—helps to account for the fact that many "nonbelieving" Jews have continued to hold Passover seders, to fast on Yom Kippur, and to circumcise their newborn sons, while their counterparts among lapsed Protestant or Catholic believers—particularly intellectuals—have generally discarded virtually all religious practice except for highly secularized forms of Christmas. The meanings accorded Jewish practice in the absence or uncertainty of faith also help explain why, even among intellectuals, religious observance has almost always remained way "out in front" of theological beliefs. Indeed, these formulations seem designed in large measure to justify and account for such practice. The rationales have rarely caught up, often dissatisfying even those who propound them, while observance in the meantime has continued undiminished—carrying meaning, generating conflict, and conferring a more or less precarious identity.

The advantages of a focus on practice for the *scholar* of modern Judaism are no less apparent. Individuals long excluded from our purview—women first among them—take on new and central interest. Issues long since treated as resolved assume an appealing complexity. The German Jewish women examined in a recent and pioneering study by Marion Kaplan, it turns out, were probably the rule rather than the exception in modernizing their faith via a twofold, back-and-forth process of *selecting* among traditional observances in the home and endowing these rituals with *altered and malleable meanings*.[2] In a similar fashion, we will discover, the intricacies of Sigmund Freud's Jewish accommodations, discards, retrievals, and repressions—recently probed by Yosef Yerushalmi—were likely shared to a degree by thousands of Jews whose relations to their Judaism are and will remain far less well known to us. For those Jews, too, it holds, as Yerushalmi writes caustically, that "the blandly generic term *secular Jew* gives no indication of the richly nuanced variety within the species."[3] I would add only that the companion term "religious Jew" conceals no less diverse an array of existential options, one which our focus on practice should help to delineate.

In sum, my first suggestion is that we discard the notion that changes in Jewish ritual behavior need not long detain the scholar bent on understanding modern Judaism since these changes can be understood quite simply as the *effect* of internalized Enlightenment ideals, which should therefore properly remain our focus. Rather, as the historian Roger Chartier argued in his recent work *The Cultural Origins of the French Revolution,* we should "[cast] doubt on two ideas: first, that practices can be deduced from the discourses that authorize or justify them; second, that it is possible to translate into the terms of an explicit ideology the latent meaning of social mechanisms."[4] Chartier's aim was to demonstrate that the Revolution was not the mere enactment of Enlightenment ideas and ideals. In our case, it is the causal sequence "Enlightenment → secularized belief → altered or discarded religious practice" that has proved inadequate and needs to be rethought. Indeed, the dichotomy Enlightenment/tradition, still far too dominant a trope in discussions of modern religious belief and behavior of whatever sort, turns out on this account to offer such a thin description of the transformation we are trying to capture that it should in many contexts *not* be refined but, instead, discarded altogether.

Modernity

Chartier's work alerts us as well to a second element of the received picture of modern Judaism in need of reconsideration: the adjective that defines the field. *Modern* has until very recently been a constant in discussions of the past two centuries of Jewish belief and practice. Its primary connotations of rationality and universality have simply been taken as givens despite undisputed and immense variation in the definition of the nouns—"Jews" and "Judaism"—which the adjective has modified. This is no longer the case. "Modernity" has in fact become the object of such intense scrutiny of late that it would be no exaggeration to say that *it* is now the commitment under siege in the academy, while study of Judaism and the Jews is flowering. The focus of scholarship has shifted from the actual or imminent disappearance of the Jews or Judaism (as of religious groups more generally) to the complex modalities of adjustment that have sustained them. Simultaneously, scholars in a variety of disciplines are paying increasing attention to the problematic character of the very concept—modernity—long used not only to describe the ostensible waning of Judaism (or Christianity) but to evaluate it.

Even if one does not go as far as to say, with Jean-François Lyotard, that "the status of knowledge is altered as societies enter what is known as the postindustrial age and cultures enter what is known as the postmodern age," leading to analysis of what Lyotard has named "the postmodern condition"[5]—even if one sides instead with Jürgen Habermas and considers modernity to be an "unfinished project" in the midst of which we all still think and work, accepting that what Habermas calls "the philosophical discourse of modernity" still deserves to hold our attention and shape our thought— even so, one notes that Habermas must labor long and hard to demonstrate the continuing relevance of this discourse, which a few decades back was utterly taken for granted. He can do so only by disavowing many of the "truths" that are still legion in studies of modernity and, particularly, in works on Jewish modernity: the supremacy of national identity, for example; the unquestioned status of claims by the natural and social sciences to rationality and universality and, so, to objective truth unmediated by history or culture; the inevitability and ubiquity of secularization.[6]

The current debate over modernity and postmodernity cannot but affect the ways we think about the definitions given to Judaism in the modern period by practitioners and scholars alike. To many Jewish scholar-practitioners, whether the nineteenth-century founders of the scientific study of Jews and Judaism or their disciples in later generations, modernity's claims have seemed largely unassailable and the goods that modernity promised or proffered of unquestionable worth. It was clear to Leopold Zunz, for example, in "On Rabbinic Literature," the programmatic essay that served to define the emergent field of Jewish studies in 1818, not only that "no new significant development is likely to disturb our survey," live Judaism having become a thing of the past, but that "a higher culture"—German—"[now] permits a more illuminating treatment" of Jewish beliefs and practices than Judaism itself could have provided. Scores of studies since Zunz's have likewise evaluated Jews and Judaism from inside the modern perspective—a perspective that their authors also claim to survey, taking the "modern" as a given, its nature fixed, while using its leverage to raise questions about modes of Jewish existence which had for centuries seemed unimpeachable. "Science steps in," as Zunz put it concisely, "demanding an account of what has already been sealed away."[7] The dead could hardly challenge the authority of what still breathed and flourished. I hope to bring the two into fruitful conversation, as it were, by juxtaposing the treatment accorded Jews and Judaism in the theories and practices of modernity that have emerged in western and central Europe over the past two centuries with the theories and practices of Judaism itself that have developed in the same societies at the same time, often in direct response to the dominant "philosophical discourse."

Zunz, like most of the intellectuals whom we shall examine, was far from an outsider to the way of life of which he gave an account; neither was he unambivalent about the modern developments that he both charted and furthered. He mourned as well as celebrated that "the Jews of Germany are seizing upon German language and German learning [Bildung] with such earnestness [that they] are thus, perhaps unwittingly, carrying [rabbinic] literature to its grave." Indeed, he allowed himself the hope that "the fate of the Jews may derive a solution, if only in part, from [his] science." A similar ambivalence, we will find, along with a similar hope in the salvific properties of good scholarship, has characterized all the leading figures in modern Jewish thought from Moses Mendelssohn onward, and never more so than when they considered how Jews should be *acting* in the new modern order: how they should dress and eat, what work they should do, whom they should marry. No less important, this same ambivalence, and the more nuanced picture of modernity that goes along with it, has characterized the greatest modern social theorists—Nietzsche and Weber, Durkheim and Freud, even Marx, on some accounts—whose voices resound clearly in contemporary debate over modernity and its discontents.

That debate, and the self-consciousness it entails, informs the present scholarly effort at every turn. We will be especially concerned here with the reconception of modernity at several points where it bears directly upon the nature of Jewish practice. One is the "invention" of nations and national traditions (traced by historians such as Eric Hobsbawm, James Sheehan, and

Theodore Zeldin), a process accomplished by intellectual and political elites who demanded Jewish compliance with emergent cultural ideals of *Bildung* or *civilisation* as the price for Emancipation. A related aspect of modernity also essential to us is the assignment of religious observance to the private sphere, where it was to remain subservient to civic duty and subject to judgment according to putatively universal Enlightenment standards. We will see this in Kant (our focus in Chapter 1), as well as in Spinoza, Hegel, and a host of lesser thinkers; it emerges no less clearly in our own day in Habermas—and accounts, I believe, for the fact (examined at length in Chapter 2) that particularistic Jewish practice is virtually invisible when the modern West is observed through the Weberian and Durkheimian lenses which have dominated religious studies in our century. This is true, I believe, in even the best work of recent theorists and represents one of the only points on which partisans of "the discourse of modernity" such as Habermas and harbingers of "postmodernity" such as Lyotard can readily agree.

The privatization and marginalization of religious practice has, of course, gone hand in hand with the belief—widespread in all the major theories of modernity—that secularization constitutes an inevitable aspect of modernization, whether as aftereffect or as driving force. However regrettable the connection might be, so this theory goes, "disenchantment" could not but accompany "rationalization"—except for those who, as Weber put it, "cannot bear the fate of the times like a man" and so enter "the arms of the old churches . . . opened widely and compassionately" to receive them. Each believer must bear his or her "intellectual sacrifice."[8] Weber's elegy to faith was an integral part of his practice of "*Wissenschaft* as a vocation." Nor was he alone in this regard. The need for qualification and refinement of "secularization theory" has generated significant controversy among sociologists and historians in recent years. Further rethinking is required, I think, if even the subtlest versions of that theory are to help us in understanding Jews. This is so not least because almost all theories of secularization, including the best of them—Peter Berger's—are rife with Protestant assumptions about religion that simply do not apply where Jews and Judaism are concerned.

Ritual
That holds as well for the third respect in which we shall attempt to revise the received picture of modern Judaism: the conception of *ritual,* which I will discuss in Chapter 3. Here the task is twofold.

On the one hand, we have the problem that almost all the anthropological literature to which scholars of religion commonly turn for help in understanding religious behavior arises out of reading about, or fieldwork among, *premodern* peoples. This is certainly the case with Emile Durkheim and Claude Lévi-Strauss, as with Mary Douglas and Victor Turner, and it is true in large measure of Clifford Geertz. Only a handful of essays by such theorists have considered how modern settings transform the meanings of ritual behavior and the ways in which that meaning is accomplished. Symbolism of the body, to take an obvious example from Douglas's work, cannot "express" the borders of a modern body politic or its subcultures as it does that of a relatively isolated clan.[9] "Liminality," a state of affairs located in between the normal structures of time or space or status, can at best turn into "liminoid," as Turner himself has conceded, when "structure" is inescapable, the collective has become the private, and the "work" of ritual has in effect become "play," a leisure-time activity.[10] The fusion that ritual effects, in Geertz's view, between "ethos" and "worldview" cannot easily proceed, as Geertz has acknowledged, in modern societies characterized by "leaps" back and forth between or among a variety of perspectives—religious, aesthetic, scientific, commonsense.[11]

On the other hand, we must come to terms with the application to Jews of theories based largely on *Protestant* notions of ritual and the sacred. Such notions, ironically enough, have not only been influential in the academy but have often been adopted by Jews themselves, who have then used them to effect the very changes in ritual practice which we shall be studying. Peter Hodgson and Robert King, among other scholars of modern Christian theology, have noted the devaluation of ritual that overtook nearly every branch of Protestantism in the centuries following the Reformation and left its mark on Judaism as well.[12] Mary Douglas has taken pains to attack this anti-ritual attitude, which became a standard element in the Enlightenment critique of religion (indeed, she has made its reversal an explicit aim of her scholarship).[13]

We will attend repeatedly in the present work to the impact of Protestant notions on the practices of Jewish individuals and communities, both in synagogues and homes. At this juncture, however, I wish to stress the impact of those notions on the practices of *modern scholarship* where ritual is concerned. Rudolph Otto's presence looms large in this field, especially in Geertz's account of "religion as a cultural system," as the presence of Otto's great teacher, Friedrich Schleiermacher, presides over Berger's account of secularization. The insights of these and other major thinkers are indispensable to the study of modern Judaism, but—particularly where ritual is concerned—they tend at times to lead us astray from the practices we seek to study. Note, for example, that ritual—contrary to Turner's theory—structures and routinizes every bit as much as, or more than, it allows for spontaneity and protest, even when it is not—as among many Jews—conceived as *law*. Note, too, that if a system of *everyday* observance is in force as it has been in every traditional Jewish community, then ethos and worldview are not—*pace* Geertz—fused primarily in weekly or cyclical "sacred" performances, if they are ever really fused at all. Rather, the frame of sanctity and meaning is fitted, from dawn to dusk, onto fundamental activities like eating, business, and sex. Douglas's very different understanding (and defense) of ritual, informed by Catholicism, will prove instructive in this regard, as will Erving Goffman's emphasis on the microdetails of everyday interaction.

Jewish thinkers throughout the modern period, we will find, have not only had to argue the virtues of *particular enactments*. They have also had to combat the various influential ideas and denigrations of *ritual itself* that made these enactments seem dispensable, hypocritical, or downright ridiculous. The present study will examine the views of scholars of religion as well as the views of Jewish religious practitioners without presuming the existence of a neutral, unbiased, "pure" conception of ritual from which critique can be ventured. Competing theories will be juxtaposed with Jewish practice as well as with one another. Indeed, for reasons I discuss at length in Chapter 3, I will generally use terms such as "practice" and "observance" alongside "ritual," the better to get at the nature and significance of *the variety of distinctive behaviors—symbolically freighted but often not merely symbolic in purpose or effect*—in which Jews have and have not engaged over the past two centuries. We will also be attentive to the competing pressures—political, economic, social, familial, moral, intellectual, and divine—which have had a bearing on Jewish decisions about practice and have thereby shaped the negotiation and construction of modern Jewish selfhood.

Commandment

This brings us to the fourth and final aspect of our rethinking: the meaning of mitzvah, or *commandment*. Scholars of modern Judaism, echoing both detractors of ritual practice and opponents of religious reform, have all too often reserved the notion of mitzvah for what has come to be known as Orthodoxy. According to this view, commandments (mitzvot) in the modern period are acts performed in accordance with halakhah—the system of laws set forth in a series of codifications based ultimately on the Torah and stretching from the Mishnah and Talmud, via medieval codes, to modern responsa composed by rabbis regarded by other Orthodox rabbis as authoritative. Even among less partisan analysts of Jewish modernity, the term "mitzvot" has often been reserved at minimum for acts which the actors believe themselves to be performing in direct response to the will of God. Practice does not count as commanded unless it enacts or expresses or flows directly out of belief. Mitzvot are defined solely as the imperatives of faith. Only in that case is the adjective "religious" applied.

This will not do. For as Franz Rosenzweig pointed out in a famous letter to Martin Buber urging him to reconsider his principled opposition to religious prescription, the restriction of "commandment" to behavior that is directly ascribed to divine decree probably misses and certainly misrepresents the vast majority of actions performed by *premodern* Jews, let alone their modern descendants. "Can we really fancy that Israel kept this Law, this Torah, only because of the one 'fact which excluded the possibility of delusion,' that the six hundred thousand heard the voice of God on Sinai?"[14] With good sociological intuition, Rosenzweig insisted instead that Jews had observed the commandments over the centuries because social reality compelled and made good sense of that observance. Practice, in turn, lent richness and meaning to lives that were often humdrum or horrid. If we ignore this wider denotation of mitzvah, we miss a great deal of reflection and activity undertaken in response to complicated sets of imperatives arising out of the distinctive Jewish identity that such Jews recognized and wished to maintain.

Ethical obligations, for example, have always constituted a major portion of the commandments and became for many Jews over the past two hundred years the principal, or even the sole, means of acting out the duties incumbent upon them. Such practitioners proudly defined their religious tradition as "ethical monotheism." To do a good deed was, in common parlance, to "do a mitzvah," whether or not it was believed that human conscience articulates divine demands. Mordecai Kaplan spoke for many twentieth-century American Jews when he "reconstructed" Judaism as a "civilization," and "revalued" the mitzvot as ethnic "folkways," but considered the mitzvot to be commandments nonetheless. We shall encounter this sort of view repeatedly as we survey the intentions underlying Jewish practice throughout the modern period.

But so too—and perhaps to a still greater extent—have Jews engaged in distinctively Jewish practice as a means of *following in the footsteps of their ancestors:* a major motif in every Jewish culture, modern and premodern, one which of course is not unknown in other religious traditions as well but which has arguably become central to a unique degree in the observances of modern Jews. Durkheim, here as elsewhere in *The Elementary Forms of the Religious Life,* may well have been characterizing his own family and fore-bears when he wrote that "native" informants, asked why they performed the ceremonies observed by anthropologists, unanimously replied, "It is be-cause our ancestors arranged things thus. This is why we do thus and not differently." In saying this, Durkheim continued, "it is admitted that [a given rite's] authority is confounded with the authority of tradition, which is a social affair of the first order." Indeed, many modern Jews would prob-ably have subscribed wholeheartedly to Durkheim's contention (though perhaps not to the way he put it) that in attending their seders, fasting on Yom Kippur, exhibiting Jewish ritual objects, studying Jewish history, or engaging in philanthropic activity and the defense of Jewish rights at home and abroad, they were working toward a "more immediate and more con-scious end" than the expression of beliefs concerning ultimate reality—namely, "assurance of the reproduction of the totemic species." This idea, Durkheim continued, "haunts the minds of the worshippers: upon it the forces of their attention and will are concentrated."[15]

In Part 2 of this book, I will attempt in a series of conceptual case studies, each grounded in the situation of a particular Jewish community of the past two centuries, to explicate the major factors which to my mind have impelled Jews toward (and away from) observance and have done much to shape that observance in concert with—and, generally, far more than—strictly theological concerns.

2. CONCEPTUAL CASE STUDIES OF MODERN JEWISH PRACTICE

We shall begin, in Chapter 4, with *politics:* perhaps the single most important factor bearing on Jewish decision making on the character and performance of ritual in western and central Europe during the nineteenth century and a factor which remains of great importance in virtually every community in the Jewish world today. I use the word "politics" to denote the impact of direct governmental edicts and/or concerted societal pressures designed to shape, elicit, or forbid distinctive Jewish ritual observance. In some cases, particularly in the German states but not only there, nineteenth-century legislation decreed matters such as what sorts of sermons could be given in what sorts of synagogues and how the rabbis delivering those sermons were to be trained. What is more, it was made clear to Jews in all of the emancipating societies of Europe (and in the nascent American society as well) that the retention or attainment of political liberties depended on the demonstration of *Bildung* or *civilisation:* dressing and eating a certain way, speaking a "pure" form of the reigning language, worshiping with proper decorum. The calculations of rabbis and laity alike about the possible and desired shape of the "reproduction of [their] totemic species" in the modern political order could not but be influenced by such demands—in part because many Jews engaged in acculturation willingly, some of them identifying the modern Gentile order with the messianic fulfillment which had long been the goal of "ethical monotheism."

These demands and calculations are still with us. Governmental intervention in the modern West is rare, though "blue laws" and Saturday public school classes of course have a direct impact on Sabbath observance. Social pressure—often from inside the Jewish community—continues. Recall Philip Roth's marvelous story "Eli the Fanatic," tracing the effect of Hasidic garb on American Jews newly relocated to the suburbs in the 1950s. It is arguably their refusal to dress (or eat or speak) like other Americans that has made Hasidim, despite their relatively small numbers, the symbolic icons of Jewry as a whole in the United States—witness Woody Allen's fantasy of himself in black garb in the movie *Annie Hall.* The decisions by individual Jewish males outside Orthodoxy about whether or not to wear a yarmulke in public have generally had as much or more to do with considerations of the desired degree of Jewish distinctiveness, and likely Gentile reactions to that, than with theological argument over whether God really cares about male head covering or has commanded it.

This is not to say that belief is not essential to Jewish ritual performances or that theological rationales are important only as symptoms or clues to the real motivations for observance lying underneath. Belief continues to matter to many modern Jews—and therein, I believe, has lain the problem for those who have sought to understand and justify observance as *symbolic expressions or enactments* which are valuable or mandatory because they *point to truth and/or inculcate virtue.* Such symbolic rationales for practice, our subject in Chapter 5, have been extremely popular over the past two centuries, for reasons which are immediately apparent. Once practice has become voluntary, once it can be compelled neither by belief in a divine Commander (and divine sanctions for disobedience) nor by the force of communal coercion, Jews must be *persuaded* (not once but repeatedly) to undertake observance. Hence the new urgency involved in carrying on the traditional Jewish practice of offering *ta'amim,* or reasons for the commandments—and the difficulty of doing so successfully.

For the persuasion must come in terms acceptable to those whose behavior it is meant to sway. In the normal course of events, this has meant appeal to beliefs, assumptions, and commitments foreign to the tradition in which the ritual arose and foreign to the beliefs often associated with a given rite explicitly through the blessings built into its performance. Shall Jews bent on joining Gentile societies thank God, as they separate the Sabbath from the rest of the week with wine, candle, and spice box, for separating light from dark, sacred from profane, "Israel from the nations"? Justifications appealing to primordial loyalties have clashed with a newly adopted universalism, just as magical accounts of observance promising effects on God, the world, or the future reward or punishment of the observer run up against the worldview of modern science. Conversely, the more universalist or scientific the rationale for a given ritual (for example, "Hanukkah celebrates freedom," or "Passover matzah represents humility"), the more it is open to the obvious objection: we know that already, as do the Gentiles (or nonpracticing Jews), who don't observe this ritual. Why then do it? Chapter 5 will probe these issues by analyzing what is to my mind the most ambitious (and, I believe, the most problematic) attempt in the modern period to answer that question with a system of symbols: that of Rabbi Samson Raphael Hirsch, the acknowledged founder of modern Orthodoxy.

In Chapter 6, we shall turn to a very different but no less influential motive for modern observance—*nostalgia,* arguably the most widespread reason for Jewish practice in America today. Evocation of the ancestors has always featured prominently in Jewish liturgy, but in the past century and a half it has taken on still more importance, both as a motivation for nontraditional observance (or rebellion against observance) and as the force behind more traditional practice. The desire to reconnect with forefathers and foremothers—putatively, by following in their footsteps—seems to grow with spatial and temporal distance from the remembered past; "nostalgia" is all the more popular a reason for observance because it is affective as much as cognitive in nature and places the emphasis on following in ancestral ways rather than on the specifics of those ways, let alone their symbolic meaning. As we would expect after Freud, ambivalence has gone hand in hand with such enactments of ritualized memory—and, in some cases, has been their driving force. In keeping with Durkheim's analysis, the appeal to ancestors has been bound up with such distinctively modern (even "scientific") practices as historical exhibitions, the collection and display of ritual objects, and travel by train or plane to the places where the ancestors lived and worshipped.

We should not, I believe, ignore the *commandedness* at work in the varieties of modern Jewish performance that I have just enumerated. Nostalgia, too, given conditions I shall set forth, can be "a mitzvah." However, we should also avoid losing critical distance from the actors and their actions. I do not for a moment wish to collapse the necessary distinctions among the various sorts of obligation which modern Jews have perceived and obeyed. But neither do I want to ignore the manifold relations among them: a multiplicity of contexts and significances that renders rigorous delimitation of "religion" or "the religious," and the unambiguous distinction of "ritual" from "commandment," extremely problematic. Limitations of scope and competence will preclude detailed investigation in this book of all the genres of commanded activity in which modern Jews have engaged. We shall not, for example, probe the impact of aesthetic norms—always an intrinsic part of traditional Jewish practice and, like attachment to the ancestors, uniquely salient in much modern observance. Nor shall we directly examine the appeal to national obligations, civic or Jewish, or the delineation of a distinctive Jewish morality. I hope, however, that the three case studies just described will provide a good sense of what it has meant for Jews to rethink ritual in the first two centuries following Emancipation and will show how that rethinking has been affected by related transformations in the structure of Jewish communities and the meanings of commandedness.

That project has become still more problematic in the present century. For one thing, nonobservance has become a real option for many Jews and, in certain groups, has even become a cause for pride rather than opprobrium. So, too, the meanings available for selected practices have multiplied, and acceptance of observance unaccompanied by belief has become widespread. Two further case studies will probe these developments and lead directly to the book's Conclusion, which will examine the dynamics of Jewish practice at century's end.

In Chapter 7, using Rosenzweig's interchange with Buber (cited above) as a springboard, we shall ask why for Rosenzweig, and many like him, practice far exceeded the justifications marshaled to account for it, while for Buber, and many like him, the *opposition* to practice far exceeded the justifications marshaled to account for that opposition—and took little notice of the practice going on all the while. Buber's hostility to ritual, I shall argue, was far from idiosyncratic (though it was that too) but was, rather, a function of his vision of how Jews should fit into the modern cultural and political orders. We can learn a lot from Buber's example about the millions of Jews throughout this century who have turned their backs, deliberately or by default, on the very same observances which had so little appeal to him. Rosenzweig's observance, I think, was likewise typical—in this case, of Jewish practice driven by imperatives other than the ultimate authority sought but rarely found. His practice, like that of many contemporary Jews, likely could not have endured if the seeker's quest had been greeted with success. The stance of seeker is crucial to the practice and vice versa; the absence of unequivocal authority is paradoxically indispensable to the conviction of commandment.

The debate between Buber and Rosenzweig will lead to consideration, in Chapter 8, of attempts by American thinkers beginning with Mordecai Kaplan to justify eclectic patterns of ritual observance in the name of "tradition," fully aware that they themselves had in large part *constructed* the visions of tradition they invoked. Kaplan, like many contemporary practitioners of Judaism, fervently believed that ritual is a far more essential aspect of religion than belief in God, that practice cannot be separated from the life of the community it serves, and that Judaism should not be reduced to the status of mere "religion" but conceived as an all-embracing "civilization." He applied this viewpoint with unflinching consistency in attempting to "reconstruct" twentieth-century American Jewry—and so inaugurated the effort, still continuing, to justify observance without apology through the communal purposes it serves and to supply meanings for observance that are self-conscious inventions without worrying overmuch about what the practices in question had meant to Jews heretofore.

That effort cannot, in the nature of the case, be entirely successful—nor can it, to my mind, be avoided. Like the impact of politics, the understanding of mitzvah as symbol, the resort to nostalgia, and the unceasing quest for authority that the quester does not wish to find, the reverence for "tradition" and "community" (despite widespread awareness that both are "constructed" rather than given) has not merely endured as we enter the third post-Emancipation century of Jewish practice but intensified. In the Conclusion of this study, I will try to account for the newfound popularity of ritual in contemporary America (and in Israel); to explain why the very same forces which have worked to produce a surge of feminist ritual innovation have also been at work in ultra-Orthodox circles, with results that are strikingly parallel; and to say where they are likely to lead American Jews in coming decades—and, given my own normative commitments, where they *should* lead.

Modern rationales for observance, I shall argue, defy coherent justification yet apparently speak in our day with a power lacking to earlier patterns of observance and their accompanying justifications. In order to understand the new patterns, we need to do more than carry forward the examination of *ta'amei ha-mitzvot* in terms of *belief* that was undertaken in this century most systematically by Isaac Heinemann.[16] We need as well (following the example of many current scholars of Judaism) to shift the focus of such examination, to widen the lens through which we look at mitzvah, and to take stock of the social, political, familial, and other imperatives that have played a major role in influencing how modern Jews have decided to walk and eat and pray and marry.

"When and why do men obey?" Weber asked in "Politics as a Vocation." "Upon what inner justifications and upon what external means does this *Herrschaft* [authority] rest?" In asking when and why modern Jewish men and women have decided upon the religious practices and abstentions that more than anything else have defined them, both in their own eyes and in the eyes of Gentile neighbors, societies, and states, we will be working from the ground up, attending to "highly robust motives of fear and hope ... and besides all this, [to] interests of the most varied sort."[17] The aim is to reopen the simplest of questions about what modern Jews have done, "religiously" and "ethnically," and why.

3. METHODOLOGICAL ISSUES

The decision to work this way, it must be confessed, involves us in a host of methodological issues and dilemmas which cannot entirely be resolved.

By far the most important is the difficulty of saying anything worthwhile about Jewish religious practice in the modern period given the fact that we know virtually nothing about how the vast majority of Jews in the West have acted religiously, let alone what *meanings* they have attached to those actions. Todd Endelman has noted trenchantly that most diaspora historians of modern Jewry, stressing "transformation rather than decline, continuity rather than disjuncture, cohesion rather than dissolution, change rather than crisis," have "shown little interest in exploring the state of Jewish religious practice—matters like synagogue attendance and observance of the dietary laws, the laws of Sabbath rest, and other domestic ceremonies that have historically been hallmarks of Jewish distinctiveness."[18] My own survey of the field confirms Endelman's generalization. We simply do not have the data that we need to characterize accurately the religious patterns adopted by modern Jewish individuals and communities as a whole. I join the historians of European and American Jewry who in recent decades have urged and returned to the task set magisterially by Jacob Katz a generation or more ago: linking Jewish religious belief and behavior to the developing *subcultures and urban communities* in which modern Jews have increasingly moved since Emancipation as well as to the *larger non-Jewish societies*—themselves racked by conflict over definitions of culture, ethnicity, and polity—with which Jews have been forced to come to terms.

This, in turn, points to several other historiographic issues. One, mentioned above, is the divide separating intellectual history from social history, the study of elites (or "virtuosi") from the study of lay (or "folk" or "mass") behavior. Intellectual history, according to Jonathan Frankel, has been favored until recently by scholars of modern Jewry in the West, while eastern Europeans and Israelis have focused on social history.[19] Paula Hyman, in her recent work on the Jews of Alsace, writes that "historians of Europe and of Jewish culture have not investigated the various responses, in different social contexts, of the masses of Jews to the circumstances they confronted in the nineteenth century." Research has, rather, concentrated on political and intellectual elites, mainly in urban areas like Paris; "the lives of ordinary Jews—most of whom, in 1800 and later, were living in villages rather than large cities," have largely been ignored.[20] Attention to practice permits and obligates us to attempt to bridge these gaps.

Jewish historiography has also been exercised of late by debate over the degree to which German Jewry should be regarded as paradigmatic for the other Jewish communities of Europe and America. No less important for our purposes is the related debate on the degree to which changes in practice and belief should be traced to external factors—the promise or granting of civil rights, the influence of Gentile schools—or to internal processes endemic to the Jewish community that long antedated any of these external developments.[21] This issue is in turn linked, as Shmuel Eisenstadt points out, to recent scholarly dispute about modernity more generally pitting those who have "stressed the importance of the traditions of different societies" against those who have instead emphasized the dynamic of international factors such as capitalism.[22] Debate over the relative influence of "colonial" or majority cultures and the relative autonomy of "subject" or minority groups will likewise be much at issue here.

Without training as a social historian, and lacking specialized competence in the particular intellectual and cultural history of any modern Jewish community except that of the United States, I cannot hope in this study to close the gaps or resolve the issues just identified. Instead, I will attempt to perform some of the conceptual labor on which that larger effort depends. Four sorts of material will be drawn upon in this project: (1) the work of experts on the various modern Jewries—particularly, the French, English, German, and American communities who will be our focus, though we shall also make reference to east European, Sephardi, and Israeli communities; (2) theoretical approaches from anthropology, sociology, and philosophy, (3) major modern Jewish thinkers for whom the nature of religious practice was of central concern; and (4) my own forays into some of the primary sources of the French, English, German, and American Jewish communities. Those Jewries were the first to seek and gain entry to the societies and cultures in which the dominant theory and practice of modernity developed; by all accounts, they have played central roles in the development of modern Judaism as well. The dominant patterns of the Reform, Conservative, and modern Orthodox movements were arguably fixed and developed among them; moreover, much of modern Jewish thought has stemmed from them. All four communities offer the added advantage for this study of having employed languages which I myself can read.

I shall not attempt a detailed or exhaustive comparative account of the several communities and their Judaisms, much less a systematic effort at fixing the degree of unity and variation among them or other segments of world Jewry. My aim here is rather a series of conceptual case studies, each based on careful unpacking of practices undertaken and/or of rationales for those practices, with the help of conceptual categories refined for just this purpose. The resulting sketch of modern Jewish ritual and mitzvah, informed by a set of reasoned inferences from the data, should provide a picture of modern Jewish practice sufficiently coherent for subsequent investigation to advance, refine, or refute.

—◦❥ ❦◦—

My hope, of course, is that this study will do far more than that. I am both a scholar of Jewish practice and a practicing Jew. As such, I want to convey a sense both of the immense costs that modernity has entailed for Western Jews and of the incalculable benefits that have accrued. I want to make sense of the fact that millions of Jews like myself carry on (and have carried on) some observances while modifying and rejecting others, at times for reasons of which we are not—and do not want to be—aware. I wish as well to dispel the commonplace notion that Jewish nonobservance is to be explained only, and quite simply, as a function of nonbelief. Other factors have played their part and should be reckoned with by scholars, practitioners, and nonpractitioners alike. This, in turn, should help to explain why—as Jacob Katz wrote in the concluding words of his classic work *Out of the Ghetto*— "it was inherent in the nature of Jewish existence that Emancipation became a turning point in Jewish history, but by no means its termination."[23]

And it was inherent, I would add, not only in the nature of *Jewish* existence. Katz's conclusion holds true as well for numerous other racial, ethnic, and religious groups who have likewise been subject to the modern calculus of gain and loss, private and public, universal and particular. Jews have not been the only people or religious group in the past two centuries forced to speak new languages, to walk (and then speed) down new roads, to outfit themselves in new clothing and conceptions. Many groups, armed with the "double consciousness" imposed by modernity—the sense, described by W. E. B. Dubois, of "always looking at one's self through the eyes of others"—have developed a similarly transformed picture of what it could mean to "attain [one's] place in the world, [to] be [one]self and not another."[24] That consciousness has both reflected and fostered the manifold activities that have informed these selves. It is by and large through distinctive patterns of practice, I believe, that the members of such minorities have learned who they are, precisely in the "twoness" that logic and ideology have so discouraged.

This "twoness" remains at century's end. Once-foreign languages have become native tongues yet have remained inflected, in prayer as in daily life, among Christians as among Jews. Walks have been altered, and in that altered state have become an integral part of ritual processions that long predated them. Suits, ties, and even top hats have become de rigueur for some commanded modes of Jewish worship—but jeans and leisurewear have of late become no less obligatory in others. The list goes on and on. To say these things is not to deny the massive transformation of Judaism in the modern period, much less of religion generally, but only to complicate our conception of it; not to sentimentalize or idealize observance, I trust, but merely to take it seriously enough to make its comprehension both possible and useful. I hope that readers of many backgrounds, scholars and practitioners alike, will find their own negotiations with modernity mirrored in the pages which follow, their own ritual abrogations and remembrances echoed, illumined, complicated, and enriched.

Part One

ONE

Founding Theories of Modernity and the Critique of Jewish Practice

We begin our inquiry into the meanings and modalities of modern Jewish practice with a footnote: half-a-dozen sentences of an eighteenth-century text that capture, with remarkable concision and directness, the issues which then and since have linked the several theories of modernity and the varieties of Jewish practice in a tense and often passionate encounter.

The footnote occurs near the end of Immanuel Kant's *Religion within the Limits of Reason Alone,* first published in its entirety in 1793 and arguably the single most influential philosophical essay on religion to have appeared in the last two centuries. Both Christianity and Judaism were recast as a result of Kant's insistence (echoed by many others) that the sole legitimate role of religion lay in the inculcation of morality, religion's promise that virtue will be rewarded in a future life lending support to the doing of ethical duty in this one. Creeds and catechisms were reformulated to emphasize ethics, sermons changed in both form and content, rituals which failed to demonstrably advance moral conduct were altered or discarded.[1] No less telling for our purposes is that, in this footnote, Kant refers his readers to Moses Mendelssohn's *Jerusalem,* first published a decade before Kant's *Religion* and unquestionably the founding text in the corpus of modern Jewish thought. *Jerusalem* quickly became crucial to the defense and definition of Jewish practice in all its forms. The essay was no less critical to the defense of Jews' right to determine this practice without the interference of state or church—a right all too often contested by new political elites in western and central Europe intent on legislating changes in Jewish ritual

observance, thereby speeding or accomplishing with state power the transformation that "reason alone" had not been sufficient to secure.

We have ample reason, then, to take careful notice of the notice Kant's
text took of Mendelssohn's—and all the more reason when we consider
that Kant severely criticized *Jerusalem* in his brief reference to it and, in fact,
utterly distorted authorial intentions which he averred were "fairly clear."
Neither the critique nor the distortion, I shall argue, was gratuitous. The
Jews and Judaism compelled attention from almost every founding theorist
of modernity because they stood as a sort of shadow in the near distance of
Enlightenment, a significant Other both too close for comfort and too potent for dismissal. Judaism, of course, was the age-old source and sometime
antagonist of Christianity. Its distinctive observances had come to seem especially bothersome to the vast majority of Enlightenment thinkers, its beliefs anachronistic at best and at worst a hopeless tissue of lies, prejudices,
and superstitions. The Jews, however, stood at the gate of Emancipation
and loudly demanded admission. Their demand had to be granted lest the
new order's pretensions to universal liberty, equality, and fraternity be
proved a sham.[2] But the ills curable in the Christian faith through a strong
dose of Enlightenment seemed in the case of Judaism to be resistant to
such a remedy. Thus challenged, reason could not allow those ills to remain
untreated. In Jewish practice the contradictions built into the theory of
modernity stood exposed; that theory, as Marx later realized, had a "Jewish
Question" all its own.

Kant's footnote attacking Mendelssohn thus marked out the terrain on
which the battle between theories of modernity and the practices of Judaism
was first waged in the late eighteenth century and where—as we shall see in
subsequent chapters—the contest between the two has continued without
interruption ever since. The critique of Jewish practice in the *Religion* points
unequivocally to what has been at stake for Jews in the various conceptions
of modernity that Kant did so much to advance. It points no less to what
has been at stake for "modernity" in the conception, and the practices,
of Judaism.[3]

I. JEWISH RELIGION AND THE LIMITS OF KANTIAN REASON

Mendelssohn makes his appearance in Kant's text, predictably enough, at
the point where Kant is arguing the utter and complete disjunction between
Christianity and the religion out of which it developed. In the preceding
chapter, entitled "The Victory of the Good over the Evil Principle," Kant
had offered a "Historical Account of the Gradual Establishment of the Sov-

ereignty of the Good Principle on Earth." That account insisted on an absolute separation between rational religion, always in service to the "good
principle," and mere "statutory religion" or "law," by definition in service
to the opposite principle. Performance of ethical duty, in Kant's conception,
means choosing freely to intend doing the right thing solely because it *is*
the right thing. Belief in a God who, in a future life, would reward virtue
was permitted and encouraged in order to strengthen individuals in their
decision to do the right thing despite their awareness that here on earth
virtue is all too often not rewarded. For that same reason, however, duty
performed out of fear of God, or coercion by God, or expectation of quid
pro quo reward by God could *not* be counted as ethical.[4] True religion
therefore necessarily excluded obedience to a "heteronomous" higher
power. It ruled out any and all belief in God that was oriented to securing
divine favor, whether in this world or the next.

This was precisely what one found in Judaism in Kant's view. Yet Christian faith had by all accounts developed out of Judaism, continued to regard
its Scripture as holy, and now as ever worshipped its one God. Hence Kant's
concern in the chapter in which the Mendelssohn footnote appears, "Concerning Service and Pseudo-Service under the Sovereignty of the Good
Principle," was to draw clear lines between the two faiths despite their apparent historical connection. Judaism was a statutory religion consisting in
coercive legislation rather than ethical teaching. As such, it could constitute
only "pseudo-service." Christianity was the one true faith. It had at first
validated Old Testament commandments so as to secure its "introduction
among the people." But that historical link to statutory religion could not
be permitted to stand. "A Christian is really bound by no law of Judaism."[5]
It is at this point that we come to our footnote:

> Mendelssohn very ingeniously makes use of this weak spot in the cus-
> tomary presentation of Christianity wholly to reject every demand
> upon a son of Israel that he change his religion. For, he says, since
> the Jewish faith itself is, according to the avowal of Christians, the
> substructure upon which the superstructure of Christianity rests, the
> demand that it be abandoned is equivalent to expecting someone to
> demolish the ground floor of a house in order to take up his abode in
> the second story.

So far so good. Mendelssohn, in the original passage from *Jerusalem,*
had been replying to the suggestion of an anonymous Christian polemicist
that the Jewish philosopher should convert, now that he has perhaps

come closer to the faith of the Christians, having torn yourself from the servitude of iron churchly bonds [that is, the commandments of the synagogue], and having commenced teaching the liberal system of a more rational worship of God, which constitutes the true character of the Christian religion, thanks to which we have escaped coercion and burdensome ceremonies, and thanks to which we no longer link the true worship of God either to Samaria or Jerusalem, but see the essence of religion, in the words of our teacher, wherever the true adorers of God pray in spirit and in truth.[6]

Kant, we now realize, has zeroed in on the absolute center of Mendelssohn's essay. He has aimed his critique precisely at the site of the polemical arrow that had caused Mendelssohn to write his work in the first place and to title it *Jerusalem*. The new covenant of Christianity, Mendelssohn insists, has not superseded the old, rendering the latter's ordinances no more and no less necessary than those of Israel's ancient neighbor the Samaritans. Mendelssohn will devote the remainder of *Jerusalem* to showing that Jewish "ceremonies" are neither "burdensome" nor "coerci[ve]." Before doing so, he pauses only long enough to make the point that if Judaism *had* become dispensable as a result of Enlightenment progress toward truth, so had Christianity, which "as you know, is built upon Judaism." If a house is about to collapse, "do I act wisely if I remove my belongings from the lower to the upper floor for safety?"[7]

Kant could not but take notice of this analogy. He had every reason to be sensitive to the charge that his critiques had undermined the foundations of the dominant faith no less than those of Judaism. Book 2 of his *Religion* had in fact been suppressed by the official censor of Berlin on grounds that it controverted the teachings of the Bible. Kant had then secured permission to print the *Religion* from the philosophical faculty at Jena, invested with the right to authorize publication of books on religious subjects. And his troubles were not to stop there.

Barely a year after the printing of this work with its footnote on Mendelssohn's analogy of the first and second stories, Kant was forced to defend himself against charges, brought in a personal letter from his monarch, that he had "misuse[d] your philosophy to undermine and debase many of the most important and fundamental doctrines of the Holy Scriptures and Christianity."[8] That letter built on a rescript of 1784, the same year that Kant had penned his famous essay defining Enlightenment as reason's independence from the tutelage of authority, in which Frederick II had laid down the state's challenge to reason's prerogatives in no uncertain terms. "A private person has no right to pass public and perhaps even disapproving judgment on the actions, procedures, laws, regulations, and ordinances of sovereigns and courts[,] . . . for a private person is not at all capable of making such judgment, because he lacks complete knowledge of circumstances and motives."[9] Kant had to demonstrate that reason (that is, a philosopher such as himself) did have that right. And to do so, he needed to prove that the critique he mounted against false religion in the name of Enlightenment did not apply to advanced forms of Christianity but *did* disqualify all other faiths—including especially the one that shared a book of Scripture with Christianity and claimed to share in the love of the one true God.

This perhaps accounts for the blatant misreading that Kant now supplies for Mendelssohn's metaphor of the building on the verge of collapse:

> His real intention is fairly clear [Kant writes]. He means to say: First wholly remove Judaism itself out of your religion (it can always remain, as an antiquity, in the historical account of the faith); we can then take your proposal under advisement.

This is astonishing—as if Mendelssohn "means to say" that Jews would consider converting to Christianity if only it were enlightened enough to divest itself of all "coercion" and "burdensome" Old Testament ceremonies! Actually, Kant continues, "nothing would then be left but pure moral religion unencumbered by statutes"—Kant's desideratum, of course, but hardly Mendelssohn's.

> Our burden will not be lightened in the least [Kant adds] by throwing off the yoke of outer observances if, in its place, another yoke, namely, confession of faith in sacred history—a yoke which rests far more heavily upon the conscientious—is substituted in its place, [though] the sacred books of this people, [no longer binding faith, would] continue to possess value for scholarship even if not for the benefit of religion.[10]

We can most usefully begin unpacking the footnote, I think, at its conclusion. The yoke of assent to "sacred history" would be harder to bear than that of "outer observances" because it pertained to *belief,* that is, the domain of reason, and not merely to behavior. Behavior was meant, in Kant's view of religion, to lead one *toward* belief or maintain one *in* belief but had absolutely no independent value. What the mind thinks or the will intends is always of far greater importance in Kant's philosophy than what the body does. This point is crucial to Kant's ethics, where good or evil rests entirely with pure intention to do one's duty, irrespective of actual performance. It could thus be no less crucial to religion, which in Kant's view existed only for the purpose of serving ethics. Compromises of the spirit could not but weigh "more heavily" upon "the conscientious" than any "yoke of outer observances."

Moreover, the observances of Judaism in Kant's view were burden enough! Earlier in the *Religion,* at a second juncture of his argument that later proved critical for Jewish belief and practice, Kant had argued (in terms reminiscent of Spinoza's *Tractatus* but apparently developed without knowledge of the earlier work) that "the Jewish faith was, in its original form, a collection of mere statutory laws upon which was established a political organization." [11] In essence, Judaism was never even meant to be a religion in the true sense of the word. This could be proved by three considerations.

First, all of Judaism's original commandments had been laid down by a political authority as "*coercive laws*"—legitimately so, since they "relate merely to external acts" and not to belief. "They are directed to absolutely nothing but outer observance." Moral teaching—the stuff of real religion—was never involved. Moses was a gifted lawgiver; his teaching, however, was seriously flawed. The development of autonomous persons was not fostered by Judaism but precluded.

Second, in keeping with their external and legal character, Jewish observances carried with them the promise of reward and punishment in *this world* and no other. In Kant's view, the only ground for our valid, inferential belief in God was the need for trust in the future reward of virtue, so as to defy human inclination and encourage us to do our duty in this world, where virtue is *not* often rewarded. "No religion can be conceived of which involves no belief in a future life"; Judaism "in its purity is seen to lack this belief." It was therefore "not a religious faith at all." The biblical stage of Judaism's development is counted as definitive here. Rabbinic and medieval traditions which do emphasize belief in a world to come are not recognized.

Third, Judaism was not suitable for admission as a "*church universal*" because it "exclude[d] *from its communion*" the entire human race." Jews believed themselves a people chosen by God, thereby showing "enmity toward all other peoples" and provoking enmity in return. [12]

Old Testament legislation, then, was (1) *coercive,* and thus opposed to the nurturing of autonomous selves; (2) *this-worldly,* and thus lacking the essential character of a true religious tradition; and (3) *exclusive,* and thus unable to meet either the requirements of universal reason or the demands of citizenship in the modern state.

These three strikes ruled out any attempt such as Mendelssohn's to pronounce Judaism a religion of reason suitable for enlightened minds and souls in the age and condition of Emancipation.[13] Jewish law blurred the boundaries of public and private so crucial to the emergent conception and creation of a public sphere, and it intruded on both of them by regulating private matters of the home and family and—in principle, at least—regulating affairs of state via its provisions for civil and criminal law. Jews demanded equal access to the rights and opportunities which Emancipation afforded; however, their tradition, by definition, denied equal access and foreclosed open and public debate.[14] Mendelssohn was to be praised for moving Judaism along the path of reform—but in order to actually serve or suit Enlightenment, Jews would have to make the decision which the polemic that prompted the writing of *Jerusalem* had urged upon Mendelssohn himself: conversion to a true religion, a truly rational religion, of which there was only one.

This did not prove an acceptable option to any but a relative handful of European Jews. The live question for the rest of the community was how Jews could define themselves, in more or less authentic continuity with their tradition, while qualifying for the rights and privileges held out to them in the promise of Emancipation and while embracing the opportunities for mind and spirit opened up to them by the advent of Enlightenment. It was clear that the only self-definition likely to prove acceptable to Gentiles in the modern order would be in terms of *religion*. Jews could not be a "nation within the nation," a "state within the state." They would have to be a community of believers, alongside Christians.

All the more reason, then, to take the Kantian challenge to their position with utmost seriousness. For it was precisely the Jewish *religion* that Kant attacked—and he attacked it not in traditional Christian terms (though he echoed those terms) but in the name and the language of Enlightenment. We should note, before proceeding to the Jewish responses, that the *content* of Kant's critique was far from new. "Carnal Israel" had been a theme of pagan polemicists even before the coming of Jesus, and a staple of Christian rhetoric at least since Paul.[15] Argument for argument, moreover, Kant's *Religion* bore an uncanny similarity to Spinoza's *Tractatus*. Kant's critique of Jewish practice also placed him in exalted company among his contemporaries. Arthur Hertzberg and other historians have documented the hostility of the time's leading French and German intellectuals toward both Jews and Judaism in excruciating detail.[16] Most philosophers of the period, Hannah Arendt notes succinctly, despised Jews as a matter of course.[17] It would have been one thing if only Voltaire, with customary acerbity, had poured scorn on the Jews' "detestable chant in your detestable jargon" and demanded that they free themselves of "hateful Jewish superstition and prejudices." Diderot, too, however—a far more tolerant spirit—condemned the Jews' "obstinate adherence to Mosaic law." Herder, more respectful of the Bible than either of the French *philosophes,* wondered how a Jew could possibly expect tolerance from others "so long as he remains so obstinately loyal to his particular national law." Tindal, Bolingbroke, and Shaftesbury were equally critical, according to Isaac Barzilay's survey, while Locke, Montesquieu, and Lessing stood forth as noteworthy exceptions to the general rule.[18]

The power of Kant's critique therefore did not lie in its novelty but in its timing, its cogency, and the immense prestige of its author. The *Religion* appeared at the very moment when French legislators were deciding on the Emancipation of French Jews and just after the matter had become a serious topic of discussion in the German states.[19] It capped a general movement in Enlightenment thought from issues of metaphysics, epistemology, and aesthetics to direct political engagement.[20] Moreover, the essay constituted the most extended statement on religion by the man recognized as the premier philosopher of his day and venerated as the hero and spokesman of Enlightenment. The book was not a dispassionate ivory tower study but an intervention aiming at far-reaching impact. And at the heart of this study, at a historical juncture of obvious importance, Kant had proclaimed in no uncertain terms that in order for Judaism to qualify as a religion—the only legitimate option for modern identity available to Jews—the Jewish *community* would have to be reconstituted (lest, in its exclusivism, it continue to constitute a "state within a state," as Fichte among others had charged). Jewish *selves* would have to be redefined (the old selves were not autonomous). And Jewish *tradition* would need to be reshaped (the old faith fell far short of rationality).[21] The terms of the contest were brutally clear.

2. COMMUNITY, SELF, AND TRADITION

Mendelssohn wrote *Jerusalem* explicitly to address his opponents' contentions on precisely these three points. Whatever else one might say about his work—his biographer Alexander Altmann has called the book "strange, powerful, and unique"[22]—it is very much an essay written in the heat of battle, charged with all the passion and confusion bound up in apologia and self-defense. Consider from Mendelssohn's viewpoint, as a further circle around Kant's footnote, the three changes which Kant demanded in Jewish religion in the name of Enlightenment and ethics.

The most basic and immediate challenge was, of course, *political*. Modernity for Jews meant above all the breakup of integral and semiautonomous communities in which they had lived, worked, and died for centuries, in return for rights—promised or awarded—to live where they pleased, earn a living just as Gentiles did, and influence state policy via office holding and elective representation. The *kehillot*—which had educated Jews, collected their taxes, arbitrated their disputes, punished their offenses, fought for their collective interests, and married, divorced and buried them— would have to go the way of all other medieval corporations. No entity or identity could legitimately stand between individuals and their rulers. The *kehillot* crumbled all the more quickly at this demand since their dissolution had been in progress for over a century already, thanks to economic hardship, political pressure, and internal religious dispute.[23] Nor were Jews especially sad to leave their backwardness and disabilities behind. The former order of variegated rights and patchwork obligations was often quite happily exchanged for uniform law codes in unified sovereign realms that seemed to promise Jews the same privileges as everyone else at exactly the same price. Mendelssohn was not alone in his enthusiasm for these developments or his willingness to pay a certain price for them in the currency of Jewish distinctiveness. Near the conclusion of *Jerusalem* he urged Jews, in the words of the majority tradition, to "give to Caesar, and give to God too!"[24]

It is immediately apparent from Kant's *Religion,* however—and it was apparent to Jews such as Mendelssohn from the outset of the period—that the political demands implicit in such Enlightenment theories, while couched in *universalist* terms, conferred sovereignty on *particular* nation-states. These, in turn, like the theories which legitimated them, rested firmly on Christian underpinnings and were subject to the influence of powerful Christian interests. Jewish partisans of Emancipation had a strong interest in the thoroughgoing application of Enlightenment political theory. They wanted the states of Europe to guarantee freedom of religion in a truly neutral, private sphere untouched by interference from either state or church.[25] Mendelssohn pleads this case eloquently in the first, the political, part of *Jerusalem* (though the version of contract theory on which he seeks to ground his argument is by all accounts seriously flawed).[26] His essay, we should recall, bears the subtitle *On Religious Power and Judaism.* Politics was clearly at the heart of its author's concerns. Indeed, *Jerusalem's* second part, the religious part, makes no sense without the first. There was no point in an emancipated Judaism without the Emancipation of the Jews, no freedom in the Enlightenment state unless it created a space that was truly free not only from Christian pressures but from those of the

state. Kant's essay makes it clear that these concerns were far from ground-
less.

Mendelssohn also welcomed—but with comparable reservations—the
second of Kant's Enlightenment presumptions: the existence of *individual
selves* obligated by contractual loyalties in the political sphere but free to
choose or not to choose loyalties in the religious sphere—allegiances which
Judaism itself (like Christianity) regarded as no less obligatory. Jewish beliefs,
Mendelssohn argued, had nothing to fear from freedom of thought and
inquiry because they were wholly in accordance with the dictates of pure
reason.[27] Jewish observances, far from attempting to coerce reason, constituted a symbolic language meant to remind one of rational truth or lead
one in its direction.[28] Rational truth was "eternal" and, as such, universal.
Jews had no unique purchase on it, no special access to God or goodness or
the afterworld. Where Kant opposed reason to "statutory religion," telling
Jews in so many words that they had to choose between humanity and
their inherited practices, Mendelssohn placed rational truth squarely inside
Judaism and so within the Jew. He explicitly offered his own example as
proof that the two could happily coexist inside a single modern mind and
soul.[29]

Both parties to this dispute understood that what was at stake was the
definition not only of Judaism but of Enlightenment. Kant's conception—
which could not (and did not) please Mendelssohn—is well-known from
his famous essay on the subject (1784). Enlightenment was "man's release
from his self-incurred tutelage," the latter consisting in "lack of resolution
and courage to use reason without direction from another."[30] Mendelssohn
took pains near the end of *Jerusalem* to aver that "we are permitted to reflect
on the law, to inquire into its spirit, and, here and there, where the lawgiver
gave no reason, to surmise a reason [for the law's observance]." However,
until God appeared to revoke the law "in as clear a voice, in as public a
manner, and as far beyond all doubt and ambiguity as He did when He gave
the law itself[,] . . . no sophistry of ours can free us from the strict obedience
we owe to the law."[31]

It is telling that in his own essay on Enlightenment—which appeared
several months before Kant's in the same journal, the *Berlinische Monats-
schrift*—Mendelssohn made the term "Enlightenment" subservient to a
higher achievement, of which it constituted only a part. "*Bildung* is the
broadest concept in Mendelssohn's presentation," Nathan Rotenstreich
writes, "while culture [*Kultur*] and enlightenment [*Aufklärung*] derive from
Bildung. Human destiny, which is not fully defined [by Mendelssohn], serves

as a measurement and as an aim of all our aspirations and endeavors." *Bildung* is crucial to that destiny in a way that *Aufklärung* is not. Note too that *Bildung* is collective rather than individual—bound up in language, which is therefore "presented as the best indicator of the *Bildung* of a certain people."[32]

What matters here is that Enlightenment can conflict with the mores of a particular group or state; in that case, Mendelssohn says obliquely, philosophy has to keep silent. Rotenstreich carefully formulates the matter this way: "In the case of a clash between the universal and the particular, or the theoretical and the practical, philosophy, being closer to theory, is obliged to demand the primacy of theory." But this it should *not* do, in Mendelssohn's estimation, for there are higher goods than Enlightenment to be served. Hence his recommendation that philosophy keep silent—meaning that "concretely or factually" philosophy would "accord primacy to practice or to the civic realm. . . . Mendelssohn does not propose an unequivocal attitude of enlightenment which would ignore the complexities of daily human existence." Accordingly, theory cedes to practice.[33]

This may explain why, in an article significantly titled "On the Common Saying: 'This may be true in theory but does not apply in practice'" (1793), Kant found it necessary to dispute Mendelssohn's conviction (in turn, disputing Lessing) that the human race was not making steady progress toward moral perfection. Individuals might evince such progress, Mendelssohn argued, but humanity as a whole has moved back and forth on the way to ethical attainment. Kant disagreed: progress in culture, he maintained, entailed progress in morality. Mendelssohn, we can see, was more respectful of cultural particularities than was Kant and less certain of reason's power to grasp truth firmly, let alone capture "eternal truths" in language. Enlightenment was a real achievement but a limited one. Theory tended to overreach itself. Practice could therefore legitimately demand its due.[34] This is consistent with Mendelssohn's conviction that Jewish selves, as we noted a moment ago, should and would remain dependent upon the guidance of the Torah—and the practice of its teachings—for their attainment of truth as well as for their acquisition of virtue.

They required, in a word, what Kant's third key presumption had pronounced dispensable: the authority of *tradition*. In Mendelssohn's view, eternal truths did not suffice. "Historical truths, or records of the vicissitudes of former ages," mattered as well (though exactly how much they mattered, and why, is a point never sufficiently clarified in *Jerusalem*). Scriptural narratives directed individual Jews toward truth and "contained the foundation for the national cohesion." As such, they were to "be accepted . . . on faith. Authority alone gives them the required evidence." [35] It would clearly not suffice, as Kant had proposed at the end of his footnote on Mendelssohn, to preserve "the sacred books of this people" in libraries—on the shelf, as it were, rather than in use. Still less could believers trust the proper interpretation of sacred books to philosophers who recognized their "value for scholarship" but denied them all "benefit [to] religion." [36]

Change was not foreign to Mendelssohn's sort of Judaism, and certainly not distasteful. [37] The degree of secularization proposed by Kant in his footnote, however—not merely appropriation of religious property and functions by the state but removal of sacred texts to "the stacks," displacement of religious influence within the self, and subjugation of sacred texts to the interpretations of philosophers—was intolerable. Jews, in Mendelssohn's very different view of the self, were nothing without their historical narratives and the practices that those narratives authorized and demanded. Individual Jews came into the world charged with obligations they could abrogate and stories they could forget only at the price of their very identity.

In consequence, it was simply not the case that "for enlightenment, nothing is required but freedom." [38] This teaching also, which in Romantic views of the self came to picture innocent individuals searching for an inner voice of truth far from the madding crowds of government or communal convention, was utterly at odds with Mendelssohn's view of the world. Autonomous selves informed only by secular cultures and subject to a modern state were not capable of constructing the "ethical commonwealth." God— and sin—still had much to say on the matter of what an individual or society might become. [39] Moreover, while Kant and other theorists of modernity maintained that the autonomous individual was a universal, a given of reason, as it were, Mendelssohn and subsequent Jewish thinkers, even as they adopted and internalized a great deal of this view of self and of culture, kept other conceptions in mind. For them it was not merely a question of which religion enlightened Jewish selves would accept but which sort of self each Jew would be, how that self would see itself in relation to its community and its past, and whether Jews could reconceive Enlightenment and the modern state so as to make room for the selves they were and wished to be.

3. FOUNDING VISIONS OF THE ETHICAL COMMONWEALTH

Consider, as a visual aid to understanding this final issue, an illustration from 1802 entitled *La Liberté des cultes* [Freedom of religions] (see figure 1). [40]

FIGURE 1. *La Liberté des cultes* [Freedom of religions] (1802). Musée Carnavalet, Paris. © Photothèque des Musées de la Ville de Paris. Photo: Olivier Habouzet.

Napoleon stands at the center of the right-hand margin, his height from foot to outstretched hand occupying almost exactly half the illustration's total vertical field. He points with that outstretched right hand toward a Masonic triangle/sun that bears a mysterious inscription and sheds beams of bright yellow light over the picture's upper half. The lower half of the illustration is occupied by a motley set of figures grouped in a semicircle around and below the sovereign, the highest of their heads on a plane exactly level with his waistband. They look up at the sun or at Napoleon with an apparent mixture of curiosity, reverence, and apprehension.

The figures are identified by a numerical key, Napoleon of course being number 1. Moving counterclockwise toward him from the near left, we see a hooded Jew bearing large tablets that are blank except for the name of Moses inscribed on them; a Catholic bishop with a miter on his head, a large cross in his left hand, and a crosier in his right, linked by hues of bright crimson and golden yellow to Napoleon's regal attire; a Quaker, dressed with evident simplicity; a Protestant minister of unidentified denomination, a book open on his chest facing outward, its lettering available for all to read; a kneeling "Chinese priest," bareheaded, his gaze apparently directed at the sun; and, his back to us, a hooded Greek (Orthodox) bishop. The final three figures are for some reason numbered in reverse order: a "Mexican," in native headdress; a "Mohammedan," also adorned with a feather, his bearing suggesting some sort of trance; and an "*Idolâtre des Indes*" bowed low to the ground, his eyes averted from Napoleon and source of light alike. A slanting palm tree on the left bows toward the triangular sun on an angle which meets that of Napoleon's hand and, with the line of figures as its base, constructs a second and larger triangle that frames the entire scene. The illustration comes with a quotation, apparently Napoleon's words to the believers assembled before him—the minisermon, as it were, that is being offered from his small mount: "A wise government protects all religions. You are all brothers; love the government under which you live."

To a remarkable degree, *La Liberté des cultes* captures not only official French ideology of the time but the connections linking political modernity, church-state relations, and Enlightenment claims to direct, unmediated, and objective contact with the truth. Napoleon was neither the first nor the only modern authority to point his audiences to the light, indeed, to effect their relation to it. We note that the triangle's beams stream into his very hand, and reach no other. His arm seems outstretched in order to receive truth and welcome it to the earth. This same pattern of relations informs *Religion within the Limits of Reason Alone* from start to finish. Kant offers an apology assuring government censors of his loyalty.[41] More subtly and significantly, he assumes that the "ethico-civil society" or "ethical commonwealth" envisioned by reason can (indeed, must) "exist in the midst of a political commonwealth and may even be made up of all its members." The modern state is the *means to* and, if perfected, the *end of* the utopian achievement that Kant urges and describes. And so long as the entire human race has not been brought to the point of doing the right thing because and only because it is the right thing to do—that is, so long as the "ethical commonwealth" has not yet come into being—state power would have to "impress these laws" upon people by other means.[42]

In *La Liberté des cultes,* Napoleon points the assembled religious leaders to the light, but his sword is conspicuous at his side. Should the sun alone not be sufficient to impose peace among the religions at Napoleon's feet, or should believers blinded to truth by their various creeds look at the light without really seeing it, his sword stands ready to assist. The legitimacy of the sovereign's rule over his diverse subjects (the spatial relations in figure 1 make the hierarchy of the preposition "over" clear) rests on his contact with the light as well as on the fact that he is one ("*un gouvernement*") as truth is one, while they, like errors, are many ("*toutes les réligions*").[43] His power rests on that difference as well. Universals in his time and place, as in our own, have potency over particulars. This was evident both in the founding theories of Enlightenment and in the actual states into whose service those theories were pressed—with or without the approval of the theorists.

Mendelssohn was made aware of this relationship between rational truth and state power by the text that seems to have lain open on his desk as he wrote *Jerusalem:* Spinoza's *Tractatus Theologico-Politicus*.[44] The whole point of that book, as stated in its preface, is to demonstrate that freedom of worship in accord with the dictates of conscience could "be granted without prejudice to the public peace." "Superstition," Spinoza's term for false religion, had engendered "many terrible wars and revolutions." Philosophy would serve the public good by setting forth criteria for true religion and convincing modern sovereigns that it, unlike the churches of lies and ignorance, posed no threat to their legitimate ambitions. To accomplish this, however, Spinoza—philosophy's advocate—must "point out the misconceptions which, like scars of our former bondage, still disfigure our notion of religion, and must expose the false views about civil authority which many have most impudently advocated."[45] He must, in other words, redefine both state and religion, the former via a theory of contract delimiting individual rights and obligations, the latter via an epistemology that makes rational knowledge utterly superior to revelation—and so, of course, makes the bearers of revelation utterly subservient to the state as well. Religion is left only with the task of arousing obedience among sectors of the population too unsophisticated for philosophy—clearly a task for functionaries supervised by government. For that reason, the final chapter in the *Tractatus,* entitled "That in a Free State Every Man May Think What He Like, and Say What He Thinks," is preceded by a chapter with the title "It Is Shown That the Right over Matters Spiritual Lies Wholly with the Sovereign, and That the Outward Forms of Religion Should Be in Accordance with Public Peace, If We Would Obey God Aright." Philosophy bends to the sovereign as well: at the conclusion of his preface, Spinoza preemptively offers to retract anything in his treatise that the political authorities might find offensive.

Note too that Spinoza directs our attention to the *"outward* forms of religion"—forms like those we have seen represented iconographically in figure 1 by the various garbs surrounding Napoleon's civic costume. Belief—an affair of the inner self and, as such, not subject to visual depiction—need not be controlled by government so long as it does not result in actions harmful to the public peace. Spinoza is confident that only a handful of "dogmas of universal faith"—almost exactly equivalent to Kant's religion of reason and Mendelssohn's "eternal truths"—are "necessary to be believed, in order that every man, without exception, may be able to obey God." People need to believe in God's existence, providence, and salvation. The sole purpose of such faith is to secure popular obedience to truths that the philosopher comes to recognize through reason alone.[46] The real issue is thus not what people *believe* but what they *do,* just as in Kant's threefold critique of Judaism the real issue is not the Jews' putative lack of belief in an afterworld (which Spinoza too lacks, of course) but the actions which allegedly transpire as a consequence of this-worldliness: coercive and exclusivist observance.

La Liberté des cultes thus helps to explain why in Spinoza, as in Kant, the "cult" of Judaism is not allowed to remain free of criticism and control. Behavior matters in a way that belief does not. Spinoza pays homage to the political as well as the cognitive power of ritual when, directly before launching into his argument that true "divine law" is utterly opposed to "ceremonial observance," he writes that Jewish collective survival over two millennia should not be taken as a miracle but, rather, ascribed to the "universal hate" excited against Jews by "outward rites, rites conflicting with those of other nations" and by "the sign of circumcision which they most scrupulously observe." Indeed, he continues,

> the sign of circumcision is, as I think, so important that I could persuade myself that it alone would preserve the nation for ever. Nay, I would go so far as to believe that if the foundations of their religion have not emasculated their minds they may even, if occasion offers, so changeable are human affairs, raise up their empire afresh, and that God may a second time elect them.[47]

The details of Spinoza's proof that divine law—a universal imperative concerned only with happiness and truth—can have nothing to do with "ceremonial observances . . . ordained in the Old Testament for the Hebrews only"[48] need not detain us here. We have already seen the essentials of the argument in Kant, along with the echo—explicit in Spinoza even more than in Kant—of Paul's critique of Pharisaic legalism, on which both philosophers expressly draw.[49] Nor, thanks to Yosef Yerushalmi's exhaustive treatment of the matter, need we dwell on Spinoza's patently tendentious explanation for Jewish survival.[50] More important for our purposes, Spinoza makes it abundantly clear that, while "inward worship" could not rightfully be regulated by the state, the "rites of religion and the outward observances of piety should be in accordance with the public peace and well-being, and should therefore be determined by the sovereign power alone." He is uncompromising on this point. Individual churches would no doubt continue or initiate particular observances in keeping with their diverse traditions. But all rites must be under the sovereign's sole control. The state should have authority over the appointment of religious functionaries, the administration of religious rites, and the task of "defining or strengthening the foundations of the Church and her doctrines."[51]

We get a hint of how a European government might regard the ceremonies of various churches—their outward garb, as in figure 1, varies considerably—from Spinoza's defense of Christian rites, on the one hand, and his dismissal of Jewish ceremonies, on the other. The former were "instituted by Christ . . . as external *signs* of the universal church . . . ordained for the preservation of a society." By contrast, Jewish ceremonies were originally established as *laws* of a political state no longer in existence and, consequently—in the absence of God's "raising up their empire afresh"—had long since become irrelevant.[52] Kant makes exactly the same distinction, to the same end.[53] Christian ceremonies, accepted freely by reason as a means to universal moral ends, were not only permitted but exemplary. Jewish ceremonies, intrinsically coercive, this-worldly, and exclusivist, were an obstacle to all that reason hoped to achieve, a barrier on the road to the ethical commonwealth.

These assumptions were widespread. Friends of Jewish Emancipation simply assumed that the ceremonies would be abandoned as a consequence of the Jews' *Verbesserung*. Opponents of Emancipation demanded an end to Sabbath observance, dietary laws, circumcision, and distinctive dress and language as a condition for the Jews' being accorded the Rights of Man.[54] For government officials, the philosophical niceties and religious details probably mattered far less than the likelihood—stated in so many words by Spinoza—that "the sign of circumcision is . . . so important, that . . . it alone would preserve the nation for ever"—no matter what the political arrangements prevailing at the time! The lesson for political elites bent on unifying disparate populations was clear. Unless Jews abandoned distinctive rituals, they might well remain a "nation within a nation," a "state within a state." This could not be tolerated. "If the foundations of their religion have not emasculated their minds"—and, we can add, if their minds did not come of their own volition to emasculate the foundations of their religion— the relevant practices would have to be altered by other means. Reason condemned such ceremonies and pronounced them an anachronism. Napoleon was not alone in brandishing the sword as well as the light, as we will see in Chapter 4.

Mendelssohn's reading of this situation facing Jewish practice evidently led him to formulate three conclusions. In the decades following *Jerusalem*'s publication, these three points proved determinative of Jewish observance.

First, *the scope available for Jewish behavior in obedience to divine commandments would henceforth be severely constricted.* It had already been progressively limited during centuries of existence in exile. The Torah's original intention, according to Mendelssohn, had been the creation of a social reality in accord with, and pointing to, eternal and historical truths. Everything a youth saw, morning, noon, and night, was meant to lead him or her constantly in that direction. "In this original constitution, state and religion were not conjoined, but *one;* not connected, but identical."[55] In exile, however, the two had been at variance. Directives other than the Torah's held sway; the rabbis had legitimated acquiescence to this order in their famous dictum "The law of the land is the law." Much civil and criminal law remained outside the halakhic domain. Emancipation was about to contract that domain still further, sweeping away Jewish courts, Jewish schools, Jewish languages, Jewish public spaces. Only the "four ells" of synagogue, on the one hand, and "home," on the other, would remain. Hence, perhaps, Mendelssohn's use of Spinoza's term "ceremonies" for the commandments despite the compromising aesthetic (and thus nonobligatory) connotation of the word. Ceremony—ritual—was virtually all that Jews had left. Mendelssohn apparently hoped that it could do the job of leading people to eternal and historical truths nonetheless, if only he and others could make the case for the commandments sufficiently compelling. It is perhaps telling that he was far less sanguine on this point in private correspondence than in public utterances like *Jerusalem*.[56]

Even in the best of scenarios—and Mendelssohn's essay, as one might guess from its title, tends to shift between elegy and utopia—major compromise from the Jewish side would be required. When Mendelssohn was summoned to meet his monarch on the holiday of Shmini Atzeret in 1771, he deemed it the better part of wisdom to appear, though this meant breaking Jewish law by riding in a carriage. He preserved a measure of dignity by descending at a distance from the ruler's residence and walking the rest of the way on foot. When, in another instance, a German state decreed that immediate burial of the dead in accordance with Jewish law was barbaric and legislated a three-day waiting period, Mendelssohn publicly argued that Jewish law conformed to the intentions of the state even with its provisions for speedier burial, but privately he found rabbinic precedent for submission to the decree, thereby arousing the wrath of a leading German authority, Rabbi Jacob Emden.[57] In *Jerusalem* itself, boxed into a corner by his own separation of belief from practice and his conviction that social contracts can bind the latter but never the former, Mendelssohn advanced the dubious argument that a person appointed to circumcise newborn males could fulfill that office—for which he had contracted—even should he lose his faith in God. "For the circumciser would enjoy his income and rank not because he approves of the doctrinal opinion [pronounced in the ceremony's blessings!] but because of the operation he performs."[58] Concessions to the demands of daily existence had long been a staple of Jewish life in exile, and observance of the commandments under conditions of Emancipation would perhaps be compromised still further. So, we might add, would clarity of thought.

Second, Mendelssohn seems to have recognized that, in his day, *reason rather than Christianity or Islam had assumed the prerogative to decide on public observance* and, indeed, to define what constituted the public sphere within which its authority held sway. *Jerusalem*'s immediate polemical opponents may have been theologians, but it was reason—spelled out by philosophy and enforced by state authority—which Jewish thinkers then and thereafter would contest most vigorously. As disputation in the medieval period had been conducted according to scriptural givens shared by both sides, Jews would now have to employ prevailing rationalist assumptions and modes of argument in an effort to persuade Gentiles that Jewish practice was, in Spinoza's terms, no threat to the public peace. No less, Jews would, using these same tools, have to persuade other Jews to undertake the limited array of observances still possible in their private sphere and to read the scriptural narratives within which those observances found their meaning and justification.

This effort—on view in *Jerusalem*—of course faced formidable obstacles. Both Enlightenment doctrine and the emergent patterns of bourgeois culture condemned Jewish forms to marginality, irrelevance, and superstition. And the only apparent alternative to Enlightenment and Emancipation for Jews—return to a political ghetto, loss of economic opportunity, coercive observance of commandments that had in many cases long since lost appeal—was to Jews such as Mendelssohn entirely unacceptable.

His aim, then, was to enter fully into the new world opened up by Emancipation and Enlightenment while quarreling with the fine points of the terms according to which truth and freedom were generally defined. He had to ensure space in the modern order for truth, eternal and historical, as he knew it from Judaism and for the freedom to pursue that twofold truth by means of the commandments.

If this effort was to have a chance of success, Mendelssohn had to drive a wedge between Enlightenment ideals of an emancipated political order and the patently Christian presumptions of some philosophers and state authorities. Kant would become the leading case in point. The best of Enlightenment theory had to be contrasted with less favorable Enlightenment practice; political theory *and* state practice had to be critiqued on the basis of principles and goals that philosophers and governments had themselves proclaimed. Liberty for the Jewish religion thus demanded what we might call the deconstruction of Enlightenment theory but what Mendelssohn regarded, not without good cause, as its fulfillment.

Hence the vigorous and thoroughgoing argument for religious freedom in part 1 of *Jerusalem,* couched in classic Enlightenment terms of contract theory; hence, too, the exercises in part 2, conducted in the spirit of Montesquieu, which were designed to get European readers to see themselves through the eyes of distant others. In one passage, Mendelssohn defends Hindu myth as an alternative and valid vessel of eternal truth. In another, he concocts the marvelous fiction of having a South Seas chieftain, brought to England by Captain Cook, gape at the strange worship conducted in the Temple of Providence at the Dessau Philanthropinum.[59] In this respect, Mendelssohn and the several generations of Jewish thinkers who followed in his footsteps took advantage of the dual status that, as Paul Mendes-Flohr has explained, has empowered modern Jewish intellectuals more generally. Mendelssohn was at once a "cognitive insider," able to manipulate the language of Enlightenment as well as anyone, having mastered and internalized its discourse, and an *"axial outsider,"* existentially committed to an identity and a set of practices that set him apart from what the surrounding society was and proclaimed to be.[60]

Third, Mendelssohn apparently realized as well that *his "theologico-political" position would not only isolate him from Gentile philosophers and theologians but would fail to secure anything like universal support among Jews.* The loss of coercive power by the Jewish community would necessarily lead to multiple patterns of observance. Leading rabbis in Mendelssohn's lifetime frequently attacked his compromises as excessive.[61] His translation of the Bible to German, for example, was denounced by some as a means to assimilation, even though the German text was written in Hebrew characters. These attacks foreshadowed still more rancorous communal divisions yet to come, as well as the dispute—which continues to this day—over whether the distinction between "acculturation" and "assimilation" is credible in theory or practice. In the generation or two following Mendelssohn's death, political and religious dispute among Jews became pronounced. Points on the ideological spectrum that had not even been identified several decades earlier were staked out, occupied, and bitterly contested, not infrequently in Mendelssohn's name. Even the relatively small group who decided that particular religious forms in service to universal truth could be traded, without cost to integrity, for majority forms could invoke the author of *Jerusalem* by citing the conversion of several of his children. Was not one "ceremonial script" as good as another?

Other Jews in the nineteenth century reached a conclusion in some ways still more radical and certainly more at variance with Mendelssohn's vision of religion and politics. It held that Jewish ritual had been intended all along to serve as a means to universal ends of truth and justice and that these ends were about to be achieved through secular means, without the assistance of a divine messiah or the guidance of divine teachings. Jewish practice should therefore take the form of *political activity*—in which Jews would engage side by side with other right-thinking people of all nationalities and creeds—and only that form, since Enlightenment and Emancipation had together rendered all religious forms, Christian as well as Jewish, archaic and dispensable.[62] Religions need not coexist—Mendelssohn's aim—because they were about to be "overcome." Judaism's universal vision of humanity would henceforth be pursued by strictly human and universal means.

4. THE JEWISH QUESTION

Marx spoke eloquently for many in these movements (albeit in advance of most, and for decades without being read by any but a few) when, in his essays "On the Jewish Question" (1843), he mounted a brilliant critique both of bourgeois Emancipation—still reluctant, at that late date, to make room for Jews—and of religion in all its forms, Jewish or Christian, Orthodox or Reform. "On the Jewish Question" marks the logical conclusion to this set of reflections around Kant and Mendelssohn because it decisively burst the bounds of the discourse of Emancipation and Enlightenment which has structured our discussion thus far.[63] It was apparent that the "Jewish question" had not been resolved by the regnant theorists of modernity (which now included not only Kant but Hegel and the Hegelians): the fault, in Marx's view, was no less modernity's than it was Judaism's. Emancipation was incomplete, Enlightenment in need of critique. As a result, the very notion of modern Jewish religious practice was fundamentally incoherent.

Marx's immediate target, Bruno Bauer, had argued (in Marx's paraphrase) that "the Christian state, by its very nature, is incapable of emancipating the Jew," while "the Jew, by his very nature, cannot be emancipated."[64] It took a secular state like France, free of theological domination, to accord religious freedom to its subjects. The Jews, as subjects, had for their part to demonstrate willingness to place duties of citizenship to their state above the demands of their religion. This they had not done. The Jewish question had yet to be resolved, Bauer maintained, because the private loyalty of the Jew still reigned supreme over political allegiance. "He is and remains a Jew, even though he is a citizen and as such lives in a universal human condition; his restricted Jewish nature always finally triumphs over his human and political obligations." The opposite would hold true, Bauer continued—"the Jew would really have ceased to be Jewish"—if, for example, "he attended and took part in the public business of the Chamber of Deputies on the Sabbath." In that case, even if the majority of Jews still felt obligated to perform their religious duties, those duties could safely be considered a private matter.[65]

Marx at once points out that Bauer had failed to take his argument far enough. Judaism had been criticized, its existence made dependent on fulfillment of certain conditions and limited to the private sphere. The state, however, the agent of this limitation in the name of humanity and justice, had been left uncriticized. Marx's aim is hardly to defend Judaism: "The existence of religion is the existence of a defect," he says pointedly. It is a mark of alienation that testifies to the incomplete Emancipation of its adherents and of the society to which they belong.[66] Indeed, in the companion essay criticizing Bauer's piece "The Capacity of the Present-Day Jews and Christians to Be Free," Marx indulges in the now infamous argument that plays (as Moses Hess and Heinrich Heine had before him) on the dual meaning of *Judentum* in German as "Judaism" and "commerce." The practical meaning of Judaism, Marx avers, is money. It is "the jealous god of Israel, besides which no other gods may exist." Christians who made money into a world power had thereby become Jews. "We discern in Judaism . . . a universal antisocial element of the present time. . . . In the final analysis, the emancipation of the Jews is the emancipation of mankind from Judaism."[67] Jewish religious observance is singled out for particular criticism. "The law, without basis or reason, of the Jew, is only the religious caricature of morality and right in general, without basis or reason; the purely *formal* rites with which the world of self-interest encircles itself."[68] Marx wants a state free of both Judaism and Christianity, a world so without alienation from the essential "species-being" of humanity that it has no need of fictive projections of human attributes and capacities onto God.

In the meantime, however—the point relevant to our concerns— within the scheme of compromises known as the bourgeois state, demands could not legitimately be made upon the Jews that the state failed to make upon others or upon itself. All citizens of the bourgeois state lived "a double existence," Marx insists, not just Jews. In the political community, people regarded themselves as communal beings, while in "civil society," life outside the realm of political theory, they acted strictly as private individuals, treated others as means to ends, degraded themselves "to the role of mere means," and became "the plaything of alien powers." "The so-called rights of man," granting Jews religious freedom within limits still under debate, "are simply the rights of a member of civil society, that is to say, of egoistic man, of man separated from other men and from the community."[69] Judaism, then, was but one (not terribly influential) instance of the "secular opposition . . . between the political state and its presuppositions . . . of the conflict between general interest and private interest."[70] As such, it could not legitimately be singled out for criticism, let alone for disprivilege. The charge of exclusivism leveled by Bauer against the Jews held for *all of civil society* as such—not despite but because of the so-called universal rights enforced by particular secular states claiming to be the agents of Enlightenment and Emancipation.

We can, I think, safely leave aside the vexing question of whether and to what degree Marx's Jewish background influenced his thought here or elsewhere; no less, I hope, we can avoid simplistic assertions or denials that self-hatred or anti-Semitism are on view in Marx's characterization of *Judentum* and his expressed desire for its "overcoming."[71] It is crucial for our purposes, however, that Marx chose to address the central issues of human versus political emancipation—and thus to challenge not only Hegelians such as Bauer but the master himself—by writing essays centered on the emancipation of the Jews. It is no less important that Marx's treatment of these issues is marked by pronounced antipathy to Jewish belief and practice as well as to the pretensions of the Jews' opponents. The point, as he described it in a letter to his colleague Arnold Ruge that same year, was "to

punch as many holes as possible in the Christian state and smuggle in rational views as far as we can"—precisely what Mendelssohn and countless
other Jews, working with very different political assumptions, had been attempting for decades.[72] Scholars who treat the Jews as a mere stand-in for a
general category carry on the false universalization that Marx condemned
in essays bearing the name of the most relevant particular he knew.

In a subsequent polemic responding to the response that Bauer had
made to his Jewish critics (Bauer's essay, unlike Marx's reply, had already
garnered immense attention),[73] Marx (now in partnership with Engels)
sharpened both his rhetoric and his argument. *The Holy Family* (1845) pur-
sues "the Jewish question" in three "campaigns." The first, approvingly citing responses to Bauer by rabbis Samuel Hirsch and Gustav Philippson,
insists contra Bauer that the Jews had played a significant role in history.
"They must have counted for something," Hirsch wrote; to which Bauer
had sarcastically replied, "An eyesore is something too—does that mean
it contributes to develop my eyesight?" Marx weighs in clearly as a Jew.
"Something which has been an eyesore to me from birth, as the Jews have
been to the Christian world, and which persists and develops with the eye
is not an ordinary sore, but a wonderful one, one that really belongs to my
eye and must even contribute to a highly original development of my eyesight." Marx has no patience for Bauer's conviction that "civil equality of
the Jews can be implemented only where Jewry no longer exists."[74]

The second campaign takes the side of the material world against the
preference of "absolute criticism" for something more ethereal. Hegelian
idealism is linked explicitly to Christianity here, materialism and socialism
to Judaism; "mass-type Jews," that is, "real Jews" whose daily activities bear
witness to their identity, are (remarkably!) the type of the human masses
to whom Marx wishes to bring human—rather than merely political—
emancipation. Compare Bauer's claim: "The Jews are emancipated to the
extent they have now reached in theory, they are free to the extent that
they wish to be free." At this juncture, Marx approvingly cites Gabriel Riesser, the leading advocate of Jewish rights in the German states, who of
course knew a great deal about the difference between freedom in theory
and freedom in practice.[75]

The third campaign reiterates Marx's conviction that the Jewish question is social and not merely religious, attacks Bauer's argument that freedom for Jews is a privilege and not a right, ridicules Bauer's belief that
Prussia constitutes the "absolute state" for which Enlightenment has
yearned, and returns to the debate in the French National Assembly over

compulsory Sunday rest as proof that equality in theory does not translate into equality in practice. "Now, according to free theory, Jews and Christians are equal, but according to this practice Christians have a privilege over Jews; for otherwise how could the Sunday of the Christians have a place in a law made for all Frenchmen?" Bauer, recognizing the contradiction, had urged only that the state leave religion to the private sphere (where Jewish practice would presumably wither away). Marx again argues that assignment of a privilege to the private sphere is hardly the abolition of the privilege; Bauer was wrong to think that if we "take from religion its exclusive power[,] . . . it will no longer exist." A state composed almost entirely of Christians remained a Christian state, its Jews a tolerated minority, even if—as in the France of the National Assembly and Napoleon—freedom and equality of all religions were enshrined in the Rights of Man.[76]

These are of course the issues with which we have been wrestling all along. Marx serves our discussion by bringing those issues into sharper focus, carrying them forward from Kant to Hegel and from the late eighteenth to the mid-nineteenth century, and divorcing critique of the prevalent conceptions of Enlightenment and Emancipation from the particularist (and religious) Jewish standpoint articulated in our survey by Mendelssohn. No less, Marx's distinction between "Sabbath Jews" and "real Jews" assists our inquiry into modern Jewish practice by precluding attribution of a specious unity to the group whose existence proved a challenge to the equally specious universality of the modern state. After Marx, the "Sabbath Jew" found in Mendelssohn's *Jerusalem* is as patently inadequate as the unreal Jews who populate Spinoza's pages, or Kant's—or Marx's own! His essays of 1843, as Julius Carlebach has pointed out, appeared in a journal filled almost entirely with essays by real Jews such as Heinrich Heine and Moses Hess whom Marx knew quite well and who, he knew, bore no resemblance whatever to his stereotype.[77] The study of modern Jewish practice, if it bears Marx's insights in mind, must do better than Marx's practice. Such study demands a theory that is adequate to the diversity of Jews and *their* practices as much as it takes account of multiple visions of modernity.[78]

5. CONCLUSION

It is fitting that having begun this chapter with Kant's footnote on Mendelssohn, we conclude with a no less problematic reference to the Jewish philosopher that occurs in the afterword to the second German edition of *Kapital* (1873). Defending his procedure of critique via textual commentary,

Marx observes that in the mid-1840s, when he began work on his magnum opus (and wrote his essays on the Jewish question),

> it was the good pleasure of the peevish, arrogant, mediocre epigones who now talk large in cultured Germany, to treat Hegel in same [*sic*] way as the brave Moses Mendelssohn in Lessing's time treated Spinoza, i.e., as a "dead dog." I therefore openly avowed myself the pupil of that mighty thinker, and even . . . coquetted with the modes of expression peculiar to him. . . With [Hegel, theory] is standing on its head. It must be turned right side up again, if you would discover the rational kernel within the mystical shell.[79]

Mendelssohn had not treated Spinoza as a dead dog—quite the contrary. Mendelssohn's role in the famous dispute over Lessing's alleged Spinozism was that of an expert witness for the defense of both thinkers. What is more, though Marx characterizes Mendelssohn as "brave," he lumps him with arrogant and mediocre contemporaries who had treated their distinguished teachers badly. Marx had acted differently, giving Hegel the deference of line-by-line textual opposition, the better to show that Hegel had gotten everything upside down and backward! Mendelssohn, archetypal Jew, earns the favor of recall in Marx's science and even the appearance of praise. However, he is denied his own voice and is subjected to an interpretation that he could not possibly condone. This is precisely the fate of Jewish practice in all the theories of modernity that we have examined thus far—and it remains the case, to a remarkable and disturbing degree, in the twentieth-century theories to which we now turn.

TWO

Twentieth-Century Theories of Modernity and the Study of Jewish Practice

Approaching the study of modern Jewish practice via the set of theoretical lenses commonly used in the contemporary academy—Weber and Durkheim, Berger and Geertz, Habermas and Lyotard, et al.—we immediately confront a methodological problem, set forth most coherently in our generation by Pierre Bourdieu. It is that the tools at our disposal are no less indispensable to the task at hand than they are inadequate. The "logic of scholarly practice" predisposes us to analyze the logic of our subjects' practice in terms of purposes and meanings too limited to "capture" what their practices are about. We know in theory that theory, like all other lenses, must be *seen through* in both senses of the words; that science necessarily involves what Weber called "blinders"; that, in Lyotard's postmodern formulation, much is inevitably excluded by a theory's "forgettings." In practice, however, a great deal of our subjects' activity and consciousness remains

> unthinkable . . . not only everything that cannot be thought for lack of the ethical or political dispositions which tend to bring it into consideration, but also everything that cannot be thought for lack of instruments of thought such as problematics, concepts, methods and techniques (which explains why good intentions so often make bad sociology) . . . [1]

I shall argue in this chapter that the "blinders" and "forgettings" of contemporary theory are particularly problematic in the case of modern *49*

Jewish practice, for two reasons. First, Durkheim, Weber, and their successors throughout the century have for understandable reasons paid far more attention to Christianity (and to secularism) than to Judaism. Sheer numbers of adherents, and the scholars' own commitments, provide adequate explanation for that bias. The result is that modern Judaism—and, particularly, Jewish practice—remain out of view in all of the most influential descriptive and normative visions of modern society. This is a function of what Bourdieu calls "ethical or political dispositions." The "values" that motivate and inform contemporary theory have not pointed the great majority of modern scholars (including the many Jews among them) in the direction of Jewish observance.

Second, and more important, such study is significantly constrained, or even precluded, by the framework of "problematics, concepts, methods, and techniques"—inherited from classical theorists—which are by and large taken for granted in the contemporary academy. One cannot, for example, take Weber's three modes of authority (rational, traditional, charismatic) or Berger's three forms of religious response to the "heretical imperative" (inductive, deductive, reductive) and simply "plug in the Jews." The prophets were not charismatic authorities, as the rabbis were not merely traditional. Rosenzweig, *pace* Berger, does not belong with Karl Barth in the deductive category. Nor, as we shall see, can a community of Jewish practice be accommodated inside Habermas's concepts of "undistorted speech" and "the public sphere." The lack of fit remains no matter how tightly one stretches those concepts or squeezes the Jews. It goes without saying that Lyotard's postmodern vision of a world free of "metanarrative" has no room whatever for any Judaism that has yet existed, modern or premodern, including the most radical versions of Reform.

Hence the dilemma stated so cogently by Bourdieu. The practices of modern Jews are rendered so much more comprehensible with the help of Weber, Durkheim, and their theoretical successors that no responsible scholar could think of turning to the subject without those theorists' mighty assistance. I certainly won't. However, a vision of our subject limited to what we can see through the usual set of lenses, those provided by the dominant theorists, leaves us blind to much that we should be seeing of Jewish practice. Indeed, it altogether prevents us from seeing what can be learned about modernity and theories of modernity by paying careful attention to precisely those actors who have eluded the mainstream categories in which scholarship has generally sought to contain them.

The context for these reflections is thus twofold. On the one hand, our discussion will consider and be shaped by the substantial revisions which have been introduced into the classical theories of modernity since Marx, particularly by recent critiques of the "philosophical discourse of modernity" that have sought to bring a host of previously excluded voices and behaviors into the dominant theoretical canon. On the other hand, Jews themselves have made immense adjustments in the name of Emancipation and Enlightenment—not least through the practice of scholarship that subjects Jewish culture and behavior to critical scrutiny and standards that claim universal, scientific validity. We possess, at century's end, a burgeoning literature on both the theory of modernity and the patterns of Jewish practice. The literature on practice more than ever stands in the near distance of prevailing discourse and, from that position, challenges the adequacy of theory's putatively universalist reports. Our purpose here is to reckon with that challenge, and so—in Bourdieu's terms once again—"to bring to light the theory of practice which theoretical knowledge implicitly applies."[2]

We shall proceed by considering three pairs of theorists—Emile Durkheim and Max Weber, Peter Berger and Philip Rieff, Jürgen Habermas and Jean-François Lyotard—and analyzing the encounters with Jewish practice which those works do and do not make possible. It is apparent from even a superficial glance at these thinkers that the evaluation of reason by reason has noticeably altered as compared with that in their classical predecessors from Spinoza to Marx. All share a widespread recognition that the word "reason" should no longer, as it were, be written with a capital *R;* all believe that reason, for all we continue to depend upon it, should be regarded as a preeminently social product rather than as a given of nature or consciousness. Utopian confidence in the potential for rational achievement, political or speculative—evident in Marx even more than in Kant—has likewise given way to a significant degree of disenchantment. The role of religion, however, remains ambiguous at best in most of the thinkers we shall consider and, to all but one of them, the Jews and Judaism remain utterly marginal. My aim once again is to check, to deploy, and where necessary to correct the theoretical lenses which such thinkers employ, so that we can in future chapters sight the practices in which modern Jews have engaged and reflect on what they might have meant.

1. DURKHEIM, WEBER, AND THE PRACTICES OF JUDAISM

We best enter both this set of issues and Durkheim's scholarship, I think, via *Suicide* (1897), which was conceived and presented to its readers as an example of why the world needed sociology and as a sample of the benefits which the new science could confer. Thus the double entendre of the book's subtitle, *A Study in Sociology*.[3] An event as seemingly individual and irrational as a person's decision to take his or her own life turns out, in Durkheim's analysis, to be a "social fact" that varies with a set of factors widely shared, wholly external to the self, and therefore subject to rational investigation.[4] *Suicide* remains a classic and great book despite major errors of fact and flaws of logic, most of which need not concern us here. Our focus will be the salvific potential of Durkheim's new science in relation to Judaism and the Jews. Truth could do more than set people free, Durkheim proclaims. It could actually save them, give them life, stave off death—so long as they did not cleave to false redemptions, enshrined in outmoded and dysfunctional practices and beliefs.[5]

Durkheim had already suggested in his first great work, *On the Division of Labor in Society* (1893), that "organic solidarity"—a voluntary union among autonomous individuals—could fully replace the premodern "mechanical solidarity." The key to achieving this regeneration was development of social scientific tools—outlined in strict analogy to the natural sciences in Durkheim's *Rules of Sociological Method* (1895)—and the deployment of those tools to revitalize collective consciousness.[6] This diagnosis is fully spelled out in *Suicide,* and the cure first indicated in the book's conclusion. Durkheim's next major work, *The Elementary Forms of the Religious Life* (1913), argued at some length the case for identity of function (and, so, of essence) between the sort of *conscience collective* that he proposed and the forms of traditional religion that he deemed outmoded. The new faith, unlike the old, would be rationally constructed with its desired moral functions in mind. Durkheim hoped to overcome "the maladjustment from which we suffer," and to relieve the "poverty of morality" afflicting his society, via a major transformation of "collective existence itself."[7] The process would be planned and directed by reason, science, sociology.

There is a problem, however: reason too has its ills. We learn of them in Durkheim's initial detailed diagnosis of the disease that his science will help to cure. "Egoistic suicide," by far the most prevalent form of self-destruction identified in the book, is shown in given areas to vary with freedom of reflection. Protestant countries or regions have the highest death rate, Catholic areas the lowest. Jews until midcentury had killed themselves even less frequently than did Catholics in every area but Bavaria and had recently tended to exceed the Catholic rate only slightly, despite an urban residential concentration and an occupational profile that should otherwise have inclined them toward Protestant-like numbers. "The only essential difference between Catholicism and Protestantism," Durkheim observes, "is that the second permits free inquiry to a far greater degree than the first." The conclusion is striking and not a little alarming to a social scientist. Protestantism's "spirit of free inquiry" was apparently causing societies and individuals to kill themselves.

Durkheim quickly adds, by way of self-defense, that this cause was really the effect of a prior cause: the weakening of "traditional beliefs." For if traditional beliefs had succeeded in retaining their hold on adherents, it would never have occurred to anyone to criticize those beliefs. The search for authority follows rather than precedes the loss of authority. Science is not responsible for the ill effects it surveys; indeed, reflection by scientists, as by laypeople, becomes imperative only when called forth by an absence that it must try to fill—"in this case a collective credo." No "religious society" can exist without such a credo. "The more extensive the credo the more unified and strong is the society." Premodern groups, by attaching individuals completely (or "mechanically") to "an identical body of doctrine," had "socialize[d] them in proportion as this body of doctrine is extensive and firm." As the doctrine was more integral, so the church—and as the church, so the society. Solidarity was high. Individual divergences were curtailed by "close and constant surveillance." Life went on.[8] We note that Durkheim holds a rather vague "spirit of free inquiry" responsible for the higher suicide rate among Protestants and that he claims it followed upon the "overthrow of traditional beliefs" rather than on the social transformation which we would expect him to emphasize. So, too, "traditional beliefs" are given sole credit for having united and socialized entire populations—except for the power of "close and constant surveillance," a qualifier he adds almost as an afterthought.

There is, however, a second major type of suicide: "anomic," caused by "anomie"—the deregulation of the passions, the failure of society to limit individual desire and to harmonize it with the requirements of the general good. Unbounded desires are always insatiable, and sudden affluence therefore results in suicide as much as sudden impoverishment. Both upset "a genuine regimen," disturb the "moral discipline."[9] We might say that egoistic suicides suffer from an excessive "I think," and anomic suicides from an overweening "I want."[10] To complicate matters still further, Durkheim insists that society can *generate* the "suicidogenic current" as well as *protect* individuals from it.[11] The proper and healthy balance between self and group is hard to find. Durkheim seems certain that the culture of individualism emerging in his own day has precluded that balance as a matter of course.

I have reviewed Durkheim's argument here because the Jews in two key respects stand midway between the individual pole and the collective pole of his analysis, the poles represented by Protestantism and Catholicism, respectively. Jews thus doubly represent, as it were, the balance essential to society's healing. In the *past,* Jews had lived in a "compact and coherent society with a strong feeling of self-consciousness and unity. Everyone thought and lived alike"—the very model of "mechanical" solidarity. Here Durkheim is careful to emphasize the role of collective behavior as opposed to belief. "Judaism, in fact, like all early religions, consists basically of a body of practices minutely governing all the details of life and leaving little free room to individual judgment." *Contemporary* Judaism, by contrast, was notable for its encouragement of (secular) education and reflection. "If the Jew manages to be both well instructed and very disinclined to suicide, it is because of the special origin of his desire for knowledge." Jews studied in order to overcome the hatred to which they were constantly exposed. Their unique sort of reflection, halfway between Protestant freedom and Catholic constraint, combined "the advantages of the severe discipline characteristic of small and ancient groups with the benefits of the intense culture enjoyed by our great societies." They had become, in a word, the model of "organic" solidarity.[12]

This is striking: Jews—through a synthesis of their premodern religious mode and their modern secular mode—turn out to be the paradigm for Durkheim's envisioned union of solidarity and reflection, *Gemeinschaft* and *Gesellschaft.* The romanticism of his vision is apparent in the idealization of both past and present Jewish society and in the unacknowledged slippage in his narrative from one to the other within the space of a single paragraph. Durkheim's identification with the Jewish struggle against anti-Semitism is explicit. Note, however, that Judaism's distinct observances are rendered irrelevant by this very same model. Jews in the past had been distinguished from all other groups—and had protected themselves from their enemies—via minutely regulated practices. In the present, Jews are distinguished—and achieve the same protection—via free and rational reflection. There could be no place for traditional Jewish forms in the modern order; witness Durkheim's cavalier dismissal of the holiday of Sukkot in *Elementary Forms.*[13] Premodern community is reduced to a specious uniformity, and premodern religious observance to a collective logic almost entirely devoid of individual judgment. Both are out of place in the present.

Durkheim's cure for the ills of modernity, prescribed in *Elementary Forms,* involves a "negative cult," which would create and maintain a strong sense of community through differentiations between sacred and profane, and a "positive cult," designed to achieve the same purpose, but through remembrances and reenactments of ancestors. The content of both cults would be far from traditional, however. God is presumed to be a fiction in no way essential to religion and, so, dispensable. Jews who had escaped the ills of the world in former eras thanks to the life-giving solidarity of their collective practices would be saved in the present era—and all humanity after them—by dint of free reflection. Syntheses of "modernity" and "tradition" are therefore quite literally out of the question. They cannot be imagined given the tools and definitions with which the theorist works.

But there is yet another factor at work, another faculty that bears on life and death in Durkheim's analysis, and it points to a second contribution to the study of religion in general, and Judaism in particular, that is both indispensable and equivocal. Recall the prominence given to anomie in *Suicide;* in *Elementary Forms,* Durkheim takes it for granted that ritual appeals to affective as well as cognitive faculties and needs. One tastes, smells, and imagines in the course of ritual; one marches, sings, and dances; one feels pain, experiences catharsis, finds a collective outlet for joy and thanksgiving. The descriptions of tribal rites in *Elementary Forms,* however romanticized, have justifiably become central to the study of religious ritual and hence will figure in the chapters which follow. But *modern* modes of ritual observance, not examined by Durkheim, also need to be seen in the context of changing emotional patterns. The register of pain and pleasure, according to several persuasive accounts, altered perceptibly in the nineteenth century—so did the pleasures of pain, the satisfactions of asceticism.[14] It also seems a reasonable inference from *Suicide* that ritual practices were in part transformed or discarded by Jews, as by Gentiles, in accordance with newly liberated desires and libidos. The search for meaning was as ever not wholly separate from the search for more immediate satisfactions. "I wants," noble and ignoble, led to rebellion against all sorts of constraints, including religiously based restrictions on eating, sexual activity, and the use of free time. Not infrequently, in the situation of anomie, "I thinks" have followed in the wake of such "I wants," justifying and rationalizing as they go.

All of this is suggested by a reading of Durkheim's text that Durkheim himself never ventures. His absolute dichotomy between sacred and profane makes one hard-pressed to recognize the interaction between the theorist's own "I want" and "I think," what we might call, following Bourdieu, the practice and the theory of religious actors and social scientists alike. Modernity, in its ideal Durkheimian form—the space in which science operates—is by definition entirely *free of both the sacred and desire*. Only thus unencumbered can it turn a neutral gaze on both, claim the objectivity needed to restore society to health, and prescribe for a period of "transition and moral mediocrity."[15] "Theory—the word itself says so—is a spectacle, which can only be understood from a viewpoint away from the stage on which the action is played out."[16] Were the dichotomy between sacred and profane *not* absolute, there would be no need for sociology to reconceive the sacred so as to reintroduce it into the social order and no possibility of its succeeding in that effort.

Durkheim's vision of his own time as one when "the old gods are growing old or already dead, and others are not yet born,"[17] thus turns out to be a doubly essential prerequisite to his project—and a guarantee of its failure. The very existence of his science depends on the death of all old gods (and particularly the last of the breed, Israel's God, still regnant over all forms of monotheism), hardly a good basis for the dispassionate study of traditional belief. Durkheim's sociology also depends on liberation from the emotional, ecstatic realm that characterized premodern religious consciousness, hardly a good basis for its replacement by a modern religious consciousness that, by his own definition, could influence the way life is actually lived only by infusing profane existence with the sanctity of collective consciousness. Durkheim mediates on these problems at length in the conclusion to *Elementary Forms* without seeing their full force, let alone resolving them.[18]

It is not surprising, then, that the faith of Durkheim's ancestors had no place in the social order which his theory was intended to promote. Durkheim located the renewal of the French *conscience collective* institutionally in occupational groups, on the one hand, and in state-sponsored civil religion, on the other. Both "universals" left no room for divergent, particularist traditions such as Judaism. Christianity no less than Judaism would compromise efficient functioning of the new faith, but the latter—as a set of minority practices—was particularly unsuited to the civil religion needed to revitalize France. One assumes that in Durkheim's staunchly secular ideal French Republic, the state-sponsored day of rest would remain Sunday (and Saturday perhaps a school day) just as the theoretical division between sacred and profane in *Elementary Forms* echoed Protestant rather than Jewish or Islamic sensibilities. Recall the color scheme linking Napoleon to the Catholic archbishop in our illustration from 1802 (see figure 1), and Marx's response to Bauer about state-sanctioned sabbath observance. The pattern of relations has not changed. Judaism remains in Durkheim's theory one of many creeds located below modern forces blessed by the light of science. Jews stand somewhere off to the side, more or less where history had already placed them.

For his part, Max Weber was well aware—up to a point—of the blinders which his ambiguous claim for rationality imposed on consideration of contemporary religion. Science, he argued, had to a significant degree emerged in the West from the culture and belief system of Puritanism.[19] Ideas of "duty in one's calling prowl about" in modern scholarship as in modern lives. Scientists, like the Puritans, sought to combat the random and the arbitrary in the world through order, proof, control. No less than the Puritans, and because of a chain of development also directly traceable to them, *all* modern selves were preoccupied with maximizing scarce advantages (*Chancen*) through a degree of methodical calculation that previous cultures could not have matched or understood. The Puritan *Berufsmensch* had put on "blinders," ordered his small area of creation, while leaving the rest of the world—which he could neither control nor transform—to God. Scientists too, ever more specialized, could master only an ever smaller area of reality, leaving the rest to other scientists—or to chance, often decisive in scholarship as in all other areas of human activity. The truths on which scientists labored all their lives would likely as not be overturned eventually.[20]

Yet practitioners of *Wissenschaft,* fully aware of their limitations and attentive to the ephemeral character of their truths, had nonetheless to meet their awesome responsibility—likewise inherited from religion—to help students (and society, more generally) achieve clarity concerning the facts and decisions confronting them. The practitioners' vocation was to assist, despite and because of unavoidable uncertainties, in determining values;[21] to affirm as Weber did that one *could* meet the demands of the day "in scholarship as in life." Although religion offered a source of values far more secure in its own terms—and thus, on the face of it, far more satisfying—Weber could not accept those terms, and he urged his readers not to accept them either. "No one will doubt in his innermost being, even if he will not admit it to himself," that "science today is irreligious."[22] The churches' certainties mocked his doubts—and his scholarship mocked their certainties. The scientific project in his view, as in Durkheim's, not only follows on faith but supplants it.

This same tragic sense of human possibility is the key to Weber's concept of political legitimation, and the authority of earthly rulers is the point at which consideration of religion first enters Weber's sociology in *Economy and Society*. Religion figures in all three of the principal forms taken by this transaction: "traditional," "charismatic," and "rational". We should note, however, that here as elsewhere in his sociology Weber did not give the three types equal time or treat them with anything like equal rigor. Even though Weber's work emphasizes the rational (that is, the goal-directed) character of much "primitive" religion and the "practical-rational" character of Confucianism, rationality's principled opposition to religion underlies and is built into all of Weber's ideal types. He explicitly warns us in "Politics as a Vocation" (1918) that his three types of religious authority are not meant to describe specific historical patterns, that "in reality, obedience is determined by highly robust motives of fear and hope" in any event.[23] Yet Weber not only finds instances of each ideal type repeatedly in his surveys of the world's religions but takes a consistent evaluative stance toward them. He is ambivalent toward rational authority but obviously identified with it; fearful of charisma though drawn to it as the only hope of salvation; dismissive of and generally hostile to frozen ritualistic tradition (the "authority of the 'eternal yesterday,' i.e., of the mores sanctified through the unimaginably ancient recognition and habitual orientation to conform").[24]

Tradition stands as a barrier to both of the other types of authority and an obstacle to innovation as such. In the fourfold typology of human action outlined at the start of *Economy and Society,* "instrumental rationality" stands at the top, followed by "value-rationality" in service to a given end. Behavior driven by "affect" stands on the border of purposive action, while behavior "determined by ingrained habituation" is over the edge, beyond purpose altogether. It is labeled "traditional."[25] In Weber's view, these strictures applied to "tradition" primarily because of its *behavioral* rather than *conceptual* cast. Tradition "stereotypes" social action in ritual. It insists that things be done ever and always in the same specific fashion. Indeed, this is the very source of its authority. The effect, Weber argues, is to preclude independent action according to general principles that the individual applies differently, through free and conscious judgment, in each given situation. Modernity once again presumes the defeat of tradition, in both formal and substantive terms. The Kantian influence here is pronounced.

Jews and Judaism, while hardly alone in the category of tradition, nonetheless occupy a special place within it—and again, as in Durkheim, the gap between Weber's extensive treatment of premodern Jews and his virtual silence on their modern descendants is striking. In *Ancient Judaism* (collecting essays originally published from 1917 to 1919), Weber celebrates the contribution made by Israel's prophets to the secularization of the cosmos and the ethical rationalization of the world. Old Testament prophets had stripped the world of its many deities and directed worship toward one God alone. This God, a Creator who stood above and beyond every reality, instructed Jews to *work on* reality as well instead of accepting and venerating it as it was. However—Weber's narrative in *Ancient Judaism* follows the Christian and Hegelian pattern—Judaism had then stultified into Pharisaic ritual.[26] Contemporary Jews, the heirs to both developments, are referred to most characteristically by the opaque quotation, from Isaiah, at the conclusion of "Science as a Vocation"—"watchman, what of the night?"—which Weber follows with the avowal that "from this we want to draw the lesson that nothing is gained by yearning and tarrying alone, and we shall act differently."

I take this to mean that "Israelites" through the ages had believed in God and put their faith into practice through rituals and ethics which had kept them apart from the larger society and its progress. Powerlessness, "pariah" status, had not helped them. Moderns, Jewish or Gentile, were by definition deprived of prophetic certainty and should act rationally and ethically to transform the world from which Jews throughout the ages had remained separate. "Precisely the ultimate and most sublime values have retreated from public life [that is, where rationality holds sway] either into the transcendental realm of mystic life"—mysticism being "the most irrational form of religious behavior"—or "into the brotherliness of direct and personal human relations"—where rational calculation is clearly out of place.[27] Religion's marginality to the modern rational project is thus well symbolized by the ancient "pariah people," the Jews. They had behaved one way in the world, waiting and tarrying in faith, whereas "we"—that is, the readers and practitioners of science—"shall act differently."

Weber's aim, after all, was the education of autonomous individuals who have internalized a universalist ethic and learned to apply it in all areas of life, thereby imposing a total, comprehensive, and meaningful pattern on experience.[28] Judaism could not but work against autonomy. Its particulars were *rituals* and, as such, bound individual action to prescribed patterns. They were also *particularist*—unique to Judaism—and, as such, ran counter to universalist demands and their realization throughout society (one of the six basic meanings of "rationality" in Weber's usage). Judaism could not be the basis of German societal or political legitimation. Neither could it provide the *Wirtschaftsethik* determinative of German civil and economic behavior, actual or ideal. Indeed, to the degree that distinctive Jewish behaviors corresponded to substantively distinctive ethical ideals, the "gods would be in conflict" not only *among* societies but *within* a given society—far from a desirable outcome in Weber's view. If, on the other hand, Jewish rituals were seen to vary only formally from Christians rituals—that is to say, merely expressed in a different way a worldview shared by other groups—Weber would likely be more tolerant of them—and far less interested. His sociology in fact gives no attention whatever to this possibility.

Substantively unique Jewish practice, then—and its study—can enter Weber's theory of modernity only through the spaces left open by his silence. It goes without saying, and therefore bears repeating, that one simply cannot approach the question of religion in the modern West *without* Weber's categories and insights. They, more than any others, have shaped the present study. Rationalization and disenchantment, "virtuosos" and the several legitimations of authority, religious rejections of and by the world, the persistence of belief and practice "in pianissimo" and in the realm of the emotions are the building blocks, it seems to me, of any useful theory of modern Western religious practice, Jewish or Christian. Contemporary theory of modernity is, justly, no less preoccupied with Weber's insistence that "the various value-spheres of the world stand in irreconcilable conflict with each other," that "different gods struggle with one another, now and for all times to come."

Note, however, that the twentieth century was not exempt from this rule in Weber's eyes. "Only the bearing of man has been disenchanted and denuded of its mystical but inwardly genuine plasticity."[29] Beneath the surface, then, modern selves—including Weber, presumably—continued to serve their various gods. Thus the puzzling declaration in the very last words of "Science as a Vocation" that meeting the demands of the day, in science and in life, was "plain and simple, if each finds and obeys the demon who holds the fibers of his very life."[30] What demon could this be? Who holds and is held by it? And what, amid the marvelous complexities revealed in and through Weber's scholarship, could possibly remain "plain and simple"?

The questions echo in Weber's silence; the religious practice of modern Jews remains by default one of the "great and vital problems" on which, as Weber put it, "forces other than university chairs" must "have their say."[31] Unless, of course, the occupants of those chairs—without abandoning scholarship for theology—expand the repertoire of conceptual tools provided us by classical sociological theory in a way that makes room for minority as well as majority voices, religious as well as secular presuppositions, behavior—habitual, affective, "value-rational" and "instrumental-rational"—as well as belief.

2. BERGER, RIEFF, AND "THE UNIVERSALIZATION OF HERESY"

The most useful recent work on secularization and the sacred offers precisely that expanded conceptual repertoire.[32] Peter Berger's influential argument in *The Sacred Canopy* (1969), developing ideas already set out with Thomas Luckmann in *The Social Construction of Reality* (1966), begins with the claim that the world is not simply given to consciousness but "constructed." Unceasing work is required to build up coherent pictures of reality and to get people to inhabit them, take them for granted, and consider them not only true but *right*. This is the labor of culture, Berger believes, assigned to religion in every period before the modern.[33] Ideas of order, to be convincing, must be conveyed and sustained by concrete and powerful institutions on the ground, ideally in a pattern of daily-life activities seconded by regular ritual observance—"objects of experience"—that make sense of our ideas and are in turn made sense of by them. Berger terms these communal and institutional realities "plausibility structures," a notion that has become crucial to all work on religion in the modern West. He adds in a parenthesis (to which we shall return) that "a theoretically important variation is between situations in which an entire society serves as the plausibility structure for a religious world and situations in which only a subsociety serves as such."[34]

With modernity, religion had, according to Berger, lost its preeminent role in the construction and legitimation of social reality; secularization is defined as "the process by which sectors of society and culture are removed from the domination of religious institutions and symbols." Note that Berger's understanding of secularization builds on the word's original connotation, "removal of territory or property from the control of ecclesiastical authorities." Modern society and culture are both secularized in this sense, and so is consciousness.[35] (David Martin, the only sociologist to have offered a full-length general theory of secularization, similarly defines the secularizing process in terms of "differentiation" in the societal realm and "alienation" of the individual.)[36] This notion too is invaluable, because it is nuanced: secularization does not mean the disappearance of religion, nor even its decline according to an absolute quantitative measure, but its removal or attenuation in some areas of collective activity (for example, politics, economic life, the arts). Religion remains of varying and perhaps increased salience in other spheres, generally private. What we have is a *contraction* in the scope of human affairs determined by religious beliefs and institutions, with a concomitant rearrangement of the "furniture of the mind."

In *The Heretical Imperative* (1979), Berger attributes these changes less to industrialization per se—closely linked to secularization in the nineteenth century, presumably because science and technology rendered religious explanations irrelevant in daily life—than to the plurality of worldviews available to individuals in modern urban centers. This is but one aspect of the *plurality of choice* in every aspect of life, which for Berger distinguishes the modern from the premodern world. He cites the Jewish move from shtetl to city, East to West, ghetto to Emancipation, as "perhaps the most important example" of the process he is describing. "Suddenly, to be Jewish emerged as one choice among others."[37] I take the general outlines of this thesis to be indisputable—but the particulars, especially where Jews are concerned, to be somewhat problematic. The questions to be asked are, what sort of choice emerged for Jews? and what factors impinged on their decisions?

"Choice" and "fate" are opposed theoretically by Berger in radical dichotomy, presuming a "removal from religion" so thoroughgoing as to be unmistakable. The "variance" *between* modern and premodern must be far greater than that *within* either category for Berger's sociology to be credible. However, Berger also describes secularization as a process that began over two thousand years ago. "The Old Testament posits a God who stands outside the cosmos, which is his creation but which he confronts and does not permeate."[38] This notion of God, he argues, facilitated the desacralization of many areas of life. As God was "physically" at a distance rather than immanent in natural forces and settings, the sacred could accordingly be imposed on or even absent from reality. In Weberian fashion, Berger traces this development forward to the Puritans and the present. Religion in the West has been the agent of its own demise: Judaism, it is clear, has declined because of a process set in motion by Judaism itself.

But why should the sacred be conceived in this way and only in this way? And why make the case of a tiny religious minority, ancient *or* modern, paradigmatic for that of dominant majorities? The two issues, we will see, are related.

Let us begin with the second. At the very end of the *Sacred Canopy*, Berger himself concedes that the claim for Judaism's paradigmatic status is counterintuitive. "Objectivity in Judaism has always been more a question of practice than of theory." The loss of the "objective" Jewish world—loss of the constructed social reality that had confronted Jews as true and right—

has therefore manifested itself more in "disintegration of religious practice than in doctrinal heterodoxy."[39] That is precisely my claim in the present study, and if it is correct, the spatial metaphors of contraction and "removal" are unsatisfactory where Jews are concerned.[40] French society, say, can be "secularized" in the sense that the state seizes church property, takes primary education out of the hands of clerics, limits the church's role in government policy, supplants its rituals with state-sponsored civil religion, and so decisively affects the ways that French men and women think, feel, eat, marry, and mourn. Religion gets "smaller" and moves aside. Group life persists, albeit with a different cast, and the sacred—religious belief and practice— persists within it, whether in the private sphere or in public culture never entirely divorced from nearly two thousand years of religious influence. But, as we have seen, Jewish society as it existed (in a variety of forms) before the onset of institutional and ideological secularization in western and central Europe was not merely transformed by those processes but severely attenuated—and in some cases destroyed. Functions were not merely redistributed from one area of Jewish society to another but transferred elsewhere—to non-Jewish institutions—when they did not cease altogether. Only weaker, smaller, and voluntarist communities remained. The members of Jewish communities migrated, both literally and figuratively, and their distinctive ways of seeing the world departed with them. Identities once sustained by particularist behaviors could not but cease or atrophy when those behaviors did.[41]

It had been crucial to those identities, moreover, as to every species of premodern Jewish society, that sacredness adhered to every conceivable aspect of Jewish life—indeed, defined collective existence itself. Jews were to be "a kingdom of priests and a holy nation." This, and not (*pace* Berger) a radical divide between a transcendent God and the world, had been the decisive aspect of biblical and rabbinic definitions of the sacred. The division between holy and profane is paralleled in Sabbath blessings by that between Israel and the nations; the former separation could not but be affected by the blurring or elimination of the latter. Jewish sacred space and time were in many cases not merely contracted but lost when restricted (to the private spaces of home or synagogue) according to a very different, modern Western, notion of holiness that deemed the according of sacred status to any national identity as inconsistent with rational and universal claims. Such "restriction" made a world of difference to the plausibility structures of Judaism: Jews, instead of living inside a Jewish construction of reality and venturing forth from it for relatively infrequent political, economic, cultural, or even social contact with the prevailing dominant reality—the case throughout the Middle Ages for Jews under Christianity or Islam—came to inhabit a fragmented, not terribly well-built construction of reality from which they venture forth so frequently that return home proves impossible without significant alteration.[42]

Home in the latter case is no longer "inside" as opposed to "outside." Identity *fuses* "we" and "they." Berger himself grasps the implication: "The peculiarity of Judaism as a religious tradition and an ethnic entity means that the problem of its plausibility ipso facto entails the so-called 'crisis of Jewish identity.'"[43] The same could not be said, for example, of the French.

The issue, I think, goes deeper still. Berger's model is Protestant through and through, even though, unlike some other theorists (Talcott Parsons, for example), he does not hail secularization as the fulfillment of Christianity rather than its downfall.[44] He does, however, explicitly regard Protestantism as the model for what it means, religiously, to modernize. Economic, political, and cultural spheres are freed from religious influence, while the "holy" remains present only in the private spheres of home and church. "It follows that the history of Protestant theology is a paradigm for the confrontation of a religious tradition with modernity." Berger does not mean that this pattern must be precisely imitated by others. He does, however, insist that "modernity is a *cognitive* condition"—a Protestant view, which no sociology could possibly offer were it to regard any tradition but Protestantism as paradigmatic.[45] And, in addition, he holds that three and only three possibilities exist for faith in the wake of secularization. These three—deductive, reductive, and inductive, represented respectively by Karl Barth, Rudolf Bultmann, and Friedrich Schleiermacher—are all based in Protestantism and, I would argue, are fully applicable to it alone.[46] Berger asserts of the first that "it would be the same in a Jewish or Muslim" context but then belies his own claim by placing Rosenzweig under the "deductive" rubric, as if his faith had anything in common with Barthian neo-Orthodoxy. The categories, while extremely useful as ideal types, are deficient even in the Protestant context (witness the treatment of Bultmann). This is all the more true when one tries to apply them *across* traditions.[47] Caution about the use of ostensibly neutral categories across traditions is, as usual, in order.

That caution in place—and the need for it is supplied often enough by Berger himself—the notion of the plausibility structure proves extremely useful in understanding the character and limits of modern Jewish practice. Mendelssohn, as we have seen, accepted both the *privatization* and the *mar-*

ginalization of Jewish practice as givens of the modern situation but sought to endow the commandments with meaning nonetheless. He argued that they could shape life as a whole even though Jewish lives would now be lived largely outside narrow communal borders, boundaries within which Jewish practices had made immediate intuitive sense. Berger helps us to understand why that attempt was doomed to something less than success. The threefold categorization of modern faith as deductive, inductive, or reductive, once corrected for the distinctiveness of Jewish patterns, is likewise helpful in accounting for the prevalence of a theological "move" that has played such a leading role in much twentieth-century Jewish thought: "inductive" appeal to experience in defiance of cognitive skepticism.

Of course, modern Jewish thinkers too have been decisively influenced by Schleiermacher, Otto, and liberal Protestantism more generally, just as Jews throughout the West have been influenced by the Protestant conceptions of faith taken for granted in their societies. No less important, Jews and Protestants have shared the problem posed to religious thought by the loss of integral communities and their precious plausibility structures, namely, that religious traditions are deprived of any hold on believers except the power of persuasion. In a society of individual consumers, persuasion comes down to the capacity to provide goods that people cannot secure elsewhere. That, in turn, has increasingly focused religious sights on two goods in particular: meaning and community or, rather, the *experience* of these two. Hence the emphasis on experience in Buber as in Rosenzweig, in Joseph Soloveitchik as in Abraham Heschel. But this experience, now as ever, comes primarily or even exclusively through *ritual*—and ritual is devalued by a modern bias toward the cognitive that Berger's sociology not only shares but helps to further.

There is a final consequence to this cognitive bias that will prove important in our study of Jewish practice: a subtle shift in Berger's conception of *culture,* reflecting a massive shift in modern societies (those that he surveys) away from the centrality of *normative* demands. In *The Sacred Canopy,* Berger presents culture as the set of "humanly produced structures" that constitute the human world. It is the "second nature" that "specializes [our] drives" and "provides [the] stability" which in all other animals is determined by instinct. "Culture consists of the totality of man's products." Such definitions, nicely synthesizing Durkheim and Weber, are conventional in contemporary social theory,[48] and Berger in this work places more emphasis than most on the normative moment of culture. "The final test of [a society's] objective reality is its capacity to impose itself upon the reluctance of individuals. Society directs, sanctions, controls, and punishes individual conduct. . . . [It] may even destroy the individual." [49] However, Berger tends to follow Weber in emphasizing religion's roles in legitimating social and political orders and addressing issues of theodicy, while he pays far less attention to religion's Durkheimian role in limiting drives and stabilizing the emotions. He devotes virtually no attention to religion's function, via culture, of telling people what good is and getting them to do it. Indeed, the word "culture" tellingly drops out of Berger's theoretical use. "Culture" does not appear in the index to *The Heretical Imperative*—where the word "heresy" loses all normative character and comes to mean simply "choice" as opposed to "fate," in accordance with the etymology from the Greek. Modernity is termed "the universalization of heresy." [50]

Nothing is heresy if everything is heresy, of course. And if everything really *is* heresy in its usual, substantive sense—a wrong choice, a normative mistake—then Berger has given us a theory of modernity and of culture utterly at variance with the general tendency in contemporary sociology and far closer, in its willingness to judge, to every Jewish notion of culture, modern or premodern, that has ever been created. Paula Hyman has noted that the Jews of Alsace, in their new public schools, received instruction not merely in a new language or culture but in *a new definition of culture*. [51] David Sorkin, analyzing German Jewry at the start of the nineteenth century, found a community "invisible" to itself in crucial respects because the notion of culture it had internalized had no place for the loyalties, norms, and institutions preserving that community and preserved by it. [52] We shall return to both examples in succeeding chapters. Clearly, a great deal has been at stake for modern Jews in the definition of culture—not least the viability and legitimacy of their "subculture," dependent for its existence on the majority's sense of these matters, a sense that has often been at some variance with their own.

These dynamics are underlined in the work of Philip Rieff, who is not only more ambivalent about modernity than any theorist we have yet discussed but is actually hostile to major aspects of the modern project: he sees that project as inherently antinomian and therefore, in his sense, *anticultural*. Rieff is also, perhaps not by coincidence, the only major contemporary sociological theorist whose work emerges in some measure from Jewish sources and articulates strong, though hardly Orthodox, Jewish religious commitments. Culture for Rieff is not a storehouse of collective knowledge or the weaving of significance (the two prevalent scholarly usages), much less the sum total of a society's artistic or creative achievement (the word's popular meaning of late). It is "a design of motives directing the self outward, toward those communal purposes in which alone the self can be realized and satisfied." Culture accomplishes this work through "the power of its institutions to bind and loose men in the conduct of their affairs with reasons which sink so deep into the self that they become commonly and implicitly understood—with that understanding of which explicit belief and precise knowledge of externals would show outwardly like the tip of an iceberg."[53]

The normative language is pronounced, as is the self's utter dependence on the community for realization and satisfaction. Faith, defined as "some compelling symbolic of self-integrating communal purpose," had done the work of culture with varying success until modern societies took the task away, ostensibly or initially to assign it to other institutions. In Rieff's view, the task in actuality has been largely abrogated. The question now is whether human personality can hang together once freed of superintending authorities and repression: not "can civilized men believe?" but "can unbelieving men be civilized?"

Rieff is not sanguine. His theory of the self, seen through a Freudian lens adjusted to account for Freud's own limitations and repressions, presumes that cultures reduced to buffet tables of information and significance available for individual choice and/or skepticism cannot perform the task that is needed.[54] This is so for two reasons. "A culture without repressions, if it could exist, would kill itself in closing the distances between any desire and its object."[55] This is Freud's point about inherent civilizational discontents. Desire is by definition infinite. Ego requires superego if we are to live together and stave off the forces of death. Substitutive satisfactions must be found—and are, in culture. Much of this work must transpire below the level of consciousness if it is to succeed. Rieff, however, is also making a second point here, quite at odds with Freud. Because human beings are imperfect, that is, sinners, any culture must provide not only interdictions— "Thou shalt not"s—but remissions as well—opportunities to do what must not be done but which, having been done, will not shatter "sacred order" because the order itself has provided for the transgression and its atonement.

Culture does not merely "raise up" or "sublimate" base desire, then— rather, it articulates authority in and through its interdictions, remissions, and atonements. It does not invent authority; it represents it, calling in debts and obligations which human beings (Freud being a notable example) would often prefer to forget—and generally do. Thus, "every culture must establish itself as a system of moralizing demands, images that mark the trail of each man's memory."[56] Culture is "the achievement of its unconscious distancing devices made conscious, yet indirect, in a variety of visual, acoustical, and plastic registrations. In a word, culture is repressive."[57]

This is not the place for a sustained presentation or critique of Rieff's theory.[58] It will suffice to dwell on several implications that directly link modernity and the Jews. First, and most important, modern culture is to Rieff's mind uniquely transgressive. "Warped and atrophied communal purposes are now being paid off at a usurious rate of interest." Our regnant—therapeutic—ethic aims at satisfaction, well-being, fulfillment, good feeling. It is unable to guide collective pursuit of the good because it has grown utterly suspicious of all attempts to define the good, let alone impose it. Cultural elites excel in criticism, "the systematic hunting down of all settled convictions," but not in articulating or imagining sacred order.

Rieff's entire oeuvre is dedicated to arguing that progress to a culture of criticism is *not* progress—and the Jews are, in his theory, the preeminent symbol and bearer of this conviction. To articulate the interdictions rather than defend the transgressions, to reinforce communal purpose rather than exalt the self, is to be a "Jew of culture." Rieff identifies himself with this group and espouses its cause. "We Jews of culture are obliged to resist the very idea" of a universal culture, for universal culture inevitably levels *downward*.[59] Heresy can be universalized, but sacred order cannot. "We mere teachers, Jews of culture . . . have no choice except to think defensively" against "that unique complex of orgy and routine which constitutes modernization."[60]

Hence the definition of a Jew as "he who resists—i.e., resists the very problem of his identity" as that problem has been posed, for example, in Marx. "On the Jewish Question," Rieff argues, aimed at the destruction of historical memory and, with it, the destruction of ideal existences that survive in historical memory as "presiding presences," instruments of moral authority. This is the meaning of Marx's denial of reality to the "Sabbath Jew" and his insistence that "the real Jew is an entirely contemporary man and, therefore, entirely sabbathless."[61]

The issue posed by Jews in Rieff's theory is not merely particular versus universal, by now well-known to us, but norm versus therapy. "How are you on the trivial old question of sabbath-keeping?" he asks sarcastically. "Is any order worthy of the name without its strict sabbaths?" No is the answer—because "no" is the word most indispensable to culture.[62] With this we reach a point in the theorizing of modernity entirely absent in the discussion thus far. Marx's anti-Judaism is, in Rieff's reading, much more than an accident of biography. The same, we might add, could be said of Kant's. "Jew" in the Christian and post-Christian West signifies law, authority, God, conscience—all of which, despite Kant's attempts to close the gap between autonomy and heteronomy, necessarily continue to stand above and beyond the freedom of the self and the dialectical processes of history. Modern, state-sponsored anti-Semitism, then, is to be understood not only as animus against a particular group that refuses to dissolve into the relevant universal as required and/or controls wealth and occupational niches desired by others. Rather, "Jew-hatred remains the deepest transgressive motif of Christian Love—and, in succession, of Western organizations of Humanity, including the Marxist." The various modern "movements toward universal equality . . . share in this impression of Israel as a distancing people"—one, that is, that separates high from low, desire from object, holy from profane, Sabbath day from the six other days of Creation.[63]

In succeeding chapters of this book, we will chart pressures brought to bear on Jews, as a condition of their Emancipation, to cease a number of observances—the Sabbath perhaps most prominent among them. If Rieff's analysis holds, the singling out of that issue (and others) was far from accidental and went much deeper than the oft-adduced, ostensible problem of Jews' capacity for performing duties in the civil service or military. We will also witness perennial Jewish debates over whether Sabbath observance should be altered or discarded or perhaps moved to Sunday—debates couched in terms of "true religion," on the one hand, and convenience of adjustment, on the other, without any reference whatever to the deeper pressures to which Rieff has drawn attention. The concealments of that reasoning also were perhaps not accidental. Rieff claims an operative factor unacknowledged on both sides: transgressive impulses—to which Jews have necessarily been subject, being as human as the next person, and of which they were a particular object, because they symbolized to Christian and post-Christian cultures the ultimate source of all "Thou shalt not"s.

While judgments of bad faith and good are notoriously difficult to make responsibly, and arguments from silence are almost always difficult to sustain, it seems impossible to escape the issue of repressed unconscious motivation entirely. The motif of transgression is, after all, explicit in and central to major theories of modernity and modernism. As an artistic movement, modernism celebrated its rejection of societal standards, propounding a view of the creative self that owes much to both Enlightenment and Romanticism.[64] Shattering conventions, shocking the bourgeoisie, rejecting standards as quickly as they were erected became the hallmarks of modernism in literature, music, the arts—the cultural "registrations" where norms would, in all premodern experience with culture, be articulated. Jews were deeply influenced by these motifs and, as a highly urban and well-educated minority, were particularly active in their advancement. This created deep tensions between the Jews themselves and all versions of their tradition, including Reform, for which norms rooted in the past were absolutely essential.

There is a still more important point here, one that does not depend either on attributions of bad faith or arguments from silence. It arises from Rieff's linkage of modernity with anti-Semitism. The theme is, of course, prominent in the historiography of modern Jews, and much attention has been given of late to the question of whether the Holocaust and lesser hatreds of the Jews should be seen as mere aberrations of modernity or developments that emerged intrinsically from the very essence of the modern project. One accordingly sees or refuses to see all of modern Jewish history in the light of the atrocities of Nazi Germany. Hannah Arendt, considering the issues of modern opposition to Jewish practice in precisely that light a generation ago, located the origins of totalitarianism in destructive patterns of thought and conduct regarding Jews, including patterns adopted *by* Jews.[65] Only Rieff, to my knowledge, has developed this insight theoretically. Auschwitz stands at the very center of *Fellow Teachers* and, I think, at the heart of his theory of modernity as a whole.[66]

It will not, however, stand at the center of this inquiry; I think unjustified to take the Gentile influences impinging on Jewish practice and consider them primarily from the vantage point of anti-Semitism or the Holocaust. Nor, to my mind, should Jewish behavior be judged by "lessons" which the Holocaust in retrospect allegedly imposes. On the other hand, we cannot entirely avoid questions of anti-Semitism, and of Jewish or Gentile association of Judaism with God and conscience, when probing what commandments Jews in the modern period chose to observe or abrogate and what pressures were applied by Gentiles to elicit those choices. Arendt's study, and many others which we shall cite in due course, place the point beyond dispute.

The two points should be seen together. First-generation departures from tradition have always involved sins of omission and commission against commandments transmitted by fathers and mothers as right action and God's will. Eating pork, for example, has had a significance for many Jews that Rieff's theory helps to clarify—as it helps to explain why the act quickly lost its significance, at least on the surface of consciousness, for the Jews who performed it. We also need to understand, however, why Gentiles should have cared enough one way or another to raise the issue of dietary laws time and again. The presence or absence of particular ritual departures from ancestral tradition—for example, having a Christmas tree—continues to be of immense importance to Jews and Gentiles alike. Without attention to dynamics of interdiction, transgression, and remission, these behaviors are far more difficult to fathom. Here, as at all other points in the study of modern Jewish history, the factor of anti-Semitism must be weighed in the balance, along with all other relevant factors, in order to make sense of what Jews did and did not do in their religious practice and why.

3. THE PHILOSOPHICAL DISCOURSE OF POSTMODERNITY

The critique of modernity's pretensions to what is called in current parlance a "totalizing discourse" is now fairly standard in scholarly literature. Stephen Toulmin, in a typical effort to expose "the hidden agenda of modernity," dismisses the notion that

> modern philosophy and science had succeeded (in John Locke's fa-
> mous phrase) in "clearing away the underbrush that stands in the way
> of knowledge." In their view, if we could only prevent ideological and
> theological issues from confusing matters, both the intellectual and
> the practical means of improving the human lot were ready to hand.

Such confidence is no longer warranted, Toulmin argues. Grand agendas for banishing ignorance with knowledge and so "improving the human lot" can no longer be pursued. Too much evil has been committed in their name. There is only the historicist program of "reconstructing an account of the circumstances in which the Modern project was conceived, the philosophical, scientific, social, and historical assumptions on which it rested, and the subsequent sequences of episodes that has led to our present quandary."[67]

For our purposes the question is not the accuracy of Toulmin's critique but the significance for the study of Jewish practice of the postmodern turn away from absolutes—the understandings that it facilitates and precludes. The answer, I think, is double-edged, just as it was in the theory that postmodern discourse claims to supersede. Jews and Judaism remain in the middle. On both sides of current debate—the side we can usefully identify with Lyotard, as well as the one most clearly articulated in Habermas—the

Jews disappear, become mere metaphor, are subsumed as before by putative universals that allow no room whatever for the particulars of their practice.

In Lyotard this is explicit. *The Postmodern Condition* (1979), a sustained attack on Habermas, argues from the outset that the issue at stake in the sovereignty of rationality is legitimation. Definitions of knowledge serve power. "The right to decide what is true is not independent of the right to decide what is just." "To speak is to fight."[68] The triumph of science is allied to the "hero" served in its subtext—"the people"—as "the sign of legitimacy is the people's consensus, and their mode of creating norms is deliberation. The notion of progress is a necessary outgrowth of this."[69] But "the people" has been created by these same elites, an effort that involved "destroying the traditional knowledge of peoples, perceived from that point forward as minorities or potential separatist movements destined only to spread obscurantism."[70] This insight—concretized, for example, in Eric Hobsbawm's work on the construction of European nations and nationalisms—is indispensable to analysis of the pressures brought to bear on Jewish ritual performance.[71]

Lyotard views the grand rationales for this labor of construction—Emancipation and Enlightenment chief among them—as "metanarratives" designed and maintained to supply legitimacy for that labor. Component elements within them are mere language games serving one or another end. The persuasiveness of these rationales has ended with our awareness of their workings: "The grand narrative has lost its credibility, regardless of what mode of unification it uses, regardless of whether it is a speculative narrative or a narrative of emancipation."[72]

Lyotard is no less suspicious of Habermas's liberal theory of modernity, according to which Enlightenment rationality can remain our framework of thought and action—a new sort of unifying narrative—if we build in consent and consensus as nonnegotiable features. This aim cannot be achieved, Lyotard argues. Pure speech acts of the sort Habermas wants, untainted by power, lie on a "horizon that is never reached." Language itself demands rules which can never be the subject of universal voluntary agreement. What is more, postulating consensus as the goal of discussion represents a nonconsensual statement forever outside the range of its own limits. The Habermas solution will inevitably involve "terror," Lyotard's term for "the efficiency gained by eliminating, or threatening to eliminate, a player from the language game one shares with him. He is silenced or consents . . . because his ability to participate has been threatened."[73]

Lyotard's critique of the Enlightenment metanarrative has much in common with Jewish and Marxist criticisms that we have noted. As such, it is extremely helpful to the project of reopening questions concerning Jewish practice presumed closed in the Kantian traditions of Durkheim and Weber. Modern Jews by the millions abandoned vernacular Jewish languages over the past two centuries in favor of new languages deemed essential to *civilisation* or *Bildung*. They eagerly adopted visions of humanity which presumed the triumph of particular cultures and the subordination of others. Appeals to the will of "the people" generally omitted the will of Jews, who, almost universally excluded during the nineteenth century from "the peoples" of Europe, were denied the legitimations that "the people" alone conferred. We shall examine these processes in detail in Chapter 4. Lyotard's critique of the metanarrative that pictures "the people" marching ever forward, making greater and greater progress to future perfection, likewise points up the problems faced by Jewish ritual practices, which resolutely looked *backward* to the past and remained obligated to it.

Lyotard, of course, has no interest in the retention of these practices, let alone of the Jewish metanarratives which they presume and sustain. Secularization is an inherent feature of his project; Lyotard not only accepts but applauds modernity's allegedly absolute break from religious traditions—the extreme and paradigmatic example, we might say, of mythic "metanarratives of legitimation." It is no surprise, then, that in Lyotard's theory, the Jews, except for their victimization in the Holocaust, entirely disappear. They even become, in his controversial lowercase styling of a recent essay, *Heidegger and "the jews"* (1988), a *symbol* of "the irremissible in the West's movement of remission and pardon. They are what cannot be domesticated in the obsession to dominate. . . . [They are] never at home wherever they are, cannot be integrated, converted, or expelled."[74] No disrespect of real Jews is intended, Lyotard adds; real Jews have merely been particularly afflicted with the dismissal signified by "the jews."

However, Lyotard has no trouble assuring us in his essay's very first paragraph that "what is most real about real Jews is that Europe, in any case, does not know what to do with them."[75] He then unwittingly bears witness to the truth he claims. Jews enter his postmodern discourse exactly as they entered Kant's modern discourse: as object, footnote, "them." In Lyotard's theory, Jews signify no independent culture, maintain no categories that challenge those by which they are silenced, believe in no God who is of more than historical interest, and so comprise no difference that is anything more than metaphor for "difference" per se. Lyotard can thus quite easily tell us "what is most real" about them. What is worse, he goes on to tell us that the real "scandal" of Heidegger's embrace of Nazism was that he "ignored the thought of 'the jews.'" Not the Jews, but "the jews"! This is asserted despite, or because of, the immediate recognition that in so doing, Heidegger joined the attempt at "making us forget forever what, in Europe, reminds us, ever since the beginning, that 'there is' the Forgotten." Real Jews remain forgotten in Lyotard's postmodern theory; this is certainly ironic, given his thoughtful reflections on how even the best historical work necessarily leaves a great deal out of its account and is ever aware of its own inadequacy, while the worst "requires the forgetting of that which may question the community and its legitimacy."[76] That is precisely what seems to be occurring in this case.

Jürgen Habermas's work offers far greater potential for the study of modern Jewish practice, at least on the face of things. The quest for a "public sphere" characterized by free, informed, undistorted, unalienated speech—standing between individuals, on the one hand, and the apparatus of state power, on the other—recalls the "neutral" or "semineutral" society in which Jews since Mendelssohn have sought to locate Jewish practice. Habermas's rejection of false universals follows directly on the critique of Emancipation and Enlightenment articulated in "On the Jewish Question." *The Philosophical Discourse of Modernity* (1985) aims to "salvage" that discourse by means of a compromise between the Enlightenment position and the postmodern critique.

Note, on the one hand, the singular definite article in his title, the "privileging" of reason implicit in the adjective, the normative as well as the descriptive connotations of the noun. On the other hand, however, Habermas acts to dissociate the phrase "from its European origins" and from any intrinsic connection with the particular historical context of western Europe. He contends that the basis for the critique—and rescue—of the theory of modernity lies within, rather than outside, that theory. Lyotard, Foucault, and company have identified not "an excess but a deficit of rationality," using a "counterdiscourse inherent in modernity itself." Habermas will use other modern resources to serve "the paradigm of mutual understanding, that is, of the intersubjective relationship between individuals who are socialized through communication and reciprocally recognize one another."[77] In this way, he will safeguard the existence of multiple "lifeworlds" independent of both capitalist consumerism and the state. "Each lifeworld must also be enabled to reproduce itself," which involves propagation of its distinctive cultural traditions, "integration of groups by norms and values, and the socialization of succeeding generations."[78] A concluding chapter, entitled "The Normative Content of Modernity," is devoted to this "telos." We seem to have here an agenda for the study of modern Jewish subcultures and the conceptual tools with which to pursue it.

The problem, however, is that Habermas's theory does not seem able to accommodate *religious* practice. Churches feature in *The Structural Transformation of the Public Sphere* only as part of the ancien régime against and outside of which the new and free arena of speech came into being in the late eighteenth century. The emergent public sphere constituted a domain of common concern and open criticism that had to break the monopoly of interpretation previously exercised by church and state. It presumed the emancipation of private individuals from the "semipublic bonds" of the church and the intermediate powers of the estates. The public sphere presumed three elements: voluntariness, a community of love, and cultivation—none of which easily accorded with religious authorities and restrictions.[79] Churches and synagogues are never mentioned in the book except as repressive institutions thankfully left behind by enlightened modernity.

Virtually all of Habermas's huge corpus leaves religious groups in total silence. Once again, the omission is not merely idiosyncratic. Habermas hopes to get beyond Weber's "false alternatives" of formal and substantive, fact and value, while remaining inside modernity's dominant philosophical discourse. He believes that he can do so only by presuming that "despite its purely procedural character as disburdened of all religious and metaphysical mortgages, communicative reason is directly implicated in social life-processes insofar as acts of mutual understanding take on the role of a mechanism for coordinating action."[80] The claim, by now quite familiar, is that we can discover in the *formal* character of speech itself—or, rather, in the process of communication as it unfolds in a society not marred by alienation or coercion—*substantive* goods which all parties will universally recognize as such. In Steven Lukes's careful formulation, Habermas "postulates the possibility of society reaching a stage of transparent self-reflection, among parties who are 'free and equal' and whose discourse has reached a stage where 'the level of justification has become reflective', in the sense that mythological, cosmological, religious and ontological modes of thought have been superseded."[81]

We observe, however, that the statement of this goal precludes its own fulfillment, just as Lyotard had warned. The process must be "disburdened of all religious and metaphysical mortgages." The ideal of mutual self-understanding depends upon the *elimination* of dogmas and "ultimate grounds."[82] Habermas's highly traditional modern theory has thus left the dichotomies of tradition versus modernity, religion versus reason, intact. "The secularization of values and norms" is built into this discourse from its opening paragraphs.[83] A lifeworld not unburdened of religion simply cannot be thought in its terms. "Habermas seems not only to exclude religion from the public square," one critic notes, "but to exclude religion from the communicatively rationalized private sphere; religion, insofar as it is to be public, is subordinated to and bound to comply with standards of truth and rightness derived through [Enlightenment] discourses."[84] Another critic observes that Habermas has failed "to analyze and to explore the resources of religion for the public sphere."[85] The theologian David Tracy has offered a particularly acute critique in this regard, writing in marked understatement that unless Habermas offers arguments against sophisticated religious positions rather than merely assuming their irrelevance, "modern theologians and philosophers will remain unpersuaded" by his comments on "the validity claims of religion and theology."[86]

We might, at best, read Habermas as saying that religious communities could contribute ideas developed inside their own particularist languages and commitments, so long as those ideas have been universalized in form and substance, that is, as long as those ideas no longer claim legitimation on "dogmatic" or other "ultimate grounds" not available to all. Religious communities even in that case, however, could *in themselves* constitute only a quasi-public sphere—and *minority* religions such as Judaism would presumably have little chance of making a significant contribution to the true public sphere of the larger society. They could not meet Habermas's requirements that, in Lukes's terms, "common interest [be] ascertained without deception" [that is, be free of religious belief] and that the consensus rationally arrived at permit "only what *all* can want[,] . . . arise only through appropriately interpreted, generalizable interests, by which I mean needs that can be communicatively shared."[87] Nor could particularist *practices,* or their complex relations to belief, be communicated. As Habermas himself concedes, "it is not so simple to counter the suspicion that with the concept of action oriented to validity claims the idealism of a pure, nonsituated reason slips in again."[88]

There is ample evidence of this tendency when Habermas touches directly on Jewish themes.[89] The discussion of "communicative versus subject-centered reason" (that is, the contest between Habermas's own view and Lyotard's) in *The Philosophical Discourse of Modernity* ends with a reference to "the covenant made by Yahweh with the people of Israel." Approvingly citing Klaus Heinrich's notion that "keeping the covenant with God is the symbol of fidelity; breaking this covenant is the model of betrayal," Habermas writes that the covenant, in its modern translation, means to "keep faith with life-giving being." Each of us is a partner to this covenant, he avers, and we must keep faith with it. Enlightenment cannot proceed without a "potentially universal confederation against betrayal."[90] We note, one final time, that the condition of covenantal fulfillment is not faith but universal rationality. For real as opposed to metaphoric Israel, the sort of fulfillment Habermas envisions is of course messianic; short of that, as Rieff reminds us, the claim to have attained it is heresy. Habermas takes a different stance on the matter, as we learn from his very next sentence: "Peirce and Mead were the first to raise this religious motif of a [covenantal] confederation to philosophical status in the form of a consensus theory of truth and a communicative theory of society," since elaborated by his own work. Covenant, "raised up" to philosophy, yields the secular vision of Habermas. The Torah's particularism has been overcome, along with its "normative content." Its God has been overcome. And, finally, the exclusive emphasis on belief has left no room for the Jewish practices through which covenant and God are still, in our day, both articulated and served.

It is telling, I think, that even Habermas's theory has no use for Jews except as instance or metaphor and no room whatever for modern Jewish practice, except, of course, in theory. Even the commitment to multiple lifeworlds has not made room for observant along with secular Jews; the critique of Kant's false universals, first articulated by Hegel and Marx and seconded in our century by the Frankfurt school, has not extended legitimacy to this particular. One is disappointed in hoping that in Habermas the covenant between Israel and God might, for once, stand only for itself and not be "raised up" to a higher theory. That this is not the case is testimony to the "deep structures" at work in the theory of modernity within which Habermas, like all the other theorists surveyed here, including even Lyotard, continues to operate. His lenses, like theirs, are both indispensable and inadequate to the study of Jewish practice. That will become clearer still as we turn to the concept most directly involved in scholarly approaches to religious observance of any sort—and, not surprisingly, most problematic—ritual.

THREE

The Distinctiveness of Modern
Jewish Practice

The concept of ritual demands special and sustained attention before we proceed with the examination of modern Jewish practice, because ritual, more than any other concept, determines what should be counted as Jewish practices in the first place and, consequently, what exactly should be examined in a study such as this one. A contemporary scholar cannot begin to talk about either religious behavior or ethnic ceremonial, both paramount concerns in the present work, without reference to the rich treasury of theory that has taught us to think in terms of sacred and profane, "parceling out," cultural systems, "liminality," purity and danger, and the like. Students of modern as well as premodern Judaism have turned to those concepts with great profit, and in this study we shall do so repeatedly.

What is more, practitioners too have been influenced by such notions. Ritual practice among Jews, as among others, has been noticeably altered over the past two centuries in accordance with changing anthropological and sociological notions of what modern individuals should or should not be doing, thinking, or feeling when they engage in ritual activity. That impact, I shall argue in the conclusion to this study, continues in our own day. Indeed, it has arguably grown of late with the resurgence of interest in ritual among scholars and practitioners alike. Theory remains a powerful guide to practice, not least by constructing relevant ritual categories and defining particular candidates for observance into or out of them.

There is, however, another and more direct impetus to careful scrutiny of the concept of ritual before we proceed (in the chapters which follow) with conceptual case studies of modern Jewish practice: the fact that that practice departs in two highly significant (and obvious) ways from the ob-

servances on which the vast majority of scholarly analysis is normally focused. It is *modern*—whereas the most widely used notions of ritual are
derived from the study of premodern and, particularly, tribal communities.
No less important, it is *Jewish*—while, as Mary Douglas and Jonathan Z.
Smith have both observed, the leading theoreticians of ritual have characteristically employed conceptions decisively influenced by Protestantism, indeed derived in major respects from Protestantism's critique of the Catholic
Church. Douglas's study of modern ritual practice, *Natural Symbols,* opens
with a critique of the "wide-spread, explicit rejection of rituals as such" in
contemporary Western societies—a legacy of Protestantism retained by the
Enlightenment—and of the use of the word by scholars and laypeople alike
to connote "empty conformity[;] . . . external gestures without inner commitment."[1] These cautions are all the more necessary when dealing with
Jewish practices, I believe, for these practices have aroused Christian ire for
almost two millennia now and have remained an object of special animus,
as we have seen, in Enlightenment discourse on the religion of reason.

The combination of the modern and the Jewish in modern Jewish practice, I shall argue, has resulted in forms and performances by Jews that both
encourage and resist categorization in the terms which dominate most ritual
theory. Our subject comprises the extremely varied sorts of behavior
through which Jews over the past two centuries have (among other things)
registered God's presence and absence, marked their own apartness and connection, celebrated their passages through the year and the years, fulfilled
their communal duties, and remembered their distant or immediate ancestors. In crucial respects, these patterns strain the most widely used concepts
of ritual (let alone of religious ritual) to the breaking point, demanding
corrections, minor and severe, which I shall suggest. In other respects,
however, such concepts are both adequate and indispensable. My working
definition of Jewish practice (adding only the qualifier "Jewish" and substi-
tuting broader terms such as "practice" or "observance") shall be the fairly
standard one supplied for "ritual" by the philosopher Lenn Goodman:

> symbolically freighted activity that bears part of its significance in the
> modalities of its performance, and that, as a matter of primary inten-
> tion, uses those modalities themselves symbolically to express certain
> attitudes toward specific values that the ritual symbolically intends.[2]

In employing this consensual definition of ritual, however, we will want to
examine, among other things, the reconception of "symbolically freighted
activity" by Jews in response to the changed condition of the Jewish and

Gentile bodies politic; the effect upon "modalities of [Jewish] performance[s]" by the forcible and voluntary relegation to private space and leisure time of a system meant by its own declarations to be public and omni-
present; and the altered "expression" through ritual of "certain attitudes
toward specific values," accompanied and shaped by *reasons* for observance
couched increasingly in terms of the assumption that symbolic expression is
what ritual necessarily is and does.

I hope, by juxtaposing major themes in the theories of thinkers such as
Durkheim and Douglas with major aspects of the Jewish reconception of
practice that began with Mendelssohn, to demonstrate the distinctiveness of
modern Jewish ritual forms and performances; I aim as well to clarify further
the choice of the conceptual case studies which constitute the major part of
this book. My object is to have theory follow where Jewish practice leads,
even as theory self-consciously registers which practices it determines to
examine and why. In the chapter's final section, after we have surveyed the
modern and the Jewish elements of modern Jewish observance, we shall
preview their joint effect on a key aspect of all Jewish ritual performance
through the ages: the belief that such observance leads to, occurs in, or
flows from the presence of God.

I. NEW LENSES FOR MODERNITY

The need for attention to the *modern* in modern Jewish ritual observance
comes into view immediately when we consider Douglas's imaginative and
influential attempt, in the tradition of Durkheim, to understand regulation
of the ritual purity of the human body in terms of the structure and situation
of the body politic in which that regulation occurs. Recall the terms in
which her claims are couched in *Purity and Danger* (1966), a veritable classic
in the field. "Some [spiritual] powers are exerted on behalf of the social
structure." Others are believed to be a danger to society. "The self is not
clearly separated as an agent" from its physical or social environment. "The
extent and limits of its autonomy are not defined." The idea of society is
"potent in its own right. . . . There is energy in its margins and unstructured
areas. For symbols of society any human experience of structures, margins
or boundaries is ready to hand." Because "primitive social structure is strictly
articulated, it is almost bound to impinge heavily on the relation between
men and women."[3]

Douglas's theory arises out of "primitive social structure" and depends
for its coherence upon the relative lack of differentiation which that struc-

ture displays. We should note that the author indulges in no romance of "primitive" paradises lost. Her theory explicitly recognizes and accounts for "the system at war with itself." Witches feed on personal jealousies and rivalries. Ritual feeds on the need for clarity as to who is in and who is out—lines drawn both within and between individual societies. Not all borders in this universe require equal guarding. Not every man or woman is a true believer. Not every ceremony is effective. Nonetheless, we are dealing in every case with a *single* social structure that, whether "highly articulated" or not, is *fairly simple* as compared to the structure of modern societies. The group has its divisions but remains *one group*. Subcultures and subcommunities are unknown. Selves do not walk about with Kantian notions of individual autonomy in their heads and legal rights to match.

The bulk of the theories of ritual in use today among scholars come from anthropologists like Douglas—well-known for her work on the Lele and Leviticus—whose data are largely or entirely premodern or even tribal in character. Clifford Geertz's primary fieldwork site has been in Java; Victor Turner's original statement of "the ritual process," "liminality," and "communitas" came through study of the Ndembu. Durkheim, father of all ritual theories, drew on tribal material exclusively in *The Elementary Forms of the Religious Life*. Such theories cannot be applied without difficulty to modern societies and selves—*not* because human nature has changed (for our purposes, we can safely steer clear of debate about the "primitive mind")[4] but because the context in which ritual emerges and functions has become radically different from what it once was.[5] For Douglas, the pattern is clear: "When the social group grips its members in tight communal bonds, the religion is ritualist; when this grip is relaxed, ritualism declines."[6] That is so because the perception of symbols and their interpretation are both socially determined.[7] It therefore stands to reason that ritual—the social action most heavily freighted with symbol—will vary not only in content but in frequency and valence with the strength of the collective consciousness. The model developed in *Purity and Danger* will no longer readily apply in the modern world. "We moderns operate in many different fields of symbolic action. For the Bushman, Dinka and many primitive cultures, the field of symbolic action is one."[8]

Douglas attempts to accommodate her theory to this development by the use in *Natural Symbols* of two variables, "group" and "grid," rather than "group" (the collective body) alone. "Grid" refers to "rules which relate one person to others on an ego-centred basis" that is said to include considerations of sex, age, and seniority.[9] We cannot give the notion adequate treatment here; suffice it to say that Douglas's theory, not without complexity in her earlier book, is now so complicated that, as she herself admits more than once, it cannot readily be confirmed or refuted empirically. "Even the difficulty of defining a social environment is great."[10] Complex social structures and highly individualist notions of self have made it so.

Modern ritual actors, we might say, and particularly members of minority groups such as the Jews, can no longer credibly see wilderness beyond their own religious or ethnic borders; indeed, such borders may no longer exist in sufficiently coherent form to be effectively symbolized by means of an individual body's entrances and exits. Many and varied societies and cultures lie beyond the borders of self and group alike, and they are found as well inside each self's own fractured and often fractious identity. Alienation from "the group" has, as Douglas notes, increased in every "ego-centered" social system. So has the "internalizing of religious experience" by individuals who piece together "on an ego-centered basis," from a variety of sources the meanings they find ultimate, there being no one source of meaning that possesses a monopoly on access to their consciousness. It is no surprise, then, that participation in collective religious ritual of the premodern sort has precipitously declined—no surprise, either, that participation in ritual has survived in the changed political context of modernity in forms and performances very different from those in preceding centuries.[11]

The consequences of this alteration for the understanding of Jewish observance over the past two centuries are neither obvious nor straightforward. Mendelssohn provides an eloquent case in point. Consider first (bearing Douglas's theory in mind) the nostalgic lament in *Jerusalem* on the damage done to human beings by the printing press. The diffusion of writing had brought incalculable benefits to humanity, Mendelssohn writes, but the loss had been no less immense. Oral instruction and spoken exchange had given way to the "rigid forms" of written characters, which "must always remain the same." Overemphasis on the written word was everywhere. Preachers now read written sermons from the pulpit. Teachers read written lectures in the classroom. Lovers pledged fealty to one another in correspondence. Friends gathered to spend an evening together reading aloud. "Everything is dead letter; the spirit of living conversation has vanished." From this patent exaggeration, Mendelssohn jumps to a still more extravagant conclusion: "Hence it has come to pass that man has almost lost his value to his fellow man." Most people could no longer even understand how a person could "educate and perfect himself without a book."[12]

Appearing as they do in a book, not to mention one written by a man whose collected works fill a shelf of some length, the charges in this passage brought against the evils of the written word seem downright comic. Yet Mendelssohn's aim is utterly serious, I believe, in keeping with the gravity of the problem to which he points and immediately proceeds; his appeal to the purity of bygone days begins a tendency that will prove pervasive in modern Jewish reflection on practice. Mendelssohn's concern is the need for a new sort of rationale for the commandments now that Jews would no longer be taught the meaning of their observance from the midst of practice but, rather, had to learn it through the far less direct and satisfying vehicle of books. God had intended Jews to understand the meaning of what they did through the doing of it. "In everything a youth saw being done," Mendelssohn explains in obvious paraphrase of Deuteronomy 6:7, "in all public as well as private dealings, on all gates and on all doorposts, in whatever he turned his eyes or ears to," the student was to find "occasion for inquiring and reflecting" on the purpose of living in accordance with the commandments.[13] Modernity had precluded that possibility—and not only, we can infer, by means of the printing press. It was the changed body politic, the very freedom from coercion that Mendelssohn himself both urged and applauded, that forced any argument for following the commandments, such as *Jerusalem,* to *compete* for Jewish allegiance and attention. In former eras, Jewish adherence and awareness could be taken for granted, but the "plausibility structure" of integral community would soon be no more. All that remained were books.

The problem was exacerbated when a Jewish thinker sought to provide a rationale for a particular commandment, such as dietary laws. Mendelssohn, we should note, did not attempt this in *Jerusalem.* We might expect, given Douglas's theory, that restrictions on what Jews ate—which had functioned for centuries to separate Jews from Gentiles—would be dropped whenever inclusion rather than exclusion became the overriding value. Jews desirous of merger with the Gentile body politic would not ritually restrict the intake of food into their physical bodies according to traditional codes, nor would they restrict the venues in which they ate to Jewish homes. This, of course, is precisely what often happened—in part, because Gentiles insisted that Jews desirous of joining their societies be willing to share meals with non-Jewish neighbors. However, a Jew might also retain dietary laws, with or without belief in their divine origin, precisely in order to mark a distinction from Gentiles which was increasingly blurred in daily life. Indeed, he or she might mark it all the more, and not only subjectively, by eating in a nonkosher restaurant but conspicuously refusing all food that has been cooked or by eating nonkosher food of any sort in a restaurant but maintaining a kosher home. These patterns too are fairly common, and they serve to distinguish Jews not only from Gentiles but also—and perhaps primarily—from other sorts of Jews. Only one thing seems certain in the complex social reality of overlapping grids and groups: the range of meanings associated with the ritual separation of "Israel from the nations," as the Sabbath is separated from weekdays, will not be the same after Emancipation as before. Borders have been moved—or erased. They are guarded, and guard, differently.[14] Theory must adjust.

Inclusion and exclusion can be marked in the very same ritual action— and increasingly would be, given the shifting borders of modern identity. Consider the recollection by Clara Geissmar, born Clara Regensburger in 1844 in Eppingen, of her mother's Sabbath observance. Mrs. Regensburger was a pious woman and kept the Sabbath strictly. However, she "had an absolute aversion to two things: warmed-up coffee and inferior fruit." So "every Saturday, my mother regularly had herself invited for afternoon coffee" at the home of Gentile neighbors whose servant girl knocked on the door punctually at four o'clock and called out, "Frau Regensburger, coffee is served." When persecutions of Jews broke out in town, Mrs. Regensburger "sought an excuse and sat at home with her gloomy ponderings." This lasted until Herr Schmidt, the Gentile neighbor, came "to check on things [and] told my mother that . . . to risk a friendship of many years because of what some gutter-snipe or some other crude person had done was a most foolish way to act." After a while, the daughter reports, "my mother's head and heart were back in their right place. She again went regularly to Saturday coffee."[15]

The details of precisely how and to what degree a Jew may benefit on the Sabbath by the labors of a Gentile seem to have been far less relevant to the meaning of the day's observance for Mrs. Regensburger than her cup of coffee at her neighbor's home. Separation from and friendship with the Gentile were enacted simultaneously in this rite, as inseparable, it seems, as the "pleasure of the Sabbath" and the pleasure of the coffee. The end to Jewish exclusivity had endowed the ritual with a meaning inconceivable in other circumstances.

Douglas's theory also reminds us, finally, that use of *bodies* as a symbolic medium for expression of the situation, worldview, or commitments of a body politic depends not only on the status of the latter "body" but on the conditions and conception of the former. Access to its entryways carries a different valence when sexual partners come and go with some frequency.[16]

It matters that more than one style of clothing dresses a body and exposes sometimes more and sometimes fewer of its parts, that (a perennial class difference) good coffee and fresh fruit are readily available, that a person can adopt various ways of walking, dancing, standing, and sitting. It matters too that "with us pollution is a matter of aesthetics, hygiene or etiquette, which only becomes grave in so far as it may create social embarrassment."[17] A host of premodern cultures, including Judaism, saw—and sees—things very differently. Does circumcision mar one of nature's creations deemed (in a common modern—and ancient pagan—view) to be perfect because it is naturally given? Or does it mark a baby boy with the inscription of God and/or community required for him to become a complete and whole male adult?

The aesthetic and normative perspectives contrasted in this example alert us to a further change in attitude toward the commandments, and rationales for them, related to the changed political conditions in which Jewish practice would be enacted after Emancipation. Whereas the premodern faithful as a rule likely understood religious ritual to be a sacred and sometimes efficacious *duty*, it has increasingly become—and has had to be explained as—a leisure-time pursuit that ornaments and adorns life, one among many ceremonies or "language games." As Durkheim put it in *Elementary Forms,* "a rite is something different from a game. It is a part of the serious life."[18] Not so when one can as easily marry in a courthouse or a room in Reno as in a church or synagogue—or have the wedding performed jointly by a justice of the peace, a minister, and a rabbi. Law is the domain of such authorities, not of ritual, in a common modern view; ethics pertains to *real* human interactions, not to symbolic observances. What and how a particular ritual means to us will necessarily vary in part with the attitude that we take toward ritual—and meaning—as such.

That is why Geertz's famous and very Durkheimian definition of religion—"a system of symbols which acts to establish powerful, pervasive, and long-lasting moods and motivations in men by formulating conceptions of a general order of existence and clothing these conceptions with such an aura of factuality that the moods and motivations seem uniquely realistic"— does not jibe with its own aesthetic orientation.[19] Geertz's rituals fuse "ethos" and "worldview" into a whole so powerful that it can serve as a model *for* as well as *of* reality.

Curiously, however, his definition lacks any normative content. The closest we get is "mood" and "motivation," the latter defined as "a persisting tendency, a chronic inclination to perform certain sorts of acts and experience certain sorts of feeling in certain sorts of situations." Geertz even adds at once that "the 'sorts' [are] commonly very heterogeneous and rather ill-defined classes." Moreover, as the essay moves from idealized *Gemeinschaft* to actual *Gesellschaft,* from descriptions by Bateson and Mead of "Balinese character" to descriptions by Alfred Schutz of "social reality" as we moderns know it, it turns out that religion is but *one among many* perspectives that inform individuals and societies. The impact of "cultural system" on "social system" and "personality system" is not straightforward. Even inside the cultural system, religion must contend with the competing perspectives of science, art, and common sense. We should see human beings, Geertz insists, "as moving more or less easily, and very frequently, between radically contrasting ways of looking at the world . . . separated by cultural gaps across which Kirkegaardian leaps must be made in both directions."[20]

Kierkegaard would not have seen things that way, of course. Nor would anyone else for whom the "aura" of religion had come to "seem uniquely realistic." The leap of faith is not so easily accomplished, back and forth, on multiple occasions. Geertz concedes two pages later that "the image is perhaps a bit too athletic for the actual facts—'slipped' might be more accurate."[21] It is the theorist who has slipped here, in a way that gives away the problem with his theory.

A "cultural system" will not have the same impact on "social systems" and "personality systems" in relatively homogeneous premodern societies (to which Geertz's definition of religion *is* appropriate) as it will in differentiated, dynamic, and multicultural contexts such as those he himself described beautifully elsewhere, most notably in his work on present-day Java. The burial ceremony, or *slametan,* he examined did not reaffirm the order of existence but, by pointing up conflicting loyalties and identities, threatened to tear the sacred order apart, and the community with it.[22] Similarly disruptive was the edict by German authorities in Mendelssohn's time that Jews cease burying their dead immediately, as Jewish law decreed, and that they instead, in a more seemly and respectful fashion, wait three days as Gentiles did—further testimony to the impact of politics on Jewish ritual performances.[23]

The rationale that Mendelssohn provides for observance in *Jerusalem* is, like Geertz's theory, demonstrably torn between the obligatory and the aesthetic. On the one hand, the author of *Jerusalem* affirms that for a Jew the commandments are utterly binding. Jews were free to reflect on the law but not to disobey it. "As long as we can point to no . . . authentic exemption from the law, no sophistry of ours can free us from the strict obedience we owe to the law; and reverence for God draws a line between speculation and practice which no conscientious man may cross."[24] On the other hand, Mendelssohn retains Spinoza's Pauline term for the commandments—"ceremony"—and describes them as a "ceremonial script." The mitzvot were one among many sets of action symbols (albeit, of course, the finest) designed to lead human beings to "eternal truths," which, Mendelssohn agreed, were by definition universal: accessible to reason and reason alone.

Given these two factors—first, the dissolution of all-embracing moods, motivations, worldviews, and bodies politic; and, second, that Jews (like members of the various Christian denominations) could no longer construe their "religion as *a* cultural system" unified in itself,[25] functioning in splendid isolation from competing systems, and serving to fuse a unified ethos, via uniform and uniformly experienced ritual, with a correspondingly coherent worldview—the commandments now had to be explained in terms persuasive to people moving in more than one such cultural system and accustomed to leaps (or slips) among them. The rabbis had always been somewhat suspicious of the enterprise of *ta'amei ha-mitzvot* (provision of "reasons" or "tastes" for the commandments), fearing that provision of a reason for practice might lead to the abandonment of practice if the reason offered were deemed unpersuasive.[26]

Mendelssohn bears witness to a heightened version of this danger: the need to justify distinctive practices, in language that is *not* distinctive, to Jews who for the first time could choose, if they remained unpersuaded, *not* to undertake traditional practices. As a result *Jerusalem* borrows from the common conceptual currency in order to purchase allegiance to Otherness for individuals to whom the Jewish ceremonial script is foreign, the language of the Gentile surroundings native. The acrobatics involved for theorist and practitioners alike are dramatic indeed.

This is not the place for a detailed account of Mendelssohn's rationale for the commandments.[27] It is striking, however, that his argument begins by citing Hobbes, Rousseau, and other major figures in the Enlightenment canon in order to demonstrate the superiority of oral over written Torah and proceeds with speculation on the origins of language that directly recalls Rousseau's *Discourse on Inequality* (translated into German by Mendelssohn some years earlier). Mendelssohn constructs his rationale for Jewish observance in terms borrowed from the greats of the Enlightenment, who are cited frequently, while Jewish authorities such as Maimonides and Yehuda Halevi, no less influential, are generally left unacknowledged.

Note too that Mendelssohn's rationale for observance is ingenious—and utterly belabored. Oral transmission has the potential, lacking in the written word, for imperceptible adjustment to "changes of time and circumstance." But confusion and indistinctness abound in the signification of words, written or oral. They can therefore not be relied on to convey precise and shared meanings; God, realizing this, had not revealed eternal truths at Sinai, let alone revealed them in words. Eternal truths were revealed, rather, in "nature and thing," grasped immediately by the mind or apprehended through reasoning from such unmediated intuitions.[28] Words could also not be used to raise inherently elusive concepts to consciousness or to communicate them to others. "Wise Providence" had therefore attached "abstract characteristics" to "perceptible signs which . . . at once recall and illuminate" them. At first the signs were things themselves (like Swift's Lilliputians, one carried around a chair to talk about a chair) or objects which represented them (like the physician's snake). Later the things gave way to images and then abstract lines, until finally the human race developed hieroglyphs and alphabets. But this progress inevitably led to misunderstanding and abuse, chiefly because signs were mistaken for what they were meant to signify. Animals came to be taken as embodiments of divine powers and worshipped; Mendelssohn confirms his suspicions on this score by a fascinating exegesis of Hindu mythology in which he makes good symbolic sense of an apparently outrageous tale of monsters, tortoises, and elephants.[29] The point, of course, is that while animals and images and even numbers could be mistaken for what they symbolized, actions could not. God had therefore given the Jews symbolic actions which would "continually . . . call attention to sound and unadulterated ideas of God and his attributes."[30]

The problems with this explanation are manifold, the most obvious difficulty being that Mendelssohn argues for the commandments as a path to the attainment of truth and the inculcation of virtue but freely admits that both truth and virtue are *available elsewhere* and can fruitfully be sought by other means. Judaism is one among a number of symbol systems, though it remains the best in Mendelssohn's view and is binding on Jews in any case. The commandments are *particularist,* the rationale which makes sense of them *universalist,* to a degree that exceeds a similar tendency in the most rationalist of the medieval Jewish philosophers. Mendelssohn has been forced to formulate a *ta'am* for the commandments which could be conveyed to Jews (or Gentiles) who had never performed them and perhaps never would. His rationale does not depend on prior experience of the good or the truth which it urges. Small wonder that the general outlines of Mendelssohn's symbolic account have often been seized upon by subsequent thinkers intent on the defense of Jewish practice—and that other Jews have availed themselves of reasons for observance not dependent on such cognitive maneuvers but, rather, couched in the *nostalgic* terms of loyalty and connection to ancestors.

The logic of both moves is brought into clearer focus by the work of anthropologist Roy Rappaport, who usefully categorizes the "messages" conveyed by ritual as either "canonial" or "indexical." Indexical messages set participants in a given ritual apart from all others, while canonical messages contain information that remains invariant across time and performances, invulnerable to the vicissitudes of the years and the dangers of deception. Certainty concerning such "highest-order meanings," Rappaport speculates, along with confidence in the social order that carries and is dedicated to those meanings might well be the most important messages that accompany observance. Individuals seek assurance through ritual performance that the "eternal truths" associated with or expressed by the rituals they enact are reliable enough to act upon and maintain. In order to provide such assurance despite variations in situation, circumstance, or belief, the truths have to be presented at a level of generality not capable of refutation.[31]

Mendelssohn did precisely that. The distinctive script bestowed by God upon the Jews, comprising 613 commandments by rabbinic count, was in his view meant in the first instance to lead them to a very few "canonical" messages, metaphysical and moral. But it was apparent to him, and a staple of Enlightenment belief, that such truths were by definition universal. As such, they were not the property of any group, least of all a small minority such as the Jews. Why then convey these truths by practices limited to that group alone? Mendelssohn is on stronger ground when he has the commandments serve as conveyors of "indexical" messages: reminders of "historical truths" pertaining to the particular existence and destiny of the Jewish people rather than to the human condition as a whole. And he gains further flexibility in symbolic explanation of the commandments by arguing that the meaning of the mitzvot at either level, eternal or historical, canonical or indexical, was not fixed but itself varied from time to time, place to place, and person to person. That being the case, there could never be one single authoritative meaning to any particular mitzvah. No interpretation could be said to be correct for all "performers and rememberers" at all times.

If this is so, however, the obvious question becomes, how would a *variety* of interpretations, changing in this fashion, yield eternal truths that are "legible and comprehensible at all times and places" or even historical truths constant throughout the ages? Presumably, Mendelssohn would reply that the meanings pointed to by observance would likely continue to fall within the range defined (and limited) by the very few principles which he had put forward as essential, that God had ordained this set of behaviors with the intention of stimulating this process of arriving at this set of meanings, and that this process had worked with a fair degree of success for many centuries. The relative constancy of the framework had kept and would continue to keep the various truths, variously arrived at, within a common and enduring boundary. To which we might well reply that it was precisely the relative constancy of the framework that had now vanished or, at minimum, was in doubt, even as the historicity of "historical truths" such as Sinai or the Exodus would increasingly be subject to challenge on scientific grounds.

In sum, Mendelssohn had fashioned an ingenious *symbolic explanation* of the mitzvot to suit the new political circumstances of freedom and diversity that he perceived and welcomed. He would not be the last modern Jewish (or Christian) thinker to do so (we shall for that reason probe the political context further in Chapter 4, and the strategy of symbolic explanation in Chapter 5). But those very circumstances were, on the face of it at least, less than conducive to the maintenance of the particular community and traditions—the Jewish "ceremonial script" and "historical truths"—to which Mendelssohn was most committed. He could persuade Jews to undertake observance only by marrying it to meanings shared with Gentiles—and Jews!—who did not undertake it. Hence the popularity of "highest-order" messages such as "ethical monotheism" or *tikkun olam,* the progressive perfection of the world. Meanings internal to the tradition, although perhaps better fitted to the distinctive details of practice, would have proven less attractive or comprehensible to the audience of readers, and so could not be invoked.

Some Jews, moreover, were bound not to like the meanings a given thinker or group imposed upon their practice, no matter what those meanings were. Many have with good reason resisted the attachment of their observance to any content whatsoever. It is a major advantage of ritual's *performative* character that it binds individuals to a group in the most palpable ways—singing together, swaying to a common rhythm, entering into a dance or procession or meal or candle-lighting with affect as well as mind—ways that keep individuals focused on symbolic action rather than on subscription to particular truths. Ritual articulates via *indirection,* pointing to truths rather than saying them outright.[32] Conventional action, precisely because it is conventional, permits us to avoid saying what we know—and allows as well for "psychic distance" from what we are doing. After all, the ritual is not our invention. We are not responsible for it; we claim nothing more by the practice than membership in the group performing it. All messages imputed to our acts therefore possess what some politicians have called "plausible deniability."[33]

That precious advantage disappears when individual ritual performance (assuming it is not coerced) is tied too strictly by others or the actor to generally accepted meanings or propositionally stated beliefs which he or she cannot embrace. The problem likely became all the more acute for Jews in the modern period because diversity of circumstance exponentially increased the array of meanings and purposes brought to a given ritual by its many actors. In addition, at the same time rabbis and theologians tried to convince Jews to undertake newly optional practices on grounds that via such undertaking they would testify to belief in highly specific matters of faith. Recall the case of the nonbelieving *mohel,* whose dismissal by the community Mendelssohn unconvincingly protested because "private belief should play no role in the fulfillment of contractual obligation."[34] In a former era, the officiant would probably not have been asked about his beliefs and would have felt no need to disclose his heresy. In the modern period, on the other hand, individuals are driven to quiz themselves about belief—and, in its absence, the justification of observance becomes difficult indeed.

This problem with symbolic rationales for the commandments accounts in large part, I believe, for the popularity of a different sort of explanation and motivation: *nostalgia,* far more a "reason of the heart" than of the mind. A recognizable area of life—located in *private* time and space, as the new rules for particularist religious loyalties demanded—is organized around regular performances which lend performers the conviction that they are carrying on the *essence* of their ancestors' faith and practice even while they alter both belief and observance to suit new circumstances. Recall Mendelssohn's elegaic invocation of the pristine Israelite past, essential to his project of redefining Judaism. Like him, modern Jews would want to be sure that nothing which truly mattered to the ancestors had been lost (or, Mendelssohn might say, conveniently forgotten), that the rhythm of their days and years had been set long before the modern workweek to which they actually moved most of the time, that their ancestors too had marched to this rhythm, tasted what they now tasted, thought the same thoughts. Mendelssohn supplied that assurance in part by passing over particular observances in silence. His account, typical of the literature proclaiming the mitzvah of nostalgia, remains at a high level of generality—no doubt a significant reason for its popularity in the nineteenth century among Orthodox, Reform, and Historical School figures alike. He has not been the last modern Jewish thinker by any means to mix elegy with utopia and to lay great stress on the unity of contemporary Jews with ancestors who lived very differently. Mitzvot were links, however fragmentary and unfinished, through which the "chain of tradition," no matter what impinged upon it, could be seen to remain unbroken.[35]

Mendelssohn well understood the political context in which Jews would henceforth, after Emancipation, have to conduct and make sense of their observances. His strategy of symbolic explanation seems calculated to address those conditions directly, and the limitations of that strategy are highlighted by his very different appeal to the ancestors, equally important in his essay. Many other modern Jews would soon walk the same path. The altered character of the modern body politic left them, as it left Mendelssohn, little choice.

2. NEW LENSES FOR JEWS AND JUDAISM

The recalibration of theoretical lenses demanded by the *Jewish* distinctiveness of modern Jewish practice is less extensive than that demanded by its modernity, I believe, both because the works of major theorists already include an immense variety of comparative material and because the practice of modern Jews has been shaped so decisively by the *modern* factors that Jews shared with everyone else in the societies to which they belonged. There are, nonetheless, several themes which should be examined, and not only because of the widespread theoretical assumption that ritual is either "merely symbolic" or altogether illegitimate. In Jonathan Z. Smith's view, that bias against ritual has "marked the study of religion as essentially a Protestant exercise, a heritage that continues to haunt theorists of religion even to the present day."[36] More important for our purposes, Judaism (like other traditions) transmits behaviors attached to particular storehouses of meanings and associations, and it patterns the attachment of meaning to behavior in a distinctive fashion. We shall focus on three examples of this distinctiveness: the *everyday* nature of Jewish observance, its status as *law,* and its *democratic* character.

First, let us consider the issue of ritual's *embeddedness in everyday experience.* Smith would remind us that the generally small and discrete ritual behaviors which time after time mark time and place and focus reflection can function (or be understood) only in relation to the realities and meanings which surround them,[37] but this reminder itself represents an intervention in a long-standing anthropological debate concerning the proper framing of ritual activity. What should be counted as its beginning? Who should be numbered among its participants? E. E. Evans-Pritchard is quite clear, for example, that "we have to distinguish between the religious rite of sacrifice [among the Nuer] and the secular rites and ceremonial acts which it accompanies and sacralizes." We would surely differentiate, Evans-Pritchard continues, between a wedding ceremony and the banquet that inevitably follows.[38] Bearing traditional Jewish practices and attitudes toward practice in mind, I am not so sure.[39]

There is an enormous difference in regard to "the holy" between observances which stand apart from everyday activity in space or time and those which structure, pervade, inform, or are superimposed upon daily activity. Only the former allow for the unbridgeable division between sacred and profane upon which Durkheim insisted in *Elementary Forms*—despite the numerous and complex exchanges between sacred and profane that he himself presented in that work.[40] Only such a view of the sacred allows Geertz to assign the "fusion" between ethos and worldview—itself a desideratum and not an achievement, according to rabbinic Judaism—to "religious symbols, dramatized in rituals or related in myths," rather than to humdrum and quotidian regulation. Milton Singer's Hindu informants, cited approvingly by Geertz, might "seem to think of their religion 'as encapsulated in these discrete performances which they [can] exhibit to visitors and to themselves.'"[41] Most Jews of Mendelssohn's day, I would wager, did not. Everyday concerns, restrictions they may well have found burdensome, probably loomed just as large in their perspective as "mysterium" or "tremendum"—until, adjusting voluntarily and involuntarily to a Protestant modern order, Jews increasingly *did* restrict their religious practice. Once-weekly or thrice-yearly services in the synagogue, along with a handful of annual celebrations in the home, then *were* seen to "encapsulate," and so to legitimately replace, the fuller calendar of practice. The politics of observance not only shaped the explanation of its meaning but delimited and framed the details of the ritual activity itself.

A second distinctive feature of Jewish practice, still more resistant to recasting in a Protestant image and still more closely tied to political considerations, is *its character as law*. This status by no means robs commandments of their symbolic dimension. Quite the opposite—as Goodman argues persuasively, all laws have a symbolic dimension, for all laws communicate social norms, expectations, and worldviews through the rich details of what they permit, prohibit, and punish.[42] Laws send messages, express attitudes, foster values. A given law's ability to perform this role is all the greater when it is part of a system; being law, its performance can be counted on, and the more all-encompassing its system's scope, the greater its chance of performing its symbolic task successfully.

That is all the more true when a ritual law claims to be *divine* in origin, albeit human and rational in the specifics of interpretation (as in rabbinic Judaism). It stands before the actor as a regimen of conduct that *necessarily* makes sense. God has commanded that it be done, and God would not do so arbitrarily. Ritual actors who believe in the law's divine origin thus stand assured that each observance serves the ultimate interests of all who maintain it whether or not they can see the point at any given moment of doing it.[43] God had given this law with love, though for reasons which have been variously understood or, in some cases, not understood at all.

The law's "heteronomous" character was never in doubt among premodern interpreters, but that character varied in its valence. Some thinkers—particularly the medieval philosophers—took pains to insist that God, though sovereign, was not a tyrant. God's decrees were entirely wise and just and beneficial. The laws' purposes could, for the most part, be ascertained through rational investigation. Other thinkers, particularly the mystics, rejoiced in the occasion offered by the law, precisely because it was law, to demonstrate exceptional obedience to God. The less apparent the reason, the better. Ordinary believers throughout the ages, less concerned with either rational proof or exhibitions of devotion, were likely comforted by the knowledge that by following divine law, they could acquire merit in the eyes of their Heavenly Judge and spend their days exactly as their Creator intended, in perennial contact with the right and true. This assurance was possible because life and the rules which regulated it—whether ritual, civil, or criminal law—derived from the same divine source, who had created the world with precisely these ends in view.

It seems fair to say that even in the modern period, when this assurance became far less reassuring, Jews have not normally weighed each individual observance for its meaning or effect. Rather, they have considered that meaning or effect as part of a total package—"Judaism" or "Torah"—to which the community in whole or in part has accepted obligation and from which individuals and community alike expect to experience reward. Indeed, individual mitzvot, though stripped of their character of revealed law in the eyes of many modern Jews, have nevertheless continued to impress such Jews as obligatory and have often remained part of an intricately cross-referenced code of meaningful behaviors, whether symbolic or nostalgic. An act such as havdalah, discriminating "Israel from the nations," could in the larger context of behaviors constituting Jewish identity become more compelling, poignant, or contentious in a context of anti-Semitism or assimilation; lighting of candles by Jewish women at the commencement of the Sabbath in recall of mothers and grandmothers could likewise assume the aspect of commandedness. Observances of lesser significance to particular ritual actors have remained linked to moments of major *personal importance* such as circumcisions, weddings, and funerals, as well as to the *collective fate* on which individual destiny has palpably depended. Rites of questionable authority have thereby continued to be bound up with others which *are* regarded as duties: whether to ancestors, to the Jewish people, to "tradition," or to ethics. Quotidian acts have, as it were, drawn from an overflow of personal as well as collective significance. "Law-governed" is not a term one would use to describe this activity in many cases, but "commandment" is not inappropriate; the act is far more than "ceremony" and cannot adequately be comprehended as symbol.

There is, however, another consequence of the inherited connotation of Judaism as law, one which has often militated *against* observance: the resistance on the part of many Jews, as of many Gentiles, to submit to behaviors that appear to demand surrender of their individual autonomy. This problem is exacerbated in the Jewish case by concerns (and charges) that the commandments' status as law posed a threat to the only legitimate juridical authority, the state. Consider in this connection the suggestions by Rieff and Rappaport that democracy—the political culture of Emancipation and Enlightenment—has inhibited the payment of obeisances to high authority. The location of authority in "horizontals" renders the acknowledgment of ultimate hierarchy problematic. The issue here is not primarily one of *belief* but of *performance*. Attitudes to hierarchy bear on a host of typical ritual actions: bowing, prostrating oneself, rising to one's feet in respect, standing at attention, inflicting pain (however symbolically), turning to face the East, kissing the cover of the Torah scroll, venerating books that contain God's name.[44]

These observations apply to all citizens of modern democracies, of course, but might have special importance to Jews, given that Jewish tradition insists on the association between mitzvah and commandment and that Jews, disproportionately an urban and highly educated group, have been especially involved in the production and consumption of secular culture. One wonders, then, whether it was perhaps not so much the aesthetic affront of *repetition* (often complained about in modern Jewish sources) that was the sticking point in performance by elites and laity alike as, rather, the patently *hierarchical* nature of those forms, conveyed not least by means of repetition. Rituals demand conformity to a certain way of acting at a certain moment—this before that, this at the same time as that, feet here, gaze in that direction, keep the holy separate from the profane—and so support a way of being that is similarly ordered and demarcated. The self not only sees itself bowing or rising but, even when doing neither, is aware of acting in conformity with one tradition rather than another, joining one community rather than another, assenting in public to a particular symbolic order of low and higher and highest.[45] Repetition, in this view, cannot be divorced from ultimate meaning: eternity, as Kierkegaard put it, "is the true repetition.[46] Opposition in the modern period to the ritual *medium* of eternity can be understood at least in part as opposition to its *message*.[47] This is Rieff's conclusion exactly:

> In its shifts within the vertical, self is an artful dodger. . . . Yet precisely what is self-evident, being sacred, occurs in constant repetitions. Repetition is authority in its form, making clear, in endless variations of such knowledge experienced, that self cannot endure a world imagined entirely profane, possibility undenied to consciousness.[48]

The argument is highly speculative, but if Rieff is at all correct, modern Jewish ritual practice enacts ambivalence about highest authority—law— not just in practices that take the place of, and progressively approximate, repressed desires—Freud's claim. It enacts ambivalence as well in *opposition* to such practices, an opposition that succeeds in part because it never once mentions its antagonism to the divine authority that the rituals, in and through their repetitions, acknowledge—a Freudian forgetting, as it were, in the opposite direction. It is one thing to regard observance as ceremony, ornament, a choice to add incremental meaning. Nonobservance in that case is a loss of whatever the ritual was meant to provide: a zero, as it were, rather than a plus. The tally is quite different when practice is regarded as obedience to a commandment. Nonobservance then becomes a minus— unless, of course, belief is denied, heteronomy is devalued, and plus and minus are declared reversed. Why opt for such a loss of option? Why freely choose an act that testifies to the ultimate denial of individual freedom?

We shall encounter such *opposition to commandment* quite often—most notably, in Martin Buber, on whom we shall focus in Chapter 7. Buber also furnishes a paradigmatic example of the performance of *mitzvah as nostalgia:* a quintessential way of acting out ambivalence toward the ancestors, of following and rebelling against them at the very same time, indeed through the very same behavior. Other Jews—like Franz Rosenzweig (our other focus in Chapter 7)—have deftly evaded the problem of ultimate authority, by regarding practice as forever in *quest* of the authority that would ultimately justify it. The search for the Commander, so long as it continues, leaves observance in a middle ground between autonomy and heteronomy, freedom and obedience. Or—yet another alternative, pioneered by Mordecai Kaplan and examined in Chapter 8—one can appeal to the authority of tradition in full awareness that one has helped to construct that tradition. This strategy, too, secures both autonomy and (selective) observance. All three patterns, as we shall see, have proved popular among Jewish elites and laity alike in the twentieth century.

I turn now to a third and final consideration essential to the "Jewishness" of modern Jewish practice: its *democratic character,* by which I seek to indicate the balance between "virtuoso" and popular observance. Despite the obvious difficulties with such generalization, it seems fair to say that Jewish ritual figured densely and intensely in the lives of ordinary folk for most of the two millennia preceding the modern period. Most observances did not require the officiation of individuals who were either professionally trained or charismatically gifted. Neither did the decision for observance require much forethought. One did what was done, with greater or lesser enthusiasm, and certain individuals at certain moments elected to do more.[49] It likewise seems fair to say that the past two centuries have seen an apparent leveling downward of observance (although several exceptions to this will shortly be noted). Prayer among most Jews of both sexes has been limited to Sabbaths and festivals, whereas once males prayed daily (or believed they should have). Of all fast-day strictures, only Yom Kippur's are still widely followed. Dietary laws have been disregarded or curtailed. And while observance has remained relatively high among Orthodox Jews and even grown higher in recent decades, members of all other denominations have tended in increasing numbers to see themselves as *audience to* rather than *actors in* public ritual performances.[50] These individuals sit as quietly in synagogues as they would in theaters or concert halls, listening to sermons or cantorial solos and singing only in unison. In part, as we will see, this is a function of increased self-consciousness concerning distinctive ritual performances; the change also comes along with a *professionalization* that, in this area as in others, has left its mark.[51] Extensive or intensive ritual practice has increasingly been conceived as a *specialized activity* best left to those well-versed in the intricacies of observance. Most Jews are no longer interested in acquiring such knowledge and, in many cases, not concerned that their rabbis acquire it either: a change of profound importance in the history of Judaism.

There are, however, exceptions to this pattern which should be noted: Orthodoxy, resurgent in recent decades in America; women, who have, thanks to feminism, been moving to reclaim their tradition through practice; a general renewal of interest in *selective* observance in the non-Orthodox movements; and the devotion by many Jews of a great number of hours to communal activities conceived as mitzvot. National or international organizations such as the Alliance Israélite Universelle, the German Jewish Gemeinde, and comparable organizations elsewhere succeeded even before the mass appeal of the Zionist movement in galvanizing widespread involvement. Synagogues, increasingly dependent on local support, have likewise summoned immense energies. Philanthropic and political work, once the province of a few Jewish "notables," now benefits from the efforts of thousands and tens of thousands. Much of the motivation and content of this activity has been social, of course. But that has always been the case; Jews presumably did not lack for fellowship in all the premodern centuries when they met to manage communal affairs, provide for the Jewish needy, and strategize about their dealings with Gentile authorities. To note this activity is not to equate modern and premodern forms but to highlight continuities in the *range* of distinctively Jewish practice, not to blur "religious" and "secular" activity but to underline the problematic character of such a dichotomy. Even while registering the overall decline in practice, its relation to political factors of acculturation and assimilation, and its effect on the explanation of practice both as symbol and as nostalgia, we should avoid simplistic graphs of observance which point only downward.

The same holds true for the related matter of *expression of emotion* in Jewish ritual contexts—another area where evidence is scarce and speculation inevitable. We can say with some assurance that the democratic character of premodern Jewish rituals was bound up with the fact that they allowed for no orgy or other total abandon (with the possible exception of drunkenness on Purim), no delirium or ecstasy (the closest approximation coming perhaps in dancing on Simḥat Torah), no infliction of pain more serious than fasting for a day (though Hasidic penitents were known to roll in the snow and take on afflictions such as exile from their homes). Jewish ritual in home and synagogue tended (in the useful categories supplied by philosopher Josef Stern) to emphasize *denotation* far more than *exemplification.* They performed that function largely through iconic features such as matzah on the Passover table rather than through actual reenactments. *Expression,* the third sort of ritual enumerated by Stern, likewise occurred metaphorically. An overflowing cup of wine expressed prosperity, while actual drunkenness, except on Purim, was studiously avoided.[52] Jews never "became" mythic characters, as Geertz's Javanese, say, "become" Rangda and Barong.[53] "On this point Judaism differs in principle with the validity of 'imitation' as a concretization of transcendental reality. . . . Worship of the mimetic object is [considered to be] idolatry."[54] Jews remained firmly anchored in real-world history, determined to remain there, with their eyes open, until the coming of the Messiah. Ritual nonetheless stimulated and channeled profound emotion, allowed and encouraged tears which might otherwise have been socially unacceptable, and elicited sensations and expressions of happiness which might otherwise have seemed inappropriate or laughable and so might actually have been unattainable.[55]

One cannot say with any certainty *if,* let alone *how,* this process changed in the modern period. It does seem, however, that the notion of religious emotion as such became for many Jews a bar to ritual performance. The demanding routines of social and occupational obligation have shunted "irrational emotion" to the corners of personal life. Jews, in particular, have displayed an antipathy toward mimesis, driven in part by commitment to the modes of behavior that Weber identified with rationality: calculation, control, logic, system. These were repeatedly demanded by Gentile political elites as the price of Jewish entry into citizenship and society, as we shall see in Chapter 4, and they loom large in symbolic explanation of the commandments from Mendelssohn onward.[56]

To other Jews, especially in recent decades, the affective character of observance has come to seem a principal attraction.[57] Immovable pews, their rows long and arranged geometrically, have lost some of their appeal; formal, constricting attire for worship has come to seem less desirable; music that elicits participation and encourages the display of emotion has achieved renewed popularity.[58] In the longer view, as Weber noted, religion in the modern West had from the start represented a refuge from rationality where emotion can hold sway. Jewish and Christian practices have been seen as a precious realm where, "in pianissimo," the spirit can still pulsate, both literally and figuratively.[59] This tendency has certainly been evident in the conception of Jewish observance as *nostalgia,* the evocation of felt connection to ancestors mattering far more than the calling to mind of abstract "eternal truths." Religious ritual might be more highly valued because of the broader than normal (albeit relatively reduced) emotional range that is still permitted and elicited within its precincts; the move of most ritual observance among Jews to the home, out of public view, allowed for continued emotional expression in a location where it is welcomed and honored.

Both tendencies, toward more emotion in synagogue and in the home, may actually have accentuated the link between ritual and affect by providing an outlet for emotion lacking at all other points of contact with the tradition and most other points of daily existence. Alternatively, or perhaps at the very same time, religious services which enforced decorum via organ, choir, architecture, or oratory may have conferred a precious order, predictability, and serenity absent in hectic urban life, giving the spirit freer rein precisely because all its movement takes place within. The art of ritual may have drawn some Jews precisely because it did *not* imitate life—in fact, dwelt markedly apart from life—in the private, mysterious, and unobservable realm increasingly held, for those very reasons, to be most authentic. These tendencies have not been limited to Jews but—like the embeddedness of observance in the everyday and the status of ritual as law—have been worked out in a distinctive manner reflecting the political situation, relation to collective ancestors, and repertoire of symbolic meaning available to modern Jews, all of which will receive further attention in the chapters which follow.

3. THE PRESENCE OR ABSENCE OF GOD

Before embarking on the case studies which will concretize these problematics and dilemmas, I want to say a few words about *relation to God,* an aspect of Jewish practice, and of modern practice more generally, that is rarely treated adequately or even mentioned in social scientific writings on the subject. That silence occurs in some cases (for example, in Weber) because the declared intent and method of those accounts is "simply" to explain the rituals under investigation, without reference to the actors' beliefs in God; in other cases (as in Durkheim or Freud), it stems from the theorists' claims to have reduced the beliefs themselves to social or psychological mechanisms. In any case, the practitioners' relation to God is too often passed over or explained away altogether by modern social scientists. The attention to "spirit" in Evans-Pritchard's work on the Nuer stands forth all the more as an exception that proves the general scholarly rule.

It must be confessed, however, that the subject of God's perceived role or lack thereof in modern Jewish practice is not easy to approach. One wants to avoid romanticizing the fervor of the ancestors or overgeneralizing the skepticism of modern observers. We have discarded the assumptions that particular behaviors correspond directly to specific beliefs and that the absence of those behaviors necessarily indicates a lack of beliefs. Our inquiry where God is concerned is further frustrated by the fact that modern Jewish thinkers, like their predecessors, have generally been loathe to speak systematically about the God who is addressed in prayer or invoked in ritual performances. Buber was not alone in making this aversion to "theology" a point of principle. "God-talk" has until very recently been more hesitant among modern Jewish elites than among Christians, and the inner experience of nonelites is, with few exceptions, simply not accessible to us. It seems to me, however, that several things can and should be said here—again, not about *conceptions of God* but about matters of *practice that bear on relation to God.*

Two such matters have already been noted: the resistance on the part of many Jews (mirroring eagerness among other Jews) to demonstrations of obedience to a divine Commander; and the difficulty of couching "highest-order meanings" at any but the most general level, irrefutable in the face of science and compatible with the majority culture in all its internal varieties. Authenticity has seemed to demand doubt, even ambivalence, where truth is concerned. The interpretations of any act are many; how then can anyone credit ritual's claim to "get things right" in a way that is impossible in "real life"? How step into the modeling of perfection that ritual affords[60] if one no longer believes that right or perfection is knowable to human beings or if one is convinced that the unity of the human self is no less a myth than the presence of God at ritual performances? Note that the problem here is not God's existence but God's commanding presence, not the power of ritual to effect changes outside the self but its ability to confer meaning on and to the self. The former were denied early on by modernizing Jewish circles. The latter have in the postmodern period remained of paramount concern.

A further problem is highlighted by Erving Goffman's exposition of the near universal practice in the modern West of rites directed at *worship of the self.* Goffman shows through innovative use of Durkheimian categories, based in turn on early anthropological theories of sacrifice, that the two sorts of worship—of God and of the self—have always been intimately related. Human beings, and not only God, are shown "deference" via rituals of "obeisance, submission, and propitiation." Paying respects to persons, as to God, can take the form of avoidance (keeping a distance, not making eye contact, eschewing second-person speech) as well as of "presentation" ("salutations, invitations, compliments, and minor services"). Human beings not only *offer* tribute to each other in this manner but *claim* tribute via "demeanor[,] . . . that element of the individual's ceremonial behavior typically conveyed through deportment, dress, and bearing, which serves to express to those in his immediate presence that he is a person of certain desirable or undesirable qualities." Rituals of deference and demeanor teach us that "the self is in part a ceremonial thing, a sacred object which must be treated with proper ritual care and in turn must be presented in a proper light to others."[61]

One cannot say with any certainty to what new lengths such obeisances have been taken in the modern period, and our analysis will not depend on such a claim. Human beings have always required and received regular signs of respect from others, augmented of course by ceremonial offerings in recognition of special authority. Indeed, Jewish rituals directed at the worship of God have commonly been modeled on the treatment of royalty at court. Goffman seems intuitively correct, however, when he maintains that "the person in our urban secular world is allotted a kind of sacredness" that is not simply a survival of premodern religiosity but a function of the self's enhanced modern status. In this case, it is *because* "many gods have been done away with" that "the individual himself stubbornly remains as a deity of considerable importance."[62] Indeed, we are able to understand the significance of the ceremony surrounding our own persons, and respond to it directly, in a way that is not available when the object of our deference is God.

The repercussions of this point extend to all the matters which we will be examining in the case studies that follow in Part 2. If *public* deference and demeanor are now paid far more frequently to the state or the self—the two principal loci of authority—than to God,[63] if middle-ground authorities, religious bodies first among them, have "lost ground"—occupy far less social time and space, consume far fewer societal resources, are held to be private and kept in that sphere—one result might be exacerbation of the sense that God is a distant rather than a familiar being, so distant as to impede the conviction of divine presence at worship or other rituals. Participation in religious ceremony might well be diminished by the belief that divine attendance is uncertain; explanations of ritual intended to elicit such participation will consequently not make reference to God's involvement.

This represents a major shift: Jewish observance, as Goodman writes, has characteristically been viewed as "a way of living 'with' God in the sense that 'ordinary' activities—eating, sleeping, dressing, doing business—are endowed with symbolic significance and by the modalities of their performance express attitudes toward the holy." A God who is near commands and elicits normative behavior by virtue of that proximity. "One who lives in the presence of God need not regard God as some mere mysterium tremendum to be called upon (or dreaded) only in emergencies."[64] Distance from God renders ritual action "merely symbolic," a performance in the usual sense, motions gone through irrespective of abstract belief in God's existence or providence.

The possibilities for modern Jewish perceptions and practice in this regard are, as usual, manifold. God as "mysterium tremendum," "Wholly Other," has no doubt seemed to some Jews so removed from the stuff of modern life as to be unapproachable. The sense of separation from God in the everyday realm of ritual may as a result have contributed to the inability to turn to God, for comfort or explanation, in emergencies such as the Holocaust. We shall find ample examples of such distance in the chapters which follow—but we shall also observe many individuals attracted to Jewish practice precisely because it possesses mystery and authority unavailable elsewhere. These same individuals, or others, may be attracted all the more to certain practices because God plays no part in them. Still other Jews, we shall discover, have been drawn to practices such as textual study which do not make explicit claims about or demands on God's presence but do make God seem present at one remove, as it were. God figures in the ritual, is a character in the texts, but leaves human beings sufficient space in which to maneuver—and perhaps even blesses their autonomy with divine silence.

The "irrelevance" of ritual—the fact that modern social and political systems do not often entrust it with "performative utterances" that can actually make a difference in the world—may not always have worked entirely against it, as we will find.[65] Nor has the skepticism of modern Jews (and Gentiles of comparable background) about claims of ritual effectiveness in anything other than the symbolic sense necessarily detracted from ritual's appeal.[66] Ritual has attracted some because of the *truths about God* that it *symbolically* expresses, while others have been drawn to the *ambivalence concerning God* that it *nostalgically* conveys and legitimates. We cannot say whether the variety or depth of meaning entering into or emerging from Jewish practice is any greater or lesser in the modern period than it was earlier. Nor can we say that piety was greater then or authenticity greater now.

All we can do, and will do in the chapters which follow, is track the numerous ways in which Jews over the past two centuries have been enacting in and through their modern performances of distinctive rituals something very different from what their ancestors did, and modern Jews have been explaining those rituals differently as well. Citizens (real or aspiring) of new bodies politic have democratized their notions of God as well as of observance. Heirs (and creators) of symbolic meanings for observance, searchers for authority they may not want to find, inventors of traditions they claim to discover, Jews have offered *ta'amim* for the commandments, and notions of commandment, well suited to the new dynamics of God's absence from or distant presence in their lives and to their own absence from or distant presence in the life of an organized Jewish community. Descendants (actual or imagined) of new as well as traditional ancestors have found innovative ways of enacting loyalty to the "God of the fathers" (and lately of "the mothers") which give full expression to rebellion or disaffection as much as to doubt or belief.

Mendelssohn, characteristically, captured all these dynamics very well in the concluding perorations of *Jerusalem.* "Adapt yourselves to the morals and the constitution of the land to which you have been removed, but hold fast to the religion of your fathers," he urged his Jewish readers, while in the very next paragraph he urged "the rulers of the earth" to allow everyone "to invoke God after his own manner or that of his fathers." In this way, Jews and their rulers could both "render unto Caesar what is Caesar's . . . [and] render unto God what is God's! Love truth! Love peace!"[67] Mendelssohn's elaborate symbolic explanation of the commandments is once more accompanied and completed by invocation of the ancestors; the work concludes, as it began, by reckoning with the political realities that first and last set the bounds both of Mendelssohn's theory and the practices it advocated. We shall begin our case studies with those political realities as well.

Part Two

FOUR

The Politics of Jewish Ritual
Observance

There is an old Jewish joke about two men who go on a journey together and after spending the night at an inn find themselves faced with a serious problem: how will they know whose horse is whose? "Easy," says the first. "I foresaw this difficulty, so I cut a swatch of hair off my horse's tail." "Aha," says the other. "That was very wise. I will do it too." The next morning they emerge from their lodgings and again wonder how they will tell the horses apart. "Easy," says the first. "I foresaw this as well, so I marked my horse behind the left ear." "Aha," says his friend. "Again very wise. I will do that too." On the third morning, however, the first traveler has no solution. He has cut no hair and marked no ear. How will they tell the horses apart? They ponder and ponder, worry and fret, until finally one of them comes up with an answer. "I know," he says. "It's easy. You take the black horse; I'll take the white one."

I shall argue in this chapter that the decisions made by Jewish individuals, movements, and groups throughout the modern period to maintain, alter, or discard distinctive Jewish observances have, in addition, ultimately represented decisions about the *marking of difference,* and thereby served to effect a greater or lesser degree of *separation from Gentile neighbors and fellow citizens.* Ritual practice, as Spinoza wrote in the *Tractatus,* is a reliable guarantor of distinctiveness, all the more crucial when a relatively tiny minority is seeking to join a larger society whose customs vary profoundly from its own. In consequence, ritual practice has inevitably borne *political* repercussions for the achievement or retention of civil liberties and social acceptance. How Jews ate and walked and talked—on the street, at home, or in the synagogue—could not but affect and reflect their own (and Gentiles') sense of whether and how much they belonged. This was equally true of Jewish celebration of the Sabbath on Saturday rather than Sunday, the refusal of Gentile delicacies and dinner invitations, the circumcision of male organs—all therefore matters of general and Jewish debate concerning Emancipation. There is ample evidence that many Jews knew themselves to be subjects of controversy. Social pressures and government demands were routinely factored into the calculus of their decision making on Jewish practice.

Hence the joke about the horses, which bears ironic witness to Jewish concern to dress and eat and speak like Gentiles, lest their differences from Gentiles appear too conspicuous, and which testifies, too, to widespread anxiety among Jews (and, for some, to the wish) that Jews *would* lose all distinctiveness from English or French or German compatriots who were not of "the Mosaic persuasion." But the joke also mocks that anxiety. It offers the assurance that no amount of adaptation was going to erase the distinctiveness of Jews. A white horse was a white horse, whether it lived in Paris or Alsace, Berlin or Bavaria. The same held true for a black horse, whether it counted itself among the Ostjuden, the immigrants from eastern Europe, or not.

My point in writing this chapter, and citing the joke, is *not* to claim, as do some Zionist and Orthodox critics, that the self-identity of western Jews in the Emancipation period can be written off as a mere exercise in self-deception. "Their condition may be justly defined as spiritual slavery under the veil of outward freedom," wrote the Zionist thinker Ahad Ha'am about French Jewry in 1891.[1] Those who regard Jewish religious adaptations over the past two centuries as mere expressions of the desire for "integration into the non-Jewish world"[2] or as gestures of outright assimilation,[3] to my mind oversimplify matters of causality and meaning that demand far greater nuance. However, it seems to me equally mistaken to ignore the roles played by *assimilatory pressures* (from inside and outside the Jewish community) and by *direct government interference* (in a host of religious matters) in altering distinctive Jewish behavior and how Jews regarded it. Ideals and ideas of statehood, culture, and civility adopted by Jews in the process of acculturation to Gentile societies likewise played a role, as did the need to make a living in conditions not conducive to inherited ways—the need to bend to realities which were not about to stretch to meet Jews halfway.

Jews were not the only group to submit to demands for *Bildung* and *civilisation* in return for the benefits of citizenship. As a group, however, they were particularly visible, even though a small minority. Jewish modes of deference and demeanor—ways of walking, eating, and speaking—changed rather dramatically in the first decades of Jewish entry into larger Gentile societies. Those new modes naturally moved back and forth, along with the Jews who carried them, between the public, Gentile sphere—in which Jews increasingly spent their days—and the private, non-Gentile sphere—to which distinctively Jewish behavior was increasingly restricted.[4] In short: Emancipation and assimilation were (in Jacob Katz's terms) "reciprocally dependent," the "inseparable halves of a *quid pro quo,* the two clauses of a complex contract."[5] The new contract with the nations promised the realization of God's intention in making the original contract—the covenant— that created the Jews at Sinai.[6] Jews were not only aware of the linkage between the two contracts but, up to a point, whether "Orthodox" or Reform, were also prepared to pay as both required, in the "currency" that both required, so as to negotiate a successful partnership between the two. That currency, in both contracts, was the pattern of observances that rendered Jews a people apart.

I. ACTING LIKE A ("CIVILIZED") JEW

The potency of both the need and the desire for greater conformity are apparent in the negative attitudes displayed by the Jews of western and central Europe toward the Ostjuden. Steven Aschheim has argued persuasively that the image of the eastern Jew was for German Jews built into the very concept of Emancipation. It constituted the negative of the picture of what they hoped, and had promised, to become if granted citizenship. New Jews would not behave as had the old. They would not be dirty, loud, or coarse. They would not live in ugly, squalid neighborhoods or engage in immoral, backward business practices such as usury and peddling. They would discard Yiddish, the "jargon" of the ghetto, in favor of a pure language. *Bildung,* declared the editor of *Sulamith,* a principal house organ of the Jewish enlightened, demanded an end to crudity and boorishness. Modernity meant more than new rights. It meant changes in how one dressed, modulation in the tone of one's speech—lowering of the decibel level—in short, the disappearance of the conspicuous ghetto Jew, epitomized by the peddler depicted in Figure 2.[7] Sander Gilman has similarly drawn attention to issues of Jewish language and gesticulation, the Jewish nose, the Jewish foot. Gentiles made it clear that they did not want to encounter otherness visibly in the bodies that crossed their paths everyday in the streets.[8]

Jews were, in general, not averse to demands for social conformity; the line between voluntary and involuntary adjustment, here as in matters of

FIGURE 2. *Jewish Street Peddler* (nine-teenth century). Courtesy of the Leo Baeck Institute, New York. Photo by Jim Strong.

religion, is often hard to draw. Did beards give way in late-eighteenth-century Berlin in conformity with current fashion or "in order to remove any outward sign of difference," as a Prussian edict of 1790 put it when demanding the change? Whatever the cause, Jews began to dress like Gentile neighbors, to uncover their heads in public, to go to the theater.[9] New schools inculcated the desired behaviors and extirpated the old through reforms of both curriculum and method.[10] Jews adopted verbal and body languages other than their "mother tongue," in accord with legal adoption by (and of) new "fatherlands."[11] A few, particularly among Berlin's most wealthy families, even took the unprecedented step of converting to Christianity.[12]

Nowhere were these processes limited to Jews. *Bildung* and *civilisation* were widely diffused cultural ideals, the markers of an emergent class (the bourgeoisie or burghers), and a necessary condition for entry to a rapidly expanding occupational group (the civil service).[13] In societies in which roles were becoming increasingly specialized, *Bildung* connoted achievement of inner harmony and coherence, a self made into a work of art, a character etched so deeply that its principles would be indelible regardless of circumstances, as well as the education and refinement required for the achievement of such integrity.[14] No less important, the two ideals functioned as an "ethic of aspiration" imposed on their respective societies by political and cultural elites; as the process of unification advanced, these elites were increasingly determined to make over the individuals newly subject to state authority, and particularly the peasantry, in their own image. James Sheehan demonstrates that the demand for *Bildung* was proportional to the perceived need for it as a tool for, and mark of, unification in German states perennially vexed by the problem of "imagining" national identity in a situation of profound ethnic diversity. "The obdurate facts of multiplicity" provoked a turn to culture, and preeminently to *language,* as the distinguishing sign of Germanness.[15]

The French case would in several respects appear very different from the German (as every society represents variations on the larger pattern), the French state having already been united and its authority centralized to a significant degree under the monarchy. But Jews in France as in Germany were the objects of concerted pressures for conformity—pressures that were applied to the population more broadly as well, and this larger pattern applied also to communities in America, North Africa, and eastern Europe.[16] Creation of the *new* French state, with Enlightenment its watchword, demanded the *civilizing* of the citizenry. Eugen Weber's masterful account of that project, in *Peasants into Frenchmen,* relates that Parisians saw the peasants as barbarians, ignoramuses, savages. Talk of civilizing them was apparently common as late as the 1850s. The peasants, for their part, refused to surrender ancient measurements to the metric system, remained hostile toward other villages and all the more so to state officialdom, and were quite content with isolation. France's immense heterogeneity found its clearest expression in a "wealth of tongues." Intellectuals like Renan joined civil servants in proclaiming that civilization could not be achieved in patois, but still the patois reigned.[17] Weber's mapping of language use indicates that the departments of Haut-Rhin and Bas-Rhin, where the vast majority of France's Jews lived in the early nineteenth century, were characterized respectively by "significant proportion of communes non-French speaking" and "all or nearly all communes non-French speaking."[18] Pressures to bring the behavior of Alsatian Jews into line with Parisian-defined norms of civilization (to be discussed in a moment) were thus by no means exceptional. French officialdom was charged with the task of strengthening it through language, festivals, and *civilisation,* a term connoting "the models of thought, behavior, and expression held in esteem in Paris."[19]

The pressure brought to bear on Jews, then, was in part so intense because it was *not* unique; the fact that the stakes were far higher than Jewish rights alone helps account for the high price demanded from Jews in return for those rights. Jews constituted a relatively tiny population that persisted in the vigorous imagination of its own countercommunity, a visible and obdurate bearer of otherness at a time when cultural hegemony was of great importance.[20] The overriding concern that Jews evinced about order and decorum likewise mirrored larger tendencies, in this case a similar concern evinced by a bourgeoisie anxious about its new rank and status.[21] It was in this context that Jewish and Gentile partisans of Emancipation, no less than their opponents, argued that "regeneration" of Jewish behavior was a necessary condition of citizenship and agreed as well that many Jews had a long way to go before they could claim a share in *Bildung* or *civilisation.* Not surprisingly, given the preferred definition of Jews as a religion and the relegation of distinctive Jewish activity to the private sphere, attention among Jewish and Gentile reformers alike focused on the synagogue and, more particularly, on its aesthetics—what could be seen, the behaviors available to view. And, here as elsewhere, Jews bent on banishing the image of the Ostjuden turned eagerly to the counterimage of the Sephardim, invoked repeatedly by rabbis, scholars, and synagogue architects as a representation of all that Jews—or Germans, for that matter—wished to be. They connoted a "religious posture marked by cultural openness, philosophic thinking, and an appreciation for the aesthetic"—traits which bespoke a Greek classical heritage that Jews could thereby claim to share with Gentile compatriots.[22]

The forces linking social and political acceptance to the ritual signs marking off Jewish "gates and doorposts" are beautifully demonstrated in an essay contest sponsored by the academy of sciences, agriculture, and arts in Strasbourg in 1824, some thirty years after Jews had been granted *les droits de l'homme.* The question posed was whether Old Testament rites and superstitions—"the belief and religious practices of the Jews"—might not present insuperable barriers to the Jews' acquisition of civilization and whether proper means could be found, despite the Jews' poor estate and the deficiencies of their tradition, "to have the Jews enjoy the benefits of civilization."[23] Respondents were instructed to consider, among other things, whether the reforms introduced in several German states presented suitable models for emulation; whether "the concordance of regular [Jewish] festivals and, in part, of extraordinary festivals with those consecrated by the laws of the State" was possible according to the "essential dogmas of Mosaism"; and whether an *école normale israélite* should be established for the training of a new breed of rabbis. The judges, all Gentile, included professors, a judge, and two *hommes de lettres*. Two of the four respondents were Jews.[24]

The judges dismissed the first response out of hand. It was written in German, exhibited faulty diction, and failed to display the "requisite compassion toward its subjects."[25] They gave more serious consideration to the essay by Prosper Wittersheim, a member of the Society of Strasbourg and the secretary of the Société d'Encouragement des Arts et Métiers of the Jews of Metz. As one might expect, it traced the progress already made by French Jews since 1789, emphasizing that Jews had applied themselves with success to the study of arts and sciences and thereby "had brought their mores closer to those of Christians," had modified the customs of their religion, and had made their faith "more compatible with the social existence in which they participate." True, peddling and poverty still prevented the civilizing of those who were thus afflicted, but Jewish young people could be directed into the arts and useful professions if French society were to adopt this as its goal. The essay detailed an educational plan that evoked the judges' admiration. They ruled, however, that Wittersheim had not sufficiently researched the question of whether Jewish belief and practice precluded ultimate success in the scheme he proposed for civilizing France's Jews. The essay was awarded honorable mention.[26]

The runner-up, Louis Blanchard, aimed to remedy the "great social incompatibility" between Jews and the nations among whom they lived through a new system of schools, the convening of another Sanhedrin which would adapt rabbinic usages, and a network of banks which could eliminate the practice of usury. The judges, dissatisfied with these strategies, awarded first prize to the remaining essay, written by Arthur Beugnot, which took account of Jewish progress since Emancipation as well as of continuing Christian hostility traced to "traditional prejudice" and to Jewish usury. Beugnot's recommendations for amelioration of the Jews' condition began with a defense of the idea that special laws should be applied in their case. "If the Jews of Alsace are themselves an exception, if they voluntarily remain outside *du droit commun,* who can be surprised that their laws remain at variance with those of the nation as a whole?" This was only fair. The judges commented that it was desirable, as much as possible, to "push" the Jews into society rather than preserve their apartness from it. They were more sympathetic to the specific reforms which Beugnot proposed: a committee to supervise the education of Jewish youth; a second committee to publish books containing a new "*catéchisme du culte mosaïque*"; and schemes for agricultural labor, apprenticeships, poor relief, reform of rabbinic education, and alteration in the timing and number of religious festivals, as in "the choice of *nourriture.*" The consistory would have to make Jews understand that while abstention from certain foods might have been useful in ancient days in Judea, it was so no longer. Such scruples were contrary to "*la fusion sociale.*"[27]

It is, of course, not clear from the essay contest whether a majority of Gentiles would have agreed with Beugnot in demanding the transfer of the Sabbath to Sunday or an end to dietary restrictions that prevented Jews from eating like, and with, other citizens. But it does seem that widespread sentiment supported some curtailment of Jewish festivals (that is, of public and private Jewish time) and the reform of Jewish behavior (in both Jewish and Gentile space, public as well as private). The burden of proof here rested on Jews: they were expected to demonstrate progress toward the goal of civilization, having conceded their distance from it at the start—to demonstrate, in other words, that both Judaism and the Jews could be significantly transformed.

The mechanics of this measured adjustment are set forth, and forcefully advocated, throughout the many volumes of the *Archives israélites de France,* a communal journal founded by its editor, Samuel Cahen, to prove that "fusion" with the national majority could be achieved without "renouncing our past." His statement of intent in the first issue (1840) derides Jews who called themselves enlightened—*éclairé*—just because they had discarded ancient practices and lapsed into a "cruel egoism." Rather, Jews should show by example that religion and patriotism were not in conflict, thereby hastening complete Emancipation. Cahen filled his paper with accounts of the consistories, learned essays about Jewish history and culture, reports on Jewish communities outside France, and especially with calls for—and descriptions of—moderate ritual reform. The epithet that he chose for the *Archives* was telling: "And God saw that the light was good."[28] Religion had nothing to fear from Enlightenment. Reason, in fact, could show the way to religion's refinement and fulfillment.

When one turns from the paper's editorial columns to its news reports, however, the problems in achieving Cahen's desired synthesis are apparent. An incident reported in the very first issue, for example, graphically demonstrated the difficulty of negotiating the new boundaries between the public and the private, the French and the Jewish, the communal and the individual. It came from the records of the central consistory, a committee of rabbis and laymen that stood at the apex of a nationwide pyramid of state-sponsored Jewish communal agencies. An Alsatian rabbi, visiting the town of Zittsheim, had found three butcher shops open for business on the Sabbath and had declared all meat purchased at those shops forbidden to Jews. He had also stipulated the twofold penitence which the butchers would have to undergo in order for their meat to be recertified: an extended fast, each day of which could be forgiven in return for a gift of forty-five centimes, and a solemn promise before the holy ark not to violate the Sabbath ever again. Two of the butchers had appealed the sentence, and the matter had eventually reached the central consistory. It ruled that "in conditions of liberty" a local rabbi was entitled only to *point out* an offense such as the butchers' violation of the Sabbath. It was his job to certify meat as kosher or withhold that certification, as Jewish law required. The withholding of certification was certainly appropriate in this case; Jews should be warned about meat they should not buy. What the rabbi did not have the right to do was *punish* the offenders. Fines were out of the question. Even the requirement of a public declaration in the synagogue was inappropriate.[29] Communal authority was still to be respected, but the means for its enforcement, now that Judaism was a private religious matter, had been severely restricted.

It is clear from this and subsequent issues of the journal that the *Archives* addressed readers for whom Jewish literacy and observance were already on the wane. Cahen chided those who had attended a fancy dress ball held in Paris on the occasion of "Carnaval" that is, Purim. The "solemnity" of the recitation of the Scroll of Esther in the synagogue had given way to revelry; the current generation had forgotten "most of the religious affections." They no longer understood Judaism, "its customs and their origin." In short, he wrote, "we have gained immensely since 1789, but we have also lost a great deal."[30] Judaism was in crisis, and the problem was not belief but "the manner of interpreting and carrying out precepts."[31] Belief was a private matter of individual conscience; observance or the lack of it was public,

there for all to see—or not to see. The temple was a desert, complained
Simon Bloch, the editor of *Univers,* another Jewish newspaper. Religion
had been abandoned by the most illustrious Jewish citizens. They spoke
French at home, dressed in their finest clothes on Sunday, and on the Sabbath were not to be found in the synagogue.[32] Cahen resigned himself to
behavior that rabbis could not and should not endorse, even if they were
not in a position to stop their congregants from engaging in it. The one
avenue left open to rabbis was silence.[33]

Cahen, along with other moderate reformers, hoped that by educating
French Jewry, on the one hand, and by altering the externals of public
observance, on the other, they could overcome the "crisis" and, as the author of an anonymous two-part essay on reform put it, *"sauver notre culte."* [34]
A little change—primarily to "make order and decency rule in the House
of God"—would go a long way. German excesses could then be avoided.
Thus an article on Hanukkah not only educated its readers about the festival's origins but called on them to transform the meaning of the holiday. It
should not be taken as a prayer for "a Jewish national restoration" but,
rather, should serve all France as an example of "the involvement of religion
in the duties of the citizen." [35] A two-part anonymous essay in the opening
issues of the journal, highly praised by Cahen, similarly urged that the abuses
which "human hands had introduced" into Judaism be corrected, particularly in the aesthetics of the synagogue. Urging an end to needless repetition, the author reported counting eighty-nine musical notes on Yom Kippur between a single verb and its object during the cantorial rendition of
the kaddish. A *"Rêve non-réalisé"* that appeared in an early issue of the *Archives* quite typically imagined a "beautiful edifice of oblong form and well-
proportioned modern construction," possessed of a spacious courtyard and
a majestic interior. The service is dignified and agreeable. Congregation and
choir responsively recited the principal psalms. The procession with the
Torah was "truly sublime and imposing." The dreamer seems to have had
no wish to alter the service in any substantive fashion but only to render it
more tasteful. He awakens to find that he had dozed off in the middle of a
sermon preached in a language that most the congregation did not speak
and was sitting in a far less exalted sanctuary than the one he had imagined.
"What a disagreeable reality after such an agreeable dream!" [36] In keeping
with Cahen's agenda, the article made no mention of the more radical steps
already taken by some congregations in Germany and restricted itself to the
sort of aesthetic changes later denounced by the Reformer David Philipson
as superficial, merely cosmetic, and untouched by concerns of principle and
conscience[37]—precisely Cahen's strategy.

It is hard to know, of course, just how successful his efforts were. The *Archives* was a journal of high quality, full to overflowing with pleas for renewal of the cult and attempts at educating the Jewish laity. Jews may well have been reinforced in their identities by the journal's elevated tone and educated about their heritage by its learned essays, all the while paying little attention to Cahen's repeated calls for greater and beautified observance. It seems that French Jews, while changing their diet and deportment, combined uneven synagogue attendance with eclectic home observance, both of which were concentrated on celebration of holidays and life-cycle events.[38] They thereby contracted the scope of Jewish practice and lessened the degree of conspicuous Jewish difference while retaining a measure of distance from the larger society and the conviction of Judaism's integrity—and their own.[39] The pattern of lay practice in Germany, despite the more ideological and theological cast of debate there, seems not to have been greatly different.[40] In Poland, too, the emerging Jewish middle class was attracted by what it saw of the aristocracy's manners and lifestyle, leading preachers to wonder, "Is not the practice of our ancestors adequate?"[41] North African and Levant Jewish communities witnessed similar patterns of ritual laxity and reproof.[42] Even in America, where, one historian has argued, Jewish rights were guaranteed almost from the outset of their settlement, making their integration into the larger society a real possibility, Jews had all the more reason to adopt the litany of middle-class civic virtues regularly laid upon them by their religious and communal leaders. American acceptance of Jews "generated a dynamic of its own," dictating the "choice of institutions and forms adopted by a group desperately seeking security."[43]

Jacob Katz's concise formulation of Jewish adjustment seems to hold for many communities in their respective eras of Emancipation or its promise: officially, Judaism was a confession of faith, and the Jewish community "a group united by its adherence to an abstract body of teachings." In practice, "adherence to Judaism scarcely depended upon a conviction of the truth of any particular set of doctrines." It was, rather, a question of Jews retaining, and marking through practice, their membership in a socially inferior minority.[44] Recalling Mendelssohn's terms, we might say that the Jewish ceremonial script abounded in hyphens, ellipses, exclamation points, and question marks. Cahen's *Archives* would of course have hoped for more, while the Strasbourg academy seemed to wish for somewhat less. European governments, as we shall now see, often had another set of expectations altogether—indeed, several different sets: each case presents a somewhat different pattern of demands and responses.

2. THE LAW OF THE LAND IS THE LAW

In France, governmental pressure came well before Napoleon. Debate in the National Assembly explicitly established *regeneration* as the quid pro quo for the full rights of citizenship, and the Terror which soon followed spelled trouble for Jewish as for all other religious observance. When Sunday was abolished as a day of rest and supplanted by *décadi,* the Jewish Sabbath also came under attack, in part from zealous Jewish Jacobins, as did other customs and distinctions.[45] Nor could Jews have found much comfort in the round of rituals organized by the successive revolutionary regimes. Mona Ozouf's remarkable study of those festivals highlights the attempt to create a uniform mass of citizens free of the ostentation and distinctions that had marked the ecclesiastical and royal ceremonies of the ancien régime. Festive spaces were to exhibit "an endless, irrepressible, and peaceful movement like the rise of tidal waters." All differences among participants were to vanish in "the enactment of the great Revolutionary baptism. The water that flowed from the 'fecund breasts' of the colossal statue, drunk from the same goblet by the envoys of the primary assemblies, promised regeneration." Iconic statues, liberty trees, meal offerings, and primal fountains were prominently featured.[46] One can easily imagine Durkheim's forebears, participant-observers at revolutionary festivals by dint of being Jews, carefully studying the events so as to avoid being swept up and carried away in the enthusiasm of the general will. A Parisian lawyer did in fact attack Jews in 1806, in part for their failure to take part in public ceremonies.[47]

In the context of Revolution and Terror, Napoleon's regulation of Jewish affairs must have seemed relievedly manageable. The "notables" and rabbis he summoned to Paris, at any rate, managed them quite well, responding to his queries about Jewish exclusivism in law, business, marriage, and observance by finessing, temporizing, and otherwise engaging in the supple art of apologetics.[48] The Jewish leaders gave up ground when it seemed unimportant or unavoidable, while preserving a significant degree of honesty and dignity—and distinctiveness.

They no doubt knew of Mendelssohn's declaration in *Jerusalem* that "as the rabbis expressly state, 'with destruction of the Temple, all corporal and capital punishments and, indeed, even monetary fines, insofar as they are only national, have ceased to be legal.'"[49] In the rabbis' famous dictum, "The law of the land is the law."

Napoleon, apparently satisfied but not fooled, responded with a decree in 1806 forgiving debts owed to Jews in Alsace and prohibiting usury and followed it with other measures that limited Jewish liberties—for example, a statute in 1808 that defined the functions of rabbis to be teaching religion, reinforcing the doctrines and decisions of the "Sanhedrin," and reminding Jews of their obligation to obey the laws of their country, especially those relating to its defense. Two of the three roles left to the rabbis—marriage and divorce—were to be exercised under state jurisdiction.[50] In former eras, Jews would have understood such restrictions as the expected wages of exile. After Emancipation, however, French Jews who identified with *la patrie* and its principles were obliged not only to accept but to legitimate the civic duties laid upon them, so long as they were also imposed upon others. Equality of treatment, not state disengagement from religion, became the burden of Jewish rhetoric, perhaps because state sponsorship of the consistories actually helped to legitimate religion in the eyes of many Jews.[51] Identification with the state only grew stronger with the years—as religious observance atrophied.[52]

All this is not to say that Jews traded one for the other. In France, as in Germany, "the proponents of conditional emancipation . . . met a united front of refusal to barter religious freedom for political equality."[53] But Jews had to reckon—and did—with a state bent on molding its population to a model of civilized humanity, and a society that for all its secularism and anticlericalism remained in many aspects of its character Christian through and through.[54] The problem was more difficult in Germany, because there was no single state and certainly no guarantee of equal rights. Jews in the various German states were subject to an *array* of authorities—including, often enough, municipal councils—which pursued varying agendas and differed on the political implications of existing and proposed Jewish observances.[55] The notion that Jews constituted a "state within the state," made such by their "espirt de corps . . . coupled with the spirit of their theocratic laws," had a venerable hold.[56] Laws designed to break down this corporate distinctiveness tended to be more straightforward than in France—at times, brutally so—even if, given the welter of authorities and powers, they were also more confusing.

Even a brief survey of the legislation bearing on Jews suffices to impress us with its intent and scope.[57] The aim, as stated explicitly in an edict of the grand duke of Baden during the Napoleonic period, was to raise the Jews' "political and moral *Bildung*" to a level commensurate with their new civic status, thereby ensuring that their "legal equality does not redound to the disadvantage of the other citizens." German states, large and small, sought to shape individual and collective Jewish decision making on religious practice so as to bring Judaism into line with governmental norms.[58] In significant measure this effort succeeded.

One prominent strategy was to mandate a particular sort of synagogue service, centered on a particular sort of sermon, to be delivered by a rabbi trained in a particular manner.[59] The position favored was Reform. Other government edicts, however, worked in precisely the opposite direction, such as those forbidding worship in private sanctuaries.[60] A Prussian decree of 1823, answering an appeal from "Orthodox" rabbis, ordered that prayers be conducted "in accordance with the traditional ritual and without the slightest innovation in language, ceremonies, prayers, or songs." Other edicts issued that year denied rabbis "ecclesiastical standing," declared that Judaism was "only tolerated," and forbade innovation in the synagogue service, including preaching in the (Gentile) vernacular.[61] Konigsburg forbade the Reform innovation of Sunday services in 1847,[62] motivated perhaps by the same desire to maintain boundaries between Jews and Gentiles that had led Prussia in 1836 to forbid Jews from taking Christian names.[63] Elsewhere, however, Reform gained ground via state power.[64]

David Philipson's attitude to these interventions, as expressed in his partisan history of Reform, is noteworthy. At times he indicates clear displeasure: the Prussian government, ignoring Orthodox pleas to block Abraham Geiger's appointment as the rabbi of Breslau in 1838, "seemed to have passed beyond the stage of petty interference with the private affairs of Jewish congregations." Reformers, too, were "guilty occasionally of compassing their object by the help of civil power," though not as often.[65] Philipson's tendency overall, however, is to attribute pro-Reform legislation to the "requirements of the day" or the "spirit of progress."[66] While government intervention in this direction was unwarranted, at least it was driven by the zeitgeist rather than by anti-Semitism, Christian bias, economic interest, or political calculation. Pro-Orthodox action, on the other hand, resulted from surrender to rabbinic pressure and reactionary political instincts. Reformers and pro-Reform governments alike obeyed higher imperatives; indeed, they obeyed the *same* higher imperatives. "Years before the reform movement took shape life had decided the question."[67] Geiger, for the same reason, voiced approval of state interference in a report written in 1849 for the Jewish Institute of Religious Instruction in Breslau. "The ethically free state has not only the right but also the duty, by authority of the reason inherent in it, to guard and preserve spiritual freedom in religious life."[68]

Neither Geiger nor Philipson seems to have considered the possibility that the state might have decisively *shaped the direction* taken by their movement or the others. We are told by Philipson, for example, that Geiger secured his rabbinic appointment in Frankfurt only after intensive lobbying of government officials. "His political status assured, he returned to Breslau and delivered his inaugural sermon on Jan. 4, 1840, in which he sounded the keynote of his thought . . ."[69] I do not mean to suggest that Geiger's sermon that day was in bad faith, tailored to suit the views of the governmental (or Jewish) patrons on whom his appointment depended. Geiger was a learned and serious thinker, consistent in his views and, as we have just seen, courageous in expressing them. His liberal beliefs about Judaism went along with liberal political opinions that could not have pleased Prussia's rulers. Even the most high-minded of souls, however, occasionally presents matters in a particular way, emphasizes one theme and downplays another, or employs certain rhetorical strategies and avoids others, depending on what his or her audience is prepared to hear. Nor is religious thought any more independent of the political conditions and political culture in which it develops than it is uninfluenced by philosophical and cultural currents—something that Geiger, for one, freely acknowledged. This is all the more true when the religious thinker has strong political views, propounds them at a time of intense political struggle, and develops them in a context where religious reform draws close and persistent scrutiny, where governments demonstrate strong interest in their citizens' religious beliefs—and even stronger interest in their practices.

3. EXILES AT HOME

That was certainly the case with the rabbis who met to shape the direction of Reform at the three rabbinical conferences held in Germany in the 1840s, a decade during which Jews had especially good reason to believe that the rights so long promised and withheld would soon be theirs. I want to review those conferences here in some detail, with an eye to understanding the political forces impinging on the rabbis' debates. State influence began with the government's determining whether or not the conferences could be held and who could attend them.[70] Nor did the politics of ritual reform end there. It is striking that the rabbis focused their deliberations entirely on matters of immense political moment, while sidestepping or ignoring other issues. Indeed, they themselves were sensitive to the charge that they were considering and in some cases enacted precisely the reforms in ritual and liturgy that successive governments in both France and Germany had stipulated as the quid pro quo for Emancipation.

No bad faith was required for this activity; indeed, good faith, as the rabbis understood it, required precisely the attention to politics that they displayed. Like other human beings, the rabbis wished to be all of a piece, and like other German Jews, they wanted their Jewish selves to be fully in harmony with the German state, society, and culture. Even more than other German Jews, reform-minded rabbis had bound up their personal identities in the triumph of a particular political order—the bourgeois liberal State—which they, along with more than one major philosopher, had pronounced the manifestation of Spirit or divine Providence. Many rabbis were often directly involved in politics.[71]

Nor were the Reformers wrong in understanding hostile Orthodox reaction to their meetings as the expression, at least in part, of a differing view on the present and future *political* status of the diaspora. If Jews were a nation in exile, awaiting miraculous messianic return to the Holy Land, existing observances were quite appropriate. If they were a religious group at home, however, blessed with an imminent (and immanent) redemption unimagined in traditional sources, very different behavior was called for. Political liberties and freedom from the "yoke of the commandments" thus went hand in hand. As the men most directly charged with carrying out Judaism's world-historical mission to spread the teachings of ethical mono-theism to the nations, the rabbis could hardly remain unmoved in the face of political developments that seemed to fulfill their highest religious aspira-tions. Paradoxically, then, Reform rabbis *had* to assume a political role, de-spite and because of their insistence (contra Orthodoxy) that Judaism consti-tuted not a national but a religious bond and, as such, had no legitimate political role to play.[72]

Michael Meyer, who, in his history of Reform, presents the three con-ferences as an attempt by the rabbis to define *religious* middle ground be-tween radical laypeople to their Left and Orthodox rabbis and laypeople to their Right, nonetheless highlights the political issues which beset the conferences from the outset. "At the very beginning [of the first meeting, held in Brunswick in 1844] two important decisions of procedure were made. The first was to use parliamentary form[;] . . . the second . . . was to make the deliberations public." Parliamentary form implied that the rabbis had granted themselves "the right to determine religious laws for German Jewry." Public debate not only generated interest but removed suspicions of hidden intent. There was, in addition, a third preliminary matter of sig-nificance: resolutions of the conferences would not bind their members. Autonomy of individual members was fiercely guarded. Only the majority was bound even "morally" by the decisions to be reached. Those who voted "no" would not be obligated by the resolutions at all.[73]

Note the fine line walked by the rabbis as they assumed a sort of authority unprecedented in Jewish tradition and, no less important, unparalleled in German religious life.[74] Previous generations of rabbis, like the Reformers' Orthodox contemporaries, derived authority from a twofold source: they studied, taught, and enforced the laws of a written and oral Torah dating back to God's revelation to Moses at Sinai; and their judgments received further legitimation from the people who lived according to their rulings. Reform rabbis broke the chain going back to Moses; they broke it not only in practice but in theory. While differing on the degree to which prior rabbinic authority should have a say in their decisions, they were unanimous that it should *not* have the *final* say. Nor would they defer to the "great ones of the day," declared such by the consensus of practitioners who taught and obeyed those rabbis' rulings. Furthermore, the Reformers could certainly not claim authority from the Jewish masses, who at that point were still overwhelmingly traditional in their observance, nor from the Jewish people as a whole, who, in the Reformers' view, did not exist *as a whole,* Jews having status only as individual believers *voluntarily* assembled in religious congregations.

If the Reformers did constitute a parliament, then, just whom did they represent? And what were they enacting if not laws? The rabbis did claim divine authority, I believe, but of the sort that required no revelation at Sinai. They were following the eternal spirit recognizable in reason and the zeitgeist. Ethical monotheism was God's invention, not theirs. The spirit of the Mosaic revelation bore witness to that truth as well, though the same could not always be said of its letter. The rabbis could not stand in their own eyes as lawgivers, for they were subject to lay (or joint lay-rabbinic) boards, which were in turn subject to government veto. Nor (given the diversity of those boards) could they act in the name of the community. Finally, their commitment to autonomy was so firm that it precluded the obligation of any rabbis not actually in attendance, let alone the members of their congregations. Strictly speaking, then, the rabbis represented only themselves and spoke not as legislators but as teachers, while claiming the highest authority of all for their teachings: the eternal principles in which they believed, the evolving religious tradition which they had mastered, the historical moment in which they participated, and the God underlying all of these. Collectively, reinforcing one another, they projected an authority none of them could have mustered alone.

It is significant in light of these dilemmas that the rabbis at Brunswick resolved early on, under prodding by Ludwig Philippson, to consider endorsing the answers given Napoleon by the Paris Sanhedrin. Assuming the mantle of that group carried obvious symbolism—in the eyes both of Jews and of Gentiles.[75] Philippson's intention "was to remove suspicion regarding Jewish loyalty to the state and thus remove any grounds for state interference in Jewish religious life." Discussion, as at the original Sanhedrin, focused on the question of intermarriage. Brunswick amended Paris on the matter. Intermarriage was permissible, the rabbis declared, but only if state law allowed the parents to raise their children as Jews—a clear counterfactual. The rabbis also took pains to reaffirm that "the Jew is bound to consider the land to which he belongs by birth and civic conditions as his fatherland, to protect it, and to obey all its laws."[76]

Other items of business bore on this theme as well. Samuel Holdheim, responding to a paper entitled, "Efforts towards the Emancipation of the Jewish Church," declared himself in favor of the absolute separation of "the religious and the political." There could be no such thing as a Christian state—and certainly not a Jewish state. "Religiously speaking, we form a closely joined community, not over against the state, but within the state."[77] Consistent with that position, the rabbis called for elimination of the Kol Nidre prayer, often "used by antisemites as evidence that the promises of Jews could not be trusted," and for an end to the humiliating *More Judaico* oath, which Jews were forced to take in Prussia until 1869.[78] A commission was formed to suggest changes in marriage laws, which had become a source of tension at a time when Jews were "striving for civil emancipation and were being incorporated in the body politic in various states."[79]

Both of the major issues debated at the conference at Frankfurt the following year bore directly on the Jews' relation to the state, and the first matter—Hebrew—also exposed tensions among the rabbis themselves. It served as the occasion for Zechariah Frankel's famous speech on "positive historical Judaism" and his subsequent departure from both the meeting and the Reform movement. The occasion was not arbitrary: debate over the "objective" and "subjective" necessity of Hebrew in the synagogue service went to the heart of Jewish self-definition. When Geiger urged prayer in the "language of the heart"—in other words, German—because "Hebrew lives no longer among the people" and David Einhorn asserted that Hebrew was "not the organ wherewith to express the feelings of the people," both men had in mind *people,* individuals, such as themselves—Germans by nationality, education, culture, sensibility—who wished the part of their lives called "religion" to be consonant with all the rest. Frankel, on the other hand, declared that the Hebrew language was "interwoven with the very life of Judaism," meaning that "Judaism" was far more than religion alone. It stood in integral relationship with *the people* who lived and created that "very life"—a different people, of course, from the Germans.[80]

Debate about whether there was an "objective legal necessity" to conduct part of the synagogue service in Hebrew, or an objective necessity "on other than legal grounds," or merely a "subjective necessity" thus proved inseparable from the questions of identity which surfaced time and again in the course of the debate. Ludwig Philippson supported use of both Hebrew and German in the service because the former was "indispensable as the point of union among Jews." Jacob Auerbach of Frankfurt said the most important issue of the day was involved: the relation of religion and nationality. Leopold Stein urged that Hebrew be retained "as a bond of union among Jews. . . . Argue against it as one will, the national element will never be entirely eliminated from Judaism. . . . We are no longer a nation, it is true, but a great religious community. . . . Hebrew, then, is the bond of union of the widely scattered sections of our great family." Einhorn said all that mattered was that the service be understood. No one understood Hebrew anymore. Holdheim voted for its use in limited sections of the service, and the majority sided with him, eighteen to twelve.[81]

Rereading the protocols of this meeting, with the hindsight of a century and a half, one readily understands why Frankel was driven to walk out. His colleagues were calmly debating the relative necessity of what for him was essential and nonnegotiable. Frankel's sense of isolation must have been all the greater upon hearing Stein, the chairman of the meeting, declare that all present agreed with Frankel's principle of "positive historical Judaism." They had obviously not understood him. The Reformers could agree with Frankel that Judaism had to be a *historical* religion. It had developed over time and would continue to develop, even as the past would continue to be respected. Maimonides and the Talmud loomed large in the Reformers' debate over Hebrew, as on other matters. They could also agree that Judaism had to remain a *positive* religion—that is to say, embodied in objective forms. The debate about Hebrew, as about Kol Nidre or second days of festivals, was from their point of view a discussion about *which* forms to retain and *what* form those forms should take. Reform never doubted the need for form—though the pun only highlights the issue's secondary character, two steps removed (as it were) from eternal essentials that really mattered and that, as such, could *not* be reformed. However, the rabbis could not subscribe to Frankel's view of Judaism as a *national* creation of the Jewish people, in partnership with God, that was meant to inform a life both national and religious. They knew full well that Frankel's position on Hebrew was connected to his stance on the other major issue debated at Frankfurt: belief in the messiah.

In 1842, commenting on the Reform prayer book adapted by the Hamburg Temple, Frankel had reasserted the importance of the messianic idea as the expression of Jewish national independence [*Selbständigkeit*]. The Jewish people had sustained itself through the ages in part thanks to the hope for this-worldly redemption. It needed that hope still. The achievement of tolerance in Germany remained far off. If German Jews were to be denied freedom of self-definition by their present homeland because they bore the name Jew, their leaders should allow them at least to live in the hope of a more accommodating homeland in the future. Indeed, Frankel contended, the Jewish people would confound those who argued that it was not a people, only a religious group, by one day reappearing to live freely and independently on God's earth.[82]

No Reformer could have written this—not because of any squabble over liturgy or revelation but because the identity expressed was so foreign to their own. Frankel's critique of Reform in 1845 appealed repeatedly to the history of the Jewish people, the heart and spirit of the Jewish people. His claim to authority rested not only on his knowledge of that history but on his status as an authentic representative of the Jewish national spirit. "Positive historical Judaism" was based on the nationalist theory of Friedrich Karl von Savigny, which assumed, like other Romantic doctrines, that each nation had a distinctive spirit that expressed itself in history, language, consciousness, and "life." If the Jewish people no longer existed, how then did or would its spirit? How would the divine continue to speak through the people's historical development if that development ceased? What authority could be claimed by those who sought to carry this development forward? Frankel's convictions did not allow for debate on subjective versus objective necessity. His viewpoint was, as he put it, "completely different from that of the assembly."[83]

Geiger had lent support to this conclusion several years earlier, when he wrote that the Damascus blood libel was not "a specifically Jewish question." For him "universal concern" meant only "whatever goes on among those Jews who comprise the upper stratum of Jewry; i.e., once again, those Jews who reside among the civilized nations, particularly in Germany." That is why the opportunity of Prussian Jews "to become pharmacists or lawyers is much more important to me than the rescue of all the Jews in Asia and Africa, an undertaking with which," he emphasized more than once, "I sympathize as a human being."[84] Geiger would reconfirm that standpoint in 1858. "There is no difference whatsoever between the Germans and the Jews as regards national features; differences of this kind are far greater between the German Jews and the French Jews than between the Jewish German and the Christian German."[85]

Religious differences simply did not carry as much weight. This seems to be the burden of the debate over Hebrew.[86] History had voted against the "objective necessity" of Hebrew and of Jewish statehood as well. Educated Jews, cultured Jews, those who represented the future and not the past of Jewish and human development, did not understand Hebrew anymore, just as they no longer spoke Yiddish. They dreamed, literally and figuratively, in German. That was the decisive consideration. Other Jews, lacking world-historical significance, did not have status in the decision.[87]

Debate at Frankfurt concerning the messiah took exactly the same path. A great deal of modern Jewish thought over the preceding sixty years, including Mendelssohn's *Jerusalem* and Hirsch's *Nineteen Letters,* had already effectively "spiritualized" the belief in Israel's redemption. Universal motifs had been highlighted, while the hope of return to Palestine—"a certain strip of territory," as Spinoza called it—had been marginalized or passed over in silence.[88] Einhorn added a uniquely Reform element to this consensus at Frankfurt when he asserted the messianic idea's inherent connection with the ceremonial law. Both had preserved Jews for centuries in exile. Now that times had changed, the law should be adjusted so as to better protect its own spirit. Accordingly, the messianic idea should retain its connotation of universal redemption but shed the hope for actual "restoration of bloody sacrifices and political independence." Holdheim and many others concurred. Stein, who had urged the conference to compromise on Hebrew, now asked for retention of prayers for a personal messiah and for the upbuilding of Jerusalem, though not for a return to Palestine. The adopted resolution read: "The Messianic idea should receive prominent mention in the prayers, but all petitions for our return to the land of our fathers and for the restoration of a Jewish state should be eliminated from the prayers."[89] The rabbis voted unanimously to eliminate related prayers for renewal of the sacrificial cult, and—another related matter—the rabbis unanimously affirmed the playing of the organ as part of Sabbath services. This too was a decision of political moment. What had been permitted in the Temple of old but forbidden by the rabbis in the synagogues of exile would again be permitted in the Reform temples of today, the members of which had ceased to pray for return to the Temple in Palestine.[90]

The major item on the agenda at the third and final conference, held at Breslau in 1846, was Sabbath observance.[91] The problem facing the rabbis was straightforward. They recognized the centrality of Sabbath observance to Judaism. Its reminders of Creation, on the one hand, and Exodus, on the other, clearly carried the essential message of ethical monotheism. But the rabbis could not persuade their congregants to observe the day itself. Work was the obstacle for many people, and leisure got in the way for others. The Sabbath was, as one historian notes, "the first observance to suffer severe compromises as German Jews moved closer to acculturation"—for reasons which perhaps went beyond both work and leisure.[92] Heine's famous depiction of the peddler Lumpchen in the *Baths of Lucca* has the Jew coming home to his hovel after a week of wandering with a pack on his back, singing "the most splendid psalms of King David," and rejoicing that all Israel's enemies were now dead "while Lumpchen is still alive and partaking of his fish with his wife and child."[93] The peddler knew what it was to celebrate the division of holy from profane, Sabbath from workweek, Israel from the nations. Gentile opponents of Sabbath observance did as well— and so, it stands to reason, did the Reformers.

Geiger's commission on the subject, reporting in 1846, emphasized the Sabbath day's essential character as absolute rest from work. It laid down the principle that biblical legislation could be modified in changed circumstances, while talmudic legislation had no standing unless it harmonized with the demands of the day. On that basis, it recommended that worthy observance of the day be restored by allowing performance of any task which was conducive to an uplifting service (for instance, playing the organ) or made it possible for an individual to attend such a service (for instance, riding in a carriage). Considerations of temporal welfare could not be ignored, however, and "participation in the welfare of the State [was] so exalted a duty that the observance of the Sabbath must yield to this in cases of collision," whether in the military or the civil service.

The rabbis divided over whether *consecration to the divine* or *cessation from work* was the essence of the day; they differed accordingly on policy. If consecration were the key, the focus of observance should be the synagogue service, and there was no need to restrict what took place outside it.[94] In the end, after vigorous debate over Holdheim's proposal to "save the Sabbath for Judaism and Judaism through the Sabbath even at the cost of surrendering the symbolical shell of transitoriness"—that is, to move the Sabbath to Sunday, when Jews would be free to observe it—the conference adopted a resolution in keeping with Geiger's report. It called for more

Sabbath observance and criticized the "over-great rigor of existing commands" as "injurious to such observance." The hope was that looser rules
and more attractive services would lure Jews back to the synagogue. Exemp-
tions were again provided for soldiers and civil servants.[95]

Holdheim saw matters very differently. His treatise *Uber die Autonomie
der Rabbinen,* published in 1843, had declared the absolute disjunction between religious law and political law in terms reminiscent of Spinoza's
Tractatus and Kant. His *Das Ceremonialgesetz im Messiasreich,* issued the same
year the rabbis gathered in Breslau, argued that "most of the biblical ceremonial laws . . . have been given solely with a view to the existence of the
other nations, and that their purpose was to separate Israel from those other
nations." Once Jews had been removed from their land, political laws could
not fulfill their original intent and so should have been abandoned by the
rabbis. Holdheim went so far as to permit mixed marriages, on the ground
that their prohibition had been a civil matter meant to maintain the Jews as
a separate and holy nation and so no longer applied.[96] It was on this avowedly political basis that he argued for moving the Sabbath to a day when it
could more easily be observed. Celebration on a particular day, that is, the
seventh day of the week, symbolized the distinctiveness of Jews as opposed
to heathens. Among monotheists it could no longer have that significance.
Nor could Jews literally believe the anthropomorphic account according to
which God created the world in six twenty-four-hour periods and rested
on the seventh. "I deny that this is a concession to Christianity; I have in
view the only possibility of a worthy celebration of the Sabbath."[97]

To a significant degree, of course, the subject of this and related debates
was, as Meyer puts it, "specific points of liturgy and ritual practice."[98] The
rabbis were exploring new religious territory, had no map to guide them,
and understandably differed over which course would take them further on
their way and which would lead them astray. On this reading, the debate
over Sabbath observance—like the debates which followed, about second
days of festivals (abolished), circumcision (reaffirmed except for *mezizah,*
sucking of the blood by the *mohel*), mourning customs (reformed in accordance with "our religious sentiment" and not, the rabbis averred, Gentile
pressure), marriage laws (*halitzah,* or levirate marriage, abolished), and the
position of women (recommendations toward equality of obligation were
made but tabled)—concerned the distinction between essence and form,
eternal and ephemeral, essential and dispensable. That distinction is at the
heart of any religious adaptation to changed circumstances.

Geiger's objection to Holdheim, that an institution of Judaism in existence for thousands of years could not be legislated out of existence by a single rabbinical conference, is readily understandable in these terms.[99] Those to the Right of Geiger would and did say, "Aha! exactly what we have been maintaining! How then permit the organ or abolish second days of festivals?" Those to his Left would ask, "Why is this reform different from all others? Why draw the line at Sunday Sabbaths?" There is much to recommend an analysis of the conferences, as of the modern transformation of Jewish practice more generally, strictly in terms of the theory and practice of religious adaptation—a project, when all is said and done, of delineating the bounds of divine and human authority.

As should by now be evident, however, there is good reason to focus on the connection Holdheim made between Sabbath observance and nationality. Mary Douglas's work can help us make sense of the rabbis' concern to adjust ritual boundaries in accordance with changed or promised redrawing of political lines; many in and around the Reform camp also articulated the relation between religion and politics in a complex fashion that precludes their dissociation of one from the other even as it defies the reduction of the former to the latter. Consider Gabriel Riesser, the most famous champion of Emancipation, who repeatedly condemned state interference in Jewish affairs, attacked rabbinic and communal coercion of observance on similar grounds, and joined the Hamburg temple. He believed, like many Reform Jews, that religious obligations such as the Sabbath and the dietary laws were products of a particular historical situation and could therefore be superseded. Yet Riesser opposed any change that seemed to stem from imitation of other religions. He strongly attacked the Frankfurt Reform Society because it had been motivated, in his view, by fear of civil authorities and the church. Jews remained morally bound by a kind of solidarity, inside and outside Germany, that he refused to define as nationhood or limit to religion alone—and that he was utterly unwilling to surrender.[100]

Or, at the opposite pole of the Reform camp, consider Leopold Zunz, who preached at the Berlin Reform congregation, supported many alterations in the service, declared German culture to be "higher" than Judaism, but became alienated from Reform when he perceived it to be turning away from the authentically Jewish—what Zunz designated as "the national." Ceremonial law had both spiritual and national significance, he argued. Circumcision and the Sabbath had been attacked because they were the symbols of the Covenant; in consequence, they were better classed as institutions than as ceremonies, since they marked Jewish life as a whole.[101] Like many others in and around the Reform camp, Zunz agitated for political change in Germany for reasons articulated in terms of Jewish faith. Unlike some others, however, he did so as a member of a people that had been attached to many different polities in the past and, if the messiah did not come soon, would no doubt belong to many more in the future.

Geiger's moving correspondence with Zunz in 1845 on the value of ceremonies, when seen in this light, reveals far more than a difference in temperament between the two or varying belief in the revealed character of written and oral law. The leader of Reform did not doubt that "any ceremony may take on a deeper meaning." None was ever "altogether devoid of significance." But observance could not rest on "a misinterpretation of certain biblical passages [or] excesses associated with charms and amulets." How could Zunz make a case in favor of circumcision, "a barbaric, gory rite which fills the infant's father with fear and subjects the new mother to harmful emotional strain"? Its only bases were habit and fear. Geiger expressed love and admiration for Holdheim's "honest conviction" and "higher moral tone," and confusion about Zunz's recent decision to keep a kosher home. Pragmatic considerations were one thing, but how justify on principle habits "that are so void of rationale and at the same time such a hindrance to the development of social relationships. Truly, the ideal of the deeper sense of brotherhood among men should have priority." Zunz replied in words that could have been written by Frankel: "The criterion for true religiosity can only be religiosity itself, that which is considered valid for all and universally cherished in a living tradition. . . . It is not religion, but ourselves that we must reform."[102]

They disagreed, as we see clearly in this exchange, about the meaning of "universally" and "all," over the identity of "ourselves" and "we," and about whether priority should be given to the distinctive marks of the Jewish people or to "social relationships" with Gentiles and a "deeper sense of brotherhood among men." For Geiger, the brotherhood of man was as much a religious as a political commitment. Judaism was a "basic truth concerning the unity of God," a grand Idea which had entered the world thanks to the genius of a particular people and had necessarily shed its "nationalistic limitations" long ago, as soon as history thrust it onto the world stage by way of the Roman destruction of Judea. That is why Geiger began his lecture series "Judaism and Its History" not with the Exodus or Sinai but with a discussion of "true religion: the consciousness of man's eminence and lowness; the aspiration to perfection, coupled with the conviction that we cannot reach the highest plane." The proper terms for the discussion of

Judaism were, in the first instance, entirely universal. Judaism was not a nation but a religion, and religion was by definition universal: the property of all humankind. It existed in "every good and noble aspiration." A person performs the "work of religion" whenever he or she overcomes selfishness, "lovingly and fervently attaches himself to his country and gives to it his own life and welfare and gladly labors for all and is filled with the desire to strive toward the Highest."[103] Ritual was a means to this end, and only that. "Too great a stress on the ceremonial" was not good for a person, or for Judaism.[104]

Thus, while Geiger agonized over breaking the fast of Tisha B'av in 1855, consistently sided with the moderates at the rabbinical conferences, wrote scholarly articles in clear, felicitous Hebrew, and as a rabbi in Berlin produced a very traditional prayer book (in part, to maintain unity among his congregants),[105] he never saw ritual as anything but a vehicle of the Idea which "raises them [the Jews] above the nations"[106] and must so raise them if the Jewish mission is to be fulfilled.[107] This, I believe, was the crux of the matter. *Peoples* had languages; faiths did not. And Geiger therefore held it a matter of the deepest religious integrity to modify the Jews' ritual distinctiveness in favor of political and religious achievements which were, in his view, inseparable. Gentile social and governmental pressure was beside the point in this regard. Emergent norms of *Bildung* and civility were valid because they expressed progress in reason and spirit that Geiger believed divine. His personal vocation as a rabbi rested on the conviction that he did not serve a particular faith, let alone a particular people, but God: the revealer of eternal, absolute, and universal truth, the enabler of redemption. Members of the Jewish faith, by joining the German people at this moment in the historical destiny of both, were not abandoning one identity for another but departing the ghetto to take part—*as* members of the Jewish faith—in the fulfillment of the entire human race.[108] Spiritual no less than material goods were at stake. Jews were going out from slavery to freedom. They were leaving exile. Without God's messiah, but with the help of the messiah's God, they were finally going to be at home.

To traditionalist Orthodox figures, by contrast, exile continued. The proof of that conviction, in the words of Julius Carlebach, was "that Jews, dissenters by choice in the political arena of the Galut [exile], [remained] subject to constant pressure by the State to move from dissent to conformity." They were of course obligated to resist those pressures, as they had for centuries, there being no difference between the nineteenth century and others in this regard, nothing sacred in its zeitgeist, nothing messianic in its promise.[109] Jacob Emden, a leading Orthodox rabbi, put the matter with striking simplicity when he complained that increasing numbers of Jews in his day "are no longer mindful of the fact that they are in galut; they mingle with non-Jews, adopting their customs, and are a great disgrace. The holy seed mixes with the peoples of the earth."[110] If 1848 really was "a day that the Lord had made," one should, as the Psalmist proclaimed, "rejoice and be glad therein." If not, one should hang back as Jews had for centuries and wait for a better day, take advantage of Emancipation but not accord it absolute value, and continue the pattern of distinctive practice that served, as always, as the principal expression and instrument of Jewish resistance.

4. CONCLUSION

A vast historical literature has accumulated over the past few decades around the comparative modernization of Jewish communities, focused in part on the question of whether the German case should be taken as paradigmatic.[111] My point here has not been to argue the latter case one way or the other but to demonstrate that the two sorts of political considerations we have described necessarily played a major role in the decisions made by Jews about the retention, adaptation, or abrogation of distinctive practices that set them apart. I hope to have shown as well that we do not cease to take religious practice seriously in its own terms merely by examining its relation to political calculations (or, for that matter, its relation to various other factors, not examined here, such as generational distance from immigration, economic niche, personal taste, and so forth). In fact, the opposite is true, all the more so in this case because many modern Jews have regarded Emancipation and Enlightenment as a fulfillment of Israel's age-old religious teachings—as, at best, the successful completion of their mission to the nations or, at the very least, the optimum condition in which their tradition and they themselves can flower.

American Jews at the end of the twentieth century seem to retain that conviction about their own society, with or without awareness that German Jews and French Jews felt similarly about theirs. In America too, despite the vast differences in condition from nineteenth-century Europe, east or west, or the Levant at the start of this century, conscious and unconscious calculations about the marking of difference continue to have their impact. Philip Roth's "Eli the Fanatic" masterfully captured these dynamics for the moment of Jewish movement to the suburbs—a moment which continues. "We didn't make the laws," the American-Jewish lawyer tells the Holocaust refugee who wants to bring a yeshiva to his neighborhood. "Woodenton is a progressive suburban community whose members, both Jewish and Gentile, are anxious that their families live in comfort and beauty and serenity. This is, after all, the twentieth century, and we do not think it too much to ask that the members of our community dress in a manner appropriate to the time and place." Eli endorses this request: "I am them, they are me, Mr. Tzuref." To which Mr. Tzuref replies, "Aach! You are us, we are you."[112] A horse is a horse, in other words, white suit or black suit. Why try to hide its distinctiveness?

The question remains definitive for American Jews, and arguably it always will; the Jews who stand apart most graphically from other Americans—Hasidim—for that very reason serve as iconic images of the community as a whole, and decisions by Jewish individuals over matters such as the wearing of a yarmulke on the street, or taking off days from work (or play) for the observance of Sabbaths or festivals, or circumcising male infants in the hospital or the synagogue will continue to be affected by societal opinion and the decisions of the Supreme Court. Law professor Stephen Carter, discussing these issues as they affect all Americans, Jewish or not, gave one of his books the subtitle *How American Law and Politics Trivialize Religious Devotion.*[113] Philip Roth, demonstrating that such matters of observance are far from trivial even among secularists, ended his novel *The Counterlife* with a stirring paean to the meaning of circumcision—a meaning that lies precisely in its being an act "quintessentially Jewish and the mark of their reality. Circumcision makes it clear as can be that you are here and not there, that you are out and not in—also that you're mine and not theirs. There is no way around it. You enter history through my history and me."[114]

The echoes of Spinoza could not be clearer. Ritual stands as a "theologico-political" matter of great moment—though that has generally not been the first meaning assigned it by modern Jewish thinkers or embraced by modern Jewish practitioners. They have generally preferred other significances for observance, to which we now turn.

FIVE

New Reasons for Old Commandments:

The Strategy of Symbolic Explanation

Geiger's transformation of the theory and practice of Jewish command-edness, like the efforts of many to his Right and to his Left on the Jewish religious spectrum in the nineteenth century, looked back explicitly to Moses Mendelssohn. As it became more and more apparent that the case for Jewish practice would have to address itself to an emancipated and enlightened audience, and so would have to be argued in terms that were immediately accessible and compelling to that audience, Jewish thinkers increasingly invoked not only Mendelssohn's name but his strategy for persuading Jews to remain inside—or enter—the framework of the commandments. The gist of that strategy can be stated quite simply, which is itself a major reason for its popularity. The commandments were presented as a "ceremonial script" that expressed universal truths in particularist symbolic language and that served, as well, to inculcate virtue through this language of ritual symbols which reminded Jews of the highest purposes directing human life. This sort of *ta'am* (reason or taste) for the mitzvot quickly came, in several varieties, to dominate elite as well as popular Jewish discourse about the commandments. In many quarters, it continues to do so today.

My purpose in this chapter is to probe that rationale for practice through an analysis of a particularly systematic form of the argument set forth in the second third of the nineteenth century by Samson Raphael Hirsch (1808–1888), generally regarded as the founder and chief theoretician of modern Orthodoxy. Hirsch, like Mendelssohn, sought to make a virtue of the necessity to argue for observance, for engagement in religious practice that until the modern era could be taken for granted. Like Mendelssohn, too, Hirsch was convinced that observance, rather than belief, was the distinguishing mark of Judaism. Devotion to an eternal practice, rather than the adaptation of Jewish doctrine to modern currents, would prove the key to Judaism's survival and renewal He, too, therefore urged his readers to regard the mitzvot as vessels which needed to be filled with content that they themselves could supply or appropriate.

But there the similarity ended. Whereas Mendelssohn had allowed for a *plurality* of meanings that would be attached by Jewish men and women to their own individual and collective practice—thereby attaching the commandments, via those meanings, to themselves—Hirsch insisted on *univocal* translations of the symbols into propositional affirmations that he, not his readers or congregants, would provide. And whereas in Mendelssohn's view the commandments *pointed to* truth, constituting a framework within which truth and virtue could successfully be pursued. Hirsch claimed that the mitzvot actually and clearly *expressed* truths, each symbolic x standing in for a specific y. The difference between the two, then, extended not merely to *what* the mitzvot symbolized but to *how* and *why* they symbolized.

Nevertheless, Hirsch's system, I shall argue, suffered no less than Mendelssohn's lack of system from the disadvantages of its particular strengths—not least because both sought to bind Jews through words and arguments to practices which, both theorists contended, were indispensable precisely because of their superiority to words and arguments. Theory, in the absence of widespread observance, would have to lead Jews back to practice and would have to do so by singing the praises of practice and denigrating the powers of mere theory! The effort could not possibly be entirely successful, and all the less so when Jews stood outside the door to observance looking in, or stood with one foot in and one foot out, or even stood just inside a door that was unlatched and ajar. Non-Orthodox thinkers, who have advanced symbolic explanations of practice no less than their Orthodox colleagues did, have therefore faced still more formidable obstacles than have either Hirsch or Mendelssohn to securing the enactments they urged. At the conclusion of this chapter, I shall reflect on the enduring popularity of the strategy and speculate on why it still remains crucial to Jewish observance and its explanation today.

I. A SCIENCE OF JEWISH SYMBOLS

Hirsch's preparation for the task of carrying Mendelssohn's program forward was, at least on the face of it, formidable. His parents combined in themselves and in their home the two tendencies already vying for control of German Jewish hearts and institutions at the turn of the nineteenth century: Enlightenment and traditional piety. Lest the latter not leave sufficient room for the former, they sent Hirsch to a non-Jewish grammar school in his formative years rather than to the Hamburg *talmud-torah* that had been organized by his grandfather, Mendel Frankfurter. Then, beginning in his thirteenth year, Hirsch received talmudic and rabbinical training from two native-born German authorities of great learning and measured openness to Enlightenment: first, from Isaac Bernays, who became the rabbi of Frankfurt in 1821, and later, in his early twenties, from Jacob Ettlinger of Mannheim. Hirsch apparently had no interest in formal yeshivah education, but he did spend a year and a half at the University of Bonn, where he and his friend Abraham Geiger organized a debating society for Jewish students. He emerged from this training with a fine methodical mind, some acquaintance with the philosophy of the day, a firm attachment to the Bible (uncommon in the yeshivah world), and a solid basis in Talmud and Shulhan Arukh that was utterly bereft of interest in or patience for the dialectics of *pilpul*.

Hirsch's service as a young rabbi in the community of Oldenburg forced him to take a stand immediately on Jewish issues of the day, particularly on the changes being introduced by Reform. In short, he, like Mendelssohn, initially assumed the role of mediator between Enlightenment culture and traditional observance because he needed to find that middle ground *for himself*. None of the spiritual and intellectual options available to Jews were adequate to "meet the demands of the day." At a relatively early age, Hirsch embarked on the attempt to do better.

His first published work, *The Nineteen Letters on Judaism* (1836), was addressed to a fictive Jewish youth on the verge of joining the ranks of what the author might well have called, echoing Schleiermacher, Judaism's "cultured despisers." The rigors of the law were a senseless burden, Hirsch's imagined young correspondent complained. Gentile culture was noble and uplifting; Judaism, by contrast, meant a history of suffering and a life without happiness. Hirsch sought to combat the attractions of assimilation (and, of course, Reform) with a new synthesis of "Torah and *derekh eretz*" (literally, the way of the land) and a new character ideal, the *Mensch-Yissroel*. He envisioned a Jew who, like himself, was trained in secular studies as well as Jewish sources, a person who spoke and dressed like Gentile neighbors, felt thoroughly at home in modern culture, but remained devoted above all to serving God through rigorous fulfillment of the commandments. His strategy for producing such people—which meant attracting the best of Jewish youth to observance—centered on convincing them that the commandments, as understood through an original six part scheme of classification and elaborate explanation in contemporary terms, could provide a meaning to life that was second to none. Nor did observance involve any sacrifice whatever of the best in non-Jewish culture.

Hirsch acknowledged his debt to Mendelssohn for this symbolic approach to the commandments explicitly in *Nineteen Letters,* though he also wrote that Mendelssohn's greatness lay chiefly in secular philosophy, because his mental development had not arisen from the "wellsprings of Judaism." He faulted Mendelssohn's successors for not carrying out his program of *ta'amei ha-mitzvot* or even comprehending it intellectually.[1] Hirsch went on to devote the bulk of his prolific writings over the next half-century to precisely those tasks.

His approach differed from Mendelssohn's, however, in several crucial and immediately obvious respects. *System* was its distinguishing characteristic and *certainty* Hirsch's predominant tone. His argument established truth through proof texts rather than philosophy. Not a whiff of Mendelssohn's endearing skepticism is to be found. Exposition of the commandments was, in Hirsch's view, not only commentary but *science.* A note at the end of *Nineteen Letters* reasoned that God is revealed in both nature and Torah. The same principles which applied to investigation of nature—and enabled us to explain the "phenomena [which] stand before us as indisputable facts"— applied to investigation of the Torah as well. Moreover, just as no fact or law discovered in nature could be denied even if science proved unable to explain it satisfactorily, so the Torah's "ordinances must be accepted in their entirety as undeniable phenomena and must be studied in accordance with their connection to each other, and the subject to which they relate." In short, they "must be law for us." Fulfillment of the commandments was a duty independent of inquiry. "Only the commandments belonging to the category of Edoth, which are designed to impress emotional and intellectual life, are incomplete without such research."[2]

Not surprisingly, Hirsch devoted the bulk of the first volume of his magnum opus, *Horeb* (published in 1837 but substantially completed before publication of *Nineteen Letters*), to *edoth*—"symbolic words or acts which bear lessons of profound significance for the individual Jew, for Israel as a whole, and for mankind in general."³ *Toroth*—"the historically-revealed ideas" concerning God, world, mankind and Israel—received only fifty pages of attention. *Mishpatim*—commanding justice toward other human beings—got little more.⁴ The reason is obvious. The commandments most laden with symbolism, those which explicitly or implicitly demanded explanation in terms of beliefs, were also the ones most "incomplete without [the] research" that Hirsch had undertaken. Equally important, they comprised the largest portion of the "ceremonial law," which in turn included the vast majority of the observances familiar to or practiced by Hirsch's readers: Sabbaths and holidays, tefillin and tzitzit, the lulav and the shofar.

Horeb's second volume, similarly, featured extended discussion of the *hukkim*—"statements concerning justice toward subordinate creatures [and] toward your own property, toward your own body and soul and spirit." This was an original formulation of the category, which in traditional Jewish parlance indicated the commandments most resistant to rational explanation: dietary laws, for example, or the mixing of species in one's garments or fields. *Mitzvoth*—love toward all living things, study of the Torah, sanctification of God's name—likewise received sustained attention because they gave Hirsch an opportunity to expound the commandments' sociological function as means of sustaining Judaism and providing a bulwark against assimilation to the ways of the Gentiles.⁵

The final category, *avodah*—divine service—was defined as "exaltation and sanctification of spiritual life by symbolic words or acts, to the end that our conception of our task may be rendered clearer, and we be better fitted to fulfill our mission on earth." We note that, as always, Hirsch's anthropocentrism was pronounced; God does not feature in the category's definition. The reason, I think, was not only that Hirsch's strategy depended on filling traditional concepts such as prayer with attractive and contemporary significance. Hirsch was by both temperament and conviction an activist, a doer. His piety was bereft of mysticism or devotionalism; his God was above all a *Commander*. While Hirsch did emphasize the need to stand before God in wholeness of heart, here as elsewhere it is not relation as much as activity that engages him. The commandments educated Jews to their "task" and "mission on earth," in fulfillment of God's will, rather than bringing God close or providing an occasion for outpourings of the soul and stirrings of the heart. Prayer, Hirsch stressed at the outset, was only one mode of divine service; all of life should serve God. What is more, the Hebrew verb for "prayer" was reflexive. It originally meant "true judgment of the self."⁶

Israel's entire existence, in Hirsch's view, was symbolic of complex propositions requiring explication. Therefore, its observance of the commandments—like his exposition of the commandments themselves, as I have stated earlier—emerged in Hirsch's oeuvre as far more a science than an art.

I will turn in a moment to two examples of the fruits of Hirsch's investigation into the commandments: his explanations for the Sabbath and for dietary laws—both, we note, observances that had been contested in the debate over Emancipation and had become the focus of the controversy stimulated by Reform—as these are set forth in *Horeb* and his biblical commentary published serially between 1867 and 1878. Before doing so, however, it will be useful to review Hirsch's most systematic exposition of the method that he employed in both works, the "Introduction to the Study of Symbolism," written in 1857.

The point of the study, Hirsch announced at the outset, was to teach the "rules for understanding abstract concepts" and "the rules for understanding symbols." Hirsch's confidence that one could be certain about a particular symbol's interpretation—so certain as to speak of "rules"—was based on the following logic. Human beings universally use symbols, he reasoned, to express concepts or emotions and to provide these expressions, otherwise ephemeral in nature, with a "lasting remembrance." A warm handshake makes a greater impression than a mere hello. A ring given us by a friend is treasured as a keepsake. Societies as well as individuals employ pictures, signs, and emblems to express ideas, truths, doctrines, or principles. "The more aware a nation is of its unity[,] ... the more prominent will be the place of symbols and symbolic acts in its political and religious life." The disadvantage of symbols as compared to words, of course, is relative lack of clarity, but we can overcome that difficulty by recognizing that symbols "derive their symbolic significance solely from the intention of the one who instituted the symbol and employed it for that stated purpose." All we need do to discover the meaning of a symbol, therefore, is uncover its originator's intention, a task which in turn depends on *etymological inquiry* into the words that name the symbols ("tzitzit" or "Shabbat" or "shofar") and on *analysis of the multiple contexts* in which the symbol appears (its association "with other factors that are either enunciated or designated by symbols of their own").

No detail was without its significance, according to this science. Every number, color, gesture, and subgesture was to be probed etymologically and contextually. As a result of this twofold investigation, interpretation of the symbol "will take an increasingly steady and sure direction" and take us to "the one idea which the symbol is really intended to communicate." "Mathematical certainty" was impossible, but one could reach the valid conclusion that out of all possible interpretations ours "might be the correct one" [*die richtige sein konne*].[7]

Thus, Hirsch's assumptions about the nature and functioning of symbols were fairly conventional. Symbols are vessels which carry meanings placed in them by individuals or groups. The way to discover a particular symbol's meaning is therefore to interrogate its creator, whether by looking into the meaning of the words attached to the symbol (the creator presumably was aware of this meaning and traded on it in his or her use of the symbol) or by examining the context(s) in which the symbol occurs (another sure clue to the intentions of the person or persons who placed it there). Hirsch's psychology seems in line with Mendelssohn's as well as the Enlightenment tradition on which Mendelssohn drew, while his view of religion as a symbolic medium that carries complex philosophical propositions in pictorial translation, as it were, was axiomatic in Hegel's enormously influential understanding of religion.[8]

There are several obvious problems with this science even if we accept the rules which Hirsch laid down for it and so leave aside vexing issues of multiple signification, overdetermination of meaning, the difficulty of arriving at "original intentions" that lie far beyond our own cultural "horizons," and the gap between such putative original intentions and the intentions of subsequent performers. None of these matters seems to have troubled Hirsch. Neither, however, did several other problems inherent in the terms of debate that he himself established.

The first is that Hirsch needed to study "the personality who instituted the symbol" in order to "discover the trend of thought from which arose the intention to convey an idea through the symbol under consideration."[9] But the "personality" in this case was God! Moses and other intermediaries of revelation are barely mentioned in Hirsch's expositions. His view of divine communication seems to have been quite literalist. God spoke the words attributed to Him. The mind that Hirsch needed to probe was divine.

His only way of getting at that mind lay in probing the commandments which it had issued. Hirsch, in common with traditionalist Jews, believed God had given commandments not only directly, in the written Torah given at Sinai, but indirectly, in the oral Torah compiled by dozens of divinely inspired rabbis over a period of many centuries. Hirsch's investigation into God's intentions therefore depended upon the correctness of the sages' understandings. Yet he announced that many, if not most, of the interpretations of the law offered by rabbis, philosophers, mystics, and commentators over the ages, including some offered in the rabbinic corpus itself, were wrong![10] Where Mendelssohn, in the spirit of the commentaries he cited, would first present Rashi's view, say, or Ibn Ezra's, and then add "but I think the verse should be read this way," Hirsch, rather like Maimonides in the Mishnah Torah, explained what the correct meaning was without much attention to other possible interpretations. Nor did he take the existence of other interpretations as cause for doubting the validity of his own findings. Perfectly good scientists, he might well have said, had for many centuries maintained that the earth was flat and that the sun was in orbit around it. They were wrong.

This exposes what was perhaps the most serious flaw in Hirsch's method: his claim to absolute and univocal correctness, as opposed to the multiplicity of error, undermined his claim to have discovered the meaning originally intended by the laws' divine author. To the degree that Hirsch and only Hirsch provided the correct interpretation of a given observance, twenty centuries of Jews had been enacting it without that interpretation. God must have been waiting for Hirsch's arrival on the scene, for someone to finally get His purpose right. Hirsch stood on firm ground only when he could demonstrate—as he often tried to do—that he was *not* innovating but merely translating into contemporary language, literally and figuratively, the understanding of the commandments that traditional authorities had expounded. Mendelssohn's avowed pluralism of interpretation avoided this problem, but it also prevented him from offering his readers the powerful incentive for observance that Hirsch supplied: a single, *scientifically* demonstrated interpretation of every commandment, aligned with modern sensibilities yet derived not from any human interpreter but directly from God.

The explications of the Sabbath in *Horeb* and the Torah commentary find Hirsch walking steadfastly in the footsteps of the rabbis, "translating" rather than innovating, and deploying an approach to the mitzvot that follows Mendelssohn's closely, at times word for word. Sabbath observance explicitly connected *shamor* (observance) and *zakhor* (remembrance) and accomplished the latter indirectly by means of the former. The purpose of the day, likewise explicit in the Torah, was to remind humanity (*zakhor*) that it was subject to God's law and, in so doing, to save the world from the evils to which human creatures were prone (for example, slavery) in the absence of proper understanding of their creation by the Creator. Kiddush, the blessing over wine, recalled the world's beginnings in the first six days as well as the redemption of Israel from Egyptian bondage (compare Exod. 20:11 and Deut. 5:15). Observance of the Sabbath (*shamor*) was required because God had chosen to withdraw "from active creation to invisible guidance of the universe." Otherwise, no reminder would have been necessary. The practice necessarily took the form of abstention from *melakhah,* the sorts of activity which most demonstrated human domination over the earth. Jews had for one day each week to eschew the making of things for human purposes, "the execution of an intelligent purpose by the practical skill of man." These commandments fell particularly on Jews because "while all mankind owe their actual physical existence to God," Israel "in addition owes its social existence to God." Jews' national identity was no less God's creation than the cosmos.

Hirsch enumerates and explains at length the thirty-nine categories of *melakhah* set forth by the rabbis, but he concludes in *Horeb* with a highly rhetorical and contemporary appeal to his readers to observe the Sabbath day despite the financial losses which this might entail. The "very non-performance of a *melachah*" implied recognition of God's ownership of one-self and the world, led to renewal of one's resolution to act accordingly all the time, and conferred both sanctity and strength. How could one possibly think of working on the Sabbath day? A livelihood "gained by depriving life of its purpose" could not truly be called a livelihood. The thought of it "could not occur to anyone who has grasped the essence of the Sabbath and observed it." [11]

This seems, on first reading, pure Mendelssohn. Practice points to propositions couched in very general and rational terms, the moral implications of which are pronounced, just as they are in Mendelssohn's own commentary on the Torah and in *Jerusalem.* Closer examination, however, reveals several obvious departures. For one thing, the Sabbath "expresses the truth" that Hirsch proceeds to put into words. Hirsch believes these words transparently clear and valid once and forever—assumptions with which Mendelssohn would have been uncomfortable. [12] What is more, Hirsch affirms not only the veracity of that truth, as he has formulated it, but the absolute necessity of every detail of the laws which regulate Sabbath observance, as these had developed from the beginnings of rabbinic exegesis until his own day. [13] Where Mendelssohn had consistently remained vague on the details of observance and implicitly offered a rationale for halakhic *reform,* Hirsch argues the *inevitability* of the law as currently practiced. Indeed, he invokes the commandments in order to attack those who have disagreed with him on either "remembrance" or "observance," especially the Reformers. His Torah commentary pours scorn on those who had interpreted Exod. 20:10 as a prohibition of hard physical work and had proclaimed the Sabbath "a day of bodily rest so that the mind might be freer to devote itself to God and spiritual matters." Abstention from *melakhah* was end, not means; the Torah forbade *melakhah* strictly but did not even mention failure to attend a synagogue service or hear a sermon! Conversely, "even the smallest work done on the Sabbath is a denial of the fact that God is the Creator and Master of the World[,] . . . a denial of the whole task of the Jew as man and as Israelite."

The rhetoric here, I believe, was not merely a function of increasing violation of the Sabbath by German Jews (similar denunciations, prompted by the same problem, occurred in every community)[14] or the result of Hirsch's desire to impress his readers with the urgency of their mission. It stemmed from nothing less than grave dissatisfaction with the balance struck by Mendelssohn and his heirs between *Yissroel* and *Mensch*—the role of observances as a marker distinguishing the Jews, as I discussed in the preceding chapter. Hirsch constantly upped the ante of observance, as it were, imputing profound and crucial significance to every last detail of the law.[15] This strategy eventually led, as Reform came to dominate more and more of Germany's state-chartered Jewish communities, to Hirsch's demand for—and recourse to—secession from the Frankfurt Gemeinde (a matter to which I will return). Israel's mission depended upon *strict* observance of its symbolic commandments and *unambiguous* recognition by Jews and Gentiles of the symbolic character of its existence. Jews could work with Gentiles, dress and speak like Gentiles, aspire to *Bildung* as Gentiles did, but they were also called to a significant degree of separation from their surroundings, indeed, perhaps to more apartness than Hirsch himself had imagined when he set out on his own path with the *Nineteen Letters*.[16] Contraction in the scope available for marking distinctiveness—as Jews, with Hirsch's blessing, entered into full participation in Gentile society—made the need for distinguishing characteristics inside the Jewish domain that remained all the more imperative.

This is still more apparent when Hirsch turns from conventional interpretations of commandments such as the Sabbath, which for obvious reasons have always lent themselves to rational interpretation, to exposition of ordinances such as the dietary laws, which have traditionally defied rational interpretation. On the matter of forbidden foods, Hirsch cleaves (albeit eclectically) to the teachings of his predecessors. Three discrete interpretations are offered.

1. Like strictures on Sabbath observance, restrictions on diet testified to the status of human beings as creatures of the Creator. One could not simply eat how, and whatever, and whenever one wanted, following one's own whims. "Do you wish to scorn God, to imply that He is not the Master of His creatures[,] . . . of yourself?"

2. Body, moreover, was connected to spirit in ways that we could not fathom. Not ingesting forbidden food perhaps saved us from physical illness, but it certainly saved us from "derogation of the sanctity of spirit and heart" that Jews, in particular, required in order to carry out their holy mission—a clear echo of the *Kuzari*.

3. Finally, God's reasons for caring about what Jews ate were not "really your affair. . . . You should obey because God has given you the command-ments. . . . That is your destiny."[17] The same was true of any command-ments for which we could supply no other compelling rationale.

However, when Hirsch came to the most baffling element of the dietary laws—the prohibition on eating milk with meat, derived by the rabbis from the command not to "seethe a kid in its mother's milk" (Exod. 23:20)—he was not at all content with obedience for its own sake. He worked long and hard to solve a puzzle that had perplexed Jewish commentators for many centuries and that had provided Reformers ammunition for opposition to all commandments which lacked rational purpose. The interpretation Hirsch presented is both complex and ingenious, and I will therefore cite it at some length.[18]

Hirsch began by stating unequivocally that the purpose of other dietary regulations was spiritual hygiene: "avoidance of the exciting or depressing effect of certain foodstuffs on one's temperament and feelings." But this did not apply to the prohibition on eating meat with milk, which, unlike the others, extended not only to eating but (according to the rabbis) to prepar-ing or making any use whatever of a milk-meat mixture. The meaning of the commandment therefore had to be symbolic. Hirsch sensibly linked it to other prohibitions on mixing species and argued that these "Laws of Nature" were designed to remind us "of the One whose order [about spe-cies] rules all created life into the very core of their existence." This particu-lar law of nature "heads the list" (its primacy was deduced by Hirsch from its occurrence at several critical junctures of the Torah)[19] because it re-minded "us of our Jewish human calling" just at the moment when Jews were about to assimilate animal matter "into the fibres of our being." At that moment they especially needed to remember "that our mission is to raise the animal parts of our bodies up to the heights at which even the human material body is meant to be kept." The body must not sink to the "instinct-bound level of animals," even though we "reproduce the tissues of our body from the animal world."

The prohibition on meat with milk was so crucial, then, because human dignity and purpose depended on a differentiation from animals that was most threatened when a person assimilated the bodies of animals into his or her own (animal) body. Unless one bore in mind what the meat-milk prohibition was meant to recall, one could not fulfill one's duties of justice toward other human beings—the *mishpatim*—which are enumerated in the section of the Torah that concludes with this very milk-meat prohibition. Note, however, that Hirsch had still not explained why the mitzvah takes this particular form—specifically, separating milk from meat rather than merely regulating the slaughter and consumption of animals, as the Torah does elsewhere. Are human beings represented by milk, say, and other animals by meat, or vice versa? In Hirsch's system, each detail had to be provided with a symbolic interpretation. Uncovering a general intention was insufficient.[20]

Hirsch supplied the requisite meaning by dividing living matter—closely following the *Kuzari*—into an ascending order of plants, animals, and human beings. He postulated that the first kingdom was marked by the functions of nourishment and reproduction, while the second exhibited powers of locomotion and thought as well. In the higher animals, Hirsch observed, the animal and vegetable systems are arranged in two discrete parts of the body, separated from one another by the diaphragm. *Milk* was the "material" that most clearly characterized an animal's vegetative half, the "specific *food* for carrying on the species." *Meat,* for obvious reasons, represented the specifically animal half. The *mixture* of the two characterized the animal world, in which motion and thought served the aims of nourishment and reproduction, and only these. But "man is different. . . . To him a third system has been granted." The breath of God made humanity an "understanding and discerning spirit," just as a unique upright position raised the animal above the vegetative part of human beings and as the head "rises heavenwards" above both.

Recall of the plant-animal-human hierarchy every time that a person ate served as a reminder that "everything on earth that ripens for Man's enjoyment is to be raised to the divine part of the human being." The command to bring first fruits of the land to the sanctuary is for this reason given in the very same verse as the meat-milk prohibition. If the opposite attitude were to prevail, the human sinking to service of vegetative purposes only, "the whole cycle of the seasons would be robbed of its purpose, the whole of life on earth would begin and end in an unfree physical cycle."

The explanation is ingenious and no more far-fetched than some others which Hirsch proffered.[21] But what has Hirsch accomplished, and lost, by this symbolic account? The lessons of his enterprise are, to my mind, far-reaching.

2. THE STRATEGY AND ITS LIMITS

Mordecai Breuer has suggested that Hirsch's aim in his science of symbols was not to probe the intentions of the divine mind or even to motivate observance in nineteenth-century Germany "by arousing 'cognitive reason.'" It was to demonstrate the sort of "mighty will" that alone "could win the fight with anti-Jewish conditions."[22] One cannot be sure, of course. My own preference is to measure the *stated* goals of Hirsch's strategy against the "conditions," Jewish and Gentile, in which it was deployed—the better to understand why other thinkers too, then and today, have relied on symbolic explanation of the commandments. In the process, we should also get a better sense of its inherent advantages and limitations.

We can usefully begin, I think, with Hirsch's frequent invocation—found as well among Reform and Historical School thinkers—of the *mission to be accomplished by Jews in exile.* The refrain of *galut* (exile) is striking in Hirsch's work, and somewhat surprising. It seems directly to contradict the stated aims of joining Torah to *derekh eretz* and joining Jews to the countries in which they lived. Nonetheless, the sixfold classification of the commandments is introduced in the *Nineteen Letters* only after Hirsch has "reconciled" his correspondent "to the fate of your people," in part by extended quotation from the "suffering servant" passage in Isaiah.[23] In *Horeb,* Hirsch asserts that the purpose of Passover is "declaration and acknowledgment of the epochal fact . . . that our fathers contributed nothing towards their liberation and that we cannot ascribe the slightest portion of it to ourselves." The Israelites of old had earned their freedom by "complete surrender to God." Jews expressed that surrender today by means of the Paschal offering.[24]

Hirsch's "Reflections on the Jewish Calendar Year," published serially in his journal *Jeschurun,* emphasized exile and mission above all else. The month of Tishre taught that Jewish spiritual reckonings were detached from the natural cycles of birth and death. Heshvan caused Jews to ask themselves whether their "weak sliding" into un-Jewish ways of life had brought real benefit or happiness. Teveth reminded Jews that their fate and life's task were linked to *galut,* that God had scattered them as a "touch-stone," un-armed and defenseless, among the nations. Shevat elicited elegaic memories of a pastoral life long gone, "faint echoes of noble precepts." Iyar taught that Judaism was not merely a religion, that is, a universal part of human culture, but a divine guide for Jews in their wanderings.

The month of Av, with its fast day on the ninth recalling the destruction of ancient Israel's two Temples, was the occasion for a magnificent ser-mon—to my mind, one of the most eloquent Hirsch ever penned—on Germany's failure to live up to the promises it had made to Jews decades before. Far from being a "political Palestine for Jews," Germany still abounded in "Jew-hatred" and restrictions on Jewish liberties. Did the de-gree of separation from Gentile society mandated by traditional observance condemn Jews to dual loyalties? No, for even while not forgetting Jerusa-lem, Jews could "seek the peace of the city to which I have banished you." The quotation from Jeremiah testified to Hirsch's highly traditional philoso-phy of exile. God's Shekhinah had gone into exile with the Jews; the ques-tion was whether the Shekhinah and the Torah would now be exiled from Jewish family life as well in return for advantages promised by the states of Europe but as yet undelivered.[25]

Breuer is therefore correct, I think, in differentiating the undoubted *patriotism* of Hirsch's Orthodox followers from the *complete identification with Germanness* articulated by Geiger and other Reformers.[26] I would add, how-ever, that there was more to this difference than divergent readings of the events in progress or even divergent "theologico-political" evaluations of history, as described at the end of Chapter 4. For Hirsch, it was axiomatic that Judaism stood apart from all other cultures and religions—and not only apart from but *above* them. The conjunction in "Torah and *derekh eretz*" did not join two equal elements but, rather, two realities assigned coexistence by Providence for the duration of Israel's modern European exile. Egypt was always the paradigm for exile in Hirsch's writings; the contrast between Israel and Egypt was one of light to dark. The contemporary meaning of the second days of festivals observed in exile was "the truth, which differ-entiates [Jews] most sharply from all paganism. The heathen knows no *hi-dush* [innovation]." The reckoning of Israel's years from spring to spring as well as from Tishre to Tishre, Hirsch wrote, constituted "an exhortation on our double nature, worked into the log-book of our lives." Everything of the earth sinks bare and blossomless into the grave. Everything holy and Jewish has its origin in light and life, and "out of darkness and death it struggles back to Light and Life."[27]

One searches in vain throughout Hirsch's prolific writings for a valuation of modernity or Enlightenment that prized more than technical achievements, even though the latter included, in Hirsch's understanding, a wider range of cultural elements than Ashkenazi Jewish authorities over the centuries (or his own more traditionalist Orthodox contemporaries) were wont to praise. Hirsch's aggressive defense of the commandments and his relentless attack on schools of thought less Orthodox than his own were so different from Mendelssohn's tolerance and goodwill not only because, as Breuer puts it, Mendelssohn wrote for a Jewry that was still almost completely rooted in the living tradition and that he wished to draw closer to the surrounding culture, while Hirsch found his vocation among a Jewry that had already taken strides on the road to modernity and whose loyalty to the tradition required renewal.[28] The point for Hirsch was to educate Jews who would *fulfill an exilic mission that required visible apartness.* The sociological purpose of the commandments evident in Mendelssohn's well-known letter to his student Herz Homberg—the separation of Jews from Gentiles—therefore loomed large in all of Hirsch's writings.[29] One might say that Hirsch's description of the people whom God intended to create by bringing the Jews out of Egypt applied as well to his view of Jews in his own time: not a "congregational church" but "a people, a nation, a 'social community,' a state, should arise from this redemption, whose 'social' existence was to have its root in God, be built up by Him, rest on Him, be arranged and constituted by Him, and be dedicated to Him."[30]

Hirsch, of course, did not desire a Jewish "state." But he did want the legal authority, and the borders marking it, that statehood provided. In the cultural sphere he aimed, as Breuer puts it, to have Jews modernize without actually being modern—a strategy of "compartmentalization" followed by many modern religious believers and movements.[31] Hirsch had no fear of driving Jews away from observance of the commandments by attaching the mitzvot firmly to interpretations from which many Jews might demur. Unlike Mendelssohn, he wrote for Jews who were willing to undertake the rigors of their mission in full acceptance of their exile. Better, in his mind, to stress the hierarchy implicit in repetition and increase the certainty conveyed by unchanging form, even if this meant fewer adherents, than to allow the "vagaries of usage" (a phrase of anthropologist Roy Rappaport) to detract any more than they already had done from Jewish distinctiveness. For Hirsch, the Jewish mission meant a life *totally* governed by the Torah insofar as this was humanly possible—and that meant a degree of *segregation* which would paradoxically be facilitated by the religious liberty granted every citizen as well as by the cultural attainments that made appreciation of Hirsch's complex symbolism possible.

However, this very apartness and, thus, the achievement of Israel's mission were prevented by the conditions of *galut* from attaining fulfillment. The plausibility structure, as we have noted more than once, was weak or absent. Hirsch's congregants worked and dressed and spoke like their neighbors, passing their days in the same streets and buildings. They could not look around and see the world that the mitzvot were meant to create. What is more, both he and they had to rest content with severe limitations on the scope of the halakhah's application. There was, and could be, no attempt in Hirsch's work to raise up a completely Jewish world—one reason perhaps that his writings evinced virtually no halakhic innovation.[32] Hirsch seems from *Nineteen Letters* onward to have regarded this situation not as aberrant but as normative for Jewish life. Jacob Katz notes that Hirsch took "Moses commanded us the Torah, an inheritance for the congregation (*kehillah*) of Jacob" (Deut. 33:4) as a reference to precisely the sort of insular social institution that he inhabited in his early years and sought to perpetuate by leading his Frankfurt followers into a separate framework for the faithful transmission of their "inheritance."[33]

Other modern Jewish thinkers have favored less separation from Gentile society and displayed more enthusiasm for the culture of Enlightenment— stances which are reflected in their explanations for the commandments. One simply cannot appeal to people weighing observance(s) from *the outside,* or to those prepared to abandon observance(s) if sufficient reason for them is not forthcoming, the same way one appeals to a community seeking more or different meaning in practices to which it is committed in any case. The striking *stylistic* differences between Hirsch's rationale for the commandments and Mendelssohn's—the former relentlessly systematic, armed with footnotes, explaining at length and then explaining once again; the latter playful, sneaking up on the reader, doubling back on itself and rambling into byways—point to divergences on the substance of Jewish distinctiveness that—a century and a half after *Horeb* and two centuries after *Jerusalem*—continue to mark the varieties of Jewish practice and its theorizing.[34] Mendelssohn sought to open the door to a plurality of individual and collective interpretations of observance, and so ascribed meaning to the mitzvot only in the most general terms. Hirsch, by contrast, lavished detail upon his readers, specified the meaning of each and every commandment at great length, and never presented alternative readings. A symbolic "science" of the commandments such as Hirsch's would assist (and has) in the founding and maintenance of a *discrete and separatist community.* In recent decades, at least, Orthodoxy has proven extremely successful in maintaining and perpetuating its distinctiveness. Mendelssohn's far vaguer symbolic approach has lent itself to adoption by a *plurality of individuals and movements,* who (with his posthumous blessing, I think) have *variously* understood both his teachings and those of Torah.

Consider, in this connection, two recent and well-known accounts of the commandments provided by Jewish thinkers in America. Abraham Heschel, seeking to move a broad and diverse audience in the direction of mitzvot, consistently stressed the existential and ethical significance of observance, all the while framing the content of that observance in extremely general terms. He rarely instructed his readers to perform commandments x or y and avoided the attachment of specific meanings to specific commandments. The Sabbath, for example, marks the creation of a "palace in time," a space for spiritual transcendence over the material concerns of everyday life. No greater specificity was ever provided; the meaning offered will appeal, and be accessible, to almost everyone. By contrast, Joseph Soloveitchik repeatedly found detailed and abstruse significance in the details of halakhah and explicitly limited full appreciation of the creative effort involved in performance of the mitzvot to the elite who are involved in the halakhah's formulation. It is no wonder that Soloveitchik's "man of faith" is by nature "lonely"—or that his marvelous phenomenology of the life of faith concludes with a declaration of the incommensurability between Jewish and modern cultures and commitments. "It is here that the dialogue between the man of faith and the man of [general] culture comes to an end."[35]

Much of modern Jewish thought and practice, I believe, can usefully be seen as following one or another of these two paths or negotiating between them. Their aim has been to provide reasons for observing the commandments to Jews who have good reasons (in terms of the cultures in which they move) for *not* observing commandments in whole or in part. But that effort, as its Jewish audiences well knew, has sought just as much to mark their individual and collective apartness from the larger society: an aim not always welcomed by modern Jews and almost never considered without deep ambivalence.

The need to provide new reasons for commandments in the first place—and to provide them to people faced with the ever present option of abandoning observance in whole or in part—points to a second problem with the strategy of symbolic explanation, likewise highlighted by Hirsch's system. Despite Hirsch's voluminous outpouring on the subject of observance, he offered *remarkably few explanations for the immense variety of commandments that he interpreted.* Repetition characterizes his writings, much as it does the commandments themselves. The meaning of the several elements into which ritual is "parceled out" remains constant across the range of observances: the number seven always means *x;* the color purple, *y.* Likewise, the teachings to which the observances point, the concepts carried by the symbolic vessels, are few. God's creation, sovereignty, providence, and redemption; humanity's assigned duties; Israel's fate and mission—this is the stuff, and virtually the only stuff, that fills Hirsch's voluminous exegeses. Paradoxically, Hirsch had no need to pay any more attention to the multidimensional character of a given practice than he did to the character, emotions, situation, and intentions of the individual actors performing that practice. The commandments are a pedagogy, and Hirsch's writings a gloss, which direct Jews over and over to the *same few truths.* Observance affirms those truths ineluctably and unequivocally.

If one rejects those truths, or rejects Hirsch's formulation of them, or does not wish to be tied as closely to them as Hirsch insists, or is not convinced that so many reminders of a simple truth are necessary, or concludes that a truth so vulnerable to forgetting could not be essential to remember, one might well reject not only Hirsch but the commandments themselves. This has been the fate of countless appeals to observance in the last century—sermons pleading for Sabbath practice on grounds of the need to remember our status as creatures of the Creator, explanations of Passover or Hanukkah as holidays celebrating freedom. Suppose one feels no need of these reminders or enacts them in other ways? Or suppose, as in Judah Leib Gordon's ringing diatribes attacking the excesses of rabbinic legalism, a holiday observance such as Passover underlines what one *despises* in the particulars of practice, thereby undermining the claims of observance as a whole?[36]

As Hirsch noted with some justice in the *Nineteen Letters,* Mendelssohn's approach also could not escape this danger —but for a different reason. Its sources were not primarily those of the halakhic tradition, meaning that Mendelssohn could not depend on maintenance of a *collective* framework of disciplined observance. How could one count on observance unless it were regarded as divine decree? *Jerusalem,* we might say, offered an interpretation that was entirely aggadic and a mode of observance to match. Each Jew endowed each commandment with individual significance. But if practice depended in fact, even if not in theory, on the *quality and salience of meaning* attached to it, Jews were likely to favor commandments endowed with meanings consonant with contemporary cultural assumptions and social practice. They would select mitzvot and *ta'amim* in proportion to their fit with non-Jewish thought and practice. No *Jewish* fusion of "ethos" and "worldview" (in Geertz's terms) would transpire; no "model of" the surrounding reality and, certainly, no "model for" it, and, therefore, no coherent "plausibility structure" that would provide the grounds for further observance. One would likely see, instead, eclectic and idiosyncratic patterns, undependable and difficult to transmit. This is, of course, precisely what has often occurred.

There are, however, at least two problems with Hirsch's critique of Mendelssohn approach. In the first place, as we have already noted, it applies to a degree to Orthodox observance as well. Even Hirsch, who constantly stressed that every mitzvah was of equal importance and that no commandment depended for its force upon interpretation, however scientific, weighted his prolific writings toward the *ceremonial private sphere*. For only that sphere remained potentially subject to Jewish law, unlike the areas of *mishpatim* already surrendered to other laws and other symbolisms. Practices such as Sabbath and dietary laws were accessible to Jews, observable in private Jewish space without disturbance of activities that joined Jews with Gentiles in shared public space. At the same time, Sabbath and diet distinguished Jews from Gentiles in a way that the rest of life no longer did, thus provoking the Gentile attacks on these observances which we have chronicled.

Second, however, Hirsch required observance, and acceptance of his interpretations for it, as *acts of obedience*. More than one interpreter has pointed to the similarity between Hirsch's pervasive symbolism and the kabbalah—and to the fact that whereas the kabbalah touched Jews on many levels and left room in its open-ended imaginative system for ever new interpretations, Hirsch functioned exclusively on the cognitive level and urged his followers to do the same. His science thus left little room for either error or invention. The commandments were a pedagogy for thought and only that. Once Hirsch had done the work of discovering the ideas placed "in" the commandments by God, no further cognitive work was required or possible.[37] "What good does all the clever and spiritual instruction do me, if every moment of life hurls me into a dead mechanism?" complained Geiger upon reading the *Nineteen Letters*.[38] The intention of Soloveitchik's *Halakhic Man* is precisely to underline the role of human agency in remaking the world and the self, but in his essay, too, true creativity is limited not only to the male gender but to the philosophically minded and highly trained legal scholars qualified to probe the divine intentions underlying the commandments. Other Jews benefit from that effort and can, to varying degrees, be taught to appreciate it; they cannot, however, join in. What is left, then, is informed obedience, and even that of course demands greater submission to traditional authority –and greater withdrawal from the secular world—than most Jews find palatable.

Hirsch's theory, it should be noted, also points in a very different direction, and it too has been a major thrust of symbolic interpretation of the commandments from his day to our own: he couched his exposition in decidedly *anthropocentric* terms. The mitzvot were intended by God entirely for the education of God's creatures rather than the maintenance of the cosmos or the delight of the Creator. Hirsch issued no call to intimate encounter with the Commander but, rather, to action undertaken on God's behalf in and upon a world where, for the moment at least, God had apparently left the progress of humanity to human agents. We might well say, following the anthropologists, that the mitzvot were given to Jews because commandments are "good to think." They carried hidden interpretations which, once brought to light by a sophisticated nineteenth-century interpreter, could be absorbed by a sophisticated nineteenth-century reader—and only by such a reader—who would then be propelled into enactment of Israel's mission.

I do not by any means wish to suggest that Hirsch indulged in the worship of the modern individual to which Erving Goffman has directed our attention, but I would point out the "demeanor" of the commentator and his "deference" to the requirements of the reader, both very much a function of the modern situation in which Hirsch found himself.[39] He knew that comprehensive practice stood a far greater chance than eclectic observance of inculcating belief and preserving the community and that individual Jews—increasingly bent on guarding autonomy from heteronomous incursion and increasingly convinced that submission to God or community threatened dignity as well—could not on their own be counted on to adopt such stringency or cleave to it.

3. CONCLUSION

Perhaps, when all was said and done, Hirsch—no less than Mendelssohn—left the outcome of his appeal for practice in other hands. Mendelssohn evinced considerably less hope for the Jewish estate in his private correspondence than he did in *Jerusalem;* Hirsch's repeated references to mission and exile reinforced the notion that Jewish survival and observance both depended on forces other than his readers' decisions. Those same references, I think, drove home the lesson that the short-term Jewish future in Germany, like the long-term Jewish past in every corner of diaspora, was probably not destined to be a happy one. This ambivalence has also proven typical of Hirsch's successors in his century and in ours. For all the pervasive optimism of modern Jewish thought, Hirsch's concern with the shortcomings of Emancipation has become well-nigh universal, particularly when Jews have considered demands, or reasons, for distinctive practice. Faithful observance of the mitzvot might help Jews to cope while awaiting the promised day of redemption, and might even bring that day closer, but no major thinker—including Mordecai Kaplan, by far the most optimistic on this score—believed that increased practice could in and of itself supply the condition for renewed collective commitment to the Covenant.

This perhaps explains the increased importance of an alternate strategy for persuading Jews to undertake observance: the connection it would afford them with their ancestors. Nostalgia cuts across and even dispenses with the varying symbolic rationales for practice. It is indifferent to content and uninterested in detail; it appeals to emotion far more than to cognition, and, far from being centered on religious observance, it makes full use of such secular cultural pursuits as literature, the visual arts, history, and museum going. We turn now to its realm, where practice (however attenuated) far more than the theory of practice (however elaborate) holds sway.

SIX

Nostalgia as Modern
Jewish Mitzvah

Perhaps the strangest passage in all of Hirsch's voluminous writings—
strange because sentimental, evocative, Romantic, and, as such, a clear departure from the rigors of Hirsch's strenuous rationalism—is the one that
opens a sermon on the month of Nisan, part of a collection of homilies
ordered according to the Jewish ritual calendar. "For lo, the winter is past,"
Hirsch quotes from the Song of Songs. "The rain is over and gone, the
flowers appear in the earth, the time of singing is come, and the voice of
the turtle is heard in the land." To which Hirsch adds at once, "By whom
is it heard? Who has an ear for the gentle whispering of the life awakening
all around?" Not the majority of humankind, for whom there is only the
"monotonous ticking of daily cares," time measured out like a pendulum,
"the gnawing of the worm burrowing in the grave, or the shrill whistle of
the creaking machine, or the thunder of the locomotive as it speeds over
the rails." No cooing turtledove could be heard by such people. "The time
of song for them does not exist." [1]

The images—and their Romantic provenance—are striking, the tropes
of elegy pronounced. No less so, I think, is the contrast drawn repeatedly
in Hirsch's writings between the pastoral perfection enjoyed by ancient Israelites and the Jews' modern urban existence in exile. There is, of course,
the possibility that we should not take these lapses into pastorale overly
seriously. By the same token, we should perhaps not take Mendelssohn too
literally when he bemoans the modern reliance on written treatises rather
than the spoken word or recalls the still more pristine life led by Israel in
the few brief moments between Sinai and the golden calf. I think, however,
that both writers *have* been captured by their own rhetoric, at least to some

extent. Advocates of Torah cannot but regret the fragility and partiality of observance in their day. Tradition inherently beckons one into a world—seemingly better, integral, more complete, almost always imaginary—denied to one's own experience.

I also think that there is more to it than that. We will see in this chapter that the nostalgia evident in the passages just cited is pervasive in modern Jewish thought and practice, both elite and popular, in ways that go beyond either rhetoric or regret. Elegy, recall of a time and place of purer faith, invocation of ancestors worthy of inhabiting that sacred world have not been marginal phenomena but utterly constitutive of the ritual experience of modern Jews: individuals increasingly cut loose from integral communities, committed to personal autonomy, and bereft of the faith of their fathers and mothers let alone that of more distant forebears. Jews in the past two centuries have wandered far, both literally and figuratively, from their childhood homes and have opted in ever greater numbers for attenuated, atavistic, and sometimes trivial modes of observance. Yet, I shall argue, modern Jewish appeals to the "merits of the ancestors" represent far more than epiphenomena of loss and degeneration. The complex set of nostalgic behaviors united by elegy for a far better past and by invocation of the ancestors who made it so has been at least as basic to *observance* of the commandments in the modern period as to *rejection* of such observance and has been just as evident in elite reflection on practice as in the most attenuated popular forms which practice has assumed. Let us begin, then, by specifying somewhat more precisely what the genre of modern Jewish nostalgia has comprised.

The compilers of the Oxford English Dictionary, writing a century ago, defined nostalgia as "a form of melancholia caused by prolonged absence from one's home or country; severe home-sickness"—precisely what we find in Hirsch's lament for innocence lost during centuries of wandering from Zion, composed in Germany not long before the OED appeared. In Webster's contemporary formulation—"homesickness; longing for something far away or long ago"—the connotation of physical or mental malady is gone, and the "home" departed is no longer necessarily literal.[2] This definition matches both current vernacular usage and the scholarship summarized and advanced in David Lowenthal's helpful study. Nostalgia, as he understands it, is a generalized looking back, a pining for the past from which one is safely distant. One conjures up memories and cleaves to mementos with admiration and enjoyment but never takes the past seriously enough to feel obligated to alter present behavior or commitments because of it.[3]

All of these tendencies loom large in the German-Jewish memoir literature collected by Monika Richarz, the Anglo-Jewish and French Jewish press of the mid nineteenth century, and the new guides to Jewish practice for the assimilated that proliferated in that same period, including a new genre of travel literature that guided Jews back to the sites where their ancestors had practiced Judaism rather than merely reading about it. This same literature, however, testifies to something more than a widespread quest for ways of carrying on the "chain of tradition" without making an all-embracing commitment to it—more too than a stretching of that chain to the breaking point without assuming the responsibility for severing it irreparably.

For one thing, Jews who had thrown off the yoke of mitzvot which claimed the authority of Sinai have been among those most visibly subject to a different and more immediate imperative, associated not with Moses but with Freud. As a consequence, I shall argue, they have remained under the sway of Moses' authority as well, their practice commanded not only in a psychological sense, their compliance and deviance both highly charged. No less important, the same patterns are evident when we turn to adherents of stricter observance or to elite thinkers devoted to justifying this observance. Such Jews, believing themselves commanded to remember the ancestors and to do, at least selectively, as they did, have made practices which seem to follow in the ways of the ancestors more salient than ever before and have awarded that reason for observance—always an important component of Jewish commandedness—a centrality that it likely never before possessed. Discontinuity with the past has rendered the memory and merits of those who inhabited it all the more precious a resource for religious and "secular" commitments alike.

When distinctively Jewish behavior is undertaken by Jews who feel that they cannot or should not do otherwise; when such activity grows out of and bears witness to a deep-seated and seemingly inescapable relation to immediate and/or extended Jewish families; when Jews act as they do in order to follow or reconnect with ancestors who demand reenactment of the past through their progeny's agency, as these ancestors connected with their own ancestors—then, I would argue, a strict dichotomy between mitzvah and nostalgia will not suffice, any more than the related dichotomies tradition/modernity and ritual/rationality will. Subtler gradations and combinations are required.

I. HOMECOMING TO ALSACE

We shall begin the attempt to provide these needed subtleties by analyzing a French text, published in 1860, that was one of the first to offer its readers a pilgrimage back in space and time to the sacred precincts of authentic ancestral Judaism: Daniel Stauben's *Scènes de la vie juive en Alsace*. The author behind the pen name was Auguste Widal, a professor at the Sorbonne, whose letters from Alsace first appeared in the *Archives israélites de France* from 1849 to 1853 and who, as one would expect from their placement in Cahen's journal, advocated both reform and "conservation" of the Jewish "past" that was then still on view in the Alsatian present. Historians Richard Cohen and Paula Hyman place Stauben's *Scènes* among the spate of mid-nineteenth-century Jewish remembrances of things past or believed past, a genre which included collections and exhibitions of Jewish ritual objects; the tales of Jewish village life by Berthold Auerbach, Leopold Kompert, and Alexandre Weill; and the depictions of Jewish vignettes and characters on canvas by Simeon Solomon and Moritz Oppenheim. The dramatic difference between Solomon and Oppenheim perhaps sums up the range of attitudes toward the "vanishing Jewish world" that was evinced by the labors of nostalgia more generally. Solomon presented decrepit Jews bereft of happiness. Oppenheim painted family scenes of warmth and charm. But much united them as well, most importantly, the assumption that the past *was* past. Ritual objects displayed on the mantelpiece were no longer taken down for routine use. Journeys to Alsatian villages were of interest to Parisian Jews ensconced for at least a generation in bourgeois urban neighborhoods precisely because they were now far enough removed from coerced observance to be curious about what it looked like.[4]

Thus Stauben tells us in his preface that he is visiting a "*sorte de civilisation*" characterized by "ancient belief" and "the miseries of the Middle Ages with its persecutions." One cannot really go back, nor would one want to. Indeed, his scenes are composed not only from what he has seen on recent voyages but from his "memories of childhood." All of this "*antiquité judaique contemporaine*" is, likewise, "alas! about to disappear."[5] The sigh is deep-felt, the regret sincere, and the interest in preserving the Judaism of the ancestors—except as a museum piece—close to nil.

And yet, of course, the analogy of the museum fails in one crucial respect. Stauben actually gets on the train at its newly completed station in Paris, changes to a local at Strasbourg, and sets foot the very same day in actual villages like Bollwiller, where tens of thousands of real Jews, his own family included, still lived in the 1860s, still spoke local Alsatian and Jewish dialects rather than French, did not dress in the latest fashion, and moved to the rhythm of the Jewish calendar that his essays tried to evoke. Stauben's travel guide proclaims and evinces a filial piety which extends to the tradition that in his pages visibly lives through the ancestors who lived by it. His readers had every opportunity to make the same voyage in his footsteps and, perhaps, affirmed similar loyalties in the very act of reading his account and entering the world of their own imaginative remembrances. The shtetl, as it were, was alive and at their door. They could and did go back to visit as tourists/pilgrims/homecomers. Emancipation in Paris, meanwhile, although an overwhelming reality possessed of powerful "plausibility structures," had been shown by the events of 1848 and subsequent years to be by no means irreversible, let alone entirely accomplished. This uncertainty about their new homes likely lent the reading of Stauben's narrative about the ancestral home a greater urgency. Its comforts were welcome, and perhaps necessary.

Several aspects of Stauben's journeys back to Judaism particularly draw my attention. The first is the idyllic account of Sabbath observance in the opening scene. As if he had read Eliade, Stauben joins the entry into sacred space with the onset of sacred time—as if in echo of the havdalah ritual, the separation of Israel from the nations, Alsace from Paris, is marked by the transition from sacred to profane, workaday week to Sabbath. The peddler who had made do with black bread and water all week sits at the table with his family for a meal of fish and beef. All enjoy the respite from daily cares, give each other the blessing of peace, join in prayer. Oppenheim, as we have seen, lavished attention on the beauties of the Sabbath, and so did Léon Cahun, in *La Vie juive* (1886), a similar portrait of Jewish life as practiced in Alsace, illustrated by Alphonse Lévy. Cahun and Lévy show us women lighting candles, fathers returning from synagogue in the snow bearing blessings for their wives and children, men reciting kiddush. "Oh, fine wine of childhood," the author sighs. "What piety and memory of grace you have left behind, and how much I regret the . . . irreligion of the present age!"[6]

The pride of place given to food in all these remembrances—Lévy's in particular—is striking. One suspects that it is what the artists and their public most vividly recalled.[7] "I have never again attained the height of belief and pleasure on which I stood as a child on the Sabbath and holiday eves. Bring back the Friday evening and you will save Judaism," writes one of Richarz's memoirists. Others concur.[8] Stauben, too, bathes his readers in

these purifying waters. Once his Alsatian Jews have recited the words "shalom aleichem," welcoming in peace the Sabbath "angels of peace," "*la
fête*"—and, with it, his book—"*est commencée.*"

However, the account of Sabbath pleasures gives way within the space
of only a few pages—via the visit of a neighbor who, we are told, habitually
visited on Friday evenings and told tales—to a much darker canvas of devils
and demonry. Stauben likewise shifts tone to a not always gentle irony. Samuel, the neighbor, tells a story about his grandfather, who had been on a
journey to a neighboring village one Saturday night and was imperiled by
demons on the way until he threw his tefillen at them, as he had been
instructed to do by "the old great Rabbi Hirsch, a master of kabbalah."
When he arrived at his destination, Samuel's grandfather discovered that a
newborn infant had vanished that very evening and had later been found
outside an open window, blue in the face but miraculously still breathing.
The old man inquired about the sin that might have exposed the family to
this near catastrophe. Had they said their prayers? Recited the psalms required in a room where mother and baby were asleep? Made the requisite
circles around the infant's head (described by Stauben in a footnote) "to
chase away the evil spirits"? Aha!—they had forgotten the circles. Fortu-
nately Samuel's grandfather had saved the baby by his kabbalistic magic on
the road. "If your child is still alive, you have me to thank for it," he told
them, and without further ado set out for home and further adventures.[9]

This is not the last that Stauben's readers will hear of magic, superstition,
or the demons of Alsace. He returns to them again and again, and even
treats us at one point to a long account of a wonder-working rabbi of
Prague. One is charmed by the stories—yet, of course, distanced by their
quite literal charms. Stauben, as the narrator, always takes care to distance
himself, by attributing the magic stories to a well-known raconteur, himself
fairly comic, who in the case of the rabbi of Prague, as of the baby outside
the window, passes on a story of *his* grandfather. The Alsatian relatives are
probably no less incredulous than their Parisian guest. Yet the Parisian reader
can henceforth not see Alsace except as a place where superstition is very
much alive and inseparable from the Jewish rituals observed there, as well it
might have been.[10] His or her own journey, like the journeys inside the tale-
within-a-tale, leads to a not yet disenchanted world where rationality still
does not hold sway over common sense.

One might well wonder, reading Stauben's account and others like it,
what Alsatian Jews believed in *besides* spirits. For the most part, Stauben
simply does not tell us. The varied interests that he had confessed at the

outset quickly pass by "ideas" in the course of the work and arrive at "rites, ceremonies, superstitions, ways of life, provincial types, and holidays." Chapter 3 takes us to preparations for a wedding, which is celebrated in chapters 4 and 5. Stauben begins his account early in the morning and ends it with the late-night banquet. The rites under the canopy play a minor part, and none of the benedictions uttered there, or any other tokens of formal belief, are even mentioned Instead we are told about the bride's jewelry, the jokes and intrigues of the characters seated at the author's table. The final tableau in the first set of scenes in *Scènes* is the funeral of a child, and there too we witness the procession, the burial, and the shivah (the formal period of mourning) that follows, all recounted tenderly but without any attempt to penetrate the mourners' heads or hearts. Instead, we are given insight into the consciousness of the elegiac narrator, and his feelings at *his* loss and that of his readers. "When I had to return to this Paris, where, for us other transplanted Alsatian Israelites, the religion and customs of the ancestors are too quickly, alas, reduced to the state of souvenirs, I promised myself to undertake a new pilgrimage at the first opportunity." [11]

Indeed, he does go back—this time to recount the "Jewish festivals of spring and autumn"—and, again, the focus is on ritual. We learn that Passover recalls the Exodus from Egypt, of course, and that Alsatian Jews observed the holiday with a "minute exactitude" which "no doubt exaggerated the intention of the Hebrew legislator." The symbolism of the apparently "bizarre" items displayed on the seder table is exposited conventionally in a phrase or two: a hard-boiled egg for the bitterness of slavery, *charoset* for the bricks the Israelites had made for Pharaoh, and so on. [12] Lévy, entirely ignoring the seder itself, presents a woman preparing matzah balls, her face suffused with inner bliss, her hands crossed to work with the matzah meal in a way reminiscent of prayer. [13] Cahun digresses from the ritual of the seder—perhaps in the spirit of the open-ended Haggadah—for a lengthy recounting of a legend about a pious tailor, told "in memory of my father," who, we now confirm, was none other than the schoolteacher Anselme, the principal subject of Cahun's vignettes. [14]

Stauben, still more remarkably, introduces us to a beggar seated at the seder table, a schnorrer and sometime bookseller called Lazare, who joined the family's celebration each year in obedience to the Haggadah's invitation "Let all who are hungry come and eat." Lazare was, Stauben remarks, the very personification of the Wandering Jew. When asked what is new with him, the beggar treats the assemblage to an attack on the Reformist sentiments which we heard Stauben expressing only a few pages before. Why bother translating the Bible or prayer book or Haggadah into French? Did God want to be entreated in any language other than the one the ancestors had spoken in Palestine? Indeed, he adds, most of the people who bought these new French books from him did not speak the language any better than those around the table! They just wanted to be in style. Misfortune was on its way. The impious reformers of Paris would lead only to "*des malheurs*." [15]

This is noteworthy: Stauben, through a character at once easy to dismiss and easy to take as a vestige of the acculturated Jew's worst nightmares, has raised the issue of actual versus vicarious observance. If Lazare was wrong and Judaism was not an all-or-nothing matter—outmoded, superstitious observance or no observance whatsoever—what then? But Stauben acts immediately to banish this suggestion. It comes via a silly beggar, and Stauben's audience, unlike Lazare's, does read French. And Parisians were no longer wandering Jews! They were at home.

Stauben takes us to synagogue, finds no meaning there worth describing, and then dwells at length on the terrors of the Omer (the seven weeks between Passover and Shavuot), when "the influence of evil spirits is felt on every side." [16] Shavuot means a new scroll for the synagogue, and the proud return of a soldier from the army—not the feast of revelation. On the high holidays, Stauben is in Witzenheim. "If you would know the austere grandeur of these religious exercises which occur every year at this time according to invariable traditions, it is again in one of the curious Jewish villages of Alsace that you must place yourself." [17] The issue of performing the rites in Paris with equal devotion does not arise.

After more superstition, we finally do get sustained attention to part of the content of one religious service, that of Rosh Hashanah, via a long account of Rabbi Amnon of Mayence and his *u'netaneh tokef* prayer, a major element in the day's liturgy. Stauben dwells almost lovingly on the persecutions of Jews over the ages and adds in a striking footnote that "even in Paris" the holiday is celebrated with particular receptivity. [18] His account of Alsace's "invariable tradition" remarkably lacks any reference to the major elements of the Yom Kippur prayers, however. It is dominated instead by the long tale of premodern martyrdom and a report of a symbolic flagellation the day before Yom Kippur in which each man beats his neighbor lightly thirty-nine times. [19]

Cahun, for his part, instructs his audience that if ever the temptation of apostasy should beset modern Jews, the memory of the *kappores* ceremony would cause the image of beloved parents to appear before their eyes, a world of innocence and tenderness that no theology or vanity could oppose. Ritual, and the memories of childhood that it evoked, would suffice to keep Jews Jewish and Judaism alive forever.[20] At Cahun's seder table, the father begs his children not to forget him, to live piously, to say kaddish for him after his death, and to be buried next to him when their own time on earth expires.[21] Fast or feast, the modern rites of remembrance focus on parental enactments, sufferings escaped, death confronted and overcome—themes prominent in traditional liturgy and practice as well.

2. REMEMBERING THE ANCESTORS

Widal's pilgrimage—like Stauben's tales—was very much a creation of its time and place. George Herbert, in a rich study situating French impressionism in Parisian society at midcentury, identifies two aspects of that artistic movement which directly bear on our own inquiry.

The first was the impressionists' renunciation of history, mythology, and religion in favor of the contemporary world. They drew their subjects from Paris and its suburbs and were attracted by "the new Paris, not by the quaint old streets or buildings." Indeed, Herbert continues, the old was increasingly no longer visible, no longer there to be depicted. It had to be seen elsewhere or to be recollected. The painters presented this new world in a detached manner that mirrored the attitude of their subjects. Think of Gustave Caillebotte's *Young Man at His Window,* from 1875 (see figure 3), in which we see the back of a pensive, solitary man standing at the window of his bourgeois apartment and gazing out at the wide street and new buildings in one of the fashionable neighborhoods constructed by Haussmann over the ashes of the old Paris razed for that purpose. "Caillebotte's figure," notes Herbert, "is the thoughtful observer, the characteristic urban person who appears in so much naturalist literature of the period, in the act of seeking the meaning of private interior versus public exterior." In Berthe Morisot's *Interior* (1872) too, the artist is a "stranger," detached, seemingly nonjudgmental in depiction, thereby adopting the urban pose portrayed on the canvas.[22] We know this type well from Peter Gay's account of bourgeois sensibility. Privacy became a passion in the mid–nineteenth century. Anxiety was kept hidden from view.[23] A new attitude toward self held that one *owned* one's emotions. There was pleasure in calling them to mind in a way that did not involve exhibition or loss of control.[24]

Yet there was of course another major subject for impressionism: the leisure-time return to pastoral haunts removed from—but easily accessible

FIGURE 3. Gustave Caillebotte, *Jeune homme à sa fenêtre* [Young man at his window] (1875). Private collection— Photographie Brame & Lorenceau, Paris.

to—the workaday urban world. Many paintings placed contemporary Parisians among living vestiges of the past and, in so doing, emphasized the gulf between the two. The opening of train service to the countryside made such depictions easily available to the artists and increasingly familiar to their audience. Advertising and travel literature sponsored by the railways worked to get Parisians on the trains. New sorts of tourist guides featured visits to village festivals and pictured locals in native costume. The latter "became living illustrations, so that visitors could find the picturesque life that proved their distance from home."[25]

The parallels to Stauben are pronounced. He too stood in between Parisian Jews detached from their inheritance and the locals still performing the past in native dress. His scenes of Alsace depicted his subjects lovingly, drew the reader close to them and their picturesque ways, but rarely surrendered an ironic distance. Emotion is rife in the vignettes Stauben portrayed and apparently was not lacking in the author himself. At times it bursts through the plane of the printed page in a way which may lead us to suspect that the rituals of the ancestors—always a directed outlet for the emotions—served something of the same function for Stauben's readers, albeit—like the impressionist canvases—at one remove. Parisians let themselves go at the seashore or in the country; when they viewed paintings of the seashore, they could recall those sentiments, feel them to a degree, while maintaining proper museum etiquette—which, of course, demanded a saving distance.

The complex relation of present to past in impressionist paintings was also mirrored in Stauben's text. Manet, Herbert explains, overturned conventions happily, "uprooted tradition in the very way he composed his picture," made fun of social and artistic traditions even as he preserved them on his canvases. Mythological figures appeared clad in contemporary costume. Artistic precedents were cited, rearranged, and of course rendered subservient to the intentions of the living artist—and yet those very borrowings sustained and kept on view the conventions against which Manet rebelled. Manet aroused (and made use of) his viewers' nostalgia, by presenting scenes that were safely contained both by the frame of his paintings and by the train schedules of their Sunday outings.[26] Tradition is similarly present on every page of Stauben's treatment of Jewish ceremonies, ordered and edited to suit his purpose. Much that we expect is *not* there, particularly that which cannot be painted on a canvas: content, belief, faith in that which—by definition, in Judaism—cannot be seen. The focus of his subjects' observances is displaced by Stauben's modern observation of them and bracketed for his readers by the fact that they see their own ancestors through his eyes and encounter them within the binding of his book. In this respect, both Stauben and the impressionists drew upon and furthered the work of folklorists such as Champfleury, whose influential *Histoire de l'imagerie populaire* (1869) anthologized and propagated verbal as well as pictorial representations of the vanishing world about which urban Frenchmen at midcentury were eager to learn.

One further commonality between Stauben's work and that of the impressionists alerts us that the past remembered and rearranged in the artistic creations of midcentury was not entirely a happy one: their use of the image of the Wandering Jew, "a key personage of mid-century realism."[27] The Jewish literature of nostalgia frequently reverted to Jewish sufferings in times past, perhaps to elicit the readers' gratitude that the past was safely past, on the far side of 1789. Only once, however, and only for a moment, do

FIGURE 4. Edouard Manet, *The Old Musician* (1862). Chester Dale Collection, ©
Board of Trustees, National Gallery of Art, Washington, D.C.

Stauben's readers confront a present challenge and glimpse a continuing
nightmare, in the person of Lazare: the beggar at the seder table, the *Ostjude*
at the door, "the very personification of the Wandering Jew." The modern
eye refocuses the tradition, we might say, sees for the most part what it
wants to see but, occasionally, that eye too can—or, perhaps, must—
wander.

Off to the far right of Manet's painting *The Old Musician* (1862) (see
figure 4), among a group of figures around a fiddler, all of whom seem
"arbitrarily clothed and placed as though they had walked on from different
dressing rooms," we find the beard, cane, long coat, and wrinkled face of
the Wandering Jew.[28] Courbet had drawn on the archetypal image in a major canvas of the 1850s, *The Meeting,* and his friend Champfleury would
place the *juif errant* on the frontispiece of *Histoire de l'imagerie populaire.* The
figure had taken on a positive valence in leftist circles by midcentury. Jews
were already the consummate Other, representing society's victims. Indeed,
in *The Meeting,* Courbet appropriated the image to depict himself as the
artist-outsider (encountering, in this instance, his burgher-patron) and, as
such, a speaker of truth.[29] One suspects that Stauben used the archetype for

FIGURE 5. *Un Iéré-chalmé* [A Jerusa-lemite]. Illustration by Alphonse Lévy for Léon Cahun, *La Vie juive* (Paris: Monnier de Brunhoff, 1886).

precisely the same purpose. Lazare served as a mouthpiece for truths and anxieties that the readers of *Scènes* would not have been willing to hear had they been uttered in his own voice or even in Stauben's. In Cahun's gallery of images, the Wandering Jew surfaces twice: once as a peddler with a pack on his back and a walking stick in his hand, and once as *"un Iéréchalmé"* resting wearily on a bench with an indistinct sword or walking stick propped at his side, his costume exotic and his days clearly numbered (see figure 5).[30]

What are we to make of the presence of the *juif errant* in works that would be seen by cosmopolitan French Jews who had hoped to leave him behind them in Alsace along with the rest of their ancestors' superstitions and sufferings? Jews were apparently no more able to banish the wandering Jewish *Ostjude* from impressionist canvases or from the French popular imagination than they were able to eliminate him from their own recollections and dark imaginings. Some of the memories of childhood that pervade Richarz's anthology of German Jewish memoirs are bathed entirely in light:

food aplenty, blessings bestowed by loving parents, the Sabbath table laid with song. But there are darker memories as well: beatings, ridicule by parents and playmates, praise of children who did not look Jewish, decrepit synagogues, "repulsive carryings-on."[31] The importance of this material for us lies not in the validity of the remembrances—their coloring by ideologies such as Reform and Zionism is often pronounced—but the repeated association of parents with negative as well as positive images of Judaism. There is a mix of love and violence, pride and ridicule, meaning and boredom, piety and arrogance, pleasant curiosity and unwelcome restraint. In French materials, too, the ambivalence—true to life, as well as to dreams and nightmares—is often enough not recognized by the memoirists themselves. One person's nightmare can easily become another's entertainment, of course, and vice versa; Jews may have internalized, and to a degree even neutralized, images current in the Gentile world that increasingly shaped their imaginations. But the symbol for the Other lauded by Courbet (or Lyotard!) could hardly have been viewed dispassionately by those whom it stigmatized and threatened. A more powerful drive to remembrance was apparently operative.

It will become clear as we probe the images and counterimages of Jewish remembrance, I think, that without Jewish nightmares there could be no Jewish nostalgia: no need for its heavily edited remembrances and belabored forgettings, no raw material for the dreams of wish fulfillment directly expressed in nostalgia or the nightmares that not infrequently appear in distorted form or at the margins of remembrance, precisely as the Wandering Jew appears on Manet's canvas. I want to attend more closely to these images and counterimages, then, to gain insight into what mid- and late-century modern Jews were simultaneously fleeing and taking such good care to remember.

3 . THE SERVICE OF THE ANCESTORS

The principal clue is furnished by the principal players in modern Jewish memory: the ancestors themselves. "Formerly our ancestors rendered important services to their contemporaries," an article in *Univers* declared in 1851.[32] Five of the services rendered to their descendants, functions served via recollection, are on view in the French- and the Anglo-Jewish press. All are uncannily continuous with roles which the ancestors have played in Jewish texts and traditions for centuries.

The first was to make vivid—to drive home, as it were—*the contrast between Judaism's past centrality to Jewish life and its present irrelevence*—a contrast attributable in large part to contemporary backsliding from the ideals and achievements of former times. No theme is more pervasive in the two French-Jewish newspapers of the period. Samuel Cahen, as we have seen, declared the restoration of Jewish practice his objective in the very first issue of the *Archives israélites de France* in 1840 and consistently advocated moderate reform of school, synagogue, and consistory as the way to achieve it. He described the conditions of the day as "indifference and irreligion on the one hand, superstition and ignorance on the other.[33] Simon Bloch's orientation in the *Univers* was more favorable to modern Orthodoxy and more hostile to Reform but no different in the evaluation of his generation and the need to recall it to the ways of the ancestors, in part by recalling those ancestors. Bloch sadly noted the contest between "*orthodoxie*" and "*les hommes du progrès,*" and he attacked the mass of indifferent Jews who would fight forcefully for the principle of religious equality but had no interest in actual religious observance and, as such, were its adversaries. "What does freedom for the synagogue matter if one never visits it . . . ,[or] the free exercise of our ceremonies, which they have forgotten or find ridiculous?"[34] The *Jewish Chronicle* of London—its editors utterly disinterested in religious observance, except when they were driven to complain of excessive rigidity on the part of the chief rabbi—was no less critical than its French counterparts about widespread alienation, ignorance, and apathy.[35]

The ridicule of practice seemed to decline over the years, if the papers are any indication, as sheer indifference grew. Jews a full generation away from observance were no longer intolerant but, instead, simply ignorant—and were in some cases willing to venture a cautious and partial return. Cahen well understood the difficulty rabbis faced in addressing sermons in 1857 to people "living this new life, accelerated, feverish, full of inventions, communications, and revolutions": congregants of diverse stations and interests for whom religion could no longer be "their entire existence" or "the sole object of their thoughts." The key to resisting these various sources of distraction lay in a yearlong round of observances.[36] Bloch, too, mourned the abandonment of Jewish life and mores, the effacement of distinctions between Jews and Gentiles. Parents who had rejected the table of their parents for "social banquets, feasts prohibited by the law of our God," found that their own children had now in turn departed "the paternal home, its teachings and traditions, in order to stray" in foreign footpaths. Did anyone still remember the pious virtues of our parents, the austerity of their conduct, the sanctity of their domestic life? "Who would dare respond to this question in the affirmative?"[37] In 1863, Bloch transmitted the chief rabbi's report that young men were celebrating their bar mitzvah in Paris without being able to read a single verse of the Torah in Hebrew—a perfect enactment of the combined remembrance and forgetting which we have discovered throughout.[38]

The young Zadok Kahn, in his inaugural address as chief rabbi of Paris in 1869, did not call for rigorous observance or traditional belief but, rather, for an end to Judaism's perceived irrelevance. "The beautiful practices of Judaism have more or less disappeared from our homes, and all we have left is the debris of our ancient piety."[39] Isadore Cahen, who assumed editorship of the *Archives* in 1862 upon his father's death, wrote in 1874 that the decline in religious observance was common to all faiths, a function of the reigning indifference, and not at all unique to Jews, an account which implicitly contained its own explanation and justification.[40] The times, and not only the Jews, were at fault. Indeed, the *Jewish Chronicle* seemed on occasion to mention traditional observances such as the Ninth of Av and Passover only to stress the degree to which contemporary Jews in England had happily departed from the woeful conditions which the holidays recalled.[41]

The generational divide separating children (and, still more, grandchildren) from their elders and more remote ancestors featured prominently in a second unfavorable comparison between present-day Jewish life and its exalted past: *the critique of the community's religious leadership.* One of Bloch's most frequent contributors, Rabbi S. Dreyfuss of Mulhouse, shrewdly characterized his colleagues in 1844 as well-intentioned, favorable to ideas of progress, and attached to well-formulated beliefs that had been sanctioned by the universalism of the times. They would defend Judaism should it be in jeopardy but lacked awareness of their own potential effectiveness.[42] Cahen, always more cautious in his criticism, noted dispassionately in 1853 that rabbis celebrated for learning and authority had become rare everywhere and particularly so in France, in part because French candidates for the rabbinate (like their German counterparts) had to dedicate so much time to acquiring "*les sciences profanes.*" He followed, in the next issue of *Archives,* with a thoughtful comparison "of the rabbi of former times and [that of] today" which highlighted not only the "strange costume, long beard, and language inspiring profound respect" of the rabbis of old but the lessons in Talmud which they provided—no longer a feature of the job description. Cahen noted by way of explanation that rabbis in former eras had not had to carry messages of consolation and instruction via pastoral work in prisons, hospitals, and homes. The matter, he concluded circumspectly, demanded the attention of the consistories.[43] Dreyfuss, in a letter to the *Archives,* was far less charitable. Jewish assimilation to the ways of their non-Jewish fellow citizens had been virtually the only goal of the consistories' official labors from their inception.[44]

Cahen's evaluation of the situation was on target—but so, however, was Dreyfuss's contention that French rabbis could not convincingly summon their congregants to return to the ways of the ancestors when they themselves were so palpably different from rabbinic predecessors. No departure from tradition was more notable or more damning than lack of command of the texts which for over a thousand years had been the source of rabbinic authority.[45]

Yet the call that resounded in the literature of nostalgia from the 1840s onward—the third service performed by the ancestors, declaimed by rabbis and laypeople alike—*summoned Jews precisely to return to, and identify with, the ways of the ancestors.* Jews were not urged back to the commandments with Mendelssohn's argument that the mitzvot structured a reality, ordered a community, inside which eternal truths could fruitfully be apprehended and virtue learned and practiced. Nor were the commandments defended, following Hirsch, as a symbolic expression of truth, a rationally defensible and completely comprehensive regimen of the highest pedagogical value. It should go without saying that almost no one spoke, in this context, of unquestioned obligation to laws given to Moses in a divine revelation at Sinai and thus binding upon every Jew ever since. Even the chief rabbi of England, urging Jews not to transgress the prohibition against eating flesh not sanctified by kosher slaughter, invoked "sanitary" and "moral" grounds before pleading, "Is it right, I ask you, to forfeit . . . eternal bliss for a mere tickling of the palate?"[46] Rather, the rabbis, editors, and publicists of France and England stressed the obligation to follow in the paths of parents, grandparents, and more distant ancestors. Few specifics were provided, and those pertained almost entirely to the realm of observance rather than belief. "Our faith contains a very small number of dogmas and devotes great effort to action," declared the *Archives* in 1869.[47] One suspects that the authors fastened on the appeal to ancestors because they believed it would be more effective than any other argument for observance that they could muster.

Thus Bloch, applauding the dedication of a small *oratoire* by a Jewish charitable society in 1857, wrote that in such modest sanctuaries, "the faithful find once again the traditions of their fathers, the pious habits of youth, the sacred chants of the village synagogue[,] . . . a religious family. . . . There one can again pray for one's dead parents, receive one's son into the covenant of Abraham, observe feasts and mourning."[48] The chief rabbi of the consistory gave voice to this convention when he asked whether the "family of Jacob," scattered around the globe, enveloped by the movement and spirit transforming the world, had "rested faithful to its mission, conserved its attachment to the antique faith of its fathers," or, rather, in its enthusiasm for progress and all that was modern, had it "broken with tradition, abjured its past."[49] Kahn made precisely the same point and used precisely the same tropes.[50] Even the *Jewish Chronicle,* no fan of "excessive" belief or observance, explained and recommended Passover observance as a way of stressing the importance of redemption and of maintaining one's "subtle yet powerful ties" to the victims of Pharaoh's tyranny.[51] The Jew, by observing the holiday, "recognizes as his own the history of his race" and demonstrates the appeal exerted by "historic consciousness." For that same reason, the Ninth of Av, too, should not be treated with indifference, even though exile was far from the reality of life in England. One should identify with the ancestors, show concern for past disasters, and work all the while to ensure that the conditions of the past would never return in England and would soon be eradicated elsewhere.[52]

Historical essays about the Jewish past, sentimental feuilletons about pious Jews of former generations, and advertisements for works of Jewish art—another emergent genre—all served as vehicles for the same appeal.[53] Bloch used the creation of a *"tableau grandiose"* to discourse upon the custom of gathering at the Western Wall on Friday afternoons before the Sabbath and upon the significance of the site itself.[54] In contrast, the *Chronicle* never devoted much space in its spare and sober columns to descriptions of religious practice and always preferred irony to sentimentality (as in a wonderful exchange concerning the Jewish delight in gefilte fish at Passover).[55] Yet it lavished attention and column inches on notable persons and events in the past, particularly on recently departed ancestors such as Mendelssohn and Zunz. The *Chronicle*'s editors held these men up as role models because they had been faithful to tradition even while altering it in accord with their awareness of the Jews' evolving history.[56] The paper even sought to excite its readers about Passover observance with news of recent archaeological discoveries that filled in and lent credence to the biblical account.[57]

No event so captured the *Chronicle*'s attention in the last four decades of the century, or was covered so generously in its pages, as the *Anglo-Jewish Historical Exhibition* held at the Albert Hall in 1887.[58] The great German-

Jewish historian Heinrich Graetz, in an address that was one of the exhibition's highlights, displeased the *Chronicle* intensely by calling for the founding of a research academy in England that would pursue scholarly inquiry into the glorious past presented so dramatically at the Albert Hall.[59] The rest of his address, however, likely captured the sentiments of the paper and its readers—articulating both dreams and nightmares—with precision. Graetz began by discoursing on the recent reworking of the myth of the Wandering Jew. A degraded outcast in its German incarnation had in France become ennobled. That was fitting, for Israel stood with downcast eyes no longer.

> This brilliant assembly, the elite of Judaism, who have established a Jewish Historical Exhibition to display to our eyes the antiquities of our past, the outward signs of our former conditions—this assembly speaks more clearly and efficaciously of our marvelous metamorphosis, of our rise and phenomenal position, than any picture in words, however dramatic it might be.

The exhibit displayed the "inner connection of your Past and your Present." English Jews were "patriots attached to this happy isle" but, as such, wanted nonetheless to "preserve connection and continuity with the long series of generations of Israel."[60]

Jews and Gentiles flocked to the Albert Hall against a backdrop of political events that had once more brought the specter of dual loyalties to the forefront of public debate.[61] Graetz's rhetorical progress from Wandering Jew through "marvelous metamorphosis" to "phenomenal present" conferred the blessing of Jewish history—already the term of authority for many English Jews—on the cognitive and behavioral moves which those Jews had enacted. They had ceased to identify with ancestors by means of performing the *religious* commandments that the ancestors had performed, adopting instead a mental and emotional identification, a felt connection with the ancestors, accomplished by viewing ritual and historical objects associated *culturally* with the ancestors' acts and lives. Advocates of that new identity, in the nineteenth century and our own, have not held up the ancestors as models of piety to be emulated—the service traditionally rendered by Jewish ancestors in this connection. Rather, such advocates have summoned loyalty to the ancestors themselves—Jews of another time and place who, like Jews in the present, had wandered far from their own homes, altered tradition in keeping with the times, but retained enough of what they inherited to pass something down. These reclaimed ancestors had provided ample material for exhibitions, and more than enough cause for celebration.

This appeal to ancestors and history, as we have seen, was characteristically lacking in specific doctrinal content—probably the reason for the rabbis' well-founded expectation that it would be effective. Rather, the genre of nostalgia provided *pictures* of traditional Jewish life—**Scènes** *de la vie juive* and **Scènes** *familiales juives*—but rarely probed beneath the surface (except to spotlight superstition) to discover what the Jews whom it portrayed did and did not believe. This tendency was integrally related to the fourth service rendered by the ancestors: an *emphasis on aesthetic reform in the synagogue,* which in England and France, unlike in Germany, was generally dissociated from any call for the overhaul of practice more generally, let alone of belief. Calls for decorum, and celebrations of its achievement, remained commonplace throughout the century.[62]

One might have thought that invocation of the ancestors in this connection would have been dysfunctional. What was the generation of mid-century abandoning, after all, if not the chaos, hubbub, genuflection, and huckstering that, according to the standard Haskalah critique, had characterized Orthodox practice for centuries? Why else the pride in grand edifices designed in cathedral style, and the distrust of smaller oratories where the manner of prayer more closely resembled eastern European ancestral precedent? And didn't the focus on aesthetics marginalize matters of belief and content that to the ancestors had been matters of life and death? Here, too, however, the ancestors were invoked in the name of tradition expressly to justify departures from tradition, in two quite different ways.

The first, mentioned in Chapter 4, was reference to Sephardic rite and architecture, which were held to be nobler—"cleaner," as it were—in their liturgical and architectural lines. Jewish critics would not appeal to the authority of Christian or Islamic models. Cahun's volume presented another model, closer to home: the sketch of an Alsatian synagogue interior that is simple, quiet, and dignified—the same qualities evident in the symmetrical portrait of a rabbi attired entirely in white, his beard neatly trimmed, his eyes directed beneficently and with great inner dignity at the prayer book held in his graceful hands (see figures 6 and 7).[63]

These idealized images of synagogues past and future are not merely selective—a feature not limited to nostalgia, of course, but rather basic to the functioning of every live tradition. They are selective in the fashion specific to adult children who skip over the nearer past of parents in favor of ancestors further removed. Elite thinkers in the modern period, following Mendelssohn's lead, have regularly engaged in precisely the same exercise. Geiger, for example, lauded and romanticized the biblical and rabbinic periods of the Jewish past, those most distant from himself, lavishing upon them

FIGURE 6. *Intérieur de synagogue* [Synagogue interior]. Illustration by Alphonse Lévy for Léon Cahun, *La Vie juive* (Paris: Monnier de Brunhoff, 1886).

such adjectives of praise as "free" and "creative." Generations and centuries nearer to hand, a "toilsome millennium," had allowed Judaism to degenerate into "rigid legalism [and] casuistry." Geiger's chosen task was to liberate Judaism, to loosen the fetters imposed in the immediately previous era, by recalling the honored ancestral dead who, when they lived, had created a Judaism admirably free and vital. More recent generations had done nothing to bring those ancestors and their tradition back to life, indeed, one might say, had killed them by abandoning their precedent of redefining Judaism. The memory of these ancient reformers, to be rekindled through the new Reformers' scholarship, would "revitalize Judaism and . . . cause the stream of history to flow forth once again."[64]

FIGURE 7. *Le Rabbin* [The rabbi]. Illustration by Alphonse Lévy for Léon Cahun, *La Vie juive* (Paris: Monnier de Brunhoff, 1886).

Ancestors thus selectively remembered, whether verbally or architecturally, conferred their blessing upon change. Grandparents are able to legitimate disobedience that parents, for obvious reasons, cannot countenance. The ancestors too had been guilty of backsliding, after all. They too had wandered, even sinned grievously, and had been forgiven. Memoirists consistently remember these departures from the previous generation's ways: the first violation of the Yom Kippur fast, the first nonkosher meal.[65] In the sort of translation pervasive in the literature of nostalgia, "forgiveness" meant that the straying ancestors had taken their place on the canvas of Jewish memory, thereby enabling their descendants to rest confident that their deeds, too, would be accepted—that is to say, remembered.

There was one final break with the past for which French Jews, in particular, required their ancestor's blessing: *the unreserved embrace of national loyalties.* This fifth service rendered by the ancestors eased the forming of an attach-

ment which—as became clear with the Franco-Prussian War of 1870—
carried with it the consequence that Jews would come into mortal conflict
with "coreligionists" who had pledged other allegiances. The pathos of this
development is extraordinary to behold. Isadore Cahen, defending his paper's engagement with a political rather than strictly religious matter—the
war between "*notre patrie*" and Prussia—noted that human beings in large
numbers were about to be killed—this, when religion saw all human beings
as brothers. What was more, many coreligionists, living on one or the other
side of the Rhine, were about to confront each other directly in battle—
this, when individual Jews occupied positions of eminence in both of the
warring countries.[66] *Univers* a month later translated verse originally in German to tell the story of a German soldier, part of the army of occupation,
who, accompanied by a pitiful and pale boy from the community, appeared
one evening for Ma'ariv services at a synagogue in Alsace. "I am in mourning," both said. They needed to say kaddish. "Only one can recite the
prayer," replied the person conducting the service (apparently because he
was unsure of the stranger's motives). The soldier deferred to the youth,
whose mouth was "certainly purer than mine for prayer." After the service,
the rabbi approached the soldier and asked him confidentially whether he
was "one of ours, even though you belong to the enemy." "*Malheur, malheur!*" the rabbi cried, upon learning that he was. "You are a Jew and you
bear *des traits de mort* which, blindly and furiously, have bloodied so many
noble Jewish hearts. Your hand has destroyed those who are triply your
brothers: in faith, in race, and in common misery. *Hélas!*"[67]

Cahun recounted the arrival back home in Alsace of a soldier from an
earlier conflict, against a different foe, who had seen a Jewish friend cradling
in his arms a Russian soldier whom he had slain. The Russian, with his
dying breath, recited the Shema Yisrael. "Why not another?" wondered
the French soldier: "Why did I have to kill a Jew?"[68] The reader wonders
if Cahun was aware of the irony in his juxtaposition of this story with the
reference, in the very same Passover section, to Israelite warriors of long ago
who had died fighting for the Israelite homeland.[69] At another point in the
volume, Cahun imagined for his readers the day when the good people of
France would retake their conquered lands from the Germans. "That night,
whether the French sublieutenant who plants the first flag on the rampart
of Strasbourg is a Jew, a Catholic, or a Huguenot, whether Picard, Bourgu-
ignon, or Gascon (for my part, I would like it if his parents were Alsatian;
his religion does not matter to me)—that night, the tricolor will be illumined upon churches, temples, and synagogues. . . . And if it is a Jew who

makes the first breach, the first German who tries to bar his way, even if he be the greatest Talmudist of Germany, the most devout rabbi of Frankfort, Berlin, or Breslau, even if the law and the prophets are attached to his helmet, will receive his six inches of French steel in the stomach."[70]

The ancestors served two essential functions in regard to this awful dilemma for their descendants—functions which could only have been served by ancestors sufficiently removed by time, by numerous generations, to be the common patrimony of both the warring Jewish parties. The first was *comfort.* Cahen, in the wake of the French defeat, evoked the bitter reflections surging into Jewish hearts at the high holiday season. Wherever one turned, there were massacres and ruins. What could it all mean? What did it portend? "As awful as these trials to which we are summoned be, can we forget, we other Israelites, that our parents submitted to things still more terrible?" He urged "our brothers in Israel, who will soon in your temples celebrate the new year, to ask pardon for our sins . . . [and to] find courage in the Israelite past."[71]

No less important, however, the ancestors provided reassurance that *the choice for national loyalties over unity with "coreligionists" had not been a mistake.* The ancestors legitimated that choice by enacting it themselves, in memory.[72] Portrait after portrait in the historical exhibition in London memorialized English Jews who had been as devoted to king and country as to "race" and religion. The French Revolution, Cahun wrote, had enabled Jews to depart from Egypt a second time. His coreligionists therefore loved France as their ancestors had loved the Jewish fatherland. He recalled that his father—the schoolteacher Anselme, the protagonist of *La Vie juive*—had recounted each Passover the story of the Revolution, which his own father had witnessed. He had blessed the memory of the Abbé Grégoire, who had raised his voice in support of Israel. Citing the chant of Had Gadya, which concludes the seder—a singsong chain of mayhem and slaughter that begins with the purchase of an innocent goat by a boy's father for two zuzim and ends with the Angel of Death—Cahun asked whether the French Revolution was not the Angel of Death. He remembered "old Chmoul" [old Samuel] remembering prerevolutionary oppression of the Jews.[73]

Most remarkable of all, Cahun reported that every Yom Kippur eve, at the meal before the fast, his father would tell the story of his own father at Valmy (the site of a famous battle to save the Revolution from foreign forces), put the best piece of food on a plate, and set it aside, saying "*Tout pour le peuple français!*"[74] Father, fatherland, and the ancestors of Israel were powerfully conjoined at these festival tables—and, even if they weren't in actual fact, had become so in nostalgic memory on the printed page—just as, for centuries, Jews had been sustained in diaspora by the memory of generations who, like themselves, had sat together on holy days and uttered prayers longing for the messiah who would take them home to Zion.

4. RITUAL OBLIGATIONS AND COMPULSIONS

One turns to Freud's *Totem and Taboo* almost ineluctably after this encounter with Jewish ancestors incessantly forgotten and remembered in religious and quasi-religious rituals characterized by great ambivalence. Indeed, given the persistent focus of these rituals on food, they might well seem to be following a lesson plan drawn up by Freud or the anthropologists he cited. I recur to Freud here without any ambition to explain reductively the phenomenon of modern Jewish nostalgia. Freud's account is too ridden with contradictions and patent inadequacies to permit such explanation in any case. My aims are far more modest. I want to use several salient aspects of Freud's theory as an aid to reflection on the meanings and motives stored up in modern Jewish nostalgia.

It seems reasonable to assume, first of all, that the ceremonials of modern Jewish nostalgia have been and remain too pervasive, as well as too patterned, to be considered either spontaneous remembrances or the result of individual decisions to recall departed ancestors. A certain compulsion is evident in the ritual performances that we have surveyed, a sense of doing things that, for whatever reason, *must be done.* That compulsion is evinced as well in a behavior that in some ways is the very opposite of the first trait Freud associated with taboo: the refusal to question traditional observance.[75] Modern Jews, as we have seen, display an inability to *cease* questioning traditional observance even for a moment, to cease finding reasons for not following it, until those very reasons have become academic because the observance itself has receded from consciousness. One might say that the questioning of tradition in the first phase of departure from prescribed behavior is inversely proportional to actual observance and that—as Freud would lead us to expect—the energy of attention (and inattention!) then shifts to those remnants of practice which *are* enacted or which individuals think they perhaps *should* enact. One may, for example, be entirely unconscious of dietary laws when eating shellfish or a cheeseburger but may agonize over the question of fasting on Yom Kippur. A Jew of the mid-nineteenth century might long since have stopped thinking of the discrepancy between his or her Shabbat observance and that of his or her parents but might well wonder whether or not to light a memorial candle or say kaddish.

In further confirmation of Freud's suggestion, the practices that *are* engaged in have rarely been lent "intelligible meaning" by the conscious motivations and reasonings of the actors, least of all by their recurrent appeal to ancestors. That appeal is hardly a satisfactory explanation of behavior that so greatly *departs* from the ways of the ancestors, unless one recalls Freud's conviction that "the obsessional act is *ostensibly* [that is, consciously] a protection against the prohibited act[;] . . . *actually* [unconsciously], in our view, it is a repetition of it."[76] Observance simultaneously marks loyalty to ancestors and their ways and rebellion against them. The *ambivalent* character of modern Jewish nostalgia is certainly pronounced. In Freud's account, the reason for ambivalence is the clash between (repressed) desire and (conscious) prohibition.[77] Modern Jewish memories have generally comprised a mixture of light and shadow, idealization and its opposite, as the observances of nostalgia involve touching and refusing to touch the tradition, remembering and refusing to remember. One wonders, too, following Freud, whether it was perhaps the guilt of departing from the ways of their ancestors that resulted, within a few generations, in widespread and remarkable "forgetting" (that is, ignorance) of the specific practices and meanings of practice which had constituted those ways.

In Freudian theory, the real object of forgetting and remembrance, wish and fear, is the father (who, in the absence of convincing explanation to the contrary, can be joined here by the mother). To carry on an observance from one's parents is to make them live in and through that observance. Nothing is remembered so distinctly by adults at Passover seders, in the accounts we have surveyed, as the seders of childhood at which parents now departed had then presided. Immediate ancestors take their place at the table alongside the Israelites who departed Egypt long ago and the rabbinic ancestors who, as recounted in the Haggadah, also sat on this night with matzah and bitter herbs before them. *Not* to tell the story and perform the ritual means not to keep the ancestors alive in memory. To abandon Judaism is, in that psychological sense, to kill the parents/ancestors, by losing touch with what they had stood for and done. Many modern Jews have taken on that onus, as in a hundred and one mundane and tangible ways they have obeyed the desire to touch forbidden objects and to enter into forbidden pleasures—food, neighborhoods, occupations, studies, sexual partners—all the while resolutely avoiding contact with much that smacked of ancestral piety or orthodox belief. It is striking that traditional Jewish taboos, as Freud well knew from his experience of violating them, were "mainly directed against liberty of enjoyment and against freedom of movement and communication"—and so could not but come into conflict with "life, liberty, and the pursuit of happiness."[78]

The ritual acts of modern Jews, then, have been "overdetermined" in their ambivalence from the outset. Sons and daughters had departed the homes of fathers and mothers for urban centers, often leaving parents behind not only literally but figuratively. Cahun rectifies this at the end of his book, doubly legitimating his own departure for Paris, by having his father settle happily in the big city as well, where he continues to attend services but accepts inevitable modifications in his observance.[79] But historical consciousness, Weber hypothesized, cannot but represent a distancing from the past it brings closer, because it by definition surpasses and relativizes the realities which for the ancestors simply *were,* thereby elevating our world above theirs.[80] That same historical consciousness has, as we have seen, enabled many modern Jews to disclaim responsibility—or even agency—for their departures from parents, village, and tradition. *History* had moved one from Alsace to Paris, as it had brought the *"sorte de civilisation"* Stauben described to the verge of extinction. Hebrew poets of rebellion spoke of being "banished from their fathers' tables" rather than of themselves picking up and leaving so as to eat a more refined cuisine elsewhere.[81] All the more reason to study history (and the literature of rebellion), thereby remaining connected to the past in and through the very act of forsaking it. In this respect, too, remembrance has proved an ally of forgetfulness. As anthropologist Renato Rosaldo has remarked, "Nostalgia is a particularly appropriate emotion to invoke when attempting to establish one's innocence and at the same time talk about what one has destroyed."[82]

The sum of these factors would have been a sufficient source of guilt for modern Jews even without the fact—here, recall not only Freud but Rieff and Goffman—that the departure from the commandments also involved rebellion, conscious and unconscious, "noisy" and silent, *against the Commander* of the ancestors. The first generation to make that awesome break, as if following Freud's instructions in *Mourning and Melancholia,* and his theory of primitive death rituals in *Totem and Taboo,* seems to have summoned immense anger against both divine and human parents. Haskalah literature overflows with it; here and there one still encounters such militancy even today, particularly in the State of Israel. By the second or third generation removed from the site of piety, however, room has generally been made for a warmer glow of affection: that is, for nostalgia. Divine and human ancestors can, as it were, be invited to the tables of the grandchildren for an evening of remembering how things used to be, when commandments really commanded. Freud seems precisely on the mark: "They could attempt, in their relation to this surrogate father"—that is, ancient Israelite, pious grandparent, the tradition as a whole—"to allay their burning sense of guilt, to bring about a kind of reconciliation with their father." But they also needed to "repeat the crime of parricide again and again"—to stray from the divine and human parents, say, by eating matzah at the seder table along with nonkosher meat or by telling of the French Revolution far more than of the Israelite Exodus. "We shall not be surprised to find that the element of filial rebelliousness also emerges, in the later products of religion, often in the strangest disguises and transformations."[83]

And yet—the final twist in Freud's argument of relevance here—there is remembrance as well as forgetting in the appeal to ancestors, fidelity to as well as rebellion against parents acted out in apparent continuity with the forebears. The continuity is often more extensive than the participants (or their parents) have realized. Recall of ancestors has *always* been central to Jewish observance. The Passover seder explicitly recalls previous generations of celebrants. Jewish prayer features the ancestors prominently. Jews for at least two millennia have asked for help from the "Defender of Abraham" on the basis of their ancestors' merits when their own were deemed insufficient. "Ancestor worship" in the Jewish case, as in many others, has not connoted worship *of* the ancestors as gods but worship of God *through* them. One dares to call on God only because of what they have done; one presumes an intimacy to which they alone had been entitled; one returns to the site of their faithfulness, puts on their dress, eats their food, goes through their motions, in the hope of gaining some of the strength—moral or even physical—that they had possessed.[84]

French and English Jews were thus obeying rather than resisting ancient imperatives when they read contemporary political loyalties into their nostalgic remembrances or quelled their horror at killing fellow Jews in obedience to those loyalties via memories of parental injunctions and acts of ritual fealty. Ancestral nightmares, no less than ancestral dreams, lived on through present remembrance. A good night's sleep, as psychologist Joseph Reimer trenchantly puts it, often requires a good nightmare.[85] The ancient "compulsions"—we might summarize, with Freud's assistance—"lifted" no less ancient "prohibitions." Nostalgic observances, taken as a whole, made the larger transgression of acculturation or assimilation permissible, did penance for it, ennobled it with the ancestors' blessing.

This would hold, finally, even if (again breaking with Freud) we assume that all of us carry around—in acceptance, rebellion, or combinations of the two—images of God which are not only formed in childhood, from parental models, but constantly revised on the basis of a host of childhood, adolescent, and adult experiences.[86] Children might, as Freud believed, want God close at hand in order to succor and protect them. Adults, particularly in the modern period, might well prefer a God who remains at a distance: a Creator who brings them to the world, gives them general guidelines as to what to do there, and then leaves them to get down to work—preferably with the promises that their labors are bound to be for the good, no matter how they seem to turn out, and that they themselves, whatever their faults, are surely deserving of blessing. Worship and invocation of precisely this sort of God, in the name of the ancestors of Israel, is evident throughout the literature that we have surveyed in this chapter. The canon of nostalgia, as we have noted more than once, is short on references to revelation at Sinai. It says little concerning the how and why of creation and redemption. Specific injunctions to behavior are largely absent. Calls to morality, spirit, and fidelity to ancestors and tradition are by contrast legion. This was perhaps perfectly suited to the needs of Wandering Jews who had roamed far from God and commandments, as well as far from home, but did not wish to deny immortality either to the ancestors or to themselves. Their observances helped them to do good in the world in the absence of God's presence by bringing the ancestors close in ritual and using them to deem works of justice and truth the true fulfillment—far more than mere ritual alone—of all that they, following God, had wished.

5. CONCLUSION

The mitzvah of nostalgia, its enactments patterned in the mid-nineteenth century, has continued and achieved new prominence in the twentieth—a tendency evinced by Martin Buber's popularization of Hasidic tales in this century's opening years. The ancestors spoke through Buber, according to his own account. He found his voice by means of their words, carried out a commission in transmitting their stories. "There was something that commanded me, yes, which even took hold of me as an instrument at its disposal." But the ancestors also, again by Buber's own avowal, animated his transgressive creativity. They sent him forth from the restrictions which Hasidim originally obeyed, and still did, "into the world."[87] True to the literature of nostalgia, Buber never converted the Hasidic message into con-

cepts. Indeed, he averred, that could not be done. The "unarbitrary testimony of the image-making vision and the image-making memory" had to
take the form of myth. It remained, for all that, a *Jewish* myth, however, its
particulars firmly in place. One could not "proclaim it as an unfettered
teaching of mankind." Note Buber's careful formulation of his stance, paradigmatic for many other modern Jews as well. "In order to speak to the
world what I have heard, I am not bound to step into the street. I may
remain standing in the door of my ancestral house: here too the word that
[is] uttered does not go astray."[88]

All of the five forms of nostalgia which we have surveyed are evident
here; all have survived into—and thrived in—late-twentieth-century
America. We will describe them at greater length in the Conclusion to this
study. For the moment, let us note several salient examples.

Grandparents are regularly remembered as exemplars of a piety that
their descendents cannot (and do not wish to) attain, at once stimulating
some observances and justifying the abandonment of others. Pilgrimages are
conducted to the sites of the piety that once was—Poland for example—
the journeys made more compelling still—and the resulting "merit" to the
descendants all the greater—by the ancestors' martyrdom at the hands of
pogromists or Nazis.[89]

Rabbis of old (or ultra-Orthodox rabbis and scholars foreign enough to
acculturated Jews that they seem a vestige of the past) are venerated as "the
real thing," their visages serving as icons of tradition, without evoking any
desire in the modern venerators to submit to their authority or conform to
their example. Jewish communal organizations of the past are likewise idealized by comparison to contemporary fragmentation, ignorance, and apathy.
The shtetl is made virtuous in remembrance, the grandparents not only
pious but their lives of a piece.

Sermons by the thousands still recall Jews to the "world of our fathers."
These have been joined of late in America by a burst of creativity in feminist
rituals that summon young Jewish women to the "ways of our mothers"—
for example, in Passover seders that feature Miriam prominently and tell
stories of Jewish heroines such as Ruth and Deborah. The anger voiced in
feminist Haggadot at male oppression, echoing the anger at Egyptians and
later enemies in the traditional text, prompts us to realize that the holidays
most widely celebrated by American Jews today are those which not only
articulate universal ideals such as freedom, and take place in a familial setting
oriented toward children, but *conjure up and redefeat ancestral enemies*—
whether Haman at Purim, or Pharaoh at Passover, or Antiochus at Hanuk-

FIGURE 8. *La Néo-ménie* [The new moon]. Illustration by Alphonse Lévy for Léon Cahun, *La Vie juive* (Paris: Monnier de Brunhoff, 1886).

kah. Jews have long articulated hostility toward their enemies by ritual recall of ancient foes and "appeased" those enemies—or, rather, legitimated their slaughter—through ritual recall of divine sanction. It remains a powerful mode of continuity.

The allure of ritual objects, museums, memoirs, and historical studies has only grown with generational distance from the past thereby "remembered." On the most popular level, Chagall's images, klezmer music, and *Fiddler on the Roof* hold sway, but endless gradations lead to more sophisticated elite reflection, critique, and recovery. Judaism's translation from religious to cultural forms—pioneered by Ahad Ha'am and Mordecai Kaplan—has, of course, played a major role in Jewish survival.

Finally, the move to America and into full participation in its ways has been justified by active custodianship of the past and the flowering of scholarship and religious creativity, both of which are vehicles of continuity with the past. The move from city to the suburbs has similarly been celebrated in return visits to what anthropologist Jack Kugelmass has termed "ethnic theme park restaurants," the schmaltz or bagels on the table and the sentimentality of the recollection going hand in hand.[90]

Through all these activities—to be probed in succeeding chapters—contemporary Jews gain the assurance that they "remain standing in the door of [the] ancestral house" despite the manifest distance they have traveled from it. Their daily practices for the most part are not distinctively Jewish, their minds by and large not furnished from Jewish storehouses, their Jewish commitments generally too inchoate for theological formulation or assent. But meaning is attached to the practices which *are* distinctively Jewish, value is located there, emotion centered and created. Picture Caillebotte's bourgeois gentleman at the window one more time, then, but imagine his head swimming with ancestral voices as he contemplates the empty street below. Now juxtapose this painting with the final print in Lévy's gallery: an old Jewish man standing on the balcony, his wife bathed in light behind and to his right by the candle he holds up to the night, reciting a prayer that—as exemplified by his candle—spreads light into the darkness (see figure 8).[91] Buber achieved what he knew of commandedness by grace of voices such as that one. This gaze into the night enabled him to walk in the darkness of God's "eclipse" and to depart radically from the ancestors' observances, convinced that he had also benefited from a light they did not see—the one that illumined his remembrances. Many Jews in our century have preceded and followed him in this, I believe, striving mightily to remember and forget at the very same time, wishing to touch and be touched by their traditions from a safe—if discomfiting—distance. We turn now to a more detailed examination of that effort.

SEVEN

Buber, Rosenzweig, and the Authority of the Commandments

The distance that Buber maintained between himself and the ancestors extended as well to the observances that the ancestors (and their descendants) practiced. Alone among major Jewish thinkers of the modern period (but together with vast numbers of twentieth-century Jews), Buber had no interest in traditional Jewish practice whatsoever. Franz Rosenzweig noted the anomaly when he read Buber's early essays on Judaism and was perplexed. The challenge he issued to Buber, published later in a well-known essay entitled "The Builders," would have applied just as forcefully to every word that Buber ever wrote, from the popularizations of Hasidism at the start of the century to his latest and most mature philosophical works.

> You have liberated [Jewish] teaching from [a] circumscribed sphere, and, in so doing, removed us from the imminent danger of making our spiritual Judaism depend on whether or not it was possible for us to be followers of Kant. And so it is all the more curious that . . . your answer to the other side of the question, the question concerning the Law: "What are we to do?" . . . should leave this Law in the shackles put upon it . . . by the nineteenth century.[1]

For Buber, observance was an all or nothing proposition. One either performed the commandments with full belief in their divine origin at Sinai and with the intention of fulfilling, by means of the mitzvah at hand, God's will for oneself at that moment of personal life and world history, or, if one lacked such full belief, one could not in good faith carry out the commandments and thus should not attempt to do so. Nonobservance, in Buber's view, was in fact *required* for obedience to the divine summons in that case, because acting with anything less than one's whole self meant turning one's back on "I-Thou" mutuality and descending into the unspontaneous, uncreative, and completely unfree realm of "I-It." There was no middle ground. "Revelation is not legislation," Buber declared categorically—and so, to the end of his days, he resolutely turned his back on the traditional observances codified in Jewish law.[2] Rosenzweig's more complicated view—"For me, too, God is not a lawgiver. But he commands"—had no appeal.[3] We are met with the fascinating phenomenon of a major Jewish thinker, a consummate exegete of the Torah and of Hasidism, a tireless advocate of Jewish communal renewal, who campaigned his entire adult life against the commandments constitutive of every Jewish community that had ever existed. Buber's thoughts on ritual observance clearly merit our careful attention.

His reflections will prove helpful in another respect as well. Understanding Buber's resolve to abandon observance enables us to better comprehend the sources of the power and appeal of observance for the many Jews in this century who, like Rosenzweig, have performed the commandments in good faith *without* the belief in Torah from Sinai upon which Buber insisted. Freed of communal constraints, yet lacking Buber's felt need to rebel against them, Rosenzweig nonetheless advocated observance from *The Star of Redemption* (his first and greatest work, completed in 1919) onward, though he more than once changed his stance about the scope and meaning of that observance. The cycle of the Jewish year is described in the *Star* with characteristic force and grandiosity; Rosenzweig claims that the structure and even the details of that cycle stemmed from the innermost essence of Jewish being, enabling Jews to attain the precious experience of eternity in time. Yet Rosenzweig wrote his fiancée the following year that he could not "take too solemn a view of kosher eating" or the Sabbath. "I look forward with pleasure to it, since we will do it together, in our house! But I can't be solemn about it or find 'educational value' in it."[4] Such statements make it abundantly clear that Rosenzweig's dispute with Buber over the "Law" concerned far more than the technicalities of how God reveals truth and what exactly was said at Sinai. His approach to the commandments—an evolving personal discipline, rather than a submission to divine decree or communal norm—has since become widespread.

I will argue at the conclusion of this chapter that Rosenzweig's observance, by the end of his life, stood in search of a theology which would adequately justify it and that in this way too he was typical of other twentieth-century Jewish thinkers and, no doubt, of countless laypeople. Practice for such Jews, we might say, was way out in front of theory, with theory struggling mightily to catch up. The search for authority had become never-ending—a state of affairs that for Rosenzweig and, we might suspect, not only for him was far from undesirable.

I. BUBER: "REVELATION IS NOT LEGISLATION"

Even a cursory reading of Buber's early addresses on Judaism makes it clear that his opposition to observance was both complex and deeply felt. "Judaism and the Jews," delivered in 1909, seems at first to open a broad space for ritual practice. "Tradition constitutes the noblest freedom for a generation that lives it meaningfully, but it is the most miserable slavery for the habitual inheritors who merely accept it, tenaciously and complacently."[5] One expects him to urge his audience to stand with the former and reject the latter. This quickly turns out not to be the case. "Jewish origin" has "planted something within us that does not leave us at any hour of our life . . . : blood, the deepest, most potent stratum of our being."[6] Observance was therefore not required for the sustenance of the community. Indeed, "freedom for [this] generation" demanded a different sort of action altogether.

The reason, spelled out in Buber's second and third addresses, can be stated in one word: *galut,* exile. Judaism meant the search for unity in the self, the community, and the world. Exile meant "barren intellectuality . . . far removed from life and from a living striving for unity," and the struggle, instead, "essentially necessary but actually sterile, . . . for the preservation of a way of life." Buber here adopted the Haskalah's historicist critique of observance, which had then been seized on by secular Zionists no less intent on defying Orthodox entrenchment. Judaism demanded ever more perfect realization of unity, and this in turn demanded the centrality of "the deed"—something not found in the "straits of prescriptions that had become meaningless." In support of this view, Buber cited Jesus as the spokesman for authentic Jewish practice: "I have not come to abolish but to fulfill the law." In Hasidism, even more than in early Christian teaching, every act had to be carried out in sanctity.

The twofold implication is explicit. If every act *must* be sanctified, *any* act *can* be sanctified. "It is not the matter of the act that is decisive but its sanctification." And in the modern world, where traditional observance was a bar to unity, response to God required an end to the fragmentation of exile. God demanded action in the world that would restore the possibility of wholeness to Jewish selves. That meant, at the very least, political engagement—and, ideally, it meant Buber's unique brand of cultural-religious Zionism.[7]

A close reading of Buber's editions of Hasidic teachings, published several years before his early lectures on Judaism, reveals that these views had been pronounced even then; Hasidism offered authority, grounding inside the tradition, for the rebellion *against* tradition which Buber sought to foment. God, according to *The Tales of Rabbi Nachman* (1906), could be found anywhere. God dwelled among the people as a whole, not among "an aristocracy of Talmud scholars, alienated from life." Nachman represented a "flowering of the soul of the exile," which tragically *but inevitably* had withered there.[8] In his next volume, *The Legend of the Baal-Shem* (1908), Buber declared that "all action bound in one and the infinite life enclosed in every action: this is *avoda*." Note the invocation of the traditional term for service, originally used for sacrifice and then extended by the rabbis to include all worship and/or service of God, in order to argue against the commandments that, for the rabbis, constituted that service. Buber introduced other Hasidic terms as well—*hitlahavut* (enthusiasm), *kavana* (intention), *shiflut* (humility)—and gave each of them a universalist interpretation that provided for authentic service in every sphere and any faith but not through the mitzvot.[9]

Decades later, Buber admitted that his retelling of the Hasidic stories had been too free in its liberation of hidden "essence" from the actual texts with which he worked. "I did not, to be sure, bring in any alien motifs; still I did not listen attentively enough to the crude and ungainly but living folktone which could be heard from this material."[10] Even in apology Buber pronounced the actual texts crude and ungainly. They required transformation at his hands in order to be worthy of attention. This was so for Jewish "deeds" as well.

In the addresses collected as *On Judaism,* Buber time and again rehearsed the standard Romantic opposition between religion and religiosity and, of course, favored the latter—unconditioned response to transcendence, burning at one's very core—to the former—seen as prescriptions and dogmas rigidly determined and handed down from olden days. Buber knew that community was possible "only where a common way of life is maintained." But he could not abide the enslavement of freedom to obligation (that is, to the commandments) that "characterizes the history of Jewish tradition." The Baal Shem Tov, despite the fact that he observed the commandments punctiliously, became in Buber's reading a fertile source of proof texts for antinomianism. Readings of the Bible offered by "official Judaism" throughout the ages to support rigorous observance were pronounced distortions.[11]

Buber's essays "The Holy Way" and "Herut," to which Rosenzweig directly responded in "The Builders," repeated this argument with greater force, singling out Jewish capitalists and profiteers for special criticism and reserving "deepest revulsion" for "the man who discusses his business prospects while wearing his *tephillin*." Buber again praised early Hasidic ritual performance, which met his requirements for proper belief and intention, and accepted Hirsch's view that "genuine affirmation of the law must be anchored in . . . certitude of the fact of revelation"—which Buber, of course, lacked. At the same time, Buber opposed reduction of "the teaching" to a "system of abstract concepts" and insisted on the centrality of Torah to Jewish life. Once again he had returned to the "living religious forces" manifest in both teaching and law without for a moment including the law along with the teaching in his vision of ideal Jewish existence.[12] Rosenzweig's reading took accurate account of Buber's inconsistencies and of the fact that Buber steadfastly refused to own up to them. His only error was in ascribing Buber's stance entirely to a principled view of revelation. Far more, as we have seen, was involved: the struggle for Thou-ness, the triumph over exile, the salvation of the spirit. While Buber's position did not alter in subsequent writings, the stakes that seemed to demand his fervent opposition to ritual got higher and higher.

In Buber's best-known work, *I and Thou* (1923), the dichotomous treatment of teaching and law reflects the all-embracing dichotomy between I-Thou and I-It, which has justly been criticized by more than one interpreter. The "portals" to I-Thou encounter enumerated in the third part of the book do not include performance of the commandments, even though Buber knew that the ritual calendar stood at the center of Jewish observance for friends such as Rosenzweig and that no form of Judaism heretofore developed had failed to award the commandments a comparable centrality. The reasons for Buber's contrary stance are beautifully articulated. One cannot count on encounter with the Eternal Thou, through ritual or any other means. "Ready, not seeking," the person in quest of I-Thou relation "goes his way." Each "finding is not an end of the way but only its eternal center. It is a finding without seeking."[13]

Characteristically, even though Buber wrote that prayer and sacrifice had proved to be means to the divine throughout the ages, he then presented the two in a way that rendered them inaccessible and undesirable to modern readers. "In prayer man pours himself out, dependent without reservation, knowing that, incomprehensibly, he acts on God, albeit without exacting anything from God." Those who offered sacrifices knew "in a foolish and vigorous way that one can and should give to God."[14] We moderns, however, had to distill the eternal essence from these outmoded forms. True revelation, Buber declared in one of the most crucial passages in all his work, vouchsafed three things and three things only. It proffered "the whole abundance of actual reciprocity." It offered "the inexpressible confirmation of meaning." And this meaning belonged to

> this our world, and it wants to be demonstrated by us in this life and this world. . . . The meaning we receive can be put to the proof in action only by each person in the uniqueness of his being and in the uniqueness of his life. No prescription can lead us to the encounter, and none leads from it. . . . I neither know nor believe in any revelation that is not the same in its primal phenomenon. . . . The eternal voice sounds, nothing more.[15]

It is clear that the presiding authority in this passage is not the Baal Shem Tov but Kant, and so it would remain. Deference to commandments meant heteronomy. Personal acceptance of the command addressed to me, and only me, constituted autonomy. Kantian obligation confronted the individual with the question of how best to treat fellow human beings as ends rather than means. Buber's parallel question was how best to maximize Thou-ness, and minimize It-ness, in one's own life and the world. Despite the fact that response to Kant's question involved a process of reasoning, whereas Buber believed that response to the divine summons was necessarily immediate and intuitive—one *knew* what was required—it remains true, in Paul Mendes-Flohr's words, that "the Kantian inflections of Buber's view of religion are apparent." That affinity is "manifest in his categorical dismissal of the mitzvot, which he deems to be a species of formalized laws, as a genuine expression of divine service."[16] Rosenzweig's critique was thus even more on target for *I and Thou* than it had been for Buber's earlier essays. The "liberation from the shackles of Kant" that Buber advocated remained, in Buber's own case, far from complete.

Ethics trumped ritual at every turn. "Put down the dictionary!" Buber urged in "Dialogue," an essay that amplified the philosophy of *I and Thou* in 1929. Genuine responsibility, real response, meant attention to everything that occurs.[17] A person must hear the message of each hour, he wrote in 1933, "stark and untransfigured." This personal assumption of responsibility was "continually threatened by the fact of so-called collective decisions." Kierkegaard supplies the proof text for this point. One can consult others, take communal norms under advisement, but one cannot yield responsibility.[18] Indeed, the problem of our age was the loss of organic communities composed of responsible selves. Technology had outpaced and smothered the flowering of spirit. "Man is no longer able to master the world which he himself brought about." In an uncanny parallel to the notion that Jewish practice in the modern period had in many cases moved way out in front of theory, Buber wrote that "I should like to call this peculiarity of the modern crisis man's lagging behind his works." The solution was for each to say Thou to the "living unknown God" by saying Thou to a fellow human being. This would reconstitute the "essential We of community," which Buber defined as "a community of several independent persons, who have reached a self and self-responsibility."[19]

The "kingdom of ends," we note, *must* be composed of and built by autonomous individuals, and God can *only* be served by their ethical and political action. Rejection of ritual practice is therefore essential to more than the transformation of Judaism. It is the prerequisite, as well, for the activity required to save the modern world from self-destruction.[20] What is more, the activity that Buber sought to motivate was universal, whereas ritual—bound to *these* forms and no other—was inevitably particular. Observance dictated by law inevitably competed with ethical activity in and on the world which, unlike ritual, is always God's will *because* it should be ours.[21]

That stance did not change once Buber, fleeing the Nazis, arrived as a refugee in Palestine, a community in formation already known throughout world Jewry for a host of nation-building rituals, songs, and dances. Instead, the opportunity to help shape a reborn "theo-political community" once more focused Buber's opposition to ritual upon its *exilic* character. He turned with new vigor to the exegesis of biblical texts, as he had turned at the start of his creativity in the *golah* to Hasidism. The contract "which YHWH makes with Israel" as a whole, Buber wrote in *Moses* (1945), opened the possibility of a comprehensive ethic not available to isolated individuals or to human beings "in general."[22] Buber's interpretations highlighted the prophetic demand that all of life be made to serve God. Ritual performances unaccompanied by social justice—condemned time and again in *The Prophetic Faith* (1942)—were hypocritical.[23] And wherever Buber found in his chosen texts a demand for ritual observance, he found reasons to render that injunction inapplicable to his own day. Thus, in *Moses,* the first Passover is taken to be the mark of Israel's new theo-political covenant with God, and the sacrifice performed at Sinai in chapter 24 of Exodus "is no pure cult act but a cultic 'pre-state' state act. . . . YHWH unites himself with Israel into a political, theo-political unity." The point was the theo-political end, not the ritual means. The Sabbath had been included in the Decalogue because it was a necessary mark of submission to divine Lordship (the point of the covenant, after all) and was all the more unlike other rituals because it was celebrated by the actual bestowal of freedom. Like the commandment to honor parents, the Sabbath was meant to "ensure the continuity of national time; the never-to-be interrupted consecution of consecration, the never-to-be-broken consecution of tradition."[24]

Buber's eloquence in praise of the Sabbath here marked the first time in all his writings that any observance was so celebrated, though it is praise of a Sabbath long past. The considerable role played by *nostalgia* in Buber's writings is joined to the preeminent part of *politics,* and together they illustrate Buber's understanding of ritual as *symbol:* the Sabbath marked submission, urged freedom, enacted consecration. Lest we be too persuaded by these "reasons for the commandments," however, Buber was careful to insist that the stipulations of the Mosaic covenant

> cannot claim any priority over those which may be proclaimed later on, and when the people declare after the reading that they wish "to do and to hear," they clearly signify that they bind themselves not in respect of specific ordinance as such, but in respect of the will of their Lord who issues His commands in the present and will issue them in the future; in the respect of the life-relationship of service to Him.[25]

The possibility of new ritual observances or the adaptation of existing observances to new covenantal conditions was, as usual, never raised. Nor did it figure in *Paths in Utopia* (1947), a work of the same period, which traced and advocated the utopian socialist quest of Proudhon, Saint-Simon, and others for true community, a secular variant of the "prophetic faith."[26]

The ethical and necessarily nonritual character of the divine covenant with Israel received only one further significance in Buber's writings. It served, in *Two Types of Faith* (1950), to distinguish Judaism from other religious traditions, particularly Christianity. The Christian tradition had been shaped not by Jesus but by Paul, who had demanded *belief* and made salvation contingent on it, whereas Jesus, following the prophets, had demanded *trust.* Paul was wrong to see the Torah as law; the word should instead be translated as "instruction." Buber even went so far as to praise the Pharisees (for the first and only time in his oeuvre, to my knowledge) because they had battled for "direction of the heart," extension of the divine world to the "whole dimension of human existence," and had criticized works done without this intention.[27] The paradox of this praise is apparent and has been perceptively analyzed by Michael Wyschogrod. Buber, the consummate modern Jewish critic of the law, attacked rather than sided with the most famous critic of the law ever to have emerged from Judaism—all the while denying the divine authority of the law that Paul had affirmed! Nor did Buber seem concerned that the attainment of a just world order (unlike the exact performance of ritual) seems hopelessly beyond human reach, occasioning guilt that bothered Paul immensely but seems to have disturbed Buber not at all.[28]

To the end, Buber held fast to the belief that redemption would come if Jews worked for it instead of looking inward to the narrow spaces of the law. The "God-side of the event whose world-side is called return is called redemption."[29] The return to Zion presented a new opportunity for that larger return, and Buber's critique of ritual played an important role in his attempt to keep Jews from missing it. *Two Types of Faith* ended with the plea that Jews become a holy nation once again.[30] This was his faith and his practice. No other faith was possible for Buber. All other practice was precluded.

2. ROSENZWEIG: "GOD IS NOT A LAWGIVER. BUT HE COMMANDS."

Buber's antipathy toward practice extended from the start of his long career to its conclusion, though, as we have seen, his reasons for nonobservance were both manifold and in flux. Rosenzweig exhibited the mirror image to this, a pattern far more widespread among modern Jewish thinkers: a more or less constant regimen of observance endowed with varying meanings over time. I hope to show that still more was involved in their dispute over the relation between revelation and commandment: a far more profound divide over the meaning of Jewish identity and Jewish existence.

Mendes-Flohr, along with other scholars of the Rosenzweig corpus, has taught us to see his lifelong project, and particularly *The Star of Redemption,* as a polemical response to the most influential German philosophical schools of the nineteenth century: Kantian and Hegelian idealism.[31] We have already noted Rosenzweig's derisive attitude toward the deference shown Kant in much Jewish philosophy of the modern period.[32] But this critique was only part of a larger agenda. Beginning with the very first words of the *Star*—"All cognition of the All originates in death, in the fear of death"—Rosenzweig proclaimed his opposition to ethical and metaphysical systems that dealt only with universals ("the All") and thus, in his view, denied individual existence (and individual death, all around him at the Balkan front during World War I) ultimate significance.[33] Judaism, committed to the meaning of individual existence, could not and should not subsume itself in such a philosophy—or in any other system content to do without God or to reduce God to a function of world or a projection of human minds. Just as Hermann Cohen had tried to demonstrate the inadequacy of an ethics not supplemented by the "religion of reason," so Rosenzweig insisted that philosophy as it was practiced in his day be replaced by a "new thinking" or "absolute empiricism" that took account of the religious reality of revelation. "This new theological rationalism . . . here adumbrated . . . [hopes to demonstrate] that both sides need something which in each case only the other party can supply."[34]

I cannot hope to do justice to Rosenzweig's masterpiece here, or even to his rich and original conception of revelation. Even a brief outline of Rosenzweig's logic in the *Star,* however, should provide a sense of why participation in ritual was so crucial to his mind—and of why "commandment" could never be synonymous with "law."

For Rosenzweig, God's presence in the world was not demonstrable empirically and, so, not "knowable" in the usual philosophical sense. But it was nonetheless undeniable, to be witnessed: no less a feature of our experience than the existence of world and humanity. None of the three could be reduced to either of the others.[35] Nor could any of the three be entirely understood. The *Star*'s first part, entitled "The Elements; or, The Ever-Enduring Proto-Cosmos," surveys virtually every major philosophical and religious tradition in the West, and some outside the West, in order to demonstrate the presence of the three elements in all these traditions as well as to argue the inadequacy of their attempts to explain the elements, often by explaining one or two of them away. Rosenzweig also wants to persuade us that the three elements are *interrelated*. There is evidence of a *creating* hand or mind. There are encounters with God, experiences of God's love—*revelation*—which announce God's activity in renewing the work of creation each day and God's role in creating us. Finally, creation and revelation lead to the reasonable conclusion that God's work and ours are unfinished and will someday be complete. They point to *redemption,* not yet knowable or describable because we live only in the present—the time, between creation and every future, that Rosenzweig urged us ever to await.

It all makes sense, Rosenzweig wants us to exclaim: fantastic, cosmic, logical sense, so that by the end of his architectonic masterpiece, with its three parts and three books within each part, book 1 of part 1 and its subsections corresponding to book 1 of parts 2 and 3 and their subsections, we are prepared for the claim that if the three elements are connected, the points forming an equilateral triangle, and the three relations among them are likewise connected to form a second triangle superimposed upside down on the first, the six-pointed Star of David that results is no coincidence but the revelation or appreciation of a fundamental fact of existence. The people Israel had been the first to recognize and proclaim the reality of God's love, expressed in creation and known through revelation. They existed eternally as the "fire . . . at the core of the star," while Christian emissaries constituted the star's rays, bringing light to the nations.[36]

The heart of the *Star*'s second part, "The Course; or, The Always-Renewed Cosmos," is a magnificent explication of the Song of Songs, which Rosenzweig reads traditionally as a declaration that revelation is love. God has not only created the world, and us within it, but creates it anew each day. In revelation, God blesses us with knowledge of the creation and makes it possible for us to experience other tokens of the divine presence. This confers inestimable meaning upon each human life. But God's love and our knowledge of it also teach us the right and necessity of the lover's demand that we, the beloved, love God in return. It is in this way and in this way only that revelation *commands* and cannot but command. The bestowal of love contains within itself the imperative "Love me!" We are commanded to "love the Lord your God" and, in large part, do so by "loving your neighbor as yourself."[37]

Rosenzweig thus counters the Kantian antinomy between heteronomy and autonomy with the rabbinic understanding of the mitzvot as the expression of God's love and our loving response to it. If we perform the commandments without that intention, they remain mere law (*Gesetz*). Animated by love, they become true commandment (*Gebot*). Christianity, too, knows and teaches this; the foil for Rosenzweig, unlike for Buber, is Islam, which insisted on "subservience by volition to the prescription established once and for all."[38] For a Jew, the commandment can never be once and for all. It must ever be heard anew, that is, interpreted anew. For God's commands come to us in the *present:* their grammatical mood is the imperative.

But the commands do come. Revelation in Judaism, necessarily accompanied by *tradition,* commands.

We are now prepared to examine the lengthy and problematic exposition of the Jewish and Christian liturgical years in part 3 of the *Star.* They are found in that part of the work, entitled "The Configuration; or, The Eternal Hyper-Cosmos," because the ritual calendar, in Rosenzweig's view, enables human beings to experience redemption in the only way that it can be experienced before the event.[39] By pointing through gesture to significances that cannot be articulated, the cycle of holy days brings eternity into time and ritual participants into eternity.

The paradox of this understanding is apparent, and multifaceted. Rosenzweig affirms no specific doctrine of creation in *The Star,* ascribes no specific or enduring stipulations to revelation, and must remain utterly vague about redemption. Human beings can know only as much as we can know. The "hyper-cosmos" must remain in the domain of the unknown. The *Star* cannot provide us with a picture of eternity or promise us a place within it. Yet Rosenzweig avers, on the basis of the Song of Songs and its interpretation, that "love is as strong as death," meaning that we are touched by God's larger order and can participate in eternity. "The cult [not only] build[s] the house in which God may take up residence, but . . . force[s] the exalted guest to move in." That claim, given Rosenzweig's inability to affirm more about creation and revelation, is immense, and he knows it. The extended introduction to part 3 is devoted to arguing "the possibility of entreating the kingdom." Since God can be addressed in prayer, God must reply! "The irresistible force of the love of neighbor . . . compels the redemptive advent of the eternal into time. God can do no other; he must accept the invitation." The ritual calendar is thus fraught with significance never before accorded it in Jewish thought of the modern period.[40]

It is all the more surprising, then, that Rosenzweig's account of the Jewish holidays in part 3 is virtually restricted to liturgy—none of the "ceremonialism" attacked by Kant, Mendes-Flohr notes, nothing "beyond the precincts of communal prayer." What is more, it is remarkably idiosyncratic. In part, Rosenzweig's schematic treatment of the holidays stemmed from the facts of biography. He had not yet embarked upon a discipline of observance but, rather, as Mendelssohn feared would be the case among modern Jews, had learned almost all he knew from books. The Siddur was easily available. Practice was not. But the major factor in Rosenzweig's approach to the ritual calendar was likely the *Star*'s tendentious and well-known argument—exactly the opposite of Buber's—that the Jews are the "eternal people," the fire burning at the core of the star, who must abide outside of the vicissitudes of history. Judaism acquired its hold on eternity by renouncing time and space. Jews did not water the soil of any homeland with their soldiers' blood but lived as exiles from their land. The Jew used the Jewish language only to pray, and "as a result he cannot speak to his brother at all[,] . . . communicat[ing] with him by a glance." Finally, Jews studied a law never renewed by any lawgiver "according to the living flux of time. . . . Even what might, for all practical purposes, be considered as innovation must be presented as if it were part of the everlasting Law and had been revealed in the revelation of that Law."[41]

One understands what Rosenzweig was getting at here. Jews could not claim eternity as their patrimony unless their way through the ages remained independent of "will and hope." One's grandchildren, for example, might not share one's nationality. They might have other politics, might differ in their beliefs about love or death or the good. But if one raised children in a "blood-community" set apart from the normal ebb and flow of history, one could with some confidence assume that, whatever else they are and do, one's descendants would observe the same round of holidays, in the same time-out-of-time as their ancestors, who thereby take on a role in Rosenzweig's system that goes far beyond the mitzvah of nostalgia. God's gift of the True Torah, passed on by the ancestors, had—again, thanks to their mediation—"planted eternal life within us"—at the expense, necessarily, of normal life. Ritual, as we have seen so often in this study, serves to mark Jews apart from all other peoples, not only in *what* it means but in *how* it means. Rosenzweig's understanding of observance serves and derives from his conception of Jewish community and destiny—a view arguably not all that different from the inchoate tribalism and celebration of Jewish survival over the centuries that seems to animate a great deal of contemporary Jewish practice.

The passivity of Jewish existence in this world as Rosenzweig imagined it is utterly striking and pervades his depiction of the ritual calendar, which is, of course, divided (somewhat mechanically) into festivals of creation, revelation, and redemption. The philosophy that he called "speech-thinking" culminates, ironically, in silence. "In eternity the spoken word fades away into the silence of perfect togetherness—for union occurs in silence only; the word unites, but those who are united fall silent." Buber, we recall, had abandoned the mystical quest for perfect union in favor of a life of dialogue in which *relation* was the ideal and *history* the domain of its achievement. Rosenzweig, within the compass of the *Star,* moves in the opposite direction. In ritual, Jews remain outside history and learn above all "how to share silence." The preparation begins with a kind of hearing that does not "stimulat[e] the speaker to speak" but, rather, "has nothing to do with a possible reply." Hence the centrality of fixed liturgy and sermons, and the necessary focus on a text, that is, on an eternal given not subject to the whim of speaker or the interests of the audience. The reading of the Torah on the Sabbath is said to establish "unanimity among the congregation" as they listen to it in silence.[42] Rosenzweig's aesthetic, heavily Romantic, uncannily conforms as well to the aesthetic of the Reform services that he rejected: a generally silent congregation, prayer in unison, a lengthy sermon.

Rosenzweig discerns a weekly progress on the Sabbath from a focus on creation in the blessing over wine on Friday evening, through the reading of the word of revelation in the synagogue on Saturday morning, to the sweet taste of redemptive rest with which one leaves the Sabbath at havdalah. The following section of the *Star* assigns one of the three themes to each of the three pilgrimage festivals, respectively, an analysis entitled "Sociology of the Community: The Meal" because eating signifies and constitutes "the re-creating of bodily life, the transformation of matter grown old." Eating together with other Jews in "silent community represents actual community alive in the midst of life." The domination evinced in this silence is now explicit. "The household is based on the circumstance that the word of the father of the family is heard and heeded." Participation of children at the Passover seder gives the whole "the form of instruction. . . . The father of the family speaks, the household listens." They listen to texts which above all recount the creation of the Jewish people in love. At Shavuot, which recalls the giving of the Torah at Sinai, revelation is, of course, the principal theme, though Rosenzweig has little to add to his commentary in part 2. Sukkot is described as Israel's issuing forth from encounter with God into the world, its required association with redemption provided by a prophetic reading (the last chapter of Zechariah) for the holiday which contains the vision of a day when "the Lord shall be King over all the earth."[43]

When Rosenzweig turns in conclusion to Judaism's most forceful integration of eternity into time, Rosh Hashanah and Yom Kippur, he places them in the rubric "Sociology of the Whole: The Greeting." People who know each other well do not need to speak when they meet. Wordless greetings are sufficient. A world in which all beings greeted one another in this fashion would truly be redeemed. It "would constitute the utmost community, the silence that can never again be broken." What is the precondition of this greeting? Rosenzweig seizes on the practice of salutes in the army—expressing both a "sense of comradeship" and shared submission to an "unrelenting discipline"—to account for the fact that on the Days of Awe, and only then, Jews prostrate themselves before God. Jews bow in "beholding the immediate nearness of God," in the knowledge that the judgment they face each year prefigures the judgment which all humankind will confront upon the advent of redemption. "Just as the year, on these days, represents eternity, so Israel represents mankind." The book has now come full circle: back to the confrontation with death. Rosenzweig interprets the wearing of a tallit for the entirety of Yom Kippur—including the evening services of Kol Nidre and Ne'ilah—as another signpost of eternity. For the tallit is also a shroud; Jewish men are traditionally buried in their prayer shawls. Death marks the limit of the realm of creation. But "revelation has the knowledge—and it is the primary knowledge of revelation— that love is as strong as death." Jewish men also wear the tallit, in a widely observed tradition, under the wedding canopy. And the first thing one does after Yom Kippur is begin work on the sukkah: "The Feast of Booths reinstates the reality of time." The way that takes one out of the divine sanctuary, Rosenzweig writes at the very end of the Star, leads "Thou knowest it not? INTO LIFE." Not a normal life: "The people remains the eternal people."[44] Wandering remains the Jewish lot, the price paid for eternity.

The dogmatic character of Rosenzweig's account of the holidays is immediately apparent. Not unlike Hirsch, he seems to declare the unequivocal meaning of each and every Jewish festival, a meaning entirely independent of the significance that individual practitioners may discover or construct.[45] One could argue that his intention is otherwise, that the Star does not attempt to prove but rather to witness, that one should therefore read Rosenzweig's positive pronouncements as if they came bracketed by doubts which do not (as in mathematics) change plus into minus but do (as in grammar) substitute question marks for exclamation points. The profound insights scattered throughout his exposition of the ritual year would in this reading intend only to demonstrate the profundity awaiting Jews in the commandments. I am not persuaded by this reading of the Star, because, according to Rosenzweig, the yearly holiday cycle (and the parallel Christian cycle, which we shall examine in a moment) are the *only* points of entry into eternity, indeed the only means by which Jews can come to know the truth to which the holidays attest. Mendes-Flohr cites a letter in which Rosenzweig confirms that "an outsider, no matter how willing and sympathetic, can never be made to accept a single commandment as a 'religious demand.'" Conversely, "only in the commandment can the voice of Him who commands be heard."[46] While Rosenzweig leaves the scope for possible commandment in part 2 of the *Star* as wide as human imaginings of acts of love toward "the neighbor" or toward God, the only specific commandments discussed in part 3 are those pertaining to the Sabbath and holiday cycle—and the *meanings* of those commandments are articulated almost always in terms of the liturgies which Rosenzweig cites. To deny these meanings is to miss the point, to fail to hear "the voice of Him who commands." Other meanings, if they diverge from these, will not do.

That is why I believe we should not dismiss the recurrent theme of *silence* as mere Romanticism, an artifact of the organic nationalism to which many thinkers of the period—including Buber—were in thrall. One learns the meaning of Israel's holy days at every step by *listening*.[47] There are allusions to other acts: one builds a sukkah, one eats a meal. But Rosenzweig has absolutely nothing to say about these. Holiday observance as he describes it lacks all taste and smell, all spontaneous family celebration. As in Buber, one finds no appreciation either of the *emotional* content of observance or of the *personal discovery of significance* in observance, both of which are essential to the building of community. Unlike Buber, however, Rosenzweig sees no need to build Jewish community, for it exists, by definition, outside of history, in the eternal time and space comprised by ritual. The call for silence, the lack of room for individual meanings of observance, the absence of respect for the chance and improvisation that animate every creative performance are all demanded by Israel's status as the eternal people, who cannot and must not change. Judaism abides forever at the core of the star, while Christianity sends its rays into and through the world: acting, altering, effective. Hence what Amos Funkenstein has called the "churchlike images Rosenzweig employs to depict the Jewish community as based on liturgy rather than law," a result of his vision of "the uniqueness and eternity of Israel . . . described in a language saturated with Christian images and terms."[48]

Rosenzweig's later writings withdrew the demand for passivity; indeed, his changed attitude toward change—that is to say, his more nuanced understanding of tradition—is already adumbrated in the *Star*.[49] But, in part because of his debilitating disease (a few years after the publication of the *Star*, he was diagnosed as suffering from amyotrophic lateral sclerosis), Rosenzweig never managed to revise his system—or to abandon it—in accord with the changes that overtook his own observance. Israel remained "a unique nation on earth," a "people dwelling alone," outside of history, its law purchasing eternity "at the cost of its temporal life." The engagement with history and politics that Buber had urged upon Jews at the expense of observance is reserved by Rosenzweig in the *Star* for Christians. Indeed, in contrast to the holy people sanctified by a ritual year, Christians are said by Rosenzweig (in a chapter title in book 2 of part 3) to walk a "Way through Time" via "Christian History," the point of which is to bring the news of creation, revelation, and redemption to the nations whose participation in truth is not guaranteed by blood. The Christian calendar promotes a common going, doing, and becoming not needed by Jews, who already abide in the precincts of eternity. In place of a "sociology of the community," the Christian "clerical year" promotes a "sanctification of the soul" achieved in part by "fine arts" and "musical arts"—architecture, drama, miracle plays, choral works—absent from the account of Judaism. They not only offer a framework organizing the life of the world but enable Christians to bear with the suffering—the cross—that is the lot of those charged with moving the world toward a goal far from realization. The "sacrament of the word" at the center of Christian worship—Rosenzweig seems to have Protestants in mind rather than Catholics—perpetually *establishes* the community of the faithful, which in Judaism is already *given* through blood.[50]

Rosenzweig's approach to Christian observance is characterized by the same abstraction that suffuses his discussion of the Jewish year, the same lack of interest in individual emotion or significance, the same confident enthusiasm that he has gotten it right, has deciphered the code. The Christian pattern must be the mirror image of the Jewish, transposed into active rather than passive mode. Christians are called to the hard work of imposing the truth on pagan souls who are often resistant to the light of the star. "The heartbeat of Judaism," on the other hand, "is community, procreation, ritual life, now as in the messianic days"—because it is *already* redeemed.[51] Rosenzweig's dispute with Buber on the issue of revelation and commandment, then, was bound up in a dispute far more profound. To Rosenzweig, Jews were Jews, and Christians were not; Jews would forever stand apart from the world in the eternity of ritual performances, while Christians acted to transform the world. In Buber's view, Israel's covenant demanded of every human being, but first and foremost of the Jews, that action be taken to transform the world—action that mere ritual functioned mainly to preclude.

3. AUTHORITY SOUGHT, FOUND, AND DISPENSED WITH

Careful examination of Rosenzweig's exchanges with Buber, in "The Builders" and in correspondence only recently published, confirms that the two differed but little on the issue of revelation. That disagreement, however, is of great relevance to Judaism, both elite and popular, in our century. For it provided Buber with good reason to opt out of the regimen of practice which Rosenzweig was seeking good reasons to secure. Buber took the seder plate off the table, as it were, and so could not ask, in the words of the Haggadah, "This matzah—what meaning has it?" Rosenzweig, from the midst of the seder, asked questions without end and found few answers satisfactory. That difference in stance, I believe, has been fundamental to Jewish practice in our century. It takes us back once more to the distinctiveness of Israel's status as a holy people and the belief—often seen as opposed to it—that one should encounter and serve the "Eternal Thou" simply as a human being, all ethnic or "racial" distinctions by way of practice being irrelevant or even harmful.

Let us begin, however, on the surface of their debate about revelation, where the issue of authority is predominant. Rosenzweig agreed with Buber, we recall, that "the way to the teaching" led through the whole of the teaching. One could not rest content with broad views from the heights—that is, ethical maxims or discourse concerning Judaism's "essence." Nor could one say, with the best of Orthodoxy—that is, rigorous learning of the Oral Law informed by the requisite sort of intention—that one had reached the goal. Judaism had yet to be lived in days not yet encountered; articulations of Judaism appropriate to those days had not yet been produced. That is why Buber's resort to the criterion of inner power was so helpful. One learned what one needed to learn, while walking the path that had no end. "Only this laborious and aimless detour through the known"—aimless, so that one did not come with a predetermined agenda to the teachings and find there only what one was looking for; laborious, because the search had to be serious—"gives us the certainty that the ultimate leap, from that which we know to that which we need to know at any price, the leap to the teachings, leads to *Jewish* teachings."[52]

The same held true, according to Rosenzweig, for practice. One knew that a particular mode of observance was Jewish *not* because it conformed punctiliously to ancient or inherited usage, and not because one had distilled essence from detail and clung to the former while altering the latter, but because one had so thoroughly informed oneself with Jewish practice on the road traveled heretofore that one's way forward could not but continue its direction. This is a far cry from the reliance on blood and isolation in the *Star.* Yet, in keeping with the *Star,* it urges Jews to step into the framework of observance and then to learn—by trial and error—what meaning they would find there. Rosenzweig now makes room for the discovery of personal significance that we noted earlier, in his correspondence with his fiancée. The personal assumption of ritual discipline—without belief in To-rah from Sinai—by no means precluded a "strict domestic rule of the Sab-bath" (no telephoning, for instance), because "an emergency breaks the Sabbath, but it also breaks it apart, and the fragments are valueless."[53] Only those involved could judge the authenticity or integrity of the observance. By the time of his exchange with Buber, Rosenzweig seems to have moved beyond the discovery of personal meaning in selected commandments to confidence that greater observance of traditional rituals would yield still greater "inner power"—in other words, a broader circumference of *Gesetz* transformed by love into *Gebot*.

On the matter of revelation, Rosenzweig was justifiably convinced that he and Buber had precious little to argue about. Had he not written in the *Star* that "God's love is present, pure and simple: how should love itself know whether it will love, whether, indeed, it has loved?" Stipulations con-cerning the duties of the beloved were impossible. The lover could com-mand only: love. The only words of the Ten Commandments which we could be sure were spoken by God were "I am the Lord thy God," or perhaps only "I"—that is, the announcement of God's presence. In a letter to Buber in 1924, Rosenzweig formulated the matter this way: "You place the dividing line between revelation and commandment. . . . I do not un-derstand that. . . . By commandment, I meant something like *lekh* [go]."[54] Abraham, in hearing God's word as he did (Gen. 12:1), had *already* heard it in love, instantaneously transforming a decree into a commandment. Rosenzweig trusted that the recipient of revelation, having taken in its de-mand for love, would lend it concreteness, just as Buber held that experi-ence of relation with the Eternal Thou inevitably issued in a summons which the human partner intuitively knew how to answer.

No, Buber replied. Rosenzweig still accorded too little weight to the self's determination of who and what commanded it. In that sense, *lekh lekha* could be a commandment *if* Abraham experienced it as such. But the order "not to have other gods before me"—applying to everyone, in every time—was purely of human authorship. Buber had to ask of every com-mand, and ask again and again, "Has that been said to me, rightly to me? So that at one time I can count myself part of *Israel,* which is being ad-dressed, and at another time, at many other times, not. And if there is any-thing that in my own life I am able to call a *mitzvah* with an undivided heart, it is just this: that I act and do not act as I do."[55]

This is telling. Buber must pass everything suggested to him as a possible commandment before the bar of his own autonomous judgment—a quite typical modern stance. He might not go through the Kantian exercise of deciding whether a particular maxim served the purpose of treating all persons as ends rather than means, but he would presumably do something akin to it: look into himself and ask whether he knew (felt?) himself to be commanded by this particular effort to maximize Thou-ness in the world. Buber, unlike Rosenzweig, sees no reason in principle to begin or end with the Jews' collective inheritance of ritual, ethical, or civil commandments. Sometimes he will feel addressed by a mitzvah already "on the books," and sometimes not; sometimes he will feel addressed by a command in some *other* culture's books! "You shall have no other gods" was not binding upon him a priori; *I and Thou,* in fact, defended the authenticity of pagan worship.[56] The ultimate authority would remain his and his alone. That was his mitzvah! As he put it in response to Rosenzweig's bafflement at this position

> I do not regard the Law as universal, but personal: namely, only what comes from it that I am forced to acknowledge as addressed to me (e.g., the older I become and the more deeply I recognize the restlessness of my nature, the more does the day of rest mean to me).[57]

To which Rosenzweig, of course, would say: "Exactly. You, Buber, have now found meaning in a traditional commandment. You could not have found this meaning unless you had chosen to observe the Sabbath. And you have observed the Sabbath (rather than, say, Easter) because it was your inheritance as a member of the Jewish people." Buber had not consulted an encyclopedia of religious rituals and selected the Sabbath as a likely source of commandment. Nor had he simply gone forth from the experience of God's presence and just happened to respond with Sabbath observance. The Sabbath involved memory of his own and his people's past. He had thus not only opened space for Jewish observance in his life but argued against the strict dichotomy of I-Thou/I-It, against which Rosenzweig had also protested.[58]

As if anticipating this reply, Buber continues at once that "the analogy you insist on [between experience or teaching, on the one hand, and law, on the other] does not hold. . . . An act does not merely carry greater weight than experience; an act has a different kind of weight. . . . I am responsible for what I commit or omit in a *different* way from the responsibility I have for what I learn and leave unlearned."[59] Action in the world was of greater moment than any inward stirrings that the teachings effected within the soul. One had to assume complete responsibility for action; law precluded such responsibility. If Buber had chosen to observe the Sabbath, that was his choice and his alone. Making it into law detracted from rather than added to its dignity.

Rosenzweig would not give up. "For me, too, God is not a lawgiver. But he commands. It is only man in his inertia who makes laws out of the commandments by the way in which he keeps them." Almost a year later, Buber again demurred. The question was "Is the Law God's law?" The answer for him, unlike for Rosenzweig, was clear. "Revelation is not legislation."[60] In the end, Rosenzweig seems to have realized that he and Buber were not really arguing over whether an enactment of love toward the neighbor did or did not contain a divine component. Their difference on that point does seem small and easily bridged. They differed, rather, on whether Jews should give prima facie credibility and priority to the pattern of ritual and ethical practices developed by Jewish individuals and communities over the centuries in direct or indirect response to an imperative that was traditionally believed to have been issued first at Sinai. This is precisely the question faced by contemporary Jews as they choose whether to opt into (or out of) the inherited framework—in many cases no longer a personal inheritance—and to what degree. Rosenzweig, by his final years, was committed in principle to the traditional pattern of observance and to a search for the authority of the divine command. Buber, from first to last, was not. He knew the sorts of things that God could command. Ritual and civil law as set forth in Jewish tradition were not among them, while—for Buber as for many contemporary Jews—ethics, liberal politics, and Jewish communal affairs all featured prominently.[61]

The debate between Buber and Rosenzweig over the authority of the commandments, then, foreshadowed a similar back-and forth on the matter of Jewish observance that has taken place in the minds and conversations of countless Jews in our century as they puzzled over their relation to Judaism. It has also proved typical in other respects. Both Buber and Rosenzweig *shifted the authority of observance from a commanding God to the individual self* who hears the commandment—exactly where it still lies for the vast majority of non-Orthodox Jews. What is more, both thinkers by the time of their debate *presumed that diverse selves would hear and practice differently:* that Jews are driven to (or away from!) observance by various individual and communal motives and inevitably discover manifold individual and collective meanings in whatever observance they do follow. This, too, is a widespread belief.

If that is so, finally, the question inevitably becomes—and actually has

become, for many Jews—*what authority does or should command observance?*
More to the point—since, for many Jews, observance has continued to
some degree despite their lack of satisfactory answers to this question, practice remaining, as I put it earlier, "out in front" of theory, and often far out
in front—*what authorities drive and command the individual in the absence of adequate authority?* To what imperatives are Jews responding while they search
for the authority that is rarely found? We lack sufficient information about
the private searchings of elite thinkers, and all the more so of the laity. It is
therefore difficult to generalize with any certainty about the search for,
wrestle with, and dismissal of authority. I believe, however, that Buber and
Rosenzweig point us to several generalizations which *can* be ventured and
which will then enable us to identify five sources of authority which have
guided and impelled the process of Jewish searching, among elites and laity
alike, while the ultimate authority sought for has proved elusive.

Many Jewish thinkers in the modern period, Buber and Rosenzweig
among them, can usefully be seen on the model of Pirandello's famous play
as characters in search of an author—an "Author"—if not God, exactly,
then some other "god-term" upon which to base their commitments. The
search preoccupies them, to say the least. We might even be tempted to say
that searching defines their thought as it had defined the major Jewish religious movements of the nineteenth century, which coalesced—according
to their avowed understanding (if not ours)—almost entirely around the
issue of what Jews were commanded to do and why and which still remain
divided over that issue today.

All theology of whatever period is concerned with the basis of religious
authority, of course. Religious thinkers aim to find new or better reasons
for existing commitments; they seek grounding in the ultimate source of
Right that obligates human beings to think and act in certain ways and, in
return, confers the precious sense that they are spending their days on earth
correctly. Jewish thought in the modern period is no exception. But it has
been disproportionately given over to this activity of justification, I believe,
and as a result has paid less attention than ever before to the explication of
texts (here, Buber is an exception) and the interpretation of rituals (here,
he is not). Modern Jewish theology has been directed outward, we might
say, far more than inward. Authority, which normally lies beneath all else,
is taken for granted as the basis of all else, has been raised to the surface as *a*
or *the* leading issue. In the twentieth century even more than in the nineteenth, Jewish thinkers have had to demonstrate why Jewish meaning and
behavior of any sort should concern modern Jews—themselves first of all—

let alone obligate them. Communal and parental practice could no longer be counted on to impel Jews to seek meaning in the framework of inherited observances. "There's no author here," says the Manager in Pirandello's play-within-a-play. "We are not rehearsing a new piece."[62] New pieces require more than good management. They require authority. Questions of content, as a result, become secondary.

Buber rarely touched them, even when dealing with texts, and not only because of his penchant for vagueness[63] and his antagonism to observance. Rosenzweig, if anything, said far too much about content in the *Star*—filling up, as it were, the vacuum created by his conversion to a realm of experience he had not yet entered. But the *Star* is entirely typical in the far greater weight it gives to the *justification* of faith and practice than to the actual *interpretation* of texts or observances. The latter exposition is, as we have seen, quite thin, often schematic, and for the most part undistinguished.

Second, as we have noted more than once, the modern Jewish search for authority initiated by Mendelssohn has, as a rule, not proven conclusive. Not only have the arguments of particular thinkers been unsatisfactory to others—the usual state of affairs—but many have often been unable to present the grounds that justify their *own* commitments. The practice of such thinkers has been far in advance of their theories, as was the case (in his later years) with Rosenzweig. It often seems to be largely self-determined. "The drama is in us," exclaims Pirandello's Manager, echoing both Buber and Rosenzweig, "and we are the drama. We are impatient to play it. Our inner passion drives us on to this."[64]

Exemplars of this pattern are numerous. Mendes-Flohr notes that Judah Magnes—an American Reform rabbi who moved to Israel, became the rector of the Hebrew University, and stood at the center of a group of intellectuals committed to shared reflection on their relation to Jewish tradition—eventually arrived at a pattern of ritual practice that resembled the ideal advocated by Conservative Judaism. "Theologically, however, he was decidedly uncomfortable with the pragmatic and sentimental-cum-cultural reasons marshalled by his American colleagues in support" of that pattern. Magnes therefore embarked on a search for other reasons—a search that never resulted in his finding them. A similar quest was undertaken by Julius Guttmann, a philosopher at the Hebrew University, who believed "that our appreciation of the mitzvot and their religious value need not await an adequate answer to these theological questions." Gershom Scholem observed far less of the mitzvot, and perhaps "believed" somewhat more, but he too evinced no strong relation between observance and theology. This lack of fit was one of the major elements of his self-described "religious anarchism."[65] I have argued elsewhere that Abraham Heschel's rationale for the commandments falters at the critical point where revelation leads to the particular "pattern of observance" set forth in halakhah.[66] In Mordecai Kaplan's thought, finally—the focus of Chapter 8—the gap between maximalist observance and minimalist justification for it is pronounced.

This suggests that the relevant authority undergirding twentieth-century Jewish practice has generally *not* been the ultimate grounding almost always sought and almost never found. It has rather been the source (or sources) of obligation that mandate the search in the first place, direct its course, and dictate the practitioner's judgment of its outcome. Modern Jewish believers in this situation, like Pirandello's characters, seem to manage quite well without an "author" determining the mode of their existence all the while their search for absolutes proceeds. Indeed, they may abandon that search altogether and still experience a relationship with God by means of their observance—and, in particular, by their *departures* from the existing store of practices and meanings. "That is the proof that I am a man," exclaims the Father in *Six Characters*. "This seeming contradiction [of past character] is the strongest proof that I stand here a live man before you."[67]

Modern ritual performers of all traditions seem distinctive in the degree to which they have pledged allegiance to multiple and therefore partial authorities, and Jews as a tiny minority have been particularly subject to this rule. In religious behavior, as in other areas of life—especially in the twentieth century—they have learned to proceed without foundational or even consensual grounding for observance. Rosenzweig pleaded for that path when he complained that "from Mendelssohn on," in search of authority for their commitments, "our entire people has subjected itself to the torture of this embarrassing questioning; the Jewishness of every individual has squirmed on the needle point of a 'why.'"[68] It was no less crucial for him to deny that Jews in previous generations had followed the commandments solely or primarily because of a belief in their divine authorship. More *had* to have been at stake for them—as it was for him. Our consideration, in this study, of the reasons for Jewish practice and the forces affecting its course has likewise ranged far beyond the justifications normally sought for religious commitment—God, revelation, reason, tradition—to include, among other things, the political pressures impinging on Jewish practice, the sense of obligation and guilt toward ancestors, and the appeal exercised by symbolic expression for truths held dear but inexpressible in words.

Buber and Rosenzweig, I think, point to sources of authority other than direct divine commandments—not least because they "squirmed" as much as anyone (and, if we take into account the sheer length of the *Star,* and the number of Buber's writings, could be said to have squirmed more than most). Five inferences regarding the operative authorities—the commanding voices to which elite thinkers and laypeople alike have been responsive while they searched for ultimate authority—seem warranted.

1. *Socially constructed reality* has continued to compel and shape observance even in the absence of all-embracing "plausibility structures." Observance continues to rest upon repeated confirmations: political, societal, familial, linguistic, architectural. Not all have been available to most Jews in the modern period or available in sufficient number and force to offer a firm foundation for observance. But Jewish institutions of various sorts have managed to create social realities strong enough to withstand the countervailing pressures toward secularism or assimilation. The Zionist movement—particularly the "cultural Zionist" party to which Buber belonged—was crucial to him in this regard. The Lehrhaus represented an attempt by Rosenzweig to create such a social reality for himself and German Jews like him.[69] Buber's appeal to Jewish mentality and blood grew into a lifelong project to imagine—and, so, to belong to—a far-flung community of intellectuals united by their total immersion in German (later, modern) culture and their rootedness (independent of practice or affiliation) in the Jewish people and tradition. Neither thinker had any interest in the sort of separatist Orthodox communities that have since developed in western Europe, America, and Israel. Walls that high, observance that extensive, did not attract or compel them. But both devoted significant energy to the creation of spaces supportive of new Jewish commitments that surrounding social realities could neither provide nor preclude. The *Star* is perhaps so long, and Buber's oeuvre so large, in part because of the recognition that their chosen task was extraordinarily difficult.

2. The need for societal "plausibility structures" to confer prima facie credibility on religious belief and observance shows the precariousness of both thinkers' reliance on the authority of religious *experience.* For encounter with God does not reach us uninterpreted, and given the "social construction of reality" dominant in Western elite and popular cultures of the century, it is perhaps a wonder that religious experience has remained available at all. Indeed, it has been accessible largely within communities that the individuals concerned could not or would not join. Buber had his formative experiences with the "God of Abraham, Isaac, and Jacob" while living as a

child near Hasidic communities in central Europe. Rosenzweig had his climactic encounter in an Orthodox service on Yom Kippur, after intellectual preparation provided by cousins who took faith so seriously that they converted to Christianity. Heschel and Soloveitchik both grew up in eastern Europe, heirs to long lineages of pietism and yeshivah learning, respectively. All found these religious experiences to be authoritative. Jews who have not had such experiences—or have not interpreted them as religious, which amounts to the same thing—have in many cases received "signals of transcendence" that conferred a vestigial authority not sufficient to undergird faith or practice in and of itself but adequate to motivate or strengthen at least a modicum of commitment when they worked in concert with other sources of authority.

3. Buber and Rosenzweig—particularly when their self-explanations are least convincing—offer testimony that *meaning* as such, significance in life that is larger than oneself, possesses its own charisma in the modern period. Charisma, like value, grows with scarcity. One clings to any ground one can, once the void has opened up in the near distance. Meaning can be received cognitively or affectively or, most likely, through both faculties together. It often resides in a text written by people of an earlier age for whom meaning was assured. One may lack such assurance but respond to its authentic articulation nonetheless, as was avowedly the case with Buber. Or one may, like Rosenzweig, find significance in a ritual despite the fact that one cannot assent in literal terms to the propositions (for example, the blessings) featured in the ritual and despite the loss of the ritual's traditional contexts (namely, a discipline of mitzvot, a community that practices them as a matter of course). Indeed, what is rendered problematic may also be rendered that much more attractive by conferring a sort of "religious virtuosity" and establishing a sort of "innerworldly asceticism," to borrow Weber's terms. "Ordinary" believers become extraordinary by definition if the rest of their social reality is determinedly secular. Minimal observance seems maximal. One relishes this degree of spiritual or behavioral apartness from the larger order even while remaining a part of it, and, conversely, one proclaims the general culture's need for the wisdom or practice that one has discovered by taking a particular and different path. This was the case with both Buber and Rosenzweig. The meaning thus transmitted and adopted carries substantial authority not only despite but because of its fragmentary character.

4. *Community,* too, possesses authority, even aside from the fact that collective commitments seem more compelling than individual experience

or conviction. Buber and Rosenzweig, deprived, like most Jews, of integral community and reveling in individual autonomy, may have been typical as well in finding themselves drawn to self-selected communities and willing, or even eager, to have those communities obligate them. Even for Buber, Jewish community remained both horizontal and vertical. It encompassed the Jewish people, as it existed in his time, "horizontally," in the diaspora and in Palestine. And it carried on the chain that "links the generations one to another," the "vertical" connection to the people whose creation took place in Egypt and at Sinai. Buber felt bound to this community no matter how far he departed from it and insisted on his right to feel that way. Indeed, his departures made him all the more intent on deriving his path from "the prophetic faith" or "the way of man according to the teachings of Hasidism." The majority, and not he, had strayed. Rosenzweig not only shared in the widespread sense among Jews of the mystery of Jewish survival over the millennia but made that survival the basis of part 3 of the *Star*.

5. If attachment to the Jewish community carries with it the enlargement of self, the anchor of meaning, the "pleasure of agreement," the sense of more than subjective rightness, it also—recall Rosenzweig's quest—possesses the powerful appeal of *immortality,* of eternity. Buber posited an essential Jewish message; identified three, and only three, points in Jewish history when that message had become the actual center of a community's existence; and declared himself in continuity with them—spokesman, as it were, for the fourth. Severance of any aspect of that attachment to the past carried guilt, which Buber (like so many others) strove mightily to assuage even as he (again, like many others) declined to engage in any of the ancestors' religious practices. Rosenzweig, for his part, also posited an essential Jewish teaching, albeit one more complex than most of the views from the "heights" that he disdained, and located its quintessential expressions in the handful of paradigmatic texts and practices featured in his long magnum opus. Whether he found particular mitzvot meaningful or not depended on whether the ancestors had, in his view, granted them paramount importance. Their way through the centuries was eternal in a way individual life might not be. Abandoning ancestral ways meant not only killing the tradition but depriving oneself of the prospect of eternity. The rays of the star burned in the world only thanks to Jews and Christians who proclaimed revelation and lived the ritual cycles that anticipated redemption.

It may well be, finally, that the metaphor of *unending search* while walking in ancestral ways, a leitmotiv of Buber, Rosenzweig, and many other twentieth-century thinkers drawn by the combination of these five sources of authority, has itself become authoritative. Its proponents have believed themselves forced by intellectual integrity to distrust any surer resolution of their doubts and to rebel against any less equivocal directive of their actions. They may also have had good reasons for preferring a distant to a proximate God, or a silent God to one issuing commandments that human selves would often rather repress or reject. Whatever the reason, the self-identity of the searcher for authority has become crucial to modern Jewish practice. It has conferred and protected a precious sense of authenticity and truth that is ideally suited for voluntarist observance in a democratic and highly individualist social context. "Searching" assists believers mightily in withstanding the very challenges to faith that have made the other sort of authority so difficult to affirm. That authority remains absent—but, as I have suggested, one doubts in many cases that it is really missed.

EIGHT

The Reconstruction
of Jewish Tradition in
Twentieth-Century America

As the quest for firmer authority continues in contemporary American Judaism, the most pervasive term and ground of authority is not "God" or "faith," not "revelation" or even "the ancestors," but "tradition." That choice clearly accords with Rosenzweig's approach to Jewish practice. It betrays as well an obvious elective affinity with numerous tendencies in late-twentieth-century American culture, both high and low.

At a time when the architecture of my newly built California condominium is listed as "traditional," and market research confirms that category's appeal; when my flannel shirt bears the label "New Traditions," which also happens to be the exact title of a journal published briefly in the 1980s by the countercultural *havurah* movement; when the *New York Times* regularly employs the word "tradition" as a synonym for any state of affairs preceding the one being reported (as in, "the breakdown of traditional cold war alliances and rivalries"); when the popular media teem with highly ambivalent visions (for example, the film *Dead Poets Society*) of a bygone era ostensibly characterized by "tradition, discipline, and rules"—at such a time it is perhaps only to be expected that religion, too, should invoke the term so regularly.[1] "Tradition" resonates as few words do in the contemporary lexicon of faith, certainly more than "faith" or "religion" themselves. It harks back to roots dearly desired without imposing obligation to any particular behavior or creed, conferring the legitimacy of connection with the ancestors and God while preserving the precious distance between honored past and life as it actually is (and, by implication, should be) lived. If we are to judge by the current usage of the word, more and more Jews are, like Rosenzweig, seeking continuity with inherited forms of practice and belief while, like Buber, claiming their right—in the name of tradition—to reform and re-construct what they have chosen to receive.

Herein lies the problem. It is one thing to place oneself in a long chain of evolution (Rosenzweig's stance, following the Historical School) or to justify radical departures from the past by appeal to the authority of an unchanging "essence" founded in reason or revelation or both (the nineteenth-century Reformers' strategy). It is quite another thing altogether to locate authority in "the tradition" despite the awareness that the past to which one appeals is, to a significant degree, a patchwork product of one's own construction, selected from a large number of pasts potentially available for use. How can one simultaneously and with utter self-consciousness both *read into* and *read out of* the "sources of Judaism"? How simultaneously "invent" the past and invoke its authority? The dilemma, I shall argue, unavoidably shadows contemporary American Jewish practice, all the more so because selective study of classical texts has itself become a major feature of Jewish practice, displacing other observances less accommodating to piecemeal "reconstruction," and thus has made the immense variety of sources better known and more widely accessible.

We shall probe the issues involved in the appeal to usable Jewish pasts by analyzing two moments of special consequence in the conception and deployment of "tradition" in our century. The first is Mordecai Kaplan's method of "functional revaluation," developed and promoted in the 1930s as American Jews of the "second generation" made their way between the two worlds of immigrant ghetto and Gentile society. Kaplan hoped to assuage their doubts about the relevance of inherited self-definitions to American circumstances—which, they recognized, were utterly unprecedented in Jewish history. The second moment to be examined comprises present-day efforts, including those of Jewish feminists, in which the approach inaugurated by Kaplan has reached mature (and divergent) fulfillment. Contemporary thinkers are free of Kaplan's need to disengage angrily from the past in order to reconstruct it, free too of the need to justify at every turn their right to appropriate that past for their own contemporary purposes. No better "god-term" is presently available to such thinkers than "tradition," given what they do and do not believe, will and will not do. None is better calculated to appeal to potential practitioners.

My aim in this chapter is to explain why that authority and that appeal are so widespread today (not only among Jews) and why both are fraught with difficulties that cannot be overcome but only—in the best of cases—confronted and understood.

I. THE AMBIGUITIES OF RECONSTRUCTION

The concept of tradition figured crucially in Kaplan's effort of reconstruction in two contradictory ways. In the first twenty-five chapters of his masterpiece, *Judaism as a Civilization* (1934)—a work devoted to thorough exposition of the problems facing Judaism and the Jews in the modern period, and a highly polemical evaluation of the inadequacies of every previous approach to solving those problems—the word "tradition" appears almost entirely with *negative* connotations. It is associated with primitive superstition, used to describe a supernatural notion of God that Kaplan dismisses, and contrasted pejoratively with scientific truth. Tradition is identified repeatedly with Orthodoxy, and with its mistaken view that Judaism had not evolved over the centuries, and is linked to otherworldliness as opposed to a modern, rational focus upon this world—the only world, Kaplan believed, in which human beings could hope to experience salvation.[2]

Kaplan's view of the Jewish past in these chapters was arguably far less charitable than that of many nineteenth-century Reformers. His periodization of history began with the "henotheistic" stage of early Israelite religion (rather than with "Revelation," as in Geiger's schema), proceeded to "theocratic" (Second Temple) and "otherworldly" stages (rabbinic and medieval Judaism), and came finally to the period driven by "modern man's demand for historic truth."[3] Moreover, Kaplan held the *entirety* of the Jewish past to be inappropriate in its current form to modernity's new realities. For Judaism was, in his view—influenced decisively by the cultural Zionist thinker Ahad Ha'am and by anthropologists such as Durkheim—not only or even centrally a religion but a *civilization,* comprising language, literature, history, arts, "folkways," and a homeland. Kaplan's break with *all* of that past—including his immediate modern predecessors—would have to be thoroughgoing. The eastern European world of his parents rarely appears in the pages of his voluminous writings, not even as nostalgia. History always interested Kaplan far less than theory. The past was largely inapplicable to his present; he would rebuild on and with its ruins.

Kaplan's aim, however, was not to found a new tradition in place of the old but to "reconstruct" the one he had inherited. An entirely new method would have to be evolved, he declared, in order to achieve continuity with the past while transforming it, "a method compatible with the evolutionary and historical conception of religion, and based upon needs of the human spirit which cannot be disregarded without danger to man's moral and spiritual health."[4] At this point in the argument, Kaplan's attitude to tradition takes a decisive turn. Where before he had referred to tradition but sparingly, and always in denigration, he must now invoke and appeal to it repeatedly in order to legitimate his project of wholesale reconstruction. The word begins to appear in this new light with astonishing regularity. Kaplan begins the crucial chapter on the "functional method of interpretation" by arguing that "the Jewish quality of the religion of the Jews . . . will consist chiefly in the fact that it will be lived by Jews." However, he apparently realizes at once that this is not sufficient.

> The religion lived by Jews can be given character and individuality by utilizing the vast storehouse of spiritual values that are implicit in its traditions. If the recorded experiences of Jewish prophet and sage, poet and saint will occupy a predominant place in the Jewish consciousness as it strives to adjust itself to life, the resulting adjustment will constitute Jewish religious behavior.[5]

Kaplan seems to intend this claim in two senses. The "resulting adjustment" will be Jewish because Jewishly informed Jews will have created it. This is a variation both on Rosenzweig's notion and on Kaplan's own initial claim that "Jewish" is what Jews do. However, the outcome he describes will also be Jewish because a group of human beings, having decided to make this particular tradition "predominant" in their "consciousness," cannot but generate beliefs and behavior continuous with that tradition and, in fact, "implicit" in it—an argument akin to Mendelssohn's in *Jerusalem*. Kaplan's attention henceforth is devoted to the latter meaning of his claim.

He now assumes, despite previous condemnations, that "traditional Jewish religion is inherently capable of engendering the most significant human attitudes" and that "utilizing traditional concepts" enables one to take advantage of the "accumulated momentum and emotional drive of man's previous efforts to attain greater spiritual power." It was therefore imperative "to develop a method of discovering in traditional Jewish religion adumbrations of what we consider an adequate spiritual adjustment to life." Kaplan would reveal and develop "the pragmatic implications of the traditional teachings." Note that in these four usages—all from a single page—tradition is very much a resource to be used rather than, as formerly, an impediment to be overcome.[6]

Not at all coincidentally, Kaplan proceeds in the following pages to link himself to his chosen intellectual and institutional tradition—the Historical School, and Zechariah Frankel more particularly—and to fault it for not going far enough in putting to good use its discovery of the "spirit that groped after self-expression in the traditional teaching."[7] Kaplan had refrained earlier in *Judaism as a Civilization* from attacking Solomon Schechter, the chancellor of the Jewish Theological Seminary and for many years Kaplan's mentor and patron, though Schechter by rights should have been subjected to a critique parallel to those directed at Samson Raphael Hirsch as the founder of modern Orthodoxy and at Kaufman Kohler, the American theoretician of classical Reform. Instead, he had picked on lesser figures who "collapsed" easily at the approach of his formidable pen.[8] Now, as Kaplan begins to lay out his own position, it becomes clearer than ever that it was Schechter who had laid its theoretical foundation. Seeking to define the commonalties of Judaism throughout the ages (despite the variations which, as a result of *Wissenschaft,* he could not deny), Schechter had argued that although Maimonides and Akiba disagreed on a great deal,

> they both observed the same fasts and feasts[,] . . . revered the same sacred symbols, though they put different interpretations on them[,] . . . prayed in the same language[,] . . . were devoted students of the same Torah[,] . . . [and] looked back to Israel's past with admiration and reverence. . . . And they both became rocks and pillars of Judaism.[9]

The continuity, in other words, lay in *practice* rather than belief— though Schechter, if pressed, would have had to concede at once that the details of that practice had also varied immensely, for historical development had not left prayer, sacred symbols, feasts and fasts, or modes of Torah study untouched. Schechter would perhaps have resisted the realization that what he pointed to as "the same" was in part a function of where he trained his lens. Kaplan, however, did not shy away from that realization—and so had to devote enormous energies to justifying his resort to the authority of "tradition" nonetheless.

His methodology for doing so is fascinating to observe from the vantage of nearly sixty years afterward: it is at once highly self-conscious and fraught with insuperable difficulties. Kaplan began with the recognition that "the task of reinterpretation consists first in selecting"—a staple of contemporary hermeneutics. One selected "from among the ideational and practical consequences of the traditional values those which are spiritually significant for our day." This crucial statement requires unpacking. Kaplan claimed, on the basis of science, to possess certain "knowledge of human nature as it functions in society and in the individual." Moreover, he believed, on the basis of social science, that human nature does not change. Human needs were accordingly constant; religious doctrines, like other aspects of culture, were formulated in order to satisfy those needs. Kaplan could therefore hope to reason back from particular ideas and institutions in the past (for example, Creation or the Sabbath) to the permanent needs or desiderata ("values") which they were meant to supply, and he then could act to supply these needs in the present with other ideas and institutions. His substitutions could be considered "equivalent," in functional terms, to the originals. Reinterpretation was not the assignment of new meaning to existing ideology and symbols but "the process of finding equivalents in the civilization to which we belong for values of a past stage," values which were admittedly qualitatively different but which "possess equivalence" when "considered morphologically"—that is, in relation to their *use*.[10]

The task was immensely complicated. Kaplan had to understand the thinking and circumstances of previous generations well enough to know how they hoped to advance unchanging human values through the adoption of particular beliefs and practices suited to the needs of their own day. He had to "reconstruct mentally the aspirations implied" in particular teachings and institutions, "disengaging from the mass of traditional lore and custom the psychological aspect which testifies to the presence of ethical and spiritual strivings." In this way, the tradition ceased to be regarded as something to be accepted or rejected and became, instead, a "symbol for a spiritual desideratum in the present."[11] The word "tradition" appears five times within a dozen lines at this point, shouting down (as it were) the doubts about continuity which Kaplan's complex methodology had to overcome. He then applies his method of revaluation to the God-idea ("as handed down," it meant one thing but would now signify something very different) and, in the following chapter, to the idea of Torah. The "traditional Torah" was no longer acceptable, Kaplan averred. He would tell us what "Torah should mean": namely, Jewish civilization as envisioned by Reconstructionism.[12]

Kaplan's approach was in several respects fully as unprecedented as he claimed it to be. Like Geiger and other Reformers, Kaplan believed that "spiritual well-being" could legitimately require the reexamination or change or abrogation of mitzvot. Tradition, as he put it in a famous dictum, should exercise a vote but never a veto. But whereas Reform thinkers altered or discarded any practice that did not further the teaching of ethical monotheism, Kaplan by and large took an opposite tack, endowing existing practices with new meaning. Moreover, where the Reformers retained belief in some sort of "progressive revelation," Kaplan allowed no other author (or authority) for the commandments than *the Jewish people*. Like Spinoza, he argued that "traditional practices," no longer regarded as divine commands, might nonetheless be called mitzvot if the term were used "in the sense that they arouse in us the religious mood." The adjective "divine" referred to the *effect* of an action rather than its *source*. Jews were both authors and objects of the commandments, "functionally revaluated" by Kaplan into "folkways."[13]

Finally, as we have noted, Kaplan maintained that *all* of Jewish culture stood at the disposal of his reconstructions, for every aspect of life could and should be transformed to better serve deep human needs—the needs which he believed every religious tradition in every age existed in order to fulfill. The commandments therefore received only a small share of Kaplan's own attention in *Judaism as a Civilization*. Far more space was devoted to stressing the full range of attitude and practice required of a "maximalist Judaism": appreciation of the Jewish arts, knowledge of Jewish history, fluency in the Hebrew language, support for the Jewish homeland. This was well suited to the expectations of eastern European immigrants, who had known a flourishing secular culture and took the national or ethnic character of their Jewish identity for granted. Thus the examples of religious ritual reconstruction in the book were few and generally quite modest. Dietary laws, as mark and sustainer of a distinctive ethnic identity, should be followed— though participation in the civilization of America allowed one the compromise of keeping a kosher home while eating nonkosher food everywhere else. Sabbath observance could be enriched (and eased) by the playing of classical music, by "entertainment" and "group singing," as well as with havdalah services. Hanukkah festivities took on greater importance in America because of the proximity of Christmas. Kaplan urged the use of distinctively Jewish names to reflect American Jewry's newly won self-respect and creativity, the presentation of Jewish dramas and pageants on Jewish stages, the design by interior decorators of "furniture, hangings and bric-a-brac in a manner that would reflect Jewish individuality."[14]

Kaplan's innovation, we might say, aimed to be no less extensive than the halakhic regimen that his folkways were intended to replace and no less comprehensive than Jewish life in the eastern European communities that he rarely mentioned.[15] In the early years of his career, Kaplan enthusiastically supported Rabbi Judah Magnes's attempt to weld a host of Jewish welfare and educational agencies in New York City into a unified *kehillah* on the European model.[16] In *Judaism as a Civilization,* written decades after the *kehillah* experiment had failed, Kaplan still persisted in the effort to have Jews differ in "entity" (that is, ethnic identity), as they had in eastern Europe, rather than in "quality" (that is, religion), as many attempted to do in the West. The latter model, he was convinced, was not viable. "What is at stake in our day is the very maintenance of Jewish life as a distinct societal entity. Its very otherness is in jeopardy."[17] The point of Jewish names and pageants, as of Sabbath and dietary laws, in Kaplan's view, was to foster a group life of common practice so compelling that attachment to Judaism could again be taken for granted as what Kaplan called an "intuitional attitude." Jewish life and practice, experienced in this way, would need no further justification: no God, no mission, no Kantian grounding in ethical aspiration.

Kaplan even allowed himself the extravagant claim that when Jews over the millennia had recited the Shema Yisrael morning and evening, "traditionally one of the most dramatically meaningful practices of Judaism," they had not done so "because of the abstract idea of absolute monotheism which it is supposed to express, but simply because it provided an occasion for experiencing the thrill of being a Jew."[18] Such was the power of collective practice in his view—and the derivative character of "abstract values and concepts"! Nothing less than the survival of the Jews and Judaism depended on his ability to revive collective practice through the provision of a rationale, at once scientific and authentically Jewish, that would lead to the re-creation of strong Jewish communities. These in turn would produce and renew Jewish practices as a matter of course.

In *The Meaning of God in Modern Jewish Religion* (1937), Kaplan rehearsed his dissatisfactions with existing versions of Judaism and then—prodded by concerns that his version of Judaism was not "religious" enough—proceeded to apply the method of functional revaluation to the yearly cycle of Jewish holidays. Where past generations had practiced "*transvaluation*[,] . . . ascribing meanings to the traditional content of a religion or social heritage, which could neither have been contemplated nor implied by the authors of that content"—Rosenzweig's essay on the significance of the Sabbath and festivals comes to mind as an example—Kaplan's method of *revaluation* would exhibit a very different relation to tradition. For "moderns," in whose name Kaplan always spoke, no other relation to tradition was possible. "Worship directed to a god who is conceived in terms that no longer satisfy the deepest spiritual insights of the age" was "idolatry."[19]

I will consider in some detail Kaplan's revaluation of the Sabbath, a virtual tour de force, the better to illustrate the self-consciousness that Kaplan brought to his task of retaining continuity with the tradition despite and because of his engagement in overhauling it—the better, as well, to understand the failure of that theory, which has forced others to reconstruct the tradition without Kaplan's "scientific" assurance of carrying on what they are changing. Let us begin by recapitulating the steps of his argument.[20]

1. "From the point of view of tradition, the Sabbath enjoys a measure of sanctity beyond that of any other occasion in the year, with the single exception, perhaps, of the Day of Atonement." Kaplan reasonably infers this from the strict prohibitions on labor in effect on the Sabbath. His reification and virtual personification of "tradition" is far from unusual in Jewish thought and even Jewish scholarship. Somewhat less convincingly, he concludes from a rabbinic statement mentioning the Sabbath in one clause and all other commandments in another that "the Sabbath is thus made coordinate with [in other words, equal in weight to] the whole system of Mosaic Law."

2. The holiday invested with the most sanctity must come to fulfill the most central human need or desideratum. "What more comprehensive purpose can there be to human life than the complete and harmonious fulfillment of all the physical, mental, and moral powers with which the human self as a social being is endowed?" Kaplan, we recall, rests confident that human nature is unchanging and that he, thanks to modern science, is equipped to understand it.

3. Self-fulfillment is the "equivalent of what in general life is expressed by the term 'salvation' and in traditional Jewish life by the phrase 'having a share in the world to come.'" The locution "general life" is obviously out of place; the context calls for a reference to something like "traditional religion." One wonders if the odd usage is coincidental. Kaplan's entire "revaluation," his claim to continuity with tradition despite radical innovation, of course stands or falls on the "equivalence" of function and meaning that he asserts. His slip comes precisely where his footing needs to be most sure.

4. Reinforcing this purported "equivalence," Kaplan argues that the tradition also regarded holidays as tools to be used for the achievement of Jewish needs. It too practiced functionalism! The Sabbath "was designed to make the Jew aware" that meaning and purpose were at hand. It was "calculated to impress the Jew" that salvation was attainable, and it had in fact

"function[ed] . . . as the symbol of salvation." True to his contrast between transvaluation and revaluation, then, Kaplan is not imposing a foreign methodology on the tradition but bringing to light what had been present, albeit latently so, all along. Observe, too, that his functionalist approach subsumes belief under the category of practice. Rabbinic thought was very much, as one might say today, performed.

5. Revaluation of the Sabbath, therefore, consists in reworking the notion of salvation linked by tradition to the Sabbath. Practice and function remain; only meaning is adapted. Kaplan aims to find a modern "equivalent" for each of the key idea's component parts: creativity, holiness, and covenant. God is "the creative life of the universe," the set of forces that comprises "the antithesis of irrevocable fate and absolute evil." Holiness is translated as "transcendent importance"; human beings and the world are both holy in this sense, that is, possessed of ultimate meaning and purpose. Covenant becomes "commitment to Judaism," that is, loyalty to the Jewish people and its civilization as Kaplan understands these.[21]

The method of reasoning back from given practice and meaning to eternal function and then to reworked practice with new meaning is obviously cumbersome. Kaplan himself abandoned it, as he made his way through the cycle of Jewish holidays, in favor of the more streamlined and conventional strategy of *translation*. We have already seen several examples of this: salvation translates as self-fulfillment, holiness as importance, divine creation as the potential for human creativity. *The Meaning of God* is as good and as bad as these translations; the holidays and symbols of Jewish tradition emerge from his presentation as attractive to the degree that Kaplan successfully invests them with appealing new meanings. (Kaplan rarely proposed new rituals, except when he joined in an ecumenical proposal for an American civil religion built around holidays such as Lincoln's Birthday and the Fourth of July.)[22] Some symbols, in Kaplan's view, possessed "inherent appeal" and so required virtually no translation. The shofar was one example, the seder another.[23] But now that sovereignty resided in the people, Rosh Hashanah's proclamation of God's kingship had to be translated as "the affirmation of faith in humanity." A rabbinic midrash on the *lulav* should be "translated into literal fact" as a thought concerning the manifestation of God's justice in our midst, and so on.[24]

Kaplan's readers may find profound significance in these "revaluations," or they may not. Some chapters in the book are, in the nature of the case, more persuasive than others. Kaplan's interpretation of Shavuot as the festival reminding Jews of God's role as the "power that makes for righteous-ness-not-ourselves" (a phrase borrowed from Matthew Arnold) is to my mind far more convincing than the presentation of Sukkot as the reminder of "God as the power that makes for cooperation." What is more, Kaplan must convince readers at every turn not only that he "translates" accurately but that his version represents an *improvement* on the original. He must join his embrace of "the tradition," his paeans to the "Jewish spirit," with the argument that obedience to the Jewish cultural heritage in its current, re-ceived forms "blinds us to new insights based on broader experience"—that is, his own.

But there is a further problem: why should one remain loyal to tradition at all? If, according to science, the same constant needs are shared by all humankind and if, according to Kaplan's sociology, these needs are met through a large number of diverse civilizations, why should American Jews follow *these* particular and particularist observances, fixed thousands of years ago? In what way does "Jewish tradition" obligate the Jew? Kaplan wavered on this point throughout his career (as, one suspects, did his readers). In the section on covenant in *The Meaning of God,* it seems that no obligation is involved. One simply makes a rational choice. Having experienced the meaning and purpose conferred by observance of Jewish holidays, the Jew comes to participate in "the feeling which was universal among the Jewish people before the so-called Emancipation, that it was a privilege to be a Jew." Here modernity is actually denigrated; the "so-called" points to de-racination, alienation, spiritual impoverishment.[25] It would be folly not to seize an opportunity for wholeness, particularly if one were convinced by Kaplan's argument that no other existing tradition was comparably equipped to offer self-fulfillment to modern individuals.

He then adds a second source of obligation to Jewish tradition: the self's demand for authenticity and integrity. Orthodoxy gave Jews adequate reason for rejecting Judaism. One could not in good faith believe what it asserted. But Reconstructionism would enable the Jew to be "as critical of Jewish tradition as he may be, provided he tries not only to criticize Jewish tradition but to correct it." That excuse for assimilation denied, Kaplan is relentless in his criticism of status seekers who abandon their people in pur-suit of social acceptance or in flight from anti-Semitism. He implicitly makes the argument (quite common after the Holocaust) that Jews are bound together in a common fate and therefore obligated to cooperate in forging their common destiny.[26]

The ancestors—and the descendants—thus provide a third source of obligation. "Our responsibility to our forefathers is only to consult them, not to obey them. Our responsibility to our descendants is only to impart our most cherished experiences to them, but not to command them."[27] The individualism and ambivalence of this appeal should by now be quite familiar to us. Kaplan simultaneously rejected the existence of a God capable of judging human beings, insisted that his ancestors had been mistaken for maintaining that belief, forgave them for their error, and urged the retention—in the name of ancestors and descendants alike—of Yom Kippur, the holiday centered on atonement before God and on pleas for forgiveness. Ancestors were censured and abandoned even as Kaplan regularly invoked the "fathers," immediate transmitters of tradition, as a source of obligation. Kaplan of course carried on, and departed from, the commitments of one father in particular.[28]

All three arguments for "tradition" have proved widespread among American Jews, and—unlike the complicated method of "functional revaluation"—are still appealed to frequently today. The linkage of tradition to the fathers, in the context of "rational choice" and the norm of authenticity, may also help us solve a sociological puzzle. Kaplan's open disbelief in our "Father in Heaven" has not proved popular among American Jews, nor have his translations equating "holiness" with "importance" or commandments with "folkways." His approach to a selective "reconstruction" of practice, however, has by and large become normative outside Orthodoxy, his definition of Judaism as a civilization has become commonplace, and leading Reform and Conservative thinkers have advocated "God-ideas" not all that dissimilar from his own. The reason, sociologist Charles Liebman speculates, is that Jews far less traditional than Kaplan in their observance may have found it all the more necessary to cleave to the vestiges of traditional belief and language accompanying observance.[29] As we noted in Chapter 6, in our examination of modern Jewish nostalgia, departures from the ways of the ancestors demand frequent assurances of their blessing. The very loyalty to ancestors that Kaplan invoked, taught, and hoped to revalue may have precluded potential adherents from following him in the *avowed* reconstruction of the ancestors' legacy.

Kaplan's program also faced a "political" obstacle still more fundamental. The inability of American Jews to develop the "intuitional attitude" toward Jewish practice that he urged was perhaps inevitable given the inability of every movement but Orthodoxy to re-create in America the sort of tight-knit communities in which distinctive observances can be absorbed as taken-for-granted elements of daily life. Kaplan's redefinition of Judaism as a civilization followed Durkheim to the letter and suffered, as that vision did, from the lack of renewed "organic community." One suspects that Kaplan's frequent recourse to the word "tradition," subsequently evinced in all quarters, stemmed in part from the term's ability, through its vagueness, to ease the tension between distinctively Jewish observance and general American norms—even as that very vagueness disguised the blurring of these boundaries in the lives of individual Jews. Folkways, selectively observed, became a major feature in the performance of both religion and ethnicity among American Jews—all the more popular because the strict connotations of "commandment," with its mandatory degree of apartness, had been stripped away, but all the more ineffective in re-creating the "otherness" that Kaplan's reconstruction of tradition not only advocated but required.[30]

2. THE REAPPROPRIATION OF TRADITION

Kaplan's successors in our own day have, as a result of his successes and failures, found his project for the use and construction of tradition at once more straightforward and more difficult. Transformation of practice in the name of tradition is now utterly commonplace and need not be elaborately explained or justified. It has become more problematic, however, because the task must be accomplished without Kaplan's faith in objective science, historical progress, or the authority of "modernity" and also without Kaplan's hope for the sort of all-encompassing community that would have made the argument in favor of tradition, however reconstructed, unnecessary.

Judith Plaskow's alertness to the dilemmas at issue here is exemplary. Indeed, the impossibility of objectively locating "the tradition" or its putative essence is crucial to her construction of a feminist Judaism substantially different from any Judaism that has existed heretofore. As a feminist, Plaskow must reject the notion that Judaism is "a given that I could fit myself into or decide to reject." Rather, she must insist that it is "a complex and pluralistic tradition involved in a continual process of adaptation and change." For she wishes to "remain within a patriarchal tradition" and yet alter it so that she can be a Jew not despite but as part of her feminism. Her work, very much like Kaplan's, is avowedly intended not only to change the tradition but to save it. "I am convinced that a feminist Judaism can restore the viability of God-talk within Judaism, providing the tradition with a language it has lost and sorely needs."[31] The dual authority to which she appeals time and again is the tradition's own legacy of repeated reinterpretation and the ground of her own experience inside an existing Jewish community: not that of American Jewry as a whole but of a far smaller group of Jewish women.

Neither Plaskow's argument nor her method can be treated adequately here, but I do want to highlight several features which illustrate her relation to Kaplan, to other contemporary understandings of tradition, and to the conceptual elements of Jewish practice that I have analyzed in previous chapters. Note, first, that she begins with a "heavy silence." Women rarely appear in historical accounts of the Jews, and they appear even more rarely as authors (or even subjects) of sacred texts. Their experiences are not part of what has until now been considered "the tradition." Plaskow must assume that what has been handed down is not a complete record of what was. It is, rather, a partial, biased record in need of correction. "Tradition" must be studied, therefore, and studied suspiciously, so that it can be rewritten.

Plaskow's blueprint for doing so—a chapter entitled "Torah: Reshaping Jewish Memory"—draws heavily on Kaplan, as well as on Buber's understanding of the biblical text as a partial record of God's encounter with ancient Israelites and on Gershom Scholem's reading of the kabbalistic notion of the hidden versus the manifest Torah. Her own chain of inheritance is clear. Moreover, she claims at more than one point (as had Kaplan, following Geiger) that her reconstruction of Judaism follows in the footsteps of the rabbis, who, like her, were not engaged in "discovering what 'really happened' but [in] projecting later developments back onto the eternal present of Sinai, and in this way augmenting and reworking Torah." The rabbis too "brought to the Bible their own questions and found answers that showed the eternal relevance of biblical truth." This justifies new practices such as feminist midrash, scholarship, ritual, and liturgy.[32]

Plaskow's continuity with classical Judaism is further highlighted by the division of her text into chapters on Torah, Israel, and God, though that "traditional" triad points to her divergence from the rabbis as well; the bounds of continuity and discontinuity are complex and do not always seem to fall where she places them. Like Kaplan, for example, she at times renders the tradition more unitary than she knows it to be, in order to exaggerate the extent of her own departure from its dictates. God has not always been, as she claims, "the beginning, the sine qua non of Jewish existence and experience."[33] More important, Plaskow feels the need to radically transform the "metaphors" which have dominated Jewish self-understanding until now. All previous renderings of God, Torah, and Israel are declared unac-

ceptable. Aware that the very extent of her innovation jeopardizes her claim
to continuity with Judaism's past, Plaskow takes pains to argue that all description of God is metaphor and that the superiority of one metaphor to
another is not a function of its truth-value but of its use.

"The experience of God in community is both the measure of the
adequacy of traditional language and the norm in terms of which new images must be fashioned and evaluated." Note the twofold novelty here.
Whereas Kaplan, too, would have regarded religious language as a cultural
product to be judged by its pragmatic adequacy, he believed nonetheless
that that language actually described *reality,* with a greater or lesser degree
of accuracy, something science had enabled us to gauge. Kaplan claimed
objectivity for his vision: he was simply experiencing, and seeing, what was
there. For Plaskow, the only standard is *communal experience.* As she explains
it, authority must rest somewhere and

> from a feminist perspective, . . . human beings are fundamentally
> communal; our individuality is a product of community, and our
> choices are shaped by our being with others. Scripture itself is a prod-
> uct of community. . . . My most important experiences of God have
> come through this community [of Jewish feminists], and it has given
> me the language with which to express them. . . . Without it I could
> not see the things that I see.[34]

That is the second difference from Kaplan. Plaskow has *decided* to remain
within the "tradition" of Judaism because she wishes to live inside a Jewish
community that also shares another nonnegotiable commitment, at once
ethical and political: feminism. Having made the decision for feminism on
other grounds (though these might well have been influenced by her Jewish
upbringing and its traditions), Plaskow then takes care (as had Kaplan before
her) to describe her experiences, if at all possible, in terms derived from
Jewish sources and to urge adoption of feminist liturgies and rituals—at
times heavily nostalgic in their invocation of the foremothers—which, similarly, draw from the storehouse furnished by Jewish tradition.

The problem of authority thus resolves itself into the question of
"whether the primary community to which I am accountable" finds her
images of God or Torah or Israel compelling—and whether the members
of her community will find meaning in the practices which those images
authorize and demand. Plaskow reasonably assumes that communities of
faith coalesce and disintegrate over time in relation to visions and metaphors
which do or do not prove adequate to their needs and experience. Her

tentative feminist theology of Judaism will prove of lasting import if it nurtures future growth. One community of readers might define itself around that vision, just as other readers might incorporate what they find useful in her vision into their own communities, ignoring elements (for example, the "theology of sexuality") which do not speak to them with "inner power." Unlike Kaplan, Plaskow need not presume a particular and unchanging conception of human nature, need not engage in the complicated work of locating "functional equivalents" to human needs and desiderata, and need not hold the success of her effort hostage to the creation of an integral American *kehillah*. Her only requirements are fellow members and readers: women and men who will, like her, be guided by the consensus of their feminist communities as they refashion Judaism through new collective practices, including midrash, scholarship, ritual, and liturgy. I will examine one such reconstruction—feminist Passover Haggadot—in detail in the Conclusion of this study.

Many of the assumptions underpinning Plaskow's work also underlie Elliot Dorff's quite different effort to articulate a Conservative Jewish ideology, and many of the same dilemmas result. Like Plaskow, Dorff seeks to turn the historical variety of Jewish belief and practice to advantage. Indeed, he claims, following *Emet Ve-Emunah,* the most recent authoritative statement of Conservative principles, that his movement alone seeks to carry on the whole of Jewish tradition rather than one element of it ("ethics" in the case of Reform, "halakhah" in that of Orthodoxy).[35] Conservative Judaism had "retain[ed] most of the tradition" even while accepting the fact and necessity of historical development: it was devoted to "tradition" *and* change.[36] For the rabbis as well, "it was clearly a matter of 'tradition and change,'" while in other movements, one or the other of these ideals had prevailed.[37]

Dorff's presentation of Jewish tradition gives prominence to the two aggadot which feature centrally in Scholem's influential essay "Revelation and Tradition as Religious Categories in Judaism" (1962) and are almost universally cited in recent centrist discussion of the issue.[38] Like Rabbi Joshua in the Oven of Akhnai story, Dorff wishes to emphasize that authority to alter the law is "not in heaven" but vested in the students of Torah. In keeping with the depiction of a Moses perplexed because he has been set down in the academy of Rabbi Akiba and cannot follow the discussion going on in his name, Dorff contends that halakhic and aggadic transformation are inevitable. Jews must follow the example of what the rabbis did as well as what they said; halakhah must be central. However, just as the rabbis saw the judges of each generation as on a par with Moses and Aaron, so we should not see ourselves as inferior to them. If Reform's credo could be stated as "Back to the Ethics of the Prophets," Conservatism should declare, "Back to the Method of the Talmud." [39]

That method is both formal *and* substantive, in Dorff's view. He stands firm on the need for halakhah—the key to tradition is traditional practice—and rejects the democratization of authority involved in Plaskow's reliance on a plurality of communities, each with its own normative consensus as to what tradition means and should comprise. In the name of his models, the rabbis, Dorff argues that "traditionally, Judaism has always been an aristocracy of the learned; laymen have not been considered able to weigh the importance of tradition accurately." In retaining this elitism, "we are simply following the Tradition." Thus, when a question of law arises, one should first examine the "traditional Jewish Codes." If all precedent proves out of keeping with contemporary needs and sensitivities, however, it should be changed forthrightly, without recourse to legal fictions. "That is a perfectly legitimate move to make in Jewish Law, as I have demonstrated above." [40]

Dorff is walking a fine line here, and its delicacy is further evidence for his claim that the path he recommends is not one which very many Jews are competent to chart. His awarding of "a vote but not a veto" to the past is, of course, consonant with Kaplan. His conception of commandment, however, is far more traditional—a subtler working out of the line begun with Frankel's reliance on the popular will of the Jewish people, Schechter's turn to the will of "Catholic Israel," and the further narrowing of that population to the Jewishly learned and observant among them by Robert Gordis, a prominent conservative theoretician of the previous generation. Differentiating his position from both Kaplan and Gordis, Dorff writes in Rosenzweigian fashion that he conceives the Torah as having been written by human beings but as constituting "the human record of the encounter between God and the People Israel at Sinai." Its authority thus rests not on God's will (Gordis), or the will of the Jewish people (Kaplan), but on the will of God as mediated by an elite of God's covenant people. "It is the rabbis, representing the community, and not every individual on his own, who must determine the content of Jewish law in our day." [41]

The identification with the rabbis and their texts—rather than with the prophets, or the authors of the Codes, or the kabbalists—is striking, and Dorff is aware that this identification is in part a function of the fact that "two generations of Conservative rabbis have been raised on a Seminary program in which Talmud has been emphasized each year, while the Codes have been given only perfunctory treatment.[42] He also seems aware that in deciding to take the Judaism of the rabbis as normative, a Jew like himself votes to "privilege" one portion of the tradition over others and to count certain readings of and within that portion as authoritative while ignoring or discounting others. This choice, while not unreasoned, cannot be defended by appeal to "the tradition" or its putative essence. Dorff has not yet to my knowledge addressed the issue of selective inheritance directly.[43] In general, however, he, like Plaskow, is aware of the difficulties in working with a constructed "tradition" rather than a given one, especially without the benefit of a method of "certain" translation such as the one that Kaplan employed.

"The point is that we maintain that we have both the right and the duty to make changes in the law when necessary, even when these changes do not follow directly from precedents." Dorff has the right because rabbinic innovations which he has decided to take as normative, according to certain texts which he has opted to "privilege," declare that precedent. He has the right, too, because scholarship, far from discerning an eternal essence or an unchanging human nature, has pointed up historical variation no more radical than his own. He hopes that the choices he makes in this regard—his selections from the past, the authorities to which he appeals—may over time come to constitute a community composed of those who assent to the same definition of tradition and identify in the same manner with the ancient rabbis. In this sense, and in this sense only, can the rabbis be said to "represent the community." This newly constituted community—once again, a far smaller community than the one that Kaplan envisioned—would in large measure be a creation of the rabbis' own selections—if, indeed, it comes into being at all—and would exist alongside others which would result from different readings of tradition. In establishing such communities of practice, Dorff states, "I firmly believe that we are doing exactly what the Tradition would have us do, if only we can muster the personal qualities necessary to carry out our program wisely."[44]

"Tradition" can be personified here in good faith, ascribed an overarching intention, and invoked as ground for contemporary behavior—all this despite a degree of awareness that it is not unitary but variegated and despite the explicit avowal that it has no essence. Dorff follows in footsteps which he has discovered through selective reading and even marked out. But the difficulties are daunting, not least because the project demands an educated and integral community rarely achieved among any Jews in America, Conservative Jews included, and unlikely to appear any time soon.

The problems are clearer still in recent Reform writings, for two reasons. First, transformation in actual practice is most apparent in that movement, since for many decades it was marked by an antipathy to ritual rivaling Buber's; and, second, Reform has always been and remains today more prolific than its rivals in the publication of statements of changing principles. A movement that as recently as 1972 could not agree to issue a "guide" to the religious practice of its members lest it infringe on their autonomy[43] was able by 1979 to build on individual rabbis' earlier "guides" and "Reform responsa" and publish *Gates of Mitzvah: A Guide to the Jewish Life Cycle,* which from its title onward speaks of commandment. Rabbi Gunther Plaut is careful to note in his foreword that Judaism "was never meant to be merely an institutional religion. Its ultimate focus remains the individual." But he then readjusts that focus to zero in on "personal observance and personal deed, at home and at work, . . . [giving] communal expression to our belief in God and . . . the significance of our membership in the historic people"—hardly the standard view in official Reform discourse or practice in the past.[46] The volume's editor, Rabbi Simeon Maslin, similarly follows the unequivocal assertion that "mitzvah is the key to authentic Jewish existence and the sanctification of life" with a footnote directing readers to four essays, included in the guide, that set forth "different points of view on why, how, and to what extent a modern Jew may feel required to perform mitzvot." Practice would be common, while the theory justifying it could vary. Individual Reform Jews, still the final arbiters of observance in the eyes of their rabbis, would then be in a position to "develop a personal rationale through which the performance of a mitzvah may become meaningful."[47]

The movement had cleared the way for this new strategy—combining the language of commandment with a reinforced commitment to autonomy—in its 1976 Statement of Principles, the first such declaration to be issued since the Columbus Platform of 1937. In almost all respects, there is no substantive difference between the statements. Only one paragraph breaks new ground: "Our Obligations: Religious Practice." It goes well beyond the 1937 affirmation of "such customs, symbols and ceremonies as possess inspirational value," paired there with "distinctive forms of religious art and music and the use of Hebrew." The aesthetic emphasis of 1937—ceremony adorns but does not obligate—gives way in 1976 to mention of "claims made upon us" that extend beyond ethical obligations to "many other aspects of Jewish living." The paragraph's concluding sentence seeks to balance newly affirmed obligation and still regnant autonomy. "Within each area of Jewish observance Reform Jews are called upon to confront the claims of Jewish tradition, however differently perceived, and to exercise their individual autonomy, choosing and creating on the basis of commitment and knowledge."[48]

One could regard this formulation as declaring the self-evident. In the modern West, and particularly in the United States, all religious observance is necessarily assumed voluntarily. What is more, if Jews who acknowledge themselves to be Jews "thereby limit their freedom to some extent," so does any parent who acknowledges that particular status.[49] Every adult knows that freedom is never absolute. Nonetheless, Maslin and Plaut have succeeded in containing the hallowed Reform commitment to autonomy within an ambitious new project of providing scope and specificity to Reform observance. The movement is now prepared to do more than simply *guide.* It affirms that God *commands,* and its rabbis are even prepared to say *what* God commands.

At times that commandment is rather equivocal. The pregnant woman considering abortion is advised to "determine" the proper course "in accordance with the principles of Jewish morality"—which are left undefined. On dietary laws, *Gates of Mitzvah* recognizes various attitudes and degrees of observance among Reform Jews and recommends that such "an essential feature of Jewish life for so many centuries" bears study by each family. At the same time, however, "it is a mitzvah" for a couple to be tested for genetic disease before marriage, to bring children into the world and thank God after doing so, and to bring children into the covenant; "it is a mitzvah" to pray on a daily basis, to affix a mezuzah to the doorpost, and to celebrate Shabbat with candles, kiddush, hallah, and appropriate blessings; "it is a mitzvah" to write an ethical will, to attend a funeral service, to prepare a first meal for mourners, and to recite kaddish when one is a mourner oneself.[50]

The source of authority of these commandments—certainly not the Shulhan Arukh or any other codification of the Oral Law—varies considerably. At times it is the application by Reform rabbis of "fundamental principles" such as "the sanctity of life" (as in the cases of abortion and genetic testing). At other points (as with circumcision or the Sabbath), it is the weight of "Jewish tradition," again as defined by Reform rabbinic interpreters. Understanding of "ultimate authority" predictably varies still more—and is not required for agreement by rabbis or congregants on the obligation of the practices mandated by "tradition." The author of one interpretive essay included in *Gates of Mitzvah* traces the authority of the commandments in Rosenzweigian fashion to a Commander, while according to a second formulation, more Buberian and Kaplanian in tone, the mitzvot "mark points of encounter by the Jewish people with God." A third, still more Kaplanian, holds that the commandments "remind us of our noblest values and stimulate us to pursue them" while serving as well to bind the religious naturalist "to his people and his tradition. They speak to him imperatively because he is Jewish and wants to remain so."[51]

These statements seem to exhaust the possible inventory of current Reform rationales for observance, which are bounded by the affirmation of individual autonomy, the rejection of halakhah, and the felt need to include more specific observances—and not merely ethical principles—within the domain of commanded Reform practice. If the movement has provided grounds for greater observance while adroitly avoiding the theological issues that have plagued such attempts throughout the modern period, its practice uncoupled from any justifying theory, it is, as we have seen, in good company. The theological technicalities need not concern us here; Reform rabbis have begun taking advantage of a new willingness among the laity to study texts and perform traditional rituals without worrying overmuch about the ultimate authority of observance or whether that authority should by rights impel them to a more thoroughgoing observance. The appeal is rather to *tradition,* which here as elsewhere works to the degree that Reform Jews prove willing to accept their rabbis' definition of that tradition through self-conscious selection from the plenitude of available options.

A footnote in *Gates of the Seasons* (a companion volume to *Gates of Mitzvah*) is telling in this respect. It reports that "the following list of mitzvot is a revision of the earlier 'Catalogue of Shabbat Opportunities.'"[52] When does an "opportunity" become a mitzvah? When a movement's rabbis (and/ or laypeople) decide to make it one. Thus it is "a mitzvah for every Jew to mark Yom Ha-atzma'ut" publicly, or to "remember the six million" on Yom Ha-shoah, but not to observe Tisha B'av. Only time will tell whether the "folk" will embrace, reject, or acquiesce in this attempt by their rabbis to guide and follow them. Elements of the elite more committed to autonomy than is the majority that voted in the new policy have already expressed their discomfort.[53] Meanwhile, the Reform movement's new prayer book, *Gates of Prayer* (1975), has run precisely the same risk, in the same manner, for the same reasons. Congregants and their rabbis are presented with a number of different services for Sabbaths and weekdays, varying in length, style, theme, and even theology. Pluralism rules. Autonomy is preserved. But at the same time, "tradition" is reasserted: there is far more Hebrew, prayers for tallit and tefillin are included, numerous references are made to

Zion. One even finds a special service for Yom Ha-atzma'ut and the return of Tisha B'av.[54] The past thus invoked, as Plaut has pointed out, helps to answer the two questions which drive many contemporary American Jews in the direction of selective observance—"What will my life say? How can I give meaning to my life?"—without requiring unequivocal affirmation of either God or revelation [55]

Ritual and observance can answer those questions convincingly, in a way that God or commandment cannot, for Jews unable in their own eyes to "believe what the ancestors believed" but fully capable in their own eyes of observing at least some of the ancestors' practices. This is all the more true when, for example, one "has a seder" without knowing the details that were involved in having a seder generations ago and, hence, need not concern oneself with observing those details. Putative "sameness" of behavior allows for departures from past belief and behavior of which one *is* aware. Moreover, the sense experience of ritual works its magic with or without belief; the power of what is performatively remembered allows all that has been forgotten to remain forgotten. Tradition continues. The blessing of the ancestors is pronounced.

3. THE THEORY OF "TRADITIONAL" PRACTICE

The theoretical contribution which more than any other has validated this move for laity, scholars, and rabbis alike is Scholem's essay "Revelation and Tradition as Religious Categories in Judaism." Scholem's scholarship as a whole aimed avowedly to overturn long-held assumptions about what was essential to or dominant in Judaism; in this essay, Scholem sought to show that while the faithful of any generation were, in the nature of the case, unconcerned with the origins of their tradition, the historian, by contrast, had to understand how traditions (in the plural) inevitably come to define the revelation from which their authority is ostensibly derived. In religious no less than in scholarly practice, the careful observer finds "the function of creativity and spontaneity in relation to that which is given."[56] This view has in recent decades received reinforcement from a number of theoretical quarters, the most influential of which has probably been Hans-Georg Gadamer's work *Truth and Method*. Gadamer, too, has argued the "indispensability of tradition" to the reading of any text and the need to become aware of one's own "horizon" of understanding (and its limits) in order to appreciate any foreign or past text or observance.[57] Self-consciousness about the constructed character of tradition, religious or scholarly, is for both

thinkers not a handicap but a necessity. Scholem quoted the Talmudic stories of the Oven of Akhnai and of Moses in Akiba's academy in full[58] to
demonstrate rabbinic awareness that no "given," whether of revelation or
tradition, is ever merely a "given." Each text or teaching has to be received
and then transmitted. Interpretation and change inevitably have their say.

I want to conclude this account of the construction of tradition in contemporary American Judaism by reflecting on the dilemmas posed by that construction not only to Jewish observance but to Jewish scholarship. The two
have been interrelated throughout the modern period, and in recent decades
it has become a truism of postmodern scholarship that it is naive to accept
any subject matter simply as a given, as independent of the definitions
through which a scholar presents it. Resultant methodological difficulties
are apparent in monographic works on particular authors or texts, and all
the more so in generalized treatments of "the rabbis" or "the kabbalists."
When one moves to surveys of "Judaism," the problems are truly immense
and generally faced in one of two ways.

In some cases, lip service is paid to the need for historical variation, but
then—given the necessity of saying something meaningful about "Judaism,"
about the "Jewish tradition" as opposed to others—the author resorts to
language that could easily be mistaken for the sort which prevailed a generation ago. One scholar, for example, began his short introduction to Judaism,
published in 1987, by explaining that the term connotes a "family relationship" among differing but related forms. Judaism cannot be reduced to a
system of beliefs; however, if we focus instead on "observable phenomena
such as worship and ritual" (the "sociological" approach), we "may well
end up by wondering whether we are studying a single phenomenon or an
apparently infinite variety of different 'Judaisms.'" The tradition has taken
different forms, but "it is also strongly felt" (note the passive voice here,
an appeal to undocumented consensus) "that there is a single thing called
'Judaism.'" Similarly, while the author warns against imposing foreign categories on Judaism, and for that reason opts for a "historical approach," he
also assumes that "from a sociological viewpoint, Jewish society is profoundly traditional. A historical approach gives full value to tradition. In
what follows we shall investigate the different traditions which have contributed to contemporary Judaism." These, it turns out, are not so much competing strands, roads not taken, victorious and silenced voices, as reified
members of the "traditional" family: "Torah and Tradition," "The Tradition
of Worship," "The Biblical Tradition," "The Legal Tradition," and so forth.[59]

The use of definite articles before the word "tradition," invoked time and again, is meant to be conclusive, as is the refusal (if only in such an introductory text) to countenance the idea that there might well be "objectively" an "apparently infinite variety of different Judaisms."

The alternative method is explored in a second introductory text, upon which Scholem's influence is pronounced. The first chapter begins with Judaism's "myth of origins"—revelation at Sinai—couched in terms of the story of Moses in Akiba's academy. Turning from revelation to tradition, we at once encounter the problem of heterogeneity. To speak of an essence would be as misleading as to argue that Judaism is merely "a disconnected miscellany of beliefs and behaviors. . . . The fact is that a fairly stable pattern of behaviors and beliefs has marked the expressions of traditional Judaism from classical times . . . to the present day." One can speak of "essential features" even if not of essence. The author proceeds to do so, first summarizing the "converging authority structures" of "the Jews," "God," and "Torah and Interpretation" (the "traditional" triad, of course) and then (after reference to the Oven of Akhnai story) arguing that "the cumulative result of the converging authority structures of God, Torah, and interpretation is tradition—itself an authority structure and religious reality of major significance in Judaism."[60]

No better "finesse" of the problems facing the historian may be available. What constitutes a "stable pattern" is, of course, subject to dispute; what counts as an "essential feature" will occasion still further argument. So long as one articulates the methodological difficulties, keeps all characterizations of "Judaism" on a high level of generality, and makes the reader aware of evidence that does not fit the categories which one proposes, one may have done all that one *can* do. The reader must then beware when he or she encounters rather bald summary of "Judaism as a Ritual System," its unity and stability ostensibility accepted as a given until the disruptions of modernity. We should be still more suspicious at the claim that "the massive scope of the Jewish tradition and its fluid extension into every aspect of life constitute for the traditionalist nothing short of the immediate covenantal Presence of God at all times."[61] Who is this "traditionalist" anyway? What "fusion of horizons" has occurred here? Such are the contemporary dilemmas of anyone who would claim to speak for, or about, "Jewish tradition." As Bourdieu warned, the practices of scholarship (here, those concerning Judaism) are inseparable from the practices of ritual. The latter have of late been greatly influenced (recall Plaskow and Dorff) by the former; the dilemmas that they share are likely to be with us for some time to come.

There is a final issue—this time, of religious or ethnic rather than scholarly performance—that seems no less inescapable. It is brought to our attention by Erving Goffman's reflections on the deference and demeanor claimed by and shown to the modern self, and clarified further by Walter Benjamin's seminal essay "The Work of Art in the Age of Mechanical Reproduction." Benjamin pointed to "the desire of contemporary masses to bring things 'closer' spatially and humanly, which is just as ardent as their bent toward overcoming the uniqueness of every reality by accepting its reproduction." That which is high must be brought low. That which is far away must be brought close. In fact, "the distinction between author and public is about to lose its basic character."[62] At the very cultural moment when a self-consciously constructed tradition assumes more and more importance among Reform, Reconstructionist, and Conservative elites, the "folk" seem increasingly inclined to practice instead a fragmentary, variable, and individualized form of what the anthropologist Samuel Heilman has dubbed "traditioning." One moves in and out of "tradition" as demanded by one's personal "lifestyle" and one's commitments of the moment—much as American Jews (and even non-Jews) periodically insert Yiddish expressions into their speech for effect and move into and out of Jewish spaces, times, and activities rather than inhabiting the largely Jewish homes, neighborhoods, fraternal organizations, and friendship networks that Kaplan and other second-generation Jews could take for granted.[63] The relevant unit of creation and authority for tradition is now the self or, at most, the family.

Geiger and Kaplan, Plaskow and Dorff all enact their innovations in the name of earlier authorities, about whom they have taken the trouble to learn. Obligation to the past, however altered, is maintained; the ancestors continue (at least to some degree) to command; the voice of the fathers—and, more recently, the mothers—remains decisive. For the average Jew—largely ignorant of Jewish history; not part of an integral community such as Kaplan imagined or a feminist or Conservative community as presumed, respectively, by Plaskow and Dorff; and therefore far more responsive to American cultural and societal pressures than to the demands of a God he or she no longer experiences as commanding in any sense—the elites' strategy of constructing "tradition" cannot work in any coherent fashion. Extremely fragmented and idiosyncratic observance seems the inevitable outcome. Those touched by "the tradition" will likely not ignore the wishes of the ancestors entirely, as they perceive them, but neither will they accord those wishes central significance in their lives. The question of a veto does not arise; the tradition's vote is one among many, weighed and counted by the self.

Indeed, armed with popular notions of tradition such as those proclaimed by *Fiddler on the Roof* and the label on my flannel shirt, Jews may well regard their stance as the only possible authentic response to the past. What else can one do, if one is not a rabbi or a scholar, except to leave Anatevka behind for whatever new worlds beckon? "Sunrise, sunset, quickly flow the years" We will survey a typical range of such behaviors in the Conclusion to this study, when we examine the utterly new and American observance of feminist Passover seders and the very different "remembrances" now widespread in the State of Israel.

Time will tell whether the "tradition," as understood by the elites, can survive the popular tendency to "traditioning" or the elites' own doubts about the authority underlying their selections. "Spontaneity in relation to that which is given" may well demand a greater restraint of spontaneity and a larger measure of submission to the given than are available to the vast majority of Jews in late-twentieth-century America. It may also require a more informed awareness of the choices involved in innovation and transmission than any foreseeable Jewish community, emancipated and enlightened, is likely to possess.

Conclusion

Gershom Scholem closed his landmark study of Jewish mysticism some fifty years ago with a story of the Baal Shem Tov, the founder of Hasidism, which Scholem saw as a parable for the current predicament of the Jews—indeed, for the contemporary religious situation more generally. The Baal Shem Tov, we are told, would go into the forest whenever faced with a dificult task. He would light a fire, say a prayer, "and what he had set out to perform was done." In the next generation, his disciple, the Maggid of Meseritz, could no longer light the fire, but he did know the place to go and the prayer to utter. The third generation could neither light the fire nor say the prayer, but it could still find the sacred place in the forest. All generations since cannot even do that. What then can they, can we, do? "We can tell the story of how it was done" and hope that, as the teller of *this* story (Scholem himself) assures us, our telling will have "the same effect as the actions of the other three."[1]

I have two very different images in mind as I conclude this examination of the impact of modernity on Jewish practice. They have not been handed down from master to disciple over the generations but witnessed firsthand by me and by people I know over the past few years. As such, they do not constitute a tale of practice lost but testimony to practice altered, created, and renewed. And while the two images I have in mind are in some ways mirror opposites of each other, and present modes of Jewish practice which are far from typical, the numerous parallels between them also suggest an emerging ritual pattern. This pattern will, I think, engage Jewish and scholarly attention alike for some time to come.

The first image is a memory from the summer of 1996. A female Conservative rabbi is instructing a group of college students about daily ritual practice. She speaks quietly, as befits the early morning hour. And, in keeping with her own practice in the morning, she places a tallit over her shoulders and slowly winds black bands of tefillin around her arm. The second image is composed of a memory from 1994, supplemented by reports by others about similar scenes. It is a picture of ultra-Orthodox men and women at a Purim party. The men are resplendent in suits of black and white, the women dressed with appropriate modesty but stylishly and in bright colors. They are dancing (separately) to very loud rock music with a Jewish flavor (or neo-Hasidic music with the volume and the beat of rock). The tables on the side of the room are laden with kosher delicacies: sushi, crudités, and luscious desserts.

Neither performance would have been possible (or even conceivable) only a few decades ago. Yet neither is especially surprising at century's end. "Large (though not all) segments of the Haredi [ultra-Orthodox] enclave, not to speak of modern Orthodoxy, [have] increasingly adopted the consumer culture and its implicit values, above all the legitimacy of pursuing material gratification," writes historian Haym Soloveitchik.[2] Conversely (we might say), many Jewish women, formerly unobservant or restricted in their observance by the tradition itself, have adopted the *Jewish* culture and its *explicit markings,* above all the legitimacy of [Jewishly] pursuing [a feminist form of] *spiritual* gratification. It would be too simple, though not entirely untrue, to say that the one group has brought its Judaism a step closer to the world, while the other has brought the world a step closer to its Judaism. For the world and Judaism, the roles of men and women, the place of ritual and the evaluation of ritual have all changed in recent, "postmodern" years—even as continuities with modern and premodern patterns have strikingly persisted. More than a tale has been told. Something ritually alive has been and still is happening, far from the woods and the fire.

My purpose in this Conclusion is twofold. I hope to assess the degree to which the modern dynamics we have examined are still evident in the varieties of more recent ritual innovation in America and Israel. That effort will, in part, take the form of more careful examination of developments in feminist and *haredi* observance, measured for fit against the categories introduced in the preceding five chapters of this study. I will then use those categories to qualify and supplement the predictors of ritual observance set forth by sociologists Marshall Sklare and Joseph Greenblum in *Jewish Identity on the Suburban Frontier,* their classic study of American Jewish identity a generation ago, the better to speculate in the final section of this Conclusion on what current trends will mean for Jewish ritual, commandment, and community in coming decades—and, given my own convictions, what I think they *should* mean. If, as Scholem reassured his readers, "the story [of Jewish practice] is not ended, it has not yet become history," one wants to know with somewhat greater specificity just what that story has become, and how its next chapter could and should be written.

I MULTIPLE LIFEWORLDS, LOCAL NARRATIVES

Let us begin by noting three major and unprecedented events of contemporary Jewish existence which have "become history" and have already altered the shape of contemporary Jewish practice.

First and foremost, the creation of the State of Israel has transformed the most basic facts of Jewish politics, demography, and religion and, in the process, has stimulated the development or reinvigoration of dozens of Jewish rituals. That is true primarily within the state's own borders, where Orthodoxy, secular practices, and a state-sponsored civil religion are all flourishing. But the state's impact on Jewish practice has been felt indirectly in the diaspora as well.

The second event of note is the postwar ascent of American Jewry to a position of affluence, secular education, cultural participation, political influence, and social acceptance (the last manifest in high rates of intermarriage) unparalleled in the history of the diaspora. American Jewry, too, has evinced great interest in ritual observance of late. The Orthodox and feminist innovations mentioned above are both part of a larger trend that is not only evident in the community as a whole but reflected in (or reflecting) a growing interest in ritual among scholars in many disciplines.

Finally, both Jewries, Israeli and American, have increasingly been constructing and observing remembrances of the third epoch-making event of recent memory: the Holocaust. Yom Ha-shoah is marked annually in many American communities, and this day of remembrance plays a far more salient role on their ritual calendars than does Israeli Independence Day (or, for many Jews, Yom Kippur). The resources being poured into building and visiting museums such as the national memorial in Washington are considerable. Pilgrimages to the sites of vanished east European communities or the death camps are common, and for many teenagers in America as in Israel, such trips function as a rite of passage. Books on the subject continue to proliferate.

These changes have been massive, I believe, and the resultant innovations in ritual highly significant. And yet, I would argue, these innovations also exhibit substantial continuities with all of the processes we have analyzed. The ground rules of Emancipation remain in force, eliciting a long-familiar and oft-practiced Jewish calculus of assimilation, acculturation, and distinctiveness. Postmodern challenges to the hegemony of a single "discourse of modernity," whether emanating from feminist Jews who voice them explicitly or from Orthodox Jews who challenge "totalizing discourse" simply by being who and what they are, carry on the Jewish retort inaugurated with *Jerusalem* and "On the Jewish Question." Habermas is, to this degree, correct: the creation of "multiple lifeworlds" (Jewish, feminist, ultra-Orthodox) is fulfilling a possibility stored up in the modern political order, and imagined by thinkers such as Mendelssohn, from its inception. Lyotard's "local narratives" have found their role alongside and within "grand narratives," the most important being those most crucial to our study, Emancipation and Enlightenment, both of which are arguably crucial to Lyotard's project as well. Tradition, for the most part, continues to be "reconstructed" and "revalued" rather than discarded outright. Authority, for the most part, is still sought, kept at a distance, and self-consciously appropriated rather than accepted without question or forgone.

The workings of these processes are clearly evident in both of the two recent movements captured in the images with which I began this Conclusion. I will recur to them in this section in order to highlight the larger dynamics in which I believe they figure. On the feminist side, ritual innovation has encompassed a broad range of adaptations or extensions of existing observances (for example, covenant ceremonies for newborn baby girls, bat mitzvah celebrations, egalitarian wedding rites, creation of midrash on female biblical characters, liturgical transformation). It has also included new calendar and life-cycle rituals (for instance, Rosh Ḥodesh gatherings on the occasion of the new month, celebrations of pregnancy or delivery, the marking of menstruation or menopause) and the recovery or renewal of long-neglected traditions (for example, *tkhines,* a genre of medieval and early modern prayers composed by and for women).[3] For purposes of this analysis, I will direct attention to one ritual in particular: feminist Passover seders, which have stimulated the production of dozens of Haggadot over the past two decades, most of them designed primarily for use at seders attended exclusively by women and intended to supplement or replace the traditional observance.[4] These haggadot are valuable to us because they offer precious insight into the intentions of Jewish ritual actors—which, as a rule, are not available to scholars. The meanings that these Haggadot enunciate, I shall argue, are far more widely shared.

On the *haredi* side, we find a recent trend toward greater stringency in observance most evident in newly rigorous *shiurim,* or "standard measurements minimally required in the performance of a religious commandment."[5] The effect is delegitimation of standards long accepted, an implicit declaration (in sociologist Menachem Friedman's words) that "the religious practices of our holy ancestors . . . were inferior to our own." A kiddush cup in use for generations, for example, is no longer good enough.[6] Established practice (as Soloveitchik puts it) "can no longer hold its own against the demands of the written word" penned by new, or newly regnant, authorities.[7] The growth of ultra-Orthodoxy is part of a larger and widely noted "move to the Right" among Jews (and Christians) in American of late. In this case too, I think, examination of one end of the religious spectrum will provide informative about points closer to the center.

All the major categories of analysis used in the present study—politics, symbolic explanation, nostalgia, quest for and denial of authority, and construction of tradition—are patently at work in the two movements just described and in the community as a whole. The question, however, is *How* are they at work?—and the answer, as we shall now see, is: in new and newly interactive ways.

Politics

The fact that distinctive religious and ethnic practice has become safe in America, at least when conducted in private time and space or in separate neighborhoods, has proved crucial to all Jewish observance, and not least to Orthodoxy. "The traditionalist minority," write two recent observers, "show[s] us that insularity and parochialism can survive quite well" even in the United States. "An ethos largely at odds with the dominant trends can be held on to with striking tenacity even by those who find themselves in the situation of modernity."[8] That is so, I would argue, because the bargain between Western states and religious minorities such as the Jews has been adjusted in recent decades, particularly in America, through compromise on both sides (a mark of postmodernity). Governments and societies have extended acceptance even to enclaves that are set apart not just spatially but by their refusal to eat, dress, or walk in total accord with modern notions of civility or *Bildung.* The minorities, for their part, have declared certain aspects of modern culture neutral as regards commandment (for example, rock music, dining out, career achievement, and lack of asceticism in the *haredi* case) while intensifying scrupulosity in the spheres that remain distinctively Jewish. Observance has in some respects become easier. The coming of a five-day workweek has eliminated the need to choose between

Sabbath and career. Dietary laws are more easily obeyed now that literally thousands of food products carry certification from rabbinic authorities—and now that Orthodox Jews, well integrated into the larger economy, can afford no less than other Jews to buy them. Conformity in some respects to the surroundings, the loss of hardship in observance, ups the ante, as it were, for distinctiveness in other areas. The borders have been redrawn by every Jewish group to take in more from Gentile culture—and to leave outside many practices of fellow Jews.[9]

The seder's unexceeded popularity among American Jews,[10] as Sklare and Greenblum suggested a generation ago, is no doubt due in part to the fact that it meets all five of the essentially *political* conditions that they believed must be satisfied in order for widespread observance to take place in this country.[11] First, the ritual carries a *message redefined in modern and universal terms.* Passover is the holiday of freedom or liberation, and its symbols and key texts have been further universalized through appropriation over the centuries by other groups, most recently the civil rights movement.[12] Second, *no social isolation is involved.* The seder takes place in the evening, outside of work hours, and in the home, the most private of spaces. Third, its observance *accords with the religious culture of the larger community and provides a Jewish alternative when one seems needed.* Passover is a spring festival that almost always falls close to Easter, as Hanukkah—the other most widely celebrated Jewish holiday in America—falls near, and relieves the pressure caused by, Christmas. Fourth, Passover is also *explicitly child-centered*—witness the "four questions" asked by the youngest participant at the start of the seder and the search for *afikomen,* a hidden piece of matzah, at the meal's conclusion. This orientation to children also makes the holiday less threatening in its proclamation of distinctiveness to outsiders and insiders alike. Fifth, and finally, the holiday meets the test of *infrequent performance.* It thus puts strict limits on the boundaries between Jews and Gentiles which it helps to sustain.

Mainstream observance in accordance with these "rules" has come to exist in symbiotic relationship with the more marked differences of separatist enclaves such as the ultra-Orthodox. Acceptance of the latter by the larger society very likely hinges on the decision by the former—the overwhelming majority of the American Jewish minority—*not* to demand equivalent distinctiveness. Most American Jews do not mark their apartness on the street with head coverings, let alone wear black head to toe. Nor do they advertise their apartness by taking off from work on Jewish holidays—including Passover (though they may forgo bread for the week or add matzah to their lunch menu). Those who do advertise a greater apartness, and do so every day in obedience to a law not the state's, can be relied on by their fellow Jews to maintain a Jewish distinctiveness that they do not wish to enact but would not wish to end.

Feminist seders make these dynamics still more apparent. Of course, the adjective that defines the genre testifies to the impact of a modern political movement of great consequence, as do the introductory ruminations standard in feminist Haggadot—patterned after the "This is the bread of affliction" passage in the traditional text—which transpose into a new key the linkage of the seder's participants to "all who are afflicted." The traditional Haggadah's "we" expands in concentric circles of inclusiveness from one seder table to all, from the contemporary generation of Jews to all generations, from Jews to human beings as a whole, as it contracts to *exclude* enemies identified with Pharaoh. In feminist seders, building on previous modern hyphenations of Jewish identity, the "we" seems constituted far less by a people and tradition deemed "patriarchal" than by Jewish or universal womenkind. These women are identified in many feminist Haggadot with the ancient Israelites—as distinguished from the men, Jewish and Gentile, who are persistently identified in these texts with Egypt.[13]

Such feminist discussions—like the all-female minyanim, Rosh Ḥodesh groups, or other ritual settings at which they transpire—are, of course, new to Jewish ritual. But they carry on the distinction between "political emancipation" and "human emancipation" set forth in Marx's formulation of "the Jewish Question" one hundred and fifty years ago. Political emancipation among women has come to connote the granting of formally equal rights in the Jewish community and in American society. Human emancipation is now pictured as full inclusion of women's needs, ideals, and consciousness(es) in the definition of Judaism *and* as the emancipation of Judaism itself (as of all other traditions) from the conditions and practices which have given rise to and sustained discrimination.[14] Moreover, while pluralism is espoused as a firm commitment in feminist seders (as in the non-Orthodox Jewish community more widely), reflection on political matters among both groups almost always follows the lines of the "philosophical discourse of modernity" enunciated by Kant. Claims to rights, truth, justice, and autonomy are ubiquitous at Passover.[15] The redemption sought for and imagined in almost every text strictly follows the lines of the Kantian ethical commonwealth. Indeed, many American texts seem uncomfortable with precisely the three aspects of Judaism that Kant singled out for critique: coercion, exclusivity, and this-worldliness (now widely taken to consist in lack of spirituality). The recital of the ten plagues arouses great discomfort, except when the plagues are recast—ritually, we might say—to cast opprobrium on acknowledged oppressors (males, in the feminist Haggadot). The traditional prayer to God to wreak vengeance on Israel's enemies is often deleted. Passover seders, like any good Kantian ritual, are clearly designed to serve moral ends and are justified only by those ends.[16] That has long been the pattern of American adjustment to the situation of Jews living inside, and on the margins of, a larger and Gentile body politic.

Such tendencies come into sharper focus when one contrasts American Haggadot with the very different texts used by Israelis, who gather at their seders first of all as members of *a political majority*. Whereas American seders or Hanukkah observances chafe at the celebration of power and, in keeping with diaspora Jewish tradition, repeatedly declare their participants double outsiders to the dominant culture, Israeli Jews celebrate the achievement of just power and mark their cultural ascendency by taking off the days of Passover—official vacation time—sometimes to shop or go to the beach. Sociologist Yael Zerubavel has recently traced the popular, religious, and state-sponsored Israeli "commemorative strategies" through which Jewish collective memory has been altered, neglected, and maintained in the Jewish state.[17] Nowhere are these strategies clearer, I believe, than at the holiday of Passover, which is linked to Israeli Independence Day thematically and tied to it as well on the national ritual calendar.[18]

The message of the Haggadah recently issued by the kibbutz movement is typical. It declares the purpose of the rite to be fulfillment of the "commandment to tell of going out of Egypt together with all Israel," but it begins with an extended meditation on *spring,* accomplished through several popular Israeli songs on the theme. Jews have left diaspora wandering, the text proclaims. They are back home in "the Land," in nature. Israel's enslavement and liberation are then recited as in the traditional text—except that stress is laid on the geographic end point of the Exodus: not Sinai but the promised land. The third of the four cups of wine traditionally drunk at the meal is dedicated to the ingathering of the exiles, the fourth to the land of Israel. "Next year in *rebuilt* Jerusalem," one sings in conclusion.[19]

Jerusalem itself need no longer be awaited. The kibbutz Haggadah celebrates a redemption that has already occurred and points to fulfillments already tasted. Bitter herbs recall only past bitterness. Matzah conjures up exilic affliction. Arabs—politically allied with the Egyptian enemies of old—do not appear. The wine and green vegetables at the table, on the other hand, are prominent: signs of departure from the exile in which all other Jews sit down to Passover. In Israel, Jews putatively celebrate the holiday at one with the world outside, the redeemed reality in which the fruits of the earth grow. The politics of Jewish ritual remembrance there, as in America, are transparent.

Symbolic Explanation

The structure and content of the Haggadah are ideally suited to the quest for innovation within the framework of the given—another likely reason for the seder's exceptional popularity among contemporary American Jewry. They are no less ideally suited to the provision of universal "highest-order" meaning through distinctive particularist symbols. "Everyone who enlarges on the story is to be praised," the Haggadah announces at the outset. Matzah, bitter herbs, and shank bone are placed on the seder table so that the group assembled around it can ask, well into the evening's recital of the Passover story, "This matzah which we eat, what meaning has it?"—and answer in a *variety* of ways.[20] Passover locates its performers between redemptions past and future, urging all who are present at the seder to undertake activities, inside and outside the framework of the festival, that will bring redemption closer. The symbols are meant explicitly to stimulate this remembrance and activity, making the enterprise of symbolic explanation that is now standard at every holiday all the more compelling.

Passover Haggadot, including feminist texts, generally send a message that combines a strong universalist thrust with a clear Jewish commitment. "We are here to relive the story of our people's slavery and freedom," the feminist texts proclaim (note, *our* people), but they add at once that "we tell the story because wherever you live, it is probably Egypt."[21] Matzah, egg, and bitter herbs in women's Haggadot are accorded traditional Jewish meanings as well as feminist and still more universal meanings (exodus and slavery, spring and fertility, and suchlike).[22] Several texts follow Marx in going beyond critique of Enlightenment ideas and of the social arrangements achieved or promised by Emancipation to universal feminist commitments that dispense with Israel's God and are hostile to Jewish forms. The ritual syntax of their seder plates is used in much the same way in which Marx deployed the rhetoric of biblical prophecy, and to a parallel effect. Modern ends transform the tradition, reject its authority, and pronounce it an anachronism.[23] Others are more traditional in the symbolic referents they assign the plagues, but almost all feminist texts resolutely and vividly employ the occasion to condemn contemporary male oppression of women, as other recent Haggadot have condemned the oppression of Soviet Jews or African Americans. The afflictions are enumerated with enthusiasm, in the apparent (and traditional) assumption that those around the table will readily identify.[24]

The particular "indexical" message of subgroup identification (for instance, feminist, Reform, Conservative, and so forth) will vary with the celebrants, of course. But the seder's function in indexically distinguishing Jewish participants from other people—even from non-Jewish friends and relatives at the seder—is quite common. Almost all contemporary Haggadot, like the texts composed for use at other rituals, conceive symbols rather didactically as shorthand statements of truths which can be translated into propositional terms, short or lengthy. This is perhaps inevitable, given that the seder, like other rituals, has as it were to plead the case for its own performance before participants who normally live outside the world of Jewish tradition. "Outsiders" such as these will enter only if and when the *meaning* of doing so is demonstrable, a case best made by symbols which possess emotional power and are used to convey truths at once relevant and uncontroversial.[25] However, once they have stepped into the Jewish framework—or if (whether Orthodox or not) they have grown up inside it—participants require a more subtle and complex set of meanings adequate to their learning and experience. They will likely delight in ambiguities and contradictions and disdain the simplicities intended for outsiders. Their satisfaction lies precisely in the repeated experience of insights they had not seen before and profundity they had not previously glimpsed.

Haredi performances savor this sort of insider knowledge, of course, but they are also in large part "indexical": designed to mark off the group clearly, both as Jews from Gentiles and as ultra-Orthodox Jews from the Jewish majority. The desire for such separation through strict adherence to the law, as well as for ever new meanings that enrich observance born first and foremost of obedience, has in recent years spawned a huge literature on practical observances, setting forth details which Jews had previously learned "mimetically" from their (not always so rigorous) Jewish surroundings. "If the *tallit katan* is worn not as a matter of course but as a matter of belief, it has then become a ritual object," Soloveitchik writes. For the intent of the ritual article is not only to obey a law but to send a message of apartness. Or, as Friedman puts it, the term *haredi* "implies precision without compromise."[26] Only observance more punctilious than the Jewish (or the Orthodox) norm can transmit the message of that identity, the relevant audience for the message being other Jews. The meaning of a given ritual therefore consists of the messages conveyed symbolically through its performance (and expressed verbally in the spate of new books) as well as of the performer's allegiance to a "higher" standard of obedience to the law than other Jews demonstrate.

Nostalgia

Ancestors present a major problem to such intensification of observance: the newly intense observer is in effect announcing that *their* ways were not sufficiently rigorous. The departure from the past is possible because it generally goes unmentioned, and the communities of eastern Europe which might have constrained the new rigor through the example of their ritual habits no longer exist. *Haredi* stringency is doubly a postwar phenomenon: replacing and supplanting observances which were destroyed in the Holocaust along with those who had observed them. Note the presence in this example (and in Orthodoxy more generally) of the five functions that the ancestors served in nineteenth-century performances of what I have called the mitzvah of nostalgia: (1) the critique of "backsliding" among the current generation; (2) the critique of backsliding particularly among its leadership; (3) the summons to a higher standard of behavior that links one to former generations (personified in the *haredi* case by the Hazon Ish, for example, and among each Orthodox group by its venerated authorities); (4) the provision of a new aesthetic meant to assist the imagining of the desired identity, a picture of the "Torah-true Jew" borrowed to some degree from preceding Jewish models but also adapted from the Gentile surroundings; and (5) the legitimation of hyphenated diaspora identity—though in the *haredi* case, this has involved their reassertion of the exilic apartness that our nineteenth-century examples rejected and their demonstration that they at least have become citizens of Gentile states without compromise of Jewish principle or practice. Note, finally, that the satisfaction which comes of rebelling against parental authority in the name of grandparents and still higher authority is not lacking even among the ultra-Orthodox.

Feminist seders of course invoke female ancestors repeatedly, in part to call down blessing on the participants, in part to provide proof of the seders' own legitimacy. Women have been there all along, the texts want to remind us, even if they have not figured in the written accounts—perhaps because they were working in the kitchen.[27] The four children in these texts are generally daughters, and they do not ask gender-neutral questions. "Why are feminist seders required?" "What has God—conceived in the feminine aspect of Shekhina—commanded?"[28] The story of Israel's enslavement and exodus become in every feminist rendering an occasion for midrashic addition of female characters who are present in the biblical account but omitted from the Haggadah, most notably, Miriam.[29] But all Passover celebrations feature the ancestors prominently. They explicitly recall the Israelites who left Egypt and the second-century rabbis who recalled that departure at an earlier seder, they identify contemporary Jews with both sets of ancestors, and they further the conviction of relation through the emotional power latent in the rite. The seder is performed at home among family; it invariably elicits memories of seders past and of participants now departed. The ritual is ideal for the commanded performance of nostalgia—no doubt a major aspect of its appeal. Hanukkah, another popular observance, works in similar fashion.

Once more, the feminist seders bring these dynamics into sharp relief. They use the ancestors (1) to critique present-day Jewish behavior, and (2) to authorize strong censure of Jewish leaders, particularly those who have failed to fulfill biblical demands for justice or have failed to follow the rabbinic precedent of innovating so as to adapt the Torah's eternal principles to changing times. Today's mothers and grandmothers, by altering Judaism in this way, will (3) help to bring wayward daughters—"banished from their fathers' table" by the alienating injustice of patriarchy—back to Judaism. The ancestors say, in effect, "It was not your fault that you have been alienated. The tradition failed you. But it has changed—and so should you. You owe it to your mothers and grandmothers to effect the transformation that they could not make or live to see." This message, essentially Kaplan's, is paralleled in "freedom seders" and many other contemporary ritual adaptations. Thus, the ancestors (4) promote an enlarged (and selective) observance focused on aesthetics: *scènes familiales* dominated by the tastes and smells of the mother's kitchen. Finally, Miriam, Sarah, and other foremothers are invoked in feminist texts (5) to justify the hyphenated identities of seder participants, which in this case include a *female* identity allegedly precluded by the tradition or inhibited by its silence. In other Haggadot, the enjoyment of the meal and the reiteration of its messages reinforce participants' satisfaction at being American Jews, at once at home in their country and at home (literally) in their tradition, all the while allowing for the vicarious enjoyment of imagining Israel's enemies punished.

How could anyone turn down the invitation to bring to life the voices of oppressed ancestors, male or female, who had been denied these opportunities? To perform the mitzvah is to remember the forefathers and foremothers, to say words they said and eat what they ate, and even in some sense to *redeem* the promise of their lives, thereby bearing witness to the liberation visible all around the seder table. The ritual is so powerful, in part, because the redemption is so palpable.[30] Explication of Passover symbols is a necessary feature of this experience of meaning, but it cannot compete with the nostalgic imperatives and rewards.

Authority

Most adult Americans have left the sway of direct parental authority by the time they ritually recall their ancestors as adults—not so, however, the sway of the Jewish people's authority. Haggadot which attempt to make ethnic loyalties into a vehicle of *tikkun olam* (universal repair of the world) also serve to reinforce those ethnic loyalties; because one is a Jew, the argument goes, a member of the people who "were strangers in the land of Egypt," one has all the more reason to treat other Others kindly. Being a Jew as well as an American, or a feminist, or all three, one has an all the greater obligation not only to work for the ethical ideals which these commitments purportedly promote but to maintain the existence of the people who for centuries have proclaimed these ideals and sought their realization. One is *commanded* to do these things: it "is a mitzvah."

The grounds of these commands, however, are—as we have seen—quite varied and not always sufficient to justify the many new forms of observance. Practice thus continues all the while firmer grounds are being sought. One source of the commandment is clearly ethical. Reason and the prophets both teach the need for truth and justice. Judaism speaks with the voice of conscience and speaks all the more loudly because of Jewish victimization by many generations of "Egyptians." Another source of authority is the felt obligation to ancestors, which implies obligation to "what they stood for" and to the tradition that defined their identity. This felt obligation has become all the greater because of latter-day success in achieving the security and influence that they lacked. Finally, the practice of a communal rite such as Passover, the use of *this* text and *these* symbols on this night "different from all others"—with this group of people, likewise "different from all others"—bespeaks at the very least an *attachment to* the extended family of the Jewish people that pulls one inward toward special obligations and responsibilities to it as well as pushes one outward to some service of "all who are needy."

God enters the matrix of obligation in contemporary texts from two directions, whether one "believes in God" or not. First, the ethical and "tribal" imperatives emanating from the seder and other rituals are often pronounced in God's name. They emerge from stories in which God is the principal character, whether acknowledged or not. Even if God does not *act* in every Passover or Hanukkah story in the present tense (the kibbutz texts provide a glaring example of God's absence, not unlike the traditional text for Purim, the Book of Esther), God has acted in most texts in the past and always stands, at the very least, in the background of the story recounted. God hardens Pharaoh's heart, sends the plagues, performs the miracle at the Red Sea, helps the Maccabees defeat Antiochus. God is likewise always present in the songs and in the blessings. "Who knows one? I know one. One is our God, in heaven and on earth." God thus figures in the calculus of obligation stimulated by the holiday. Second, and no less important to my mind, participants are repeatedly reminded that God had been an active presence in the lives of the venerated ancestors recalled during the ritual. God is thus a major part of the legacy passed down for reception by later generations. The latter need not "believe in God" if they wish to partake of that inheritance, but they cannot avoid mentioning God's name, blessing God, thanking God, and thinking about the ancestors' relation to God. In a rite still widely practiced, Jews remember their parents and loved ones annually by saying kaddish—a prayer of praise to God.

Rituals thus become frameworks for more sustained theological reflection than is afforded most American Jews (or allowed by them) in daily life. Feminist texts must, of course, deal with theological matters explicitly, both in deciding what attributes to ascribe to God and, if the texts use or translate Hebrew, in determining what gender to employ for divine predicates. Only a handful of strategies are available. One can, following Kaplan's method, retain most of the traditional divine attributes (which need not be gendered in English) while "revaluing" them.[31] One can employ God's most common feminine appellation, the Shekhinah. One can omit reference to God wherever possible or reduce God's involvement to formulaic cliché.[32] Another approach, more ambitious, systematically feminizes God's names and attributes: "Blessed are you, O Shekhina, our mistress queen of the universe."[33] A final strategy moves from second person singular address to first person plural statement, solving the problem of gendered address by depersonalizing God. Thus Marcia Falk's blessing, "Let us bless the source of life that brings forth bread from the earth."[34]

Most feminist Haggadot, like other Haggadot and American Jewish ritual texts more generally, are not dogmatic on the point of God's "personality" or attributes. God is simply "there" in the ways that I have noted. Individuals are left to make what they will of that presence in the ritual and on the page. But this points, however, to a matter of authority more significant than God's gender: God's presence in—or absence from—the rituals or the events that they recount. Soloveitchik reports his reflection, upon visiting a *haredi* yeshivah at the high holidays in 1959, that "there was something missing. . . . There was introspection, self-ascent, even moments of self-transcendence, but there was no fear in the thronged student body." He is led to ask "to what extent God was palpably present on Yom Kippur among the different generations of [Orthodox] congregants in Boston and Bnei Brak," and he concludes that there has been a diminution of the sense of God's natural involvement in mundane everyday affairs in recent generations. The "perception of God as a daily, natural force is no longer present to a significant degree in any sector of modern Jewry, even the most religious." [35]

My own study of contemporary American ritual activity supports this speculation; indeed, ritual is perhaps attractive because it continues even in the absence of God's felt presence and compensates for that absence with the invocation of God's name in song, text, and blessing. A student of contemporary mourning rites has observed that these rites "have great appeal today because of their ability to meet the emotional needs of mourners"— this, even though "the pervasive theme in almost all prayers relating to death is that God decides the length of a person's life and that His decision, always a just one, is determined by the person's moral and religious behavior." Both ideas are foreign and unacceptable to "contemporary sensibilities," but the wounds are healed by the rituals nonetheless. [36] So too, obligations are imposed and accepted in the course of ritual performances more generally— despite the absence of belief in a divine commander—so long as the sources of authority detailed in Chapter 7 are in place. *Community* must be constructed or reinforced by the ritual in order to exercise its authority. *Meaning* must be built in, through symbolic messages that enjoin universal as well as particularist obligations. *Religious experience* must be provided, at least in the sense just described: God inhabits the ritual and the stories, regardless of an individual's level of belief. The sanction of the ancestors must be pronounced, rendering the ritual a gateway into *immortality,* the eternal. Finally, the ritual must provide a *plausibility structure* for its own claims by linking them to realities outside the ritual framework that are known to the participants.

Belief in God's revelation or providence enters into ritual performances only when (and to the degree that) practice demands. Highly observant Jews will generally (though not always) possess belief in God's existence and the divine authority of the law they recognize. However, we know very little about contemporary Jewish belief, and what we do know suggests that much observance does not derive from or depend on that belief that God had commanded it. Observance at century's end seems to have moved even farther out in front of belief than was the case previously in twentieth-century Judaism and seems not terribly concerned about whether belief will struggle, in the manner of Rosenzweig or Kaplan, to catch up. Ultimate truths held or not held are a matter of no great urgency so long as Jews are able to sit down at a Passover table or join in other ritual celebrations and find the performances a source of meaning. Indeed, any statement of ultimate truths might prove divisive or preclude some individuals from participating. Far better to stick to matzah and bitter herbs, as most American Jews probably do at their seders, and leave theology aside, to dance with Miriam rather than to wrestle overmuch with God. The seder itself, structured in terms of questions and never content with answers, positions Jews exactly where they have most wished to be for some time now in relation to authority: ever seeking, always in quest, rather than at home with authority or content with their own obedience. That is no doubt one reason they feel so comfortable observing the holiday.

Tradition

For the very same reason, seders constitute a proof text for the constructed character of Jewish tradition. The Haggadah builds improvisation into its every performance. *Haredi* strictures, even if they deny their own innovation, likewise know themselves to rest on laws which obligate Jews who choose to obey (or disobey) them somewhat differently. Observant American Jews as a whole, unabashedly selective, generally hold themselves obligated to re-create only the "spirit" of a commanded performance and to heed only as much of the "letter" of the law as they need to rekindle that spirit. Even the feminist Haggadot least committed to "traditional" forms evince a striking fidelity to that letter, insofar as they retain the seder's most venerable symbols and component rituals. If Jews want to have a seder, they cannot not set the table with matzah and bitter herbs, or open with recitation of four questions, proceed with the depiction of four children, enumerate the ten plagues, sing Dayyenu, and conclude with Had Gadya. It is as if all the authors of these new texts—as well as the American Jewish performers of other rituals—had read Mordecai Kaplan (who himself published a "new Haggadah" in 1942) and signed on to his strategy of ritual continuity combined with ideational "revaluation".[37] One Haggadah puts it clearly: "Embracing the challenge of tradition, we clear new paths to the future. Ours is a holy journey, a journey towards new song. . . . Next year in Jerusalem."[38] The givens of tradition are, as always, not merely a foil for ritual innovation; they are its vehicle. Each new message seeks to draw power from the medium, which remains unchanged. The medium invariably (in part, through invariance) leaves its imprint on the message.

Other Jewish rituals serve similar purposes in similar fashion, and are likewise enjoying new, if not comparable, popularity. A recent *New York Times* article on sukkah building in the suburbs was aptly titled "Symbols of a Desert Exile Bloom in Jews' Backyards."[39] Churches which have declined for many of the same reasons that synagogues have—liberal education, pluralism, individualism, privatism, anti-institutionalism, resistance to obligation, and so forth—are more recently experiencing a resurgence fueled by many of the same factors that have been leading Jews back to seders and sukkot and, occasionally, even to synagogue. Churches offer *meaning*— "compelling teaching," as one study of the Protestant revival calls it, and "inspiration." They provide *community:* "Strong religions are also characterized by the 'shoulder-to-shoulder solidarity' of those who have committed themselves to the movement." Churchgoers are looking for "social contacts and a suportive community." That is certainly an attraction of both Orthodoxy and feminism, and—recall Plaskow's reconstruction of tradition—an explicit ground of authority. Finally, the study of churchgoers reports, the latter want "personal support, reassurance, and help."[40] Although this need is not often acknowledged in Jewish rituals, it has been brought to the fore in feminist seders and met in some of them through new elements such as the participants' washing of each other's hands at the start of the service.[41]

The fact that the trend toward renewed, self-conscious, and selective observance of tradition goes beyond Jews, and perceptibly so, likely plays a role in reinforcing it *among* Jews. Little credence is given outside Orthodoxy to the claim that Jews stand in a unique relation either to God or to the good.[42] If Protestants and Catholics, too, are in search of meaning and community, and are locating it through a renewed relationship to tradition, their quest satisfies an ever present Jewish need for reassurance that they are a *part of* and not only *apart from* the larger society. Protestant church attendance, in particular, seems to turn on *belief in* God and *beliefs about* God; this correlation also highlights a likely reason for continued low synagogue attendance among all but Orthodox Jews. Those not in the pews lack the requisite belief and, thus, the requisite "comfort level" of good feeling. But this also helps to explain the growing interest among Jews in rituals which do *not* place a premium on belief and which make participants feel very good indeed, all the while keeping God regularly accessible through stories, songs, and blessings. Providing access to God has been a function served by Jewish ritual since time immemorial, and making Jews feel good no doubt has a long history as well.

2. THE MAKING OF POSTMODERN JEWISH RITUALS

We arrive, then, at a set of five predictors for postmodern Jewish ritual performance (quite likely applicable to many non-Jewish religious services as well). They take the five conditions set forth by Sklare and Greenblum a generation ago one step farther, as contemporary observance arguably builds on the modern pattern that those researchers delineated.

Politics

A ritual will be observed to the degree that, and in the fashion in which, it establishes and reinforces the desired measure of inclusion in, and apartness from, the larger society. It will take account of Gentile opinion about legitimate and illegitimate differences and the display of difference, but it will be sensitive as well to Jewish opinion about what constitutes crossing the line which the ritual is meant to draw. The Christmas trees common in Jewish homes a generation ago were not generally perceived to cross that line, but they would be today—hence their role in disputes about observance among intermarried couples. Conversely, greater observance may be demanded because others, too, are observing more and an individual wants to mark a border that leaves them outside. The late historian Gerson Cohen observed in 1981 that "we have made traditional ritual respectable, so that every Jewish communal function today offers at least the option of kosher food."[43] He was at once applauding the achievement and noting that its value as a demarcation of distinctiveness had declined.

Symbolic Explanation

Rituals must plead the case for their own performance, all Jewish attachment now being voluntarist, by means of the explanations of symbols that they proclaim or display. "Canonical" messages proclaimed by the ritual— "eternal truths"—will be universal and personalist rather than tribal, even if the ritual vehicle that "carries" these truths is particularist and the "historical truth" it recalls pertains specifically to Jews. To most American Jews, therefore, Passover is "about" freedom or liberation from bondage rather than God's salvation of one people through the infliction of deadly plagues on another. Sukkot is "about" wandering or exile; Shavuot is "about" divine revelation or ethical aspiration rather than the giving of the Torah. "Indexical" messages will vary with the performers' apartness from other Jews but remain inside the framework of perceived legitimate difference, even as the messages attract Jews with meaning(s) not readily available elsewhere. Those who have moved inside the tradition, or who grew up as insiders and received a substantial Jewish education, require more than basic meanings to hold their interest and affirm the ultimate value of their commitment. Ambiguities, contradictions, multiple readings of a given text will offer them satisfaction that straightforward "this means that" symbolisms cannot. Indeed, the latter may well occasion scorn.

Nostalgia
Rituals must wrap participants in memories of previous ancestral performances, linking present-day observers to the ancestors, giving the sense of following in their ways, legitimating anger against internal "backsliders" or external enemies, and allowing for the expression of ambivalence toward parents, more distant forebears, and their demands. The "child-centered" character of much Jewish ritual, noted by Sklare and Greenblum, literally drives home the relation to ancestors even as it gives adults an excuse for performance and minimizes the importance of the particularism it displays. What is more, performance of the ritual at home locates it in the most private of spaces and in the place most identified by contemporary Americans with "who they really are," free from the public arena of role-playing and professional occupation.

Authority
The ritual should provide meaning through the vehicles that I have detailed, principally through the authority of meaning and community themselves, while leaving Jews free to search for an ultimate authority which can direct their rituals and their lives. Practice cannot dispense with that search or—even among the Orthodox—presume it completed. Revelation, even if undisputed, must provide latitude for varying communal or individual interpretation. God, even if believed to be present and close at hand, must be sufficiently distant to encourage and allow for independent human agency. God's presence in songs and blessings, which as late as a generation ago drove many Jews to reject ritual activity in the name of modern intellectual integrity, is in the postmodern period no longer a barrier and often an attraction—validating the quest and providing the assurance of transcendence.

Tradition

Finally, the ritual should be enshrined in the imagination as part of "the tradition," something the ancestors would have done and were known for doing. The term can, in some cases, serve to legitimate departures from former norms: if the ancestors "kept kosher," for example, that was "the tradition then," but now "times have changed." In other cases, however— particularly where ritual performance is not a matter of an absolute yes or no, kosher or *trefe,* but of occasional distinctions (kosher for Passover only; kosher at home but not outside the home) or of holidays which can be altered without perceived loss of the tradition (as in greatly shortened Passover seders or Sabbath observance restricted to Friday evenings)—the blessing of tradition encourages and even compels observance.

One might be tempted to add a sixth predictor of ritual observance: *celebration of the self or group and of what they have become.* Consider, in light of our focus on Passover, the demonstration of total release from bondage perceived by anthropologist Jack Kugelmass in the nostalgic visits by Jewish suburbanites to a kosher-style steakhouse located in the basement of a Lower East Side tenement. Kugelmass shows us Jews who come to the restaurant in fancy cars for a putative return to mama's kitchen, who heap their plates with *schmaltz* and other good things, and who then—sated by the extravagant portions—return happily to real life, far away from the old neighborhood. They are engaged, he argues, in a performance of ethnic identity. The chicken fat, the music, and the curios on the wall are Jewish vehicles for an exercise of generalized ethnic nostalgia that is permitted and, indeed, mandated by American culture in our day. That exercise can be played out only through the sort of ethnic particulars that the restaurant provides. By performing it, American Jews also tell the timeless tale, as American as it is Jewish, of the rise from humble origins to great success, of pioneers who left home to seek their fortune and have now found it. The proof of their success is their ability to pay the bill.[44]

We recognize this tale as a variation on the Passover theme of exodus and redemption—and may therefore be tempted all the more to view many American seders, feminist or otherwise, and much of Jewish ritual activity along with them, as a similar species of ethnic performance. Many seders are "kosher-style," after all, not only in cuisine but in content (little or none of the Haggadah is recited). Perhaps, then, I have imputed too much value to these and other ritual performances by modern and contemporary Jews. The messages these performances transmit about identity may in truth be no more substantial (even if no less) than those pronounced in visits to ethnic restaurants or attendance at klezmer music concerts or Israeli film festivals. This would explain why more Jews are open to sending these messages and to receiving them: it is not that greater distinctiveness can now be marked at lower cost, perhaps, but that higher cost (in other words, more ritual exertion) now carries lower distinctiveness—which is just as the actors wish it.

I am not entirely persuaded by that argument, however, and not only because I refuse to undervalue even minimal enactments of the distinctiveness inherent in ethnic or religious attachment. A seder, for all its adaptation to changing circumstances, promises (and often delivers) a measure of authenticity unavailable at the steakhouse. It constitutes a traditional framework that links Jews to a history not always pleasant and to a religion which demands that life be serious. Stepping into the ritual constitutes a statement about identity, particularly when one knows that the Haggadah—like Jewish history—inevitably makes claims upon its Jewish performers. The location of the seder in the home or synagogue hall adds a further decree of *sacredness,* both in the Durkheimian sense of that which is set apart from the normal and in the Jewish sense of that which is holy: that which raises one up is more resistant to trivialization and appropriation for the self's own purposes. Finally, God is invoked in the blessings, figures in the stories, hovers over the events they describe. Routinization inevitably overtakes ritual performances: ignorance of traditional layers of meaning is inevitable when performance is not restricted to an elite; even the reduction of high ceremony to kitsch is not entirely out of keeping with ritual intentions to offer a dose of heavy seriousness sugarcoated in a tale or children's song, so that it goes down as easily as sponge cake. That might be a parable for a great deal of ritual performance by contemporary American Jews. Ritual has always offered comfort and reassurance as much as challenge and reproof. And, arguably, it offers many American Jews far more than that.

There is, of course, no way to know what meanings, intended and unintended, accompany the individual performances of any rite, modern or postmodern. It does seem, however, that the vitality of Judaism in contemporary America rests precisely on the dynamics of ritual practices that allow for multiple messages, indirect avowals, and significant emotional investment. *Belief* in revelation has not kept the vast majority of Jews Jewish over the past two centuries, and it does not do so today. Neither has lack of belief in revelation driven them away. Other factors have been at work. A Jewish community intent on securing its own future will proceed, then, not by seeking to convince people of the truths (unique or shared) for which it stands, much less by accusing fellow Jews of betraying those truths if they choose not to stand inside the tradition. Rather, it will offer them experiences of meaning and community in *practices* satisfying both intellectually and emotionally in the five ways I have described and hope that they will choose to come back, again and again, for more. Many American Jews, perhaps the majority, will likely not opt for more than occasional entry into this minority framework, for no other reason than that it *is* a minority framework. Others, perhaps hungrier for meaning and/or community, "differently qualified religiously" as Weber put it, more attached to ancestors or more actively questing after authority, will choose more frequent observance, and thus find more of the meaning they seek in the terms that Jewish observances impress upon them.[45]

It seems probable to me—assuming that true pluralism in the United States can be achieved, real difference valued, and a more thoroughgoing multiculturalism attained—that more and more Jews *will* opt for observance to some degree, thereby rendering Scholem's story of a tale reduced to the telling of it—a substitute for the performances it recounts—entirely premature. I have repeatedly urged that we not idealize or sentimentalize the modern practices surveyed in this study, and I certainly would not declare the contemporary renewal of interest among religious actors and scholars alike the revival of the genuine religiosity which Scholem awaited (and, I think, advocated). But neither should we denigrate these efforts—or imply the same by romanticizing the observance of the ancestors. Ritual now, as ever, offers Jews possibilities for adherence denied by creedal affirmations. Commandment continues to evince a robust independence of divine revelation, a diversity of sources, an array of enactments. Community provides satisfactions too palpable to be sacrificed or gainsaid—despite and because of the individualism fostered by Emancipation and the autonomy demanded by Enlightenment.

Modern Judaism, then, like its rethinking, thankfully remains very much a work in progress.

INTRODUCTION

1. Max Weber, "The Social Psychology of the World Religions," in *From Max Weber: Essays in Sociology,* ed. Hans H. Gerth and C. Wright Mills (New York: Oxford University Press, 1969), 287.

2. Marion A. Kaplan, *The Making of the Jewish Middle Class* (New York: Oxford University Press, 1991).

3. Yosef Yerushalmi, *Freud's Moses: Judaism Terminable and Interminable* (New Haven, Conn.: Yale University Press, 1991), 9.

4. Roger Chartier, *The Cultural Origins of the French Revolution,* trans. Lydia C. Cochrane (Durham, N.C.: Duke University Press, 1991), 18.

5. Jean-François Lyotard, *The Postmodern Condition: A Report on Knowledge,* trans. Geoff Bennington and Brian Massumi (Minneapolis: University of Minnesota Press, 1984), 3, xxiii.

6. See Jürgen Habermas, *The Philosophical Discourse of Modernity,* trans. Frederick Lawrence (Cambridge, Mass.: MIT Press, 1991), 310.

7. Leopold Zunz, "On Rabbinic Literature," in *The Jew in the Modern World: A Documentary History,* ed. Paul R. Mendes-Flohr and Jehuda Reinharz (New York: Oxford University Press, 1980), 197.

8. Weber, "Science as a Vocation," in *From Max Weber,* 155.

9. See Mary Douglas, *Purity and Danger* (London: Routledge & Kegan Paul, 1966), 62, and *Natural Symbols: Explorations in Cosmology* (New York: Pantheon Books, 1982).

10. See Victor Turner, *Process, Performance, and Pilgrimage: A Study in Comparative Symbology* (New Delhi: Concept Publishing Company, 1979), chap. 1.

11. See Clifford Geertz, "Religion as a Cultural System," in *The Interpretation of Cultures* (New York: Basic Books, 1973), 87–125; see, in particular, 119–22.

12. See Peter C. Hodgson and Robert H. King, *Christian Theology: An Introduction to Its Tradition and Tasks* (Philadelphia: Fortress Press, 1985), 288.

13. See Douglas, *Natural Symbols,* 1–18.

14. Franz Rosenzweig, "Teaching and Law" (originally published in "The Builders"), in *Franz Rosenzweig: His Life and Thought,* ed. Nahum Glatzer (New York: Schocken Books, 1976), 239.

15. Emile Durkheim, *The Elementary Forms of the Religious Life,* trans. Joseph Ward Swain (New York: Free Press, 1965), 401, 415–16.

16. See Isaac Heinemann, *Ta'amei Ha-Mitzvot* [The reasons for the commandments in Jewish literature] (Jerusalem: Jewish Agency, 1966).

17. Weber, "Politics as a Vocation," in *From Max Weber,* 78–79.

18. Todd Endelman, "The Legitimization of the Diaspora Experience in Recent Jewish Historiography," *Modern Judaism* 11, no. 2 (May 1991): 201–3. See also David Sorkin, *The Transformation of German Jewry, 1780–1840* (New York: Oxford University Press, 1987), 4.

19. Jonathan Frankel, "Assimilation and the Jews in Nineteenth-Century Europe: Towards a New Historiography," in *Assimilation and Community: The Jews in Nineteenth-Century Europe,* ed. Jonathan Frankel and Steven J. Zipperstein (Cambridge: Cambridge University Press, 1992), 1–37.

20. Paula Hyman, *The Emancipation of the Jews of Alsace* (New Haven, Conn.: Yale University Press, 1991), 1–5.

21. See Shulamit S. Magnus, "German Jewish History," *Modern Judaism* 11, no. 1 (February 1991): 125–30.

22. Shmuel N. Eisenstadt, ed., *Patterns of Modernity,* vol. 1, *The West* (New York: New York University Press, 1987), 1–11.

23. Jacob Katz, *Out of the Ghetto* (New York: Schocken Books, 1978), 219. That work and Katz's approach to the investigation of modern Jews and Judaism more generally are the principal inspiration for this study.

24. W. E. B. Dubois, *The Souls of Black Folk,* in *Three Negro Classics,* ed. John Hope Franklin (New York: Avon Books, 1965), 215, 218.

ONE

1. Kant's leading role in the transformation of Jewish belief and practice has long been recognized; see Michael A. Meyer, *Response to Modernity* (New York: Oxford University Press, 1988), 17, 64–66, 69, 73, 205–7; Nathan Rotenstreich, *Jewish Philosophy in Modern Times* (New York: Holt, Rinehart and Winston, 1968), and *Jews and German Philosophy: The Polemics of Emancipation* (New York: Schocken Books, 1984), 3–70; and Emil Fackenheim, *Encounters between Judaism and Modern Philosophy* (New York: Basic Books, 1973), 31–77.

2. See Jacob Katz, *Out of the Ghetto* (New York: Schocken Books, 1978), chaps. 4–5, and *Emancipation and Assimilation: Studies in Modern Jewish History* (Westmead: Gregg International Publishers, 1972) 21–45.

3. The larger story of modernity's effect on Jewish observance and belief is well-known and, in its general outline, beyond dispute; see, for example, Katz, *Out of the Ghetto;* Meyer, *Response to Modernity,* and *The Origins of the Modern Jew: Jewish Identity and European Culture in Germany, 1749–1824* (Detroit: Wayne State University Press, 1967); Joseph Blau, *Modern Varieties of Judaism* (New York: Columbia University Press, 1966); and, for an annotated collection of sources documenting the impact of modernity on Judaism, Paul R. Mendes-Flohr and Jehuda Reinharz, eds., *The Jew in the Modern World: A Documentary History,* 2d ed. (New York: Oxford University Press, 1995).

4. Immanuel Kant, *Religion within the Limits of Reason Alone,* trans. Theodore M. Greene and Hoyt H. Hudson (New York: Harper and Row, 1960), 3–10, 40–49, 54–128. On this point, see also the exposition in Kant, *Foundations of the Metaphysic of Morals,* trans. Lewis Beck (Indianapolis: Bobbs-Merrill, 1959); the discussion in Fackenheim, *Encounters,* 33–53; and John R. Silber, "Introduction, Part 2: The Ethical Significance of Kant's Religion," in Kant, *Religion,* lxxix–cxxxiv.

5. Kant, *Religion,* 153–54.

6. Moses Mendelssohn, *Jerusalem,* trans. Allan Arkush (Hanover, N.H.: University Press of New England, 1983), 86–87.

7. Ibid., 87.

8. Theodore M. Greene, "Introduction, Part 1: The Historical Context and Religious Significance of Kant's *Religion,*" in Kant, *Religion,* xxxii–xxxvii.

9. Frederick II, cited in Jürgen Habermas, *The Structural Transformation of the Public Sphere,* trans. Thomas Burger (Cambridge: MIT Press, 1994), 25.

10. Kant, *Religion,* 154. Arkush, the translator of this edition, notes elsewhere that Kant's comments "have not received the attention they deserve" (*Moses Mendelssohn and the Enlightenment* [Albany: State University of New York Press, 1994], 254–81, particularly 275–79). Alexander Altmann, in his commentary on Arkush's translation of *Jerusalem,* observes only that Kant "misjudged . . . Mendelssohn's attitude to the historical element in Judaism" (*Jerusalem,* 203–4 n. 87). Mendelssohn was not about to take conversion to Christianity "under advisement." Kant had for whatever reason gotten it wrong.

Rotenstreich is admittedly baffled by Kant's remarks and puts them in the context of the compliments which Kant had addressed to Mendelssohn ten years earlier upon *Jerusalem*'s publication. Kant very much admired the book, praising its "penetration, subtlety, and wisdom." Rotenstreich avers that "there is no point in questioning his [Kant's] sincerity" (*Jews and German Philosophy,* 23; and see 23–36). He suggests that Kant may have "overinterpreted" Mendelssohn then as later because he quite reasonably understood him in accordance with the views of Mendelssohn's protégé David Friedlander.

It was Friedlander who had sent Kant a copy of *Jerusalem* and who, perhaps acting on his own reading of Mendelssohn, would several years after publication of Kant's *Religion* propose the mass conversion of Berlin Jewry to an enlightened form of Christianity. Arkush rightly decides, after a survey of Friedlander's writings, that Rotenstreich's conjecture, though ingenious, is ultimately unconvincing. Perhaps, Arkush speculates, the author of *Jerusalem* had admitted in private conversation with Kant—"a reasonable man, if ever there was one"—that he too had become a deist bereft of real belief in revelation and that he feigned adherence to traditional faith in order to retain the confidence of the coreligionists whom he hoped to transform. In the end, however, Arkush concludes that "Kant simply suspected that a man who was as thorough a rationalist as he believed Mendelssohn to be could not possibly have been a genuine believer in the validity of biblical revelation and the eternally binding character of the Mosaic law. Read with a skeptical eye[,] . . . Mendelssohn's writings provide ample cause for entertaining at least some such doubts" (*Moses Mendelssohn and the Enlightenment,* 275).

However, for a reading of Mendelssohn that supports (with ample quotation from his public and private writings) the view that his protestations of belief in the divine revelation of Scripture at Sinai were sincere, see David Sorkin, *Moses Mendelssohn and the Religious Enlightenment* (Berkeley and Los Angeles: University of California Press, 1996), 83. It seems more credible, I agree, to read Kant with a skeptical eye than to read Mendelssohn that way. There seems no reason whatever—given the arguments brought by Arkush, Leo Strauss, Yirmiyahu Yovel, and others—to accept Rotenstreich's judgment that Kant's sincerity in the footnote is beyond question. Pose, double entendre, veiled allusion, and blatant distortion were all standard practice in the Enlightenment critique of religion. Kant's animus against Judaism—and, particularly, Jewish law—is presented in his *Religion* with no concealment whatever. Friendship for Mendelssohn would likely have encouraged a certain blurring of Mendelssohn's thinking with his own, and it would not have precluded more egregious misrepresentation if the end were true religion's triumph over false. Kant was "a reasonable man"—and reason's authority and power in the emergent order were at stake. For that evidence, see Arkush, *Mendelssohn,* 274–83; Strauss, *Persecution and the Art of Writing* (Glencoe: Free Press, 1952), 33, and *Spinoza's Critique of Religion* (New York: Schocken Books, 1982); and Yovel, *Spinoza and Other Heretics,* vol. 2, *The Adventures of Immanence* (Princeton: Princeton University Press, 1989), 3–26, as well as the sources Yovel cites on 188 n. 8.

11. Kant, *Religion,* 116; and see Shlomo Pines, "Spinoza's *Tractatus Theologico-Politicus,* Maimonides, and Kant," *Scripta Hierosolymitana* 20 (1988): 48; and Yovel, *Adventures of Immanence,* 9.

12. Kant, *Religion,* 116–17.

13. Note, however, Hans-Georg Gadamer's contention, after his summarizing of Mendelssohn's position, that "one who hears Mendelssohn argue in this manner will understand that the modern Enlightenment can more easily be reconciled with the religious tradition of Judaism than with the Christian tradi-

tion which contains an unsolvable contradiction impossible to hide between reason and revelation." This was precisely the claim of countless nineteenth- and twentieth-century Jewish thinkers, most notably Hermann Cohen, whom Gadamer immediately mentions. Kant's attack on Judaism might well have been motivated in part by the need to fend off precisely this suspicion. See Dieter Misgeld and Graeme Nicholson, eds., *Hans-Georg Gadamer on Education, Poetry, and History,* trans. Lawrence Schmidt and Monica Reuss (Albany: State University of New York Press, 1992), 160.

14. This comes out clearly in the historical account of the notions of public and public sphere provided in Habermas, *Structural Transformation of the Public Sphere,* chaps. 1–5; see, especially, 46, 85.

15. On this theme, see, most recently, Daniel Boyarin, *Carnal Israel* (Berkeley and Los Angeles: University of California Press, 1995).

16. See Arthur Hertzberg, *The French Enlightenment and the Jews* (New York: Schocken Books, 1968). See also Isaac Barzilay, "The Jew in the Literature of the Enlightenment," *Jewish Social Studies* 18, no. 4 (October 1956): 243–61. Gary Kates criticizes Hertzberg's account of the treatment accorded Jews during the French Revolution for not distinguishing among the Revolution's very different phases; see Kates, "Jews into Frenchmen: Nationality and Representation in Revolutionary France," *Social Research* 56, no. 1 (spring 1989): 213–32, especially 223–26. However—the point crucial for my claims—Kates agrees that the French were not really talking about Jews at all in these debates. The Jews were "symbols of something else"—the definition of Emancipation and representation—and as such were not denied the "rights of passive citizenship" but only those of "active citizenship."

17. Hannah Arendt, *The Origins of Totalitarianism* (New York: Harcourt Brace Jovanovich, 1973), 46.

18. See Barzilay, "The Jew in the Literature of the Enlightenment," 243–44, 252–56. Arendt, with some exaggeration, calls Diderot "the only eighteenth-century French philosopher who was not hostile to the Jews and who recognized in them a useful link between Europeans of different nationalities" (*Origins of Totalitarianism,* 23).

19. See, for example, Ferenc Feher, "Practical Reason in the Revolution: Kant's Dialogue with the French Revolution," *Social Research* 56, no. 1 (spring 1989): 161–85.

20. See Sorkin, *Mendelssohn and the Religious Enlightenment,* 108, and the sources which he cites, preeminently James Sheehan, *German History, 1770–1866* (Oxford: Clarendon Press, 1989), 190–206.

21. Fichte, quoted in Katz, *Emancipation and Assimilation,* 62; see also 47–76.

22. Altmann, *Moses Mendelssohn: A Biographical Study* (Philadelphia: Jewish Publication Society, 1973), 552.

23. On this point, see the classic studies by Katz, *Tradition and Crisis* (New

York, Schocken Books, 1961), and *Exclusiveness and Tolerance* (New York: Schocken Books, 1961). See also Eliezer Schweid, *Toledot He-hagut ha-yehudit B'et Ha-ḥadasha* [A history of Jewish thought in modern times] (Jerusalem: Keter, 1977), 12; and Sorkin, *The Transformation of German Jewry, 1780–1840* (New York: Oxford University Press, 1987), 41–54.

24. Mendelssohn, *Jerusalem,* 133.

25. See Katz, *Out of the Ghetto,* 42–56.

26. See Altmann, *Moses Mendelssohn,* 514–52; Julius Guttmann, "Mendelssohn's *Jerusalem* and Spinoza's *Theologico-Political Treatise*," in *Studies in Jewish Thought,* ed. Alfred Jospe (Detroit: Wayne State University Press, 1981), 361–86; Simon Rawidowicz, "Ha-philosophia shel *Yerushalayim*" [The philosophy of *Jerusalem*], in *Iyyunim b'maḥshevet Yisrael* [Studies in Jewish thought] (Jerusalem: Rubin Mass, 1971), 2:70–117; and Rotenstreich, "Mendelson v'ha-ra'ayon ha-medini" [Mendelssohn and the political idea], in *Sefer ha-yovel likhvod Mordecai Menaḥem Kaplan* [Jubilee volume in honor of Mordecai Kaplan] (New York: Jewish Theological Seminary of America, 1953), 237–48.

27. See Mendelssohn, *Jerusalem,* 89–92.

28. See ibid., 93–121.

29. See Altmann, "Moses Mendelssohn as the Archetypal German Jew," in *The Jewish Response to German Culture,* ed. Jehuda Reinharz and Walter Schatzberg (Hanover, N.H.: University Press of New England, 1985), 17. See also Sorkin, *Mendelssohn and the Religious Enlightenment,* 45, 282–295.

30. Kant, "What Is Enlightenment?" in *Metaphysics of Morals,* 85–92.

31. Mendelssohn, *Jerusalem,* 133. Arkush apparently finds this avowal suspect (*Mendelssohn and the Enlightenment,* 270–74, 281–83); I do not. It was crucial to Mendelssohn's life, as to his work, that Jewish selves become enlightened, seek "eternal truth" like everyone else through rational means, yet avail themselves of the assistance in pursuing truth and practicing virtue afforded by the "ceremonial script" of the commandments.

32. Rotenstreich, *Jews and German Philosophy,* 37–42; see also 45–59. *Kultur* is "directed toward the practical sphere and has as its objectives goodness, refinement and beauty in artifacts, in art, as well as in objective social mores." Its field is social intercourse. *Aufklärung* comprises rational knowledge as well as "skill[,] . . . man's rational ability to reflect." Mendelssohn characterizes different groups of people on the basis of the distinction he has drawn. Residents of Nuremberg (like the French) have more culture, while Berliners (like the English) have more Enlightenment. The Greeks were "*eine gebildete Nation.*"

33. Rotenstreich, *Jews and German Philosophy,* 42–44. This point pervades Mendelssohn's Jewish writings; see Sorkin, *Mendelssohn and the Religious Enlightenment,* 15–17, 100–111, 161, 241. See also Sorkin's explanation (225 n. 31) of why he translates Mendelssohn's usages of *Kultur* as "applied knowledge" rather than "culture."

34. Rotenstreich, *Jews and German Philosophy*, 24–25. For a statement of Mendelssohn's point of view, see *Jerusalem*, 127. For a recent discussion of these issues, see Sorkin, *Mendelssohn and the Religious Enlightenment*, chaps. 1–2.

35. Mendelssohn, *Jerusalem*, 127.

36. Kant, *Religion*, 154. On this point see Sorkin, *Mendelssohn and the Religious Enlightenment*, chaps. 4–6.

37. On this point, see Sorkin, *Transformation of German Jewry*, 41–54, as well as his *Mendelssohn and the Religious Enlightenment*, chap. 1.

38. Kant, "Enlightenment," 86.

39. On these issues, see Charles Taylor, *Sources of the Self: The Making of the Modern Identity* (Cambridge, Mass.: Harvard University Press, 1989), chaps. 1–4, 11, and 17–24, especially chaps. 20–21.

40. The illustration appears in Beatrice Philippe, *Etre juif dans la société française* (Paris: Editions Montalba, 1979), 124, where it is credited to the Musée Carnavalet.

41. Kant, *Religion*, 7–10; for Mendelssohn's comparable attempt to demonstrate fidelity to his monarch, see *Jerusalem*, 78.

42. Kant, *Religion*, 86. Habermas points to the tension—common in much Enlightenment political theory—between law as the expression of will, on the one hand, and of reason, on the other; see *Structural Transformation of the Public Sphere*, 81.

43. Marx makes precisely the same point with reference to Hegel, who had written that "in order for the state to come in to existence as the self-knowing ethical actuality of spirit, it is essential that it should be distinct from the forms of authority and of faith. But this distinction emerges only in so far as divisions occur within the ecclesiastical sphere itself. It is only in this way that the state, above the *particular* churches, has attained to the universality of thought—its formal principle—and is bringing this universality into existence" (Hegel, *Grundlinien der Philosophie des Rechts*, in *Hegel's Philosophy of Right*, ed. T. M. Knox [Oxford: Clarendon Press, 1942], 173); see Karl Marx, "Bruno Bauer, *Die Judenfrage*," in *Karl Marx: Early Writings*, trans. and ed. T. B. Bottomore (New York: McGraw Hill, 1964), 12.

44. See Guttmann, "Mendelssohn's *Jerusalem*."

45. Benedict Spinoza, *A Theologico-Political Treatise*, trans. H. M. Elwes (New York: Dover Publications, 1951), 6.

46. Ibid., 186–89.

47. Ibid., 56.

48. Ibid., 69.

49. See, for example, Spinoza's comment that Paul's "doctrine is the same as ours . . . so that Paul teaches exactly the same as ourselves" (Ibid., 53).

50. Yosef Yerushalmi, *Assimilation and Racial Anti-Semitism* (New York: Leo Baeck Institute, 1982).

51. Spinoza, *Theologico-Political Treatise*, 245, 252.

52. Ibid., 76.

53. Kant, *Religion*, 167 n.

54. On *Verbesserung* and disparagement of Jewish behavior, see, for example, Katz, *Emancipation and Assimilation*, 32–36, 56–75, and *Out of the Ghetto*, 80–103; David Vital, *The Future of the Jews* (Cambridge, Mass.: Harvard University Press, 1990), 8–20; and Chapter 4 of the present work. Amos Funkenstein argues cogently that even though they had been subject to Gentile rule for centuries modernity posed a unique problem for Jews because Jews and non-Jews alike assumed that the acquisition of political rights demanded some degree of social and cultural assimilation, resulting in a measure of social integration; see Amos Funkenstein, *Perceptions of Jewish History* (Berkeley and Los Angeles: University of California Press, 1993), 221–223, 235.

55. Mendelssohn, *Jerusalem*, 119, 128.

56. See Mendelssohn's famous letter to his student Herz Homberg, written soon after the publication of *Jerusalem*, in which Mendelssohn argued that the commandments were necessary in order to unify "true theists" in their continuing battle against "polytheism, anthropomorphism, and ecclesiastical authority" (Mendelssohn, *Gesammelte Schriften: Jubilaumsausgabe* [Stuttgart: F. Frommann, 1983], 13:132–34; the letter is also conveniently available in full as an addendum to the Hebrew translation of *Jerusalem* [Ramat Gan: Masada, 1977], 226–28).

57. See Altmann, *Moses Mendelssohn*, 276, 288; and Sorkin, *Mendelssohn and the Religious Enlightenment*, 97.

58. Mendelssohn, *Jerusalem*, 82.

59. See ibid., 113–15.

60. See Mendes-Flohr, "The Study of the Jewish Intellectual: A Methodological Prolegomenon," in *Divided Passions* (Detroit: Wayne State University Press, 1991), 23–53.

61. See Altmann, *Moses Mendelssohn*, 403.

62. Mendelssohn, as much as Kant or Spinoza, had believed atheism inimical both to right living and to the demands of citizenship; he had pronounced religious ritual an essential means of fostering the ethical commonwealth (see Mendelssohn, *Jerusalem*, 63).

63. Funkenstein, who calls Marx's essay "a caricaturized version of Mendelssohn's" work, notes that Marx was virtually the only thinker during the struggle for Emancipation who did not share the axiom that Emancipation and social integration had to go hand in hand; see Funkenstein, *Perceptions of Jewish History*, 231.

64. Marx, "On the Jewish Question," in *Early Writings*, 4.

65. Ibid., 5–7.

66. Ibid., 9–11.

67. Ibid., 36–40.

68. Ibid., 38.

69. Ibid., 10–13, 22–24. Habermas highlights the fact that Marx's critique follows directly on Hegel's in the *Philosophy of Right*. Habermas's own critique in turn follows closely on "On the Jewish Question" and parallels to a remarkable degree the analysis of Kant offered in the present essay; see Habermas, *Structural Transformation of the Public Sphere,* chaps. 13–14, especially pp. 117–32.

70. Marx, "On the Jewish Question," 14.

71. On these issues, see Julius Carlebach, *Karl Marx and the Radical Critique of Judaism* (London: Routledge and Kegan Paul, 1978); and a recent thoughtful essay, Dennis Fischman, *Political Discourse in Exile: Karl Marx and the Jewish Question* (Amherst: The University of Massachusetts Press, 1991).

72. Marx, quoted by David McLellan, *Karl Marx: His Life and Thought* (New York: Harper and Row, 1973), 86, cited in Fischman, *Political Discourse in Exile,* 15.

73. See Carlebach, *Karl Marx and the Radical Critique of Judaism,* 147, 261.

74. Marx and Frederick Engels, *The Holy Family; or, Critique of Critical Criticism: Against Bruno Bauer and Company,* trans. Richard Dixon and Clemens Dutt, in *Collected Works* (London: Lawrence and Wishart, 1975), 4:88; for Marx's sources, see 4:688 n. 25. One is driven to read this passage as confession that Judaism has been an eyesore to Marx from birth—"a wonderful one"—and that Judaism both belongs and contributes to the way Marx sees the world. Were it not for the paucity of references to Jews and Judaism in Marx's oeuvre, and the hostility evident in the equation of Judaism with huckstering, this recognition would not be surprising from a man descended on both sides of his family from three centuries of rabbis and whose extended family remained populated by many—and prominent—Jews. See Fischman, *Political Discourse in Exile,* 16–18; and Carlebach, *Karl Marx and the Radical Critique of Judaism,* 5, 151, 385).

75. Marx and Engels, *The Holy Family,* 94–99. A similar point is made in the very first of the "Theses on Feuerbach" (1845), where Marx attacks the latter's assumption that "the theoretical attitude [is] the only genuinely human attitude, while practice is conceived and fixed only in its dirty-judaical manifestation." Feuerbach's preference for theory over practice is likened to ancient Christian prejudice against carnal Jews in the name of spirit. See Marx, "Theses on Feuerbach," in *The Marx-Engels Reader,* ed. Robert Tucker (New York: W. W. Norton, 1978), 143.

76. Marx and Engels, *The Holy Family,* 106–18.

77. See Carlebach, *Karl Marx and the Radical Critique of Judaism,* 152, 158. Heine's scathing attack on the conceptions of Jews and Judaism popular among his radical acquaintances applies in large measure to Marx: "Some think they know the Jews because they have seen their beards, which is all they have ever revealed of themselves" (quoted in ibid., 190).

78. On class divisions among Jews, and their impact upon observance, see Arendt, *Origins of Totalitarianism,* 12–14, 24–27, 62–65. The impact of class on modern Jewish religious behavior has been considerable; see, for example, Todd Endelman, *The Jews of Georgian England* (Philadelphia, Jewish Publication Society, 1979), 132–35, and *Radical Assimilation in English Jewish History, 1656–1945* (Bloomington, Ind.: Indiana University Press, 1990), 86; and Hugh McLeod, *Class and Religion in the Late Victorian City* (Hamden, Conn.: Archon Books, 1974), and *Religion and the Working Class in Nineteenth-Century Britain* (London: Macmillan, 1984).

79. Marx, *Capital: A Critique of Political Economy,* trans. Samuel Moore and Edward Aveling (New York: International Publishers, 1967), 1:19–20. I am pleased that Fischman, drew the citation to my attention (*Political Discourse in Exile,* 85–86), and I am baffled by his note: "We might wonder why Marx has an attack by Mendelssohn, an assimilated Jew, on Spinoza, a Jewish heretic, on his mind at this time" (133 n. 35). Mendelssohn was hardly an assimilated Jew, and his purpose in the dispute with Lessing over Spinoza was hardly to brand the latter a heretic. On the facts of the case, see Altmann, *Moses Mendelssohn,* 35, 611.

TWO

1. Pierre Bourdieu, *The Logic of Practice,* trans. Richard Nice (Stanford, Calif.: Stanford University Press, 1990), 5.

2. Ibid., 27.

3. Emile Durkheim, *Suicide: A Study in Sociology,* trans. John A. Spaulding and George Simpson (New York: Free Press, 1951). See Steven Lukes, *Emile Durkheim: His Life and Work* (New York: Harper and Row, 1972), 193; and Robert Nisbet, *Emile Durkheim* (Englewood Cliffs: Prentice-Hall, 1965), 45.

4. See Durkheim, *The Rules of Sociological Method,* trans. Sarah A. Solovay and John H. Mueller (New York: Free Press, 1966), 14, 31, 44; and *Suicide,* 41–45.

5. See Durkheim, *Suicide,* 212.

6. Durkheim, *On the Division of Labor in Society,* trans. George Simpson (Glencoe, Ill.: Free Press, 1933); and see his *Rules of Sociological Method,* xxxix.

7. Durkheim, *The Elementary Forms of the Religious Life,* trans. Joseph Ward Swain (New York: Free Press, 1915), 386–87.

8. Durkheim, *Suicide,* 156–60.

9. Ibid., 246–58.

10. For a discussion of the third type of suicide, the "altruistic," see ibid., 219–23, 234. Whereas "egoistic" suicides are characterized by too much self in relation to society, "altruistic" suicides are characterized by too little, as when women kill themselves upon the deaths of their husbands or when soldiers are driven to suicide because their training has led them to deny the self and its needs.

11. Ibid., 209, 215, 323.

12. Ibid., 160, 167–68.

13. Durkheim, *Elementary Forms,* 50. Durkheim remarked in *Suicide* that while Protestantism is the "freest from material practices and consequently the most idealistic," Judaism "still clings to the most primitive religious forms in many respects" (376).

14. See Theodore Zeldin, *France: 1848–1945,* vol. 2, *Intellect, Taste, Anxiety* (Oxford: Clarendon Press, 1977), 784. William James noted trenchantly that susceptibility to pain is neither a cultural nor a biological constant; see *The Varieties of Religious Experience* (Cambridge, Mass.: Harvard University Press, 1985), 115–16. Peter Gay and Theodore Zeldin have argued that especially high levels of anxiety afflicted the nineteenth-century bourgeoisie; see Gay, *The Bourgeois Experience: Victoria to Freud,* vol. 1, *Education of the Senses* (New York, Oxford University Press, 1984), 17, 38, 56–58; and Zeldin, *France,* 823, 983. Christopher Lasch has pointed to the "rehabilitation of desire" introduced by Adam Smith, a striving after the goods of this world that became a pervasive feature of Enlightenment society; see Lasch, *The True and Only Heaven* (New York: W. W. Norton, 1991), 502. See also Charles Taylor, *Sources of the Self: The Making of the Modern Identity* (Cambridge, Mass.: Harvard University Press, 1989), chaps. 17–23.

15. Durkheim, *Elementary Forms,* 475.

16. Bourdieu, *Logic of Practice,* 14.

17. Durkheim, *Elementary Forms,* 475.

18. Ibid., 462–87.

19. See Max Weber, *The Protestant Ethic and the Spirit of Capitalism,* trans. Talcott Parsons (New York: Scribners, 1958), 180. On Weber's confusing but coherent use of the word "rationality" in that and succeeding works, see Arnold Eisen, "The Meanings and Confusions of Weberian Rationality," *British Journal of Sociology* 29, no. 1 (March 1978): 61–67; David Beetham, *Max Weber and the Theory of Modern Politics* (London: George Allen & Unwin, 1974), 274; Herbert Marcuse, "Industrialization and 'Capitalism,'" in *Max Weber and Sociology Today,* ed. Otto Stammer, trans. Kathleen Morris (Oxford: Basil Blackwell, 1971), 133–52, 184–86; and Steven Kalberg, "Max Weber's Types of Rationality," *American Journal of Sociology* 85, no. 5 (1980): 1145–80. See also Peter Hamilton, ed., *Critical Assessments of Max Weber* (London: Routledge, 1991).

20. See Weber, "Science as a Vocation," in *From Max Weber: Essays in Sociology,* trans. and ed. Hans H. Gerth and C. Wright Mills (New York: Oxford University Press, 1969), 129–43; and Eisen, "Called to Order: The Role of the Puritan *Berufsmensch* in Weberian Sociology," in *Critical Assessments of Max Weber,* 101–16.

21. See Weber, "Science as a Vocation," 134, 138.

22. Ibid., 138, 142.

23. Weber, "Politics as a Vocation," in *From Max Weber,* 79.

24. Ibid., 78–79. See also Weber, *The Sociology of Religion,* trans. Ephraim Fischoff (Boston: Beacon Press, 1963), 77, 199, 259, and *Ancient Judaism,* trans. Hans Gerth and Don Martindale (New York: Free Press, 1952), 12, 253.

25. See Weber, *Economy and Society,* ed. Guenther Roth and Claus Wittich (Berkeley and Los Angeles: University of California Press, 1978), 4, 22–26.

26. See Weber, *Ancient Judaism;* especially parts 4–5.

27. Weber, "Science as a Vocation," 155. See also Weber, "Religious Rejections of the World and their Directions" (1915), in *From Max Weber,* 342, 346, 348.

28. See Weber, *Economy and Society,* 578; and *Protestant Ethic,* 119.

29. Weber, "Science as a Vocation," 147–48.

30. Ibid., 156.

31. Ibid., 148.

32. For a critique of midcentury theories of secularization that conceive of that process as uniform, global, and inevitable, see Shmuel Eisenstadt, "Post-Traditional Societies and the Continuity and Reconstruction of Tradition," *Daedalus* 102, no. 1 (winter 1973): 1–25. See also the signal contributions of R. J. Zwi Werblowsky, *Beyond Tradition and Modernity* (London: Athlone, 1976); and Edward Shils, *Tradition* (Chicago: University of Chicago Press, 1981). Among the huge recent literature on secularization, see especially K. Dobbelaere, "Secularization: A Multi-Dimensional Concept," *Current Sociology* 29, no. 2 (1981): 3–213, "Secularization Theories and Sociological Paradigms: Convergences and Divergences," *Social Compass* 31, nos. 2–5 (1984): 199–219, and "Secularization Theories and Sociological Paradigms: A Reformulation of the Private-Public Dichotomy and The Problem of Societal Integration," *Sociological Analysis* 46, no. 4 (1985): 377–389; F. Lechner, "The Case against Secularization: A Rebuttal," *Social Forces* 69, no. 4 (1991): 1103–19; Bryan Wilson, "Secularization: The Inherited Model," in *The Sacred in a Secular Age,* ed. Philip Hammond (Berkeley and Los Angeles: University of California Press, 1985), 9–20; and Robert Wuthnow, "Recent Patterns of Secularization: A Problem of Generations?" *American Sociological Review* 41, no. 3 (1976): 850–67.

33. See Peter Berger, *The Sacred Canopy: Elements of a Sociological Theory of Religion* (Garden City, N.Y.: Doubleday, 1969), 25. On Berger, see James Davidson Hunter and Stephen C. Ainlay, eds., *Making Sense of Modern Times: Peter L. Berger and the Vision of Interpretive Sociology* (London: Routledge and Kegan Paul, 1986); and Robert C. Fuller, "Religion and Empiricism in the Works of Peter Berger," *Zygon* 22 (December 1987): 497–510.

34. Berger, *Sacred Canopy,* 48; and see 46–48.

35. Berger, *The Heretical Imperative* (Garden City, N.Y.: Doubleday, 1979), 106–7.

36. See David Martin, *A General Theory of Secularization* (Oxford: Basil Blackwell, 1978), 69–88.

37. Berger, *Heretical Imperative,* 26–27.

38. Berger, *Sacred Canopy,* 115.

39. Berger, *Sacred Canopy,* 170; see also 108.

40. One critic of Berger, however, has argued persuasively that this unitary model, presuming "religion, like politics, to be a property of the whole society," is ill fitted to the description of America over the past two centuries because this country, far from presenting a single "sacred canopy" or the absence thereof, has rather been characterized by "the disestablishment of the churches and the rise of an open market for religion"; see R. Stephen Warner, "Work in Progress Towards a New Paradigm for the Sociological Study of Religion in the United States," *American Journal of Sociology* 98, no. 1 (March 1993): 1044–51.

41. In eastern Europe and the Sephardi communities of the Mediterranean, western Asia, and North Africa, ethnic/national distinctiveness remained primary, and acculturation to Gentile cultures was slower and more partial. The general pattern, however, was similar. On the parallels and divergences among Sephardi communities, see Aron Rodrigue, *Images of Sephardi and Eastern Jews in Transition* (Seattle: University of Washington Press, 1993); and Norman A. Stillman, *The Jews of Arab Lands in Modern Times* (Philadelphia: Jewish Publication Society, 1991). On eastern European Jews, see Michael Stanislawski, *Tsar Nicholas I and the Jews* (Philadelphia: Jewish Publication Society, 1987); and Steven Zipperstein, *The Jews of Odessa* (Stanford, Calif.: Stanford University Press, 1988). Comparative issues are addressed explicitly in Pierre Birnbaum and Ira Katznelson, eds., *Paths of Emancipation: Jews, States, and Citizenship* (Princeton, N.J.: Princeton University Press, 1995). Finally, for a Durkheimian analysis that disputes the Weberian account of secularization that I have presented above, following Berger, see Calvin Goldscheider and Alan S. Zuckerman, *The Transformation of the Jews* (Chicago: University of Chicago Press, 1984).

42. On this point, see Jacob Katz, *Exclusiveness and Tolerance* (New York: Schocken, 1973).

43. Berger, *Sacred Canopy,* 170.

44. Parsons maintained that Christian values and commitments in the modern West were no longer segregated in churches but "diffused" via differentiation throughout the "secular city," a consummation of Protestant ambitions that he called the "Christianizing of society"; see "Christianity and Modern Industrial Society," in *Sociological Theory, Values, and Sociocultural Change,* ed. Edward Tiryakian (New York: Harper & Row, 1963), 44–49, 62–67. Cf. Warner, "Work in Progress," 1047.

45. Berger, *Heretical Imperative,* 53.

46. The first type, the "deductive," aims "to reassert the authority of a tradition in the face of modern secularity"; the second, the "reductive," "to reinterpret the tradition in terms of modern secularity"; the third, the "inductive," characterized by "the turn to experience as the ground of all religious affirma-

tions," is attributed to Friedrich Schleiermacher (Berger, *Heretical Imperative,* 56–58; and see the detailed discussion in chaps. 3–5).

47. Why then use these categories? The answer perhaps lies in the fact, explicit in Berger's work, that his sociology is inseparable from his normative religious commitment to liberal Protestantism. Secularization means the relocation of the sacred, and "the classic description of the experience of the sacred is the one by Rudolf Otto"—*mysterium tremendum et fascinans.* Schleiermacher is the presiding presence in Otto's theology, and he retains that position in Berger's sociology. In fact, his theology of religious experience is the only strategy Berger believes workable for preserving faith despite the privatization of religious authority. For a Christian, "an unambiguous identification with the line of liberal Protestantism that originated with Schleiermacher" is "the only viable option." Berger's entire analysis is colored by this commitment. His description of religious evolution as a progressive "routinization of charisma" presumes a founding event in which "religious experience posits its own authority." See Berger, *Heretical Imperative,* 42–44.

Jews and Muslims have not tended to see things that way. Nor would any modern Jewish thinker of my acquaintance agree with the statement in Berger's most recent avowal of faith, *A Far Glory,* that "the various doctrines and ideologies that divide us today" are from a religious point of view "quite unimportant, indeed irrelevant. The Gospel is not of this world . . ." (*A Far Glory* [New York: Doubleday, 1993], 15). On these issues, see also Michael A. Morgan, "Judaism and the Heretical Imperative," *Religious Studies* 17 (March 1981): 109–20; and Thomas Kerlin, "Crossing Berger's Fiery Brook," *Thomist* 40 (July 1976): 366–392.

48. See the related and influential conception of culture in Clifford Geertz, *The Interpretation of Cultures* (New York: Basic Books, 1973), 11, 54.

49. Berger, *Sacred Canopy,* 11.

50. Berger, *Heretical Imperative,* chap. 1.

51. See Paula Hyman, *The Emancipation of the Jews of Alsace* (New Haven, Conn.: Yale University Press), 121.

52. See David Sorkin, *The Transformation of German Jewry, 1780–1840* (New York: Oxford University Press, 1987), chap. 1.

53. Philip Rieff, *The Triumph of the Therapeutic: Uses of Faith after Freud* (New York: Harper & Row, 1968), 4–5.

54. For Rieff's presentation and critique of Freud, see, in particular, the most recent edition of, and new afterword to, *Freud: The Mind of The Moralist,* 3d ed. (Chicago: University of Chicago Press, 1979).

55. Rieff, *Triumph of the Therapeutic,* 11.

56. Ibid.

57. Rieff, *Freud,* 362.

58. For concise statements of Rieff's viewpoint, see his *The Feeling Intellect:*

Selected Writings, ed. Jonathan B. Imber (Chicago: University of Chicago Press, 1990), chaps. 47–48.

59. Rieff, *Fellow Teachers* (New York: Dell Publishing Company, 1973), 46.

60. Ibid., 112–13.

61. Ibid., 78–79.

62. Ibid., 136.

63. Ibid., 170–72.

64. On modernism, see Hans Ulrich Gumbrecht, "A History of the Concept 'Modern,'" in *Making Sense in Life and Literature,* trans. Glen Burns (Minneapolis: University of Minnesota Press, 1991; and Matei Calinescu, *Five Faces of Modernity* (Durham, N.C.: Duke University Press, 1987).

65. See Hannah Arendt, *The Origins of Totalitarianism* (New York: Harcourt Brace Jovanovich, 1973), chaps. 1–3.

66. See, for example, Rieff, *Fellow Teachers,* 138–39.

67. Stephen Toulmin, *Cosmopolis: The Hidden Agenda of Modernity* (New York: Free Press, 1990), 3.

68. Jean-François Lyotard, *The Postmodern Condition: A Report on Knowledge,* trans. Geoff Bennington and Brian Massumi (Minneapolis: University of Minnesota Press, 1984), 8, 10.

69. On this first point, cf. Yaron Ezrahi, *The Descent of Icarus* (Cambridge, Mass.: Harvard University Press, 1990), 14.

70. Lyotard, *Postmodern Condition,* 30.

71. See E. J. Hobsbawm, *Nations and Nationalism since 1780: Programme, Myth, Reality* (Cambridge: Cambridge University Press, 1990).

72. Lyotard, *Postmodern Condition,* 30, 37.

73. Ibid., 60–65.

74. Lyotard, *Heidegger and "the jews,"* trans. Andreas Michel and Mark Roberts (Minneapolis: University of Minnesota Press, 1990), 22.

75. Ibid., 3.

76. Ibid., 3–8.

77. Jürgen Habermas, *The Philosophical Discourse of Modernity,* trans. Frederick Lawrence (Cambridge, Mass.: MIT Press, 1991), 310.

78. Ibid., 299. Modernity in Habermas's view, as in Weber's, had tragically specialized all knowledge and assigned each its own mutually inaccessible canon of validity. The 'spheres of knowing' were separated from belief as from "legally organized and everyday life" (19). Habermas wants to overcome these divisions, as he wants to move beyond Weber's false dichotomy of formal and substantive rationality (see 315); he is concerned, rather, with multiple and local "life-worlds," each of which is constituted by mutual understanding and true communication (see 296).

79. See ibid., 36, 47, 90, for example.

80. Ibid., 315–16.

81. Lukes, "Of Gods and Demons: Habermas and Practical Reason," in *Habermas: Critical Debates,* ed. John B. Thompson and David Held (Cambridge, Mass.: MIT Press, 1982), 134.

82. Ibid., 134.

83. Habermas, *Philosophical Discourse of Modernity,* 2.

84. Thomas Walsh, "Religion, Politics, and Life Worlds: Jurgen Habermas and Richard John Neuhaus," in *Secularization and Fundamentalism Reconsidered,* ed. Jeffrey K. Hadden and Anson Shupe (New York: Paragon House, 1989), 3:100.

85. Francis Schüssler Fiorenza, "Introduction: A Critical Reception for a Practical Public Theology," in *Habermas, Modernity, and Public Theology,* ed. Don S. Browning and Francis Schüssler Fiorenza (New York: Crossroad Press, 1992), 9.

86. David Tracy, "Theology, Critical Social Theory, and the Public Realm," in *Habermas, Modernity, and Public Theology,* 36.

87. Lukes, "Gods and Demons," 136. On these issues, see also *Habermas, Modernity, and Public Theology.*

88. Habermas, *Philosophical Discourse of Modernity,* 322.

89. See, aside from the example cited in the text, Habermas, "Gershom Scholem: The Torah in Disguise," in *Philosophical-Political Profiles,* trans. Frederick G. Lawrence (Cambridge, Mass.: MIT Press, 1983), 199–211, particularly 205, 210. On this point, see also the essays in *Habermas, Modernity, and Public Theology.* For Scholem's theological views, see, for example, his "Reflections on Jewish Theology," in *On Jews and Judaism in Crisis,* ed. Werner Dannhauser (New York: Schocken Books, 1984).

90. Habermas, *Philosophical Discourse of Modernity,* 325.

THREE

1. Mary Douglas, *Natural Symbols: Explorations in Cosmology* (New York: Pantheon, 1982), 1.

2. Lenn Goodman, "Rational Law/Ritual Law," in *A People Apart: Chosenness and Ritual in Jewish Philosophy and Thought,* ed. Daniel H. Frank (Albany: State University of New York Press, 1993), 155–56

3. Douglas, *Purity and Danger* (London: Routledge and Kegan Paul, 1966), 99, 83, 114, 140.

4. Cf. Emile Durkheim, *The Elementary Forms of the Religious Life,* trans. Joseph Ward Swain (New York: Free Press, 1915), 13, 20; Mary Douglas, *Implicit Meanings: Essays in Anthropology* (London: Routledge and Kegan Paul, 1973), xi; E. E. Evans-Pritchard, *Nuer Religion* (New York: Oxford University Press, 1977), 123–43, 311–22; and Bryan Wilson, ed., *Rationality* (New York: Harper Torchbooks, 1971).

5. See, on this point, Joseph R. Gusfield and Jerzy Michalowicz, "Secular

Symbolism: Studies of Ritual, Ceremony, and the Symbolic Order in Modern Life," *Annual Review of Sociology* 10 (1984): 417–18. Douglas has demonstrated that many of the conceptions standard in the field arose out of their authors' attempts to differentiate modern religious beliefs from primitive rites and super-stitions which were putatively lower on the evolutionary ladder; see Douglas, *Purity and Danger,* chap. 1; see also Howard Eilberg-Schwartz, *The Savage in Judaism* (Bloomington: Indiana University Press, 1990), chaps. 1–4.

6. Douglas, *Natural Symbols,* 13–14; see also 24–33.

7. Ibid., 9.

8. Douglas, *Purity and Danger,* 68–69.

9. Douglas, *Natural Symbols,* viii, 57.

10. Ibid., 63–64; see also 119.

11. Ibid., 7. The effect of changed Jewish circumstances on halakhic attitudes toward the crucial matter of exogamy is probed in David Ellenson, *Tradition in Transition: Orthodoxy, Halakhah, and the Boundaries of Modern Jewish Identity* (Lanham, Md.: University Press of America, 1989), 81–85.

12. Moses Mendelssohn, *Jerusalem,* trans. Allan Arkush (Hanover, N.H.: University Press of New England, 1983), 102–4.

13. Ibid., 119.

14. See Jacob Katz, *Exclusiveness and Tolerance,* (New York: Schocken Books, 1961), chap. 1. Katz has demonstrated that Emancipation altered not only the meaning of observance but its details and affected not only choices by individual Jews to obey or disregard a given law but the arguments used by the authorities in reformulation of the law. Whether lenient or strict, a *posek* in the fractured Jewish body politic of modernity "knew that his rulings obligated only those who had remained faithful to the ancestral tradition or who had determined, after hesitation, to accept the yoke of the halakhah." Each individual Jew "had to decide for himself if he was willing and able to live accordingly," his personal decision being final. See Katz, *The "Shabbes Goy": A Study in Halakhic Flexibility,* trans. Yoel Lerner (Philadelphia: Jewish Publication Society, 1989), 134, 154–55.

15. Monika Richarz, ed., *Jewish Life in Germany: Memoirs from Three Centuries,* trans. Stella P. Rosenfeld and Sidney Rosenfeld (Bloomington: Indiana University Press, 1991), 156.

16. Inherited symbols may even lose their meaning altogether; cf. Douglas, *Natural Symbols,* vii. On this point, see also Caroline Walker Bynum, *Holy Feast and Holy Fast: The Religious Significance of Food to Medieval Women* (Berkeley and Los Angeles: University of California Press, 1987).

17. Douglas, *Purity and Danger,* 73; see also 140.

18. Durkheim, *Elementary Forms,* 423; see also Douglas, *Natural Symbols,* 43–53.

19. Clifford Geertz, "Religion as a Cultural System," in *The Interpretation of Cultures* (New York: Basic Books, 1973), 90.

20. Ibid., 120; and see 96, 114–20.

21. Ibid., 122.

22. Geertz, "Ritual and Social Change: A Javanese Example," in *Interpretation of Cultures,* 142–69; see also Geertz, "Religious Belief and Economic Behavior in a Central Javanese Town," in *The Protestant Ethic and Modernization,* ed. S. N. Eisenstadt (New York: Basic Books, 1968), 309–42.

23. Alexander Altmann, *Moses Mendelssohn: A Biographical Study* (Philadelphia: Jewish Publication Society, 1973), 288. Rabbi Jacob Emden, one of the leading German authorities of the day, strongly disagreed with Mendelssohn's concession on the matter and accused him in a sharp rebuke of abandoning ancient custom for the sake of adopting Gentile behavior. Mendelssohn, for his part, believed that the insistence on immediate burial stemmed from superstitious notions that the soul could not enter paradise or be freed of torment by demons until the body was at rest. For a beautiful depiction of how traditional and modern cultures and subcultures clashed around a funeral, see Anthony Kwame Appiah, *In My Father's House* (New York: Oxford University Press, 1992), 190–92.

24. Mendelssohn, *Jerusalem,* 103.

25. The allusion here is, of course, to the Geertz essay of that title, but the point holds equally for Victor Turner's well-known theory of ritual as a "liminal experience" of "anti-structure" and "communitas" that occurs in the intervals between times or places where structure is, as per normal, rigidly enforced; see Turner, *The Ritual Process: Structure and Anti-Structure* (Ithaca, N.Y.: Cornell University Press, 1982), chap. 3. Turner recognized that modernity has not been kind to liminal experience. The theory, by his own admission, is patently inapplicable to societies so highly structured and individualist that "liminality" becomes metaphorical. At best, moderns are offered occasions for a *glimpse* of true communitas and experience "liminoid" moments of collective fantasy and imagination that promise—and at times even achieve—an overturning of normal possibilities and expectations. Ritual has moved along the continuum from work to play, obligation to option, collective to individual, centrality to marginality; see Turner, *Process, Performance, and Pilgrimage: A Study in Comparative Symbology* (New Delhi: Concept Publishing Company, 1979), 15, 23, 27; see also 28–54, especially 52.

26. See Isaac Heinemann, *Ta'amei Ha-Mitzvot* [The reasons for the commandments in Jewish literature] (Jerusalem: Jewish Agency, 1966), 12–20, 34, 129–44; and Ephraim E. Urbach, *The Sages: Their Concepts and Beliefs,* trans. Israel Abrahams (Jerusalem: Magnes Press of Hebrew University, 1979), 1:365–99.

27. I have treated these issues in detail elsewhere; see Eisen, "Divine Legislation as 'Ceremonial Script': Mendelssohn on the Commandments," *AJS Review* 15, no. 2 (fall 1990): 239–67. See also Altmann, *Mendelssohn,* 514–52; Altmann's

introduction and commentary to Mendelssohn, *Jerusalem;* Julius Guttmann, "Mendelssohn's *Jerusalem* and Spinoza's *Theologico-Political Treatise*," in *Studies in Jewish Thought,* ed. Alfred Jospe (Detroit: Wayne State University Press, 1981), 361–86; Simon Rawidowicz, "Ha-philosophia shel *Yerushalayim*" [The philosophy of *Jerusalem*], in *Iyyunim b'mahshevet Yisrael* [Studies in Jewish thought] (Jerusalem: Rubin Mass, 1971), 2:70–117; and Nathan Rotenstreich, "Mendelson v'ha-ra'ayon ha-medini" [Mendelssohn and the political idea], in *Sefer ha-yovel likhvod Mordecai Menahem Kaplan* [Jubilee volume in honor of Mordecai Kaplan] (New York: Jewish Theological Seminary of America, 1953), 237–48. On Mendelssohn's tortuous explanation of the "divine legislation" as "a kind of living script," see Heinemann, *Ta'amei Ha-Mitzvot,* 9–46; and, for a more cogent treatment which is at times critical of my own approach, see Allen Arkush, *Moses Mendelssohn and the Enlightenment* (Albany: State University of New York Press), 167–239.

28. Mendelssohn, *Jerusalem,* 102. Mendelssohn thus takes the famous midrash about God's revelation at Sinai coming simultaneously in seventy languages to mean that the revelation was beyond language altogether. His emphasis on the historical rather than the metaphysical truth revealed at Sinai closely follows Judah Halevi's argument in the *Kuzari,* though his enthusiasm for miracle, unlike the *Kuzari*'s, is muted at best. See Halevi, *Kuzari,* trans. Hartwig Hirschfeld (New York: Schocken Books, 1964), 1:1–25.

29. See Mendelssohn, *Jerusalem,* 105–15.

30. Ibid., 117–18.

31. Roy Rappaport, "Logos, Liturgy, and the Evolution of Humanity" paper presented at the ICAES symposium "Evolutionary Ecology and the Human Condition," Zagreb, July 1988), 8, 19–20; and *Ecology, Meaning, and Religion* (Richmond, Calif.: North Atlantic Books, 1979), 179–197, 229.

32. Cf. Rappaport, "The Construction of Time and Eternity in Ritual" (Department of Anthropology, University of Michigan, photocopy), 2, 16; see also his *Ecology, Meaning, and Religion* 178; and Goodman, "Mythic Discourse," in *Myths and Fictions,* ed. Shlomo Biderman and Ben-Ami Scharfstein (Leiden: Brill, 1993), 99.

33. Stanley Jeyaraja Tambiah, "A Performative Approach to Ritual," in *Culture, Thought, and Social Action* (Cambridge, Mass.: Harvard University Press, 1985), 132–34.

34. Mendelssohn, *Jerusalem,* 80, 82.

35. Cf. Rappaport, *Ecology, Meaning, and Religion,* 199.

36. Jonathan Z. Smith, *To Take Place: Toward Theory in Ritual* (Chicago: University of Chicago Press, 1987), 98–103; see also Goodman, "Rational Law/Ritual Law," 178.

37. See Smith, *To Take Place,* 114; Smith draws on the notion of "parcelling out"—breaking ritual actions down into component parts—used by Claude

Lévi-Strauss in *The Naked Man,* trans. John and Doreen Weightman (New York: Harper and Row, 1981), 672. On the issue of embeddedness, see also Pierre Bourdieu, *The Logic of Practice,* trans. Richard Nice (Stanford, Calif.: Stanford University Press, 1950), 7–8; Edmund R. Leach, *International Encyclopedia of the Social Sciences,* ed. David L. Sills (New York: Macmillan, 1968), s.v. "ritual," 13:522; Don Handelman, *Models and Mirrors: Towards an Anthropology of Public Events* (Cambridge: Cambridge University Press, 1990); and David Hall, *Worlds of Wonder, Days of Judgment: Popular Religious Belief in Early New England* (Cambridge, Mass.: Harvard University Press, 1989), 3, 17–19. Smith's account of how bits and pieces of ordinary activity and experience are "borrowed" and patched together for ritual use is strikingly similar to descriptions of animal ritual. Greeting ceremonies, for example, are described (in Philip Whitfield, ed., *The Animal Family* [New York: W. W. Norton, 1979]) as "a patchwork of small behavioral scraps gleaned from many functional contexts and sewn together to create a fabric of fascinating complexity" (56).

38. Evans-Pritchard, *Nuer,* 144, 285.

39. For a very different view of the relation between a ritual such as wedding vows and the feast that follows, see Maurice Bloch, *Hunter into Prey* (Cambridge: Cambridge University Press, 1994).

40. See Durkheim, *Elementary Forms,* 53–55, but also the chapters on "positive and negative cult," which make it clear, as he puts it, not only that "some things are sacred while others are not" but that "there are inequalities and incompatibilities between sacred things"—in other words, a continuum of sacredness and profaneness (340).

41. Geertz, "Ethos, World View, and the Analysis of Sacred Symbols," in *Interpretation of Cultures,* 127, and "Religion as a Cultural System," 113. Compare Geertz's account to Smith's argument that ritual is generally "no big deal" (Smith, "The Domestication of Sacrifice," in *Violent Origins: Ritual Killing and Cultural Formation,* ed. Robert G. Hamerton-Kelly [Stanford, Calif.: Stanford University Press, 1987], 194). If ritual is superimposed on everyday experience, Smith adds elsewhere, "there is nothing that is inherently sacred or profane. These are not substantive categories, but rather situational ones" (*To Take Place,* 104). On ritual as focusing device, cf. Douglas, *Purity and Danger,* 63.

42. See Goodman, "Rational Law/Ritual Law," 173–75.

43. Ibid., 113, 119. The following discussion also draws on Heinemann, *Ta'amei Ha-Mitzvot;* and Daniel C. Matt, "The Mystic and the *Mizwot,*" in *Jewish Spirituality from the Bible through the Middle Ages,* ed. Arthur Green (New York: Crossroad, 1986), 367–404.

44. See Rappaport, *Ecology, Meaning, and Religion,* 200.

45. Ibid., 117; "Construction of Time and Eternity in Ritual," 3–4.

46. Søren Kierkegaard, *Repetition,* trans. Walter Lowrie (New York: Harper Torchbooks, 1964), 15.

47. See Rappaport, "Construction of Time and Eternity in Ritual," 22; "Logos, Liturgy," 29; *Ecology, Meaning, and Religion,* 116.

48. Philip Rieff, *The Feeling Intellect: Selected Writings,* ed. Jonathan B. Imber (Chicago: University of Chicago Press, 1990), 333.

49. My thinking about "elite" versus "folk" religion among Jews is indebted to an unpublished paper by Michael Stanislawski, "Towards the Popular Religion of Ashkenazi Jews" (Columbia University, photocopy). Catherine Bell has observed correctly that "relatively little attention has been paid to how the presence of specialists affects ritual practices"; see her *Ritual Theory, Ritual Practice* (New York: Oxford University Press, 1992), 130.

50. See Mordecai Breuer, *Modernity within Tradition,* trans. Elizabeth Petuchowski (New York: Columbia University Press, 1992), chap. 1.

51. This is especially evident in musical performances in the synagogue by trained organists and choirs. One of the few accounts of religious ritual to pay serious attention to its musical component is Tamiah, *Culture, Thought, and Social Action,* 123–25.

52. Josef Stern, "Modes of Reference in the Rituals of Judaism," *Religious Studies* 23:109–14.

53. Geertz, "Religion as a Cultural System," 114–18.

54. Michael Govrin, "Jewish Rituals as a Genre of Sacred Theater," *Conservative Judaism* 36, no. 3 (spring 1983):17. Govrin notes that we have no record of dramatic or musical presentations in the premodern Jewish community; perhaps there was no room inside or outside the synagogue for festive recollection of the deeds of "gods" or heroes. This changed fairly quickly in the modern period. The context for Jewish practice came to include both Jewish and Gentile dramatic and musical performances. One effect may have been competition among cultural performances for the opportunity to express and reaffirm identity, mourn collective sufferings, or exult in communal achievements.

55. Richard Schechner's theory of ritual as performance takes pains to demonstrate that emotion can be reliably evoked upon command, with corresponding physiological changes that can also be induced by bodily movements and/or stimuli. The means to the arousal of emotion are readily available and widely employed. See Richard Schechner, "Magnitudes of Performance," in *The Anthropology of Experience,* ed. Victor W. Turner and Edward M. Bruner (Urbana: University of Illinois Press, 1986), 344–69. Particular rituals—like actors on stage—seem to shift easily from one emotion to another, as, say, Shmini Atzeret with its memorial prayer and its solemn plea for rain gives way at sunset to the revelry of Simḥat Torah, or as Israelis move on command in a single interval of twilight from the Day of Remembrance of fallen soldiers to the celebrations of Independence Day. Religious Israelis, unlike diaspora Jews, observe Shmini Atzeret on the very same day as Simḥat Torah, making the transition from emo-

tion to emotion, and back, still more abrupt. On the Israeli festivals, see Handelman, *Models and Mirrors,* 191–233.

56. Hence the especially major import, where modern Jews are concerned, of the question that Nietzsche posed so powerfully in *The Birth of Tragedy:* not so much whether one could *believe in* myths of the gods after the rise of "theoretical man" but whether one could participate in performances, like Greek tragedy, that allowed one to glimpse the "primal unity"; see Nietzsche, *The Birth of Tragedy,* trans. Walter Kaufmann (New York: Vintage Books, 1967), sec. 20.

57. See the discussion of *havurah* Judaism, an American development influenced by the counterculture of the 1960s, in Riv Ellen Prell, *Prayer and Community* (Detroit: Wayne State University Press, 1989). On ultra-Orthodoxy, see Haim Soloveitchik, "Rupture and Reconstruction: The Transformation of Contemporary Orthodoxy," *Tradition* 18, no. 4 (1994): 64–130.

58. Outright embrace of mystery and emotion—a species of Romanticism frowned upon by nearly all Jewish movements, from Reform to ultra-Orthodoxy—has played a major role in the fascination with Hasidism among Western Jews. Only in recent decades, however, and particularly in America, have mainstream Jewish groups and thinkers been receptive to anything like Nietzsche's attacks on "the desert of our exhausted culture" and accordingly felt an attraction, however cautious, to the prospect of "a tempest [that] seizes everything that has outlived itself" and carries it off in "sublime ecstasy" and "distant melancholy."

59. See Max Weber, "Science as a Vocation," in *From Max Weber: Essays in Sociology,* trans. and ed. Hans H. Gerth and C. Wright Mills (New York: Oxford University Press, 1969), 155.

60. See Smith, "Domestication of Sacrifice," 224.

61. Erving Goffman, "The Nature of Deference and Demeanor," in *Interaction Ritual* (New York: Pantheon Books, 1982), 58, 72, 77, 91.

62. Goffman, "Nature of Deference," 47, 95. See the excellent use made of Goffman's categories in Samuel Heilman, *The People of the Book: Drama, Fellowship, and Religion* (Chicago: University of Chicago Press, 1983); cf. Ellenson, "A Sociologist's View of Contemporary Jewish Orthodoxy: The Work of Samuel Heilman," *Religious Studies Review* 21, no. 1 (January 1995): 14–18.

63. While religious processions have declined in the modern West, especially in comparison to their frequency during the Middle Ages, parades celebrating the state or society (or the various groups which represent or compose society) have continued and perhaps even grown more frequent. Presidential inaugurations, like rock concerts and sporting events, still offer great spectacle to late-twentieth-century Americans (inaugurations, of course, are framed by an invocation of the deity at the start and a benediction at the close) while ecclesiastical installations generally receive little attention and public *religious* ceremonial of all sorts is far less prominent.

64. Goodman, "Rational Law/Ritual Law," 183–84.

65. On performatives in ritual, see Rappaport, *Ecology, Meaning, and Religion,* 193; and Tambiah, *Culture, Thought, and Social Action,* 128–30.

66. Modern Jews would likely not have clung so determinedly to the rite of circumcision, for example, had they approached it via the confluence of mystical intentions apparently common among medieval kabbalists; see Eliot Wolfson, "Circumcision, Vision of God, and Textual Interpretation: From Midrashic Trope to Mystical Symbol," *History of Religions* 27, no. 2 (1987): 189–215; and "Circumcision and the Divine Name: A Study in the Transmission of Esoteric Doctrine," *Jewish Quarterly Review* 78, nos. 1–2 (July–October 1987):77–112.

67. Mendelssohn, *Jerusalem,* 133, 139.

FOUR

1. Ahad Ha'am, "Slavery in Freedom," in *Selected Essays of Ahad Ha'am,* ed. and trans. Leon Simon (New York: Atheneum, 1970), 175–77.

2. See, for example, the treatment of Reform as an ideological adjustment prompted largely by the desire for "integration into the non-Jewish world" by Shmuel Ettinger, "The Modern Period," in *A History of the Jewish People,* ed. H. H. Ben-Sasson (Cambridge, Mass.: Harvard University Press, 19), 825–46. Michael Meyer cites a number of sources that betray this bias, including classic accounts by Simon Dubnow and Raphael Mahler, in his *German Political Pressure and Jewish Religious Response in the Nineteenth Century* (New York: Leo Baeck Institute, 1981), 24 n. 3. Meyer writes that "not surprisingly, it has often appeared to historians of the Jews that the movement for religious reform was at bottom a persistent effort to deliver an acceptable down payment for so highly valued a commodity" as Emancipation. "Yet . . . it was far more complex." The present chapter aims to articulate that complexity, in a manner that concurs with the analysis of Ismar Schorsch, *Jewish Reactions to German Anti-Semitism, 1870–1914* (New York: Columbia University Press, 1972), 1–13; and of David Ellenson, *Between Tradition and Culture* (Atlanta: Scholars Press, 1994), xi–xix.

3. On this matter, cf. Michael Marrus, *The Politics of Assimilation: A Study of the French Jewish Community at the Time of the Dreyfus Affair* (Oxford: Clarendon Press, 1971); and Hannah Arendt, *The Origins of Totalitarianism* (New York: Harcourt Brace Jovanovich, 1973); with Phyllis Cohen Albert, *The Modernization of French Jewry: Consistory and Community in the Nineteenth Century* (Hanover, N.H.: Brandeis University Press, 1972), and her "Ethnicity and Jewish Solidarity in Nineteenth Century France," in *Mystics, Philosophers, and Politics: Essays in Honor of Alexander Altmann,* ed. Jehuda Reinharz and Daniel Swetschinski (Durham, N.C.: Duke University Press, 1982), 249–73.

4. The historian most influential in this regard has been George L. Mosse; see his *German Jews beyond Judaism* (Bloomington: Indiana University Press, 1985),

"German Jews beyond Liberalism in Retrospect: Introduction to Year Book 32," *Year Book of the Leo Baeck Institute* 32 (1987):xiii–xxv, and "The Secularization of Jewish Theology," in *Masses and Man: Nationalist and Fascist Perceptions of Reality* (New York: Howard Fertig, 1980), 250–56. My analysis also follows the work of Steven E. Aschheim, *Brothers and Strangers: The East European Jew in German and German Jewish Consciousness, 1800–1923* (Madison: University of Wisconsin Press, 1982); Sander Gilman, *The Jew's Body* (New York: Routledge, 1991), and *Jewish Self-Hatred: Anti-Semitism and the Hidden Language of the Jews* (Baltimore: John Hopkins University Press, 1986); Jay R. Berkovitz, *The Shaping of Identity in Nineteenth-Century France* (Detroit: Wayne State University Press, 1989); and Paula Hyman, *The Emancipation of the Jews of Alsace* (New Haven, Conn.: Yale University Press, 1991).

5. Jacob Katz, *Emancipation and Assimilation: Studies in Modern Jewish History* (Westmead: Gregg International Publishers, 1972), 19. As Katz put it succinctly in another work, the Jews were on probation; see his *Out of the Ghetto* (New York: Schocken Books, 1978), 192. Steven M. Lowenstein writes that "in the German lands, proposals on the position of the Jews were rarely based purely on abstract considerations of human rights. The question of the Jews was very much a practical political and social question": in return for rights, the Jews were to regenerate themselves, which meant giving up cultural, economic, and religious traits that stood in the way of integration (*The Berlin Jewish Community: Enlightenment, Family, and Crisis, 1790–1830* [New York: Oxford University Press, 1994], 70–71). For a fine analysis of a pictorial representation of the bargain struck by Jews in Germany, see Russell Berman, "Citizenship, Conversion, and Representation: Moritz Oppenheim's *Return of the Volunteer*," in *Cultural Studies in Modern Germany: History, Representation, and Nationhood* (Madison: University of Wisconsin Press, 1993), 46–72.

6. I follow recent historiography in regarding the transformation of Jewish belief and practice as the outcome, in part, of intellectual developments internal to the Jewish community rather than thrust upon it from the outside. Cf. David Sorkin, *The Transformation of German Jewry, 1780–1840* (New York: Oxford University Press, 1987), 44–59; and see the classic analysis by Azriel Shohet, *Im Hilufei Tekufot* [Beginnings of the Haskalah among German Jewry] (Jerusalem: Bialik Institute, 1960). Sorkin and other scholars make it clear that no simple causal sequence linked particular political pressures, achievements, or aspirations, on the one hand, with particular patterns of religious practice, on the other. Nor can one ignore factors impinging on patterns of observance such as generational distance from immigration, class, and regional differences—or personal taste. In England, for example, the practice of tradition was regarded more positively among successful middle-class merchants and professionals than in the working-class surroundings of peddlers and artisans. Successive waves of immigrants were more likely to be observant than those acculturated, but this

did not mean "scrupulous observance," notes Todd Endelman, since most were poorly educated and rather "careless in religious matters"; Jewish aristocrats were observant but far from Orthodox by traditional standards (*Radical Assimilation in English Jewish History, 1656–1945* [Bloomington: Indiana University Press, 1990], 35; and see 47, 80–81, 86). See also Endelman, *The Jews of Georgian England, 1714–1830: Tradition and Change in a Liberal Society* (Philadelphia: Jewish Publication Society of America, 1979), xi, 119–56, 167; Hugh McLeod, *Class and Religion in the Late Victorian City* (Hamden, Conn., Archon Books, 1974), and *Religion and the Working Class in Nineteenth-Century Britain* (London: Macmillan, 1984); and Geoffrey Alderman, *Modern British Jewry* (Oxford: Clarendon Press, 1992), 9–10, 12. Bill Williams's analysis of Manchester Jews convincingly demonstrates the desire of differing economic groups to exhibit "civic and social behavior" appropriate to their several stations, as well as the importance of regional pride expressed in defiance of the London-based chief rabbinate; see his *The Making of Manchester Jewry, 1740–1875* (Manchester: Manchester University Press, 1976), 37, 62, 80, 132–37, 164, 221.

7. See Aschheim, *Brothers and Strangers,* 3–10.

8. See Gilman, *Jew's Body,* 3, 14, 193. For Mendelssohn's less than praiseworthy comments on Polish Jews, see Gilman, *Jewish Self-Hatred,* 93. Ruth Gay notes that Jewish retail establishments in Germany in the latter decades of the century, in another demonstration of the demeanor befitting citizenship, proudly exhibited the polar opposites of the traits stereotypically associated with the peddlers of old: fixed prices, no haggling, customers encouraged to browse, no high-pressure sales tactics, the option to return unwanted goods. All such changes came gradually: "In their appearance, as in their language, the old continued to coexist with the new for long stretches" (Gay, *The Jews of Germany: A Historical Portrait* [New Haven, Conn.: Yale University Press, 1992], 122; and see 122–24, 189).

9. See Lowenstein, *Berlin Jewish Community,* 44–53; Gay, *Jews of Germany,* 122. Gay notes of a scene depicting a crowd in front of the synagogue at Furth about 1800 that "the men and boys . . . are still wearing the medieval barrette first prescribed for south German Jews in the fifteenth century. Known irreverently as the *Shabbes deckel,* or Sabbath lid, it remained a staple of male dress" (122). The men are wearing old-fashioned pleated collars and have beards; the older married woman has her head covered, while the younger women, more attuned to current fashion, do not. David Ellenson reports that the son of Rabbi Esriel Hildesheimer, founder of the Orthodox Rabbiner-Seminar, not only went bareheaded on occasion but told others that covering the head in certain situations would be regarded in Germany as a display of bad manners; see Ellenson, "Jewish Religious Leadership in Germany: Its Cultural and Religious Outlook," in *Critical Issues of the Holocaust,* ed. Alex Grobman and Daniel Landes (Chappaqua, N.Y.: Roseel Books, 1983), 16.

10. See Sorkin, *Transformation of German Jewry,* 30. The case in France was analogous. On the rapid Sephardi acculturation in Bordeaux, see Berkovitz, *Shaping of Identity,* 259 n. 5. Had the quid pro quo of their Emancipation contract been known in advance, one historian speculates, the Jews of Alsace might well have decided against it; see Simon Schwarzfuchs, *Les Juifs de France* (Paris: Albert Michel, 1975), 213. See also Berkovitz, *Shaping of Identity,* 91; Beatrice Philippe, *Etre juif dans la société française* (Paris: Editions Montalba, 1979), 406; Hyman, *Jews of Alsace,* 1–5, and *From Dreyfus to Vichy: The Remaking of French Jewry, 1906–1939* (New York: Columbia University Press, 1979), 139; and Albert, *Modernization of French Jewry,* 20, 38.

11. On the use of Yiddish, see Lowenstein, *Berlin Jewish Community,* 46–48, and *The Mechanics of Change: Essays in the Social History of German Jewry* (Atlanta: Scholars Press, 1992), 14.

12. See Gay, *Jews of Germany,* 139; Katz, *Out of the Ghetto,* 205–6; Sorkin, *Transformation of German Jewry,* 97; and Monika Richarz, ed., *Jewish Life in Germany: Memoirs from Three Centuries,* trans. Stella P. Rosenfeld and Sidney Rosenfeld (Bloomington: Indiana University Press, 1991), 18. Lowenstein provides the most complete account; see *Berlin Jewish Community,* 120–33, 180, 188.

13. See Peter Gay, *The Bourgeois Experience: Victoria to Freud,* vol. 1, *Education of the Senses* (New York: Oxford University Press, 1984), 22; Otto Brunner, Werner Conze, and Reinhart Koselleck, eds., *Geschichtliche Grundbegriffe,* (Stuttgart: Ernst Klett Verlag, 1972), 1:508–51; and Sorkin, *Transformation of German Jewry,* 4–5, 14–17.

14. See Mosse, *German Jews beyond Judaism,* 3.

15. See James Sheehan, *German History, 1770–1866* (Oxford: Clarendon Press, 1989), 1–14. On the influence of Herder in this connection, see Mosse, *Masses and Man,* 255. See also Benedict Anderson, *Imagined Communities: Reflections on the Origins and Spread of Nationalism,* rev. ed. (London: Verso, 1993), 6. Sheehan has also demonstrated that the ideal of *Bildung* effectively excluded the vast majority of Germans, who, during the first half of the nineteenth century, overwhelmingly had little or no direct experience with big cities or their emergent ethos; see Sheehan, *German History,* 204ff, 485.

16. Cf. Roger Chartier, *The Cultural Origins of the French Revolution,* trans. Lydia C. Cochrane (Durham, N.C.: Duke University Press, 1991), 3–19. The elites who propounded those ideas also created a new civil religion to legitimate their rule, complete with its own calendar and festivities, and imposed the French language (via a national school system) on populations which had hitherto conversed in regional dialects. E. J. Hobsbawm estimates that in 1789 half the population of France did not speak French at all and only about 12 percent spoke it "correctly"; see *Nations and Nationalism since 1780: Programme, Myth, Reality* (Cambridge: Cambridge University Press, 1991), 60.

17. See Eugen Weber, *Peasants into Frenchmen: The Modernization of Rural*

France, 1870–1914 (Stanford, Calif.: Stanford University Press, 1976), 3–94. Efforts at unification were marked by the frequent proclamation that the goal so assiduously pursued had already been achieved. France was "one and indivisible," its unity the expression of a "general will." Weber notes, however, that as late as 1882, Ernest Renan rejected the German conception of nationhood worked out earlier in the century by Herder, Fichte, and Humboldt because it relied upon four basic elements that in the French case were still patently problematic: language, tradition, race, and state (see *Peasants into Frenchman,* 112).

18. Ibid., 68.

19. Theodore Zeldin, *France, 1848–1945,* vol. 2, *Intellect, Taste, Anxiety* (Oxford: Clarendon Press, 1977), 6; and see 3–25, 178, 316. See also Gordon Wright, *France in Modern Times* (New York: W. W. Norton, 1981), 5; and Zeldin, *Conflicts in French Society* (London: George Allen Unwin, 1970).

20. Recall Nietzsche's comment in *Beyond Good and Evil* that the Jews "are beyond any doubt the strongest, toughest, and purest race now living in Europe," while the Germans remained a "weak and indefinite" type that could easily be blurred or extinguished by a stronger race (*Beyond Good and Evil,* trans. Walter Kaufmann [New York: Vintage Books, 1966], sec. 251). For the larger context of Nietzsche's ambivalent attitude toward Jews and Judaism, see my "Nietzsche and the Jews Reconsidered," *Jewish Social Studies* 48, no. 1 (1986):1–14.

21. See Gay, *Education of the Senses,* 17.

22. Ismar Schorsch, "The Myth of Sephardic Supremacy," *Year Book of the Leo Baeck Institute* 34 (1989): 47, 66.

23. "Rapport de la Commission chargée d'examiner les mémoires qui ont concouru pour le prix proposé en 1824, par la Société des sciences, agriculture, et arts du département du Bas-Rhin," in *Journal de la Société des Sciences, Agriculture, et Arts, du Département du Bas-Rhin, Séant à Strasbourg* (Strasbourg: F. B. Levrault, 1825), 2:303, 307; my translation, here and throughout, unless noted otherwise. The contest is discussed in Berkovitz, *Shaping of Identity,* 48–54, but the reading I present here is independent of his.

24. "Rapport," 297–99; and see Berkovitz, *Shaping of Identity,* 48–54.

25. Ibid., 299.

26. Ibid., 300–303. Wittersheim's appeal followed the lines of Zalkind Hourwitz's submission to the contest sponsored by the Metz Royal Academy in 1785–1787; see Frances Malino, "The Right to Be Equal: Zalkind Hourwitz and the Revolution of 1789," in *From East and West: Jews in a Changing Europe,* ed. Frances Malino and David Sorkin (Oxford: Basil Blackwell, 1990), 91–93.

27. "Rapport," 303–18.

28. *Archives israélites de France* 1 (1840):1–3; my translation, here and throughout, unless noted otherwise.

29. Ibid., 67–68.

30. Ibid., 157–58.

31. Ibid., 241.

32. *Univers* 2 (1845):194–95.

33. *Archives* 16 (1855):135–37.

34. Ibid., 1 (1840):648; and see Berkovitz, *Shaping of Identity,* 138.

35. *Archives* 1 (1840):641–42. On the Ninth of Av, similarly, Jews should recall the destruction of the Jerusalem Temple "as befits free men," thanking Providence that they (unlike other Jews) had a *patrie* and resolving to make themselves worthy of God's protection by loving both God and country; see *Archives* 3 (1842):367–70. The two loyalties of French Jews could thus reinforce one another rather than conflict. Cahen would no doubt have approved of ritual objects that bore the tricolor of the flag; see Hyman, *Jews of Alsace,* 124.

36. *Archives* 1 (1840):581, 647, 645; and see 581–89, 642–48. Concern about unnecessary repetition was expressed in Orthodox circles as well; see the compendium of synagogue customs *Sefer Melitz Yosher* (Amsterdam: n.p., 1808), 2–3.

37. David Philipson, *The Reform Movement in Judaism* (New York: Macmillan, 1907), 45–46.

38. See Albert, "The Right to Be Different: Interpretations of the French Revolution's Promises to the Jews," *Modern Judaism* 12, no. 3 (October 1992): 244–45; and Berkovitz, *Shaping of Identity,* 230–32. In this, they were not unlike British Jews, whose path to Emancipation included little active persecution or rampant discrimination by society or government and was characterized by a near total absence of ideological warfare within the Jewish community or of prolonged political agitation by Jews on their own behalf. Once legal disabilities affecting Catholics were removed in 1829, full liberties for Jews were not long in coming; perhaps, as a result, Cecil Roth was able to write without complete exaggeration that "fullest collaboration is possible in the Anglo-Jewish community among elements who do not see eye to eye regarding the minutiae of religious observance" (Roth, ed., *Anglo-Jewish Letters* [London: Soncino Press, 1938], 286). On the process of Emancipation in England, see Endelman, *Jews of Georgian England,* and "The Englishness of Jewish Modernity in England," in *Toward Modernity: The European Jewish Model,* ed. Jacob Katz (New Brunswick, N.J.: Transaction Books, 1987), 226–31; and Paul H. Emden, *The Jews of Britain* (London: Sampson, Low, Marston, 1993), 133–35. It is characteristic of the pattern described by Endelman and others that the chief rabbi's singular ban on members of the new Reform congregation in London in the 1840s seems not to have been much admired or respected and that the disputes fueling the new group's formation seem to have been largely aesthetic rather than ideological in nature; see Endelman, *Jews of Georgian England,* 3–36, 104, 107, 176; and Roth, *Anglo-Jewish Letters,* 281–86. The ban was soon lifted.

39. On the difficulty of separating private from public and safeguarding distinctiveness in the former while surrendering it in the latter, see Sheehan, *German History,* 798–99.

40. See Michael A. Meyer, *Response to Modernity* (New York: Oxford University Press, 1988), x–xxi. Worshipers in Reform services moved their bodies very little in the course of the service—as they had begun, in the same period, to sit quietly in the concert hall. Stillness during prayer highlighted the spiritual movement meant to occur, in both settings, invisibly. This was but one of many ways in which Judaism came to be conceived and experienced very differently once it was limited to a single, intense, and focused hour or two on a single day of the week, uncluttered with the quotidian minutiae of eating, dressing, and industry. See also Mordecai Breuer, *Modernity within Tradition,* trans. Elizabeth Petuchauski (New York: Columbia University Press, 1992), vii, 5, 32–44. Lowenstein surveys an array of alterations in ritual, liturgy, and synagogue ordinances in *Mechanics of Change,* 86–87, 118–31.

41. David E. Fishman, *Russia's First Modern Jews: The Jews of Shklov* (New York: New York University Press, 1995), 51.

42. See Norman A. Stillman, *The Jews of Arab Lands in Modern Times* (Philadelphia: Jewish Publication Society, 1991), 27, 186–89, 223, 243; and Aron Rodrigue, *Images of Sephardi and Eastern Jews in Transition* (Seattle: University of Washington Press, 1993), 8–10, 74–78.

43. Naomi Cohen, *Encounter with Emancipation: The German Jews in the United States, 1830–1914* (Philadelphia: Jewish Publication Society, 1984), xii, 111, 158.

44. Katz, *Out of the Ghetto,* 209.

45. See Zosa Szajkowski, "Jewish Religious Observance during the French Revolution of 1789," in *Jews and the French Revolutions of 1789, 1830, and 1848* (New York: Ktav, 1970), 785, 792, 820; and see 785–94, 809–21. See also Schwarzfuchs, *Les Juifs de France,* 215.

46. Mona Ozouf, *Festivals and the French Revolution,* trans. Alan Sheridan (Cambridge, Mass.: Harvard University Press, 1988), 126; and see 3–18, 54, 126–54, 164.

47. See Berkovitz, *Shaping of Identity,* 41.

48. See the Assembly of Jewish Notables, "Answers to Napoleon"; Count Molé, "Summons for Convening the Paris Sanhedrin (September 18, 1806)"; and the Parisian Sanhedrin, "Doctrinal Decisions," in *The Jew in the Modern World: A Documentary History,* ed. Paul R. Mendes-Flohr and Jehuda Reinharz (New York: Oxford University Press, 1980), 116–24.

49. Moses Mendelssohn, *Jerusalem,* trans. Allan Arkush (Hanover, N.H.: University Press of New England, 1983), 130. Alexander Altman has noted, in his commentary on Allan Arkush's translation of *Jerusalem,* that Mendelssohn's statement of the venerable Jewish principle "The law of the land is the law,"—that is, that Jews had to accommodate to circumstances, faute de mieux—"does not fully correspond to the facts" (232). The Hatam Sofer expressed praise for the Sanhedrin's position validating the work of the Assembly of Notables (see Jacob Katz, "Towards a Biography of the Hatam Sofer," in *From East and West,* 157–58).

50. On the policing function of the rabbis, see Albert, *Modernization of French Jewry*, 61, 122; and Hyman, *Jews of Alsace*, 9. For changes in Alsatian Jewish practice, see Schwarzfuchs, *Les Juifs de France*, 234–38. Poignantly, the very same issue of the *Archives israélites* that recounts the case of the kosher butchers reports on an address by Adolphe Cremieux appealing for an end to the More Judaico oath—as it turned out, unsuccessfully. See also Philipson, *Reform Movement*, 216.

51. Traditional and Reform Jews alike therefore supported keeping rabbis on the national payroll; Cf. Berkovitz, *Shaping of Identity*, 238.

52. The Dreyfus affair at century's end apparently did not appreciably weaken identification with the state and neither did the fact that fallen Jewish soldiers in World War I had their graves marked with a cross or, upon appeal by the consistory, with plain stones but could not lie in plots marked with six-pointed stars; see Hyman, *From Dreyfus to Vichy*, 51.

53. Meyer, "German Political Pressure," 14.

54. Cf. Schwarzfuchs, *Les Juifs de France*, 222.

55. Jacob Toury, "Types of Jewish Municipal Rights in German Townships: The Problem of Local Emancipation," in *Year Book of the Leo Baeck Institute* 22 (1977):55–80. See also Shulamit S. Magnus, "'Who Shall Say Who Belongs?': Jews between City and State in Prussian Cologne, 1815–1828," *AJS Review* 16, nos. 1–2 (spring–fall 1991): 57–105.

56. Ernst Traugott von Kortum (1795), quoted in Katz, *Emancipation and Assimilation*, 64; and see 47–76.

57. Major treatments of the subject are cited by Meyer, "German Political Pressure," 24 n. 5.

58. Sorkin, *Transformation of German Jewry*, 29–35.

59. Cf. the restrictions in Westphalia cited by Jakob Petuchowski, *Prayerbook Reform in Europe* (New York: World Union for Progressive Judaism, 1968), 106–10. On Israel Jacobson's reforms, see Meyer, *Response to Modernity*, 30–36; on the prohibition of worship outside the synagogue, see Lowenstein, *Mechanics of Change*, 105.

60. See Philipson, *Reform Movement*, 33–35; and Lowenstein, *Berlin Jewish Community*, 136–37.

61. Philipson, *Reform Movement*, 35–36.

62. See ibid., 298.

63. See Lowenstein, *Mechanics of Change*, 16.

64. See ibid., 13; and Philipson, *Reform Movement*, 51–52, 104–05.

65. Philipson, *Reform Movement*, 34, 76.

66. Ibid., 43, 103.

67. Ibid., 44.

68. Abraham Geiger, "Report for 1849," in *Abraham Geiger and Liberal Judaism: The Challenge of the Nineteenth Century*, ed. Max Wiener, trans. Ernst J. Schlochauer (Cincinatti: Hebrew Union College Press, 1981), 172.

69. Philipson, *Reform Movement,* 76.

70. See Lowenstein, *Mechanics of Change,* 97; and Philipson, *Reform Movement,* 313.

71. See Robert Lieberles, "Was There a Jewish Movement for Emancipation in Germany?" *Year Book of the Leo Baeck Institute* 31 (1986): 38.

72. On Orthodox response to the conferences, see Ellenson, "Traditional Reactions to Modern Jewish Reform: The Paradigm of German Orthodoxy," in *Routledge History of Jewish Philosophy,* ed. Daniel Frank and Oliver Leaman (New York: Routledge, 1997); for details concerning the individual rabbis participating in the conferences, see Lowenstein, *Mechanics of Change,* 95–100, 110–13. On the rabbis' political role, see Liberles, "Was There a Jewish Movement for Emancipation in Germany?" *Year Book of the Leo Baeck Institute* 31 (1986): 38. For more on the political context of the time, see Michael Anthony Riff, "The Anti-Jewish Aspect of the Revolutionary Unrest of 1848 in Baden and Its Impact on Emancipation," *Year Book of the Leo Baeck Institute* 21 (1976): 27.

73. Meyer, *Response to Modernity,* 134. Esriel Hildesheimer, a leading Orthodox rabbi, attacked the conferences precisely on this ground; see Ellenson, *Rabbi Esriel Hildesheimer and the Creation of a Modern Jewish Orthodoxy* (Tuscaloosa: University of Alabama Press, 1990), 34.

74. Cf. Ismar Schorsch, "Emancipation and the Crisis of Religious Authority: The Emergence of the Modern Rabbinate," in *Revolution and Evolution: 1848 in German-Jewish History,* ed. Werner E. Mosse, Arnold Paucker, and Reinhard Rürup (Tübingen: J. C. B. Mohr, 1981), 205–47; see especially 207–13.

75. David Philipson explains that by declaring the Paris Sanhedrin a precedent for its own activities, the rabbinical conference at Brunswick "consciously or unconsciously, declared itself the official voice of the modern spirit" (*Reform Movement,* 211); the original discussion can be found in *Protokolle der Ersten Rabbinerversammlung abgehalten in Braunschweig* (Brunswick, 1844), appendix 1, 94–98. Liberles writes that the rabbis thereby "extended the commitments made by those earlier Jewish leaders of primary loyalty to the State and the society in which they lived" ("Jewish Movement for Emancipation," 40).

76. Meyer, *Response to Modernity,* 234; Philipson, *Reform Movement,* 212.

77. Samuel Holdheim, quoted in Philipson, *Reform Movement,* 211–12.

78. Meyer, *Response to Modernity,* 134.

79. Philipson, *Reform Movement,* 217.

80. On the Frankfurt conference, see Philipson, *Reform Movement,* 233–46; and Meyer, *Response to Modernity,* 136–38; the original transcriptions can be found in *Protokolle und Aktenstücke der zweiten Rabbinerversammlung abgehalten in Frankfurt am Main* (Frankfurt am Main: n.p., 1845).

81. Liberles believes that Stein's vote may have stemmed from local congregational issues; see "Leopold Stein and the Paradox of Reform Clericalism, 1844–1862," *Year Book of the Leo Baeck Institute* 28 (1983): 261–64. See also Ellenson, *Between Tradition and Culture,* 76–78. On Holdheim, see Petuchowski,

"Abraham Geiger and Samuel Holdheim: Their Differences in Germany and Repercussions in America," *Year Book of the Leo Baeck Institute* 22 (1977): 139–59; see also Michael Meyer, ed., *Avraham Geiger: Mivḥar Ketavav 'al Tikkunim Bedat* [Abraham Geiger: selected writings on religious reform] (Jerusalem: Zalman Shazar Center, 1991), 74.

82. See Zechariah Frankel, "'Al Ra'ayon Ha-Meshiḥi Ve-'Atzmaut Yisrael" [On the messianic idea and Jewish independence], in *Zekharya Frankel Ve-Reshit Ha-Yahadut Ha-Pozitivit Historit* [Zachariah Frankel and the beginnings of Positive Historical Judaism], ed. Rivka Horwitz (Jerusalem: Zalman Shazar Center, 1984), 111–15. See also Baruch Mevorakh, "She'elat Ha-Mashiah Be-Pulmusei Ha-Imansipazia Ve-Ha-Reforma, 1781–1819" [The problem of the messiah in the Emancipation and Reform controversies] (Ph.D. diss., Hebrew University, 1966).

83. Cf. the selections in Frankel, *Zacharias Frankel,* 45–67, 83–110; and Horwitz's introduction to *Zacharias Frankel,* 16, 28.

84. Geiger, letters to Joseph Naftali Dernburg, 3 August and 22 November 1840, in *Abraham Geiger and Liberal Judaism,* 90, 87, 90; and see 86–90. See also Meyer, ed., *Abraham Geiger,* 74.

85. Geiger, "On Renouncing Judaism," in *Abraham Geiger and Liberal Judaism,* 292. See also Meyer, "Universalism and Jewish Unity in the Thought of Abraham Geiger," in *The Role of Religion in Modern Jewish History,* ed. Jacob Katz (Cambridge: Association for Jewish Studies, 1975), 91–104.

86. Cf. the related comment on the subjective or objective character of Jewish chosenness in the Berlin prayer book of 1844, in Guenther Plaut, ed., *The Rise of Reform Judaism: A Sourcebook of Its European Origins* (New York: World Union for Progressive Judaism, 1963), 57.

87. A preacher at the Berlin *Reformgemeinde* put the matter most clearly when he explained that "Hebrew has become a foreign language for us, and German the language of our homeland"; cited in Petuchowski, *Prayerbook Reform in Europe,* 59.

88. Cf. Arnold M. Eisen, "Off-Center: The Concept of the Land of Israel in Modern Jewish Thought," in *The Land of Israel: Jewish Perspectives,* ed. Lawrence A. Hoffman (Notre Dame, Ind.: Notre Dame University Press, 1986), 263–71.

89. Quoted in Philipson, *Reform Movement,* 255–56.

90. See ibid., 255–59. Meyer notes that the rabbis were "aware of the argument that use of the organ represented an ostensible imitation of the Gentiles" but chose to base their preference for it on its similarity to the *magrefah,* a musical instrument used in the Temple (*Response to Modernity,* 138).

91. On the Sabbath question and the Breslau meeting as a whole, see Philipson, *Reform Movement,* 261–316; and Meyer, *Response to Modernity,* 138–41. The original transcriptions of the conference can be found in *Protokolle der dritten Versammlung deutscher Rabbiner* (Breslau: n.p., 1846).

92. Gay, *Jews of Germany*, 125; and see Mosse, *German Jews beyond Judaism*, 8.

93. Gay, *Jews of Germany*, 54; on the attempt to rehabilitate and ennoble the image of the Jewish peddler, see 226.

94. See Philipson, *Reform Movement*, 272–85.

95. See ibid., 282–302.

96. See Petuchowski, "Geiger and Holdheim," 142–45.

97. Holdheim, quoted in Philipson, *Reform Movement*, 292–95, see also 90, 160; and see Meyer, *Response to Modernity*, 80, 413; and Petuchowski, *Prayerbook Reform in Europe*, 117.

98. Meyer, *Response to Modernity*, 138.

99. See Philipson, *Reform Movement*, 313.

100. See Moshe Rinott, "Gabriel Riesser," *Year Book of the Leo Baeck Institute* 7 (1962): 20–23; and Meyer, "German Political Pressure," 12.

101. See Samuel S. Cohon, "Zunz and Reform Judaism," *Hebrew Union College Annual* 31 (1960): 252–76; and Nahum Glatzer, "Leopold Zunz and the Revolution of 1848," *Year Book of the Leo Baeck Institute* 5 (1960): 122–29.

102. Geiger, letter to Leopold Zunz, 19 March 1845, and Zunz's reply, 4 May 1845, in *Abraham Geiger and Liberal Judaism*, 113–15. See also Cohon, "Zunz and Reform Judaism," 267; and Lowenstein, *Mechanics of Change*, 16.

103. Abraham Geiger, *Judaism and Its History*, trans. Charles Newburgh (New York: Bloch, 1911), 21–22.

104. Geiger, letter to Dernburg, 20 July 1841, in *Abraham Geiger and Liberal Judaism*, 92.

105. See Geiger, *Judaism and Its History*, 68; Wiener, "Biography of Abraham Geiger," in *Abraham Geiger and Liberal Judaism*, 52; and Ellenson, *Between Tradition and Culture*, 71–76.

106. Geiger, *Judaism and Its History*, 51.

107. See Geiger, "On Renouncing Judaism," 291; see also Geiger, *Judaism and Its History*, 68. Philipson put the matter more starkly still: Judaism was either a universal religion, in which case the "dead hand of the past" had to be removed, or a "national religion," in which case the Prophets of old, often invoked by reform, "had dreamed vain things and uttered foolish babblings" (*Reform Movement*, 120). Geiger's view of German destiny appears in *Judaism and Its History*, 70, 155–59.

108. Many Jews still alive in the 1840s remembered the ghetto all too well (see the reminiscence by Ludwig Borne, cited in Gay, *Jews of Germany*, 71) and had no illusions concerning its spiritual superiority over the conditions of Emancipation. Indeed, the vast majority of German Jews still lived in rural areas where neither material conditions nor social intercourse with Gentiles had much improved and looked forward all the more longingly to the exodus still to come.

109. Cf. Julius Carlebach, "The Foundations of German-Jewish Orthodoxy: An Interpretation," *Year Book of the Leo Baeck Institute* 33 (1988): 68. After Bruns-

wick, for example, Orthodox spokesmen attacked not only the specific changes introducted by the Reformers but the sacrifice of obligations in force until the messiah's coming in order "to purchase temporal and political contentment." Ironically, the only acceptable Reform resolution in their eyes was the one affirming Jewish loyalty toward the German states. Cf. Philipson, *Reform Movement,* 225–27; and Meyer, *Response to Modernity,* 135. The two groups literally and figuratively spoke entirely different languages. The Reform conferences were of course conducted in German; the Orthodox attack was mounted in Hebrew. A fine account of Orthodoxy's attitude to Germany and Emancipation is provided by Breuer, *Modernity within Tradition,* 296–309.

110. Jacob Emden, quoted in Mordecai Breuer and Michael Graetz, *German-Jewish History in Modern Times* (New York: Columbia University Press, 1996), 238.

111. See, for example, Katz, ed., *Toward Modernity: The European Jewish Model* (New Brunswick, N.J.: Transaction Books, 1987); and Pierre Birnbaum and Ira Katznelson, eds., *Paths of Emancipation: Jews, States, and Citizenship* (Princeton, N.J.: Princeton University Press, 1995).

112. Philip Roth, "Eli the Fanatic," in *"Goodbye Columbus" and Five Short Stories* (New York: Vintage Books, 1993), 247–48, 261–62, 264.

113. Stephen L. Carter, *The Culture of Disbelief: How American Law and Politics Trivialize Religious Devotion* (New York: Doubleday, 1993); see, in particular, on Jewish observance, 5–6, 12–13, 132, 269.

114. Roth, *The Counterlife* (New York: Farrar, Straus, Giroux, 1986), 323; and see 322–24.

FIVE

1. Samson Raphael Hirsch, *The Nineteen Letters on Judaism,* ed. Jacob Breuer, trans. Bernard Drachman (Jerusalem: Feldheim Publishers, 1969), 123, 142–43. I have borrowed the term "cultured despisers" from Friedrich Schleiermacher (*Speeches on Religion to Its Cultured Despisers,* trans. John Oman [New York: Harper Torchbooks, 1958]) because of the parallels between the audiences whom Hirsch and Schleiermacher addressed. The substance of Hirsch's rational defense of Judaism in terms of commandments ordained by the revelation of a personal God was utterly at variance with Schleiermacher's Romantic defense of Christianity in terms of a feeling of unity with or absolute dependence upon the whole of nature. In his most systematic account of the commandments' symbolic content and method, Hirsch paused to attack "so-called religions which stem from man's feelings of dependence" and "direct man towards the night" (Hirsch, *The Collected Writings,* vol. 3, *Jewish Symbolism* [New York: Philip Feldheim: 1984], 88).

2. Hirsch, *Nineteen Letters,* 143–44.

3. This and the other definitions of the six types of commandments presented here are found in Hirsch, *Nineteen Letters,* 75–76. Noah Rosenbloom notes that Hirsch repeatedly apologized for publishing *Horeb* before *Moriah,* an exposition of Jewish doctrine that he had hoped to make his first published work but that appeared only in outline form as *Nineteen Letters.* Hirsch's ambition, Rosenbloom argues persuasively, was to be the nineteenth century's Maimonides. Hence the writing of a philosophically grounded and systematically organized code of law that its author hoped would be consulted whenever problems of religious observance arose, and hence the title *Horeb,* which—like the term "Mishnah Torah"—derived from Deuteronomy. See Rosenbloom, *Tradition in an Age of Reform: The Religious Philosophy of S. R. Hirsch* (Philadelphia: Jewish Publication Society, 1976), 125–47.

4. See Hirsch, *Horeb: A Philosophy of Jewish Law and Observances,* 2 vols., ed. and trans. I. Grunfeld (London: Soncino, 1962). The German title, *Versuche uber Yissroels Pflichten in der Zerstreuung,* is significant for its implied parallel to scientific investigation rather than philosophical theorizing (*Versuche*), its explicit acknowledgment that it is intended for a diaspora audience (and, the subtitle makes clear, for a young one at that), and for the use of *Pflichten*—obligations, duties—rather than *Gesetzen* (laws), on the one hand, or *Zeremonien* (Mendelssohn's term of choice), on the other.

5. Hirsch, *Horeb,* 1:379.

6. Hirsch, *Horeb,* 2:471–72.

7. Hirsch, "Introduction to the Study of Symbolism," in *Jewish Symbolism,* 3–14, 125–27; *Gesammelte Schriften* (Frankfurt am Main: Kauffmann, 1906): 3:226. The hesitation indicated by the word "might" here is unusual—compare the other language used in the text—and is belied by the tone of certainty throughout Hirsch's voluminous writings. The relevant question facing the interpreter of the commandments, Hirsch wrote later in the essay, was whether one could assign a concept to the symbol such that "all these separate regularities and circumstances can be defined in a single, uncontrived manner as logical consequences emanating from it" (66). For a graphic example of Hirsch's systematic exposition, see the chart diagramming the meaning of the annual cycle of festivals in *Horeb,* 1:89–90. Rosenbloom believes that Hirsch firmly bore in mind the distinction between law and "aggadata" or homiletics, and remained humble about the "conjectural and non-mandatory" character of his speculative reflections. This goes along with his depiction of the Hirsch of the 1830s as restrained, moderate, and conciliatory in character and tone, as opposed to the older Hirsch, whom he describes as "controversial, belligerent," and militant in his advocacy of separation between traditional and nontraditional Jews. See Rosenbloom, *Tradition in an Age of Reform,* 188–94, xii. While the contrast has some validity, I find the Hirsch of *Horeb* to be preachy, extremely directive, and consistently puritanical. The tone throughout belies the suggestion that his

interpretations are merely conjectural. Hirsch exhibited no more humility in this regard than did his model, Maimonides. See, for example, *Horeb,* 2:301, 362, 551; and see note 74, below.

8. For useful background on nineteenth-century notions of symbol, see Hans-Georg Gadamer, *Truth and Method,* trans. and ed. Garrett Barden and John Cumming (New York: Seabury Press, 1975), 147–73; and Emil Fackenheim, *The Religious Dimension in Hegel's Thought* (Boston: Beacon Press, 1967).

9. Hirsch, "Symbolism," 14.

10. "Even the most clever, ingenious explanation must be rejected as soon as it is found to be at variance with any one of these essential aspects of the symbol. We will categorically reject any obvious misinterpretation" (Hirsch, "Symbolism," 14). One sees from this dependence on the interpretations of the sages—embodied, to Hirsch's mind, in their legal rulings—why he was so fervently opposed to the notions of historical development within the earliest legal corpus, the Mishnah. Hirsch bitterly attacked Zechariah Frankel's scholarship on this matter; see Hirsch, "A Provisional Statement of Accounts," "Postscript," and "On Dr. Frankel's Statement," in *Collected Writings,* 5:278–314.

11. Hirsch, *Horeb,* 1:61–72; *The Pentateuch: Translated and Explained by Samson Raphael Hirsch,* vol. 2, *Exodus,* trans. Isaac Levy (London: Isaac Levy, 1960), 266–74.

12. Hirsch, *Horeb,* 1:64.

13. "With a little thought, all these examples, which have been selected [from the thirty-nine forbidden *melakhot*] with a practical end in mind, may easily be traced back to the general principles which we tried to expound above, and will appear clearly as their practical fulfillment"; these exact performative implications of God's command to remember and observe the Sabbath "had to be drawn . . . by the legal authorities" (Hirsch, *Horeb,* 1:76). The same certainty is evident in his explanation of the festivals (1:84–89) and in the precise explanation of the spices and the candle used in havdalah (1:105). Neither multiple significations nor a divine intention to stimulate emotion rather than merely thought is considered.

14. Cf. Norman Stillman, *The Jews of Arab Lands in Modern Times* (Philadelphia: Jewish Publication Society, 1991), 186–89, 223.

15. See Hirsch, *Exodus,* 270; and *Horeb,* 1:63. For further examples of raising the stakes of nonobservance, see, for example, the passages in *Horeb* where lying is deemed a violation of one's highest duty toward God (2:249), or where the person who commits the "great sin of speaking during prayer" by the *hazan* is pronounced guilty of "degrading the House and Worship of God" (2:551).

16. On this matter, and the polemical context in which Hirsch adopted his stance on many other issues, see Robert Liberles, *Religious Conflict in Social Context: The Resurgence of Orthodox Judaism in Frankfurt Am Main, 1838–1879* (Westport, Conn.: Greenwood Press, 1985).

17. Hirsch, *Horeb*, 2:318–19; Cf. Hirsch, *The Pentateuch*, vol. 3, pt. 1, *Leviticus*, trans. Isaac Levy (London: Isaac Levy, 1958), 266–79, at Lev. 11:1–23.

18. See Hirsch, *Exodus*, 408–12. Rosenbloom notes correctly that Hirsch's rationales for commandments such as the dietary laws became more complex as the observance of a ritual's details became more precarious; see *Tradition in an Age of Reform*, 203).

19. The *Mekilta*, a halakhic rabbinic commentary on Exodus, offers a variety of interpretations of the threefold repetition of the prohibition; see *Mekilta d'rabbi Ismael*, ed. H. S. Horovitz and I. A. Rabin (Jerusalem: Bamberger and Wahrman, 1960), 335–39; or, in English, *Mekilta de-Rabbi Ishmael*, trans. Jacob Lauterbach (Philadelphia: Jewish Publication Society 1976), "Tractate Kaspa," chap. 5, 186–96, at Exod. 23:19. This matter apparently does not interest Hirsch as much as the content of the prohibition, where he innovates not only relative to the rabbis but, so far as I am aware, to all previous commentators. Nachmanides, for example, interprets the literal prohibition on seething a kid in its mother's milk as a statute against cruelty; this interpretation is then extended to include any animal and any milk; see his commentary at Deut. 14:21 (*Commentary on the Torah: Deuteronomy*, trans. and ed. Charles B. Chavel [New York: Shilo Publishing House, 1976], 172).

20. See Grunfeld, introduction to *Horeb*, by Hirsch, 1:105; and Rosenbloom, *Tradition in an Age of Reform*, 202.

21. For other readings which, to my mind, are not persuasive (subjectivity is, of course, inevitable in such judgments), see Hirsch's elaborate explication of "what the Jewish festivals teach and what resolutions they aim to evoke," in *Horeb*, 1:88–93; his more elaborate explication and justification of the observance outside Israel of a "second day of festivals," in his commentary in *Exodus*, 126–27, at Exod. 12:1; his still more complicated reading of circumcision, which interprets the ceremony as a twofold injunction to avoid evil and do good, in his *Collected Writings*, 3:74–83; the correlation in that same essay of the Eighteen Blessings uttered in daily prayer with particular parts of the animals offered twice daily in the temple, in *Collected Writings* 3:241; the interpretation of the number and type of shofar blasts on Rosh Hashana, in *Horeb*, 1:136–41; and his account of tithes, in *Horeb*, 1:201–3.

22. Mordecai Breuer points to the "show of insistent, emphatic emotion and rhetoric," the "warm sincerity," and "aggressively affirmative joy and enthusiasm for tradition and duty"—all of which contrasted with Mendelssohn's "coolly rational and often apologetic tone." Will, not worldview, was the key: "Hirsch's opponents soon recognized that his strength lay not in his system of thought but in the powerful conviction of his presentation" (Breuer, *Modernity within Tradition*, trans. Elizabeth Petuchowski (New York: Columbia University Press, 1992), 64–65.

23. Hirsch, *Nineteen Letters*, 62–72.

24. Hirsch, *Horeb*, 1:111–12.

25. Hirsch, "Reflections on the Jewish Calendar Year," in *Judaism Eternal,* ed. and trans. I. Grunfeld (London: Soncino, 1956), 1:5–145; cf. Breuer, *Modernity within Tradition*, 293.

26. Such guarded patriotism was by no means limited to adherents of Orthodoxy, however; see Breuer, *Modernity within Tradition*, 302–5.

27. Hirsch, *Exodus*, 126–29, at Exod. 12:1–2; see also 146, at Exod. 12:20 21. Once more the influence of the *Kuzari* is pronounced.

28. See Breuer, *Modernity within Tradition*, 72–74.

29. See, for example, Hirsch, *Horeb*, 2:329. For Mendelssohn's letter to Herz Homberg, see Mendelssohn, *Gesammelte Schriften*, 22 vols., ed. Alexander Altmann (Stuttgart: F. Frommann, 1973), 13:132–34; see also the discussion in Arnold M. Eisen, "Divine Legislation as 'Ceremonial Script': Mendelssohn on the Commandments," *AJS Review* 15, no. 2 (fall 1990): 260.

30. Hirsch, *Exodus*, 131 at Exod. 12:4.

31. See Breuer, *Modernity within Tradition*, 81.

32. Cf. Eliezer Schweid, "Two Neo-Orthodox Responses to Secularization, Part 1: Samson Raphael Hirsch," *Immanuel* 19 (winter 1984–85): 115–16.

33. Jacob Katz, "Rabi Shimshon Refael Hirsch, Ha-meyamin U-mismail" [Rabbi Samson Raphael Hirsch, On the Right and the Left], in *Ha-Halakha Be-meizar: Mikhsholim 'al Derekh Ha-Ortodoksia Be-Hithavuta* [Halakhah in straits: Obstacles to Orthodoxy at its inception] (Jerusalem: Magnes Press, 1992), 232–34. See also Katz, *Ha-Kera' she-lo nit'ahah: Perishat Ha-ortodoksim mi-kelal ha-kehilot be-Hungaryah uve-Germanyah* [The unhealed breach: The secession of Orthodox Jews from the German community in Hungary and Germany] (Jerusalem: Merkaz Zalman Shazar, 1995).

34. Cf. Breuer, *Modernity within Tradition*, 64–65.

35. Joseph B. Soloveitchik, *The Lonely Man of Faith* (New York: Doubleday, 1992), 106, and see *Halakhic Man*, trans. Lawrence Kaplan (Philadelphia: Jewish Publication Society, 1983). See also Abraham Heschel, *Man Is Not Alone* (New York: Farrar, Straus and Giroux, 1991), and *The Sabbath* (New York: Farrar, Straus and Giroux, 1995).

36. See Michael Stanislawki, *For Whom Do I Toil: Judah Leib Gordon and the Crisis of Russian Jewry* (New York: Oxford University Press, 1988), 79–81, 94–95.

37. Hirsch's symbolism, Breuer writes, was a thoroughly creative achievement but too subjective to set a precedent, and it bore the stamp of certainty and finality to such a degree that although some mechanically repeated his achievement, none created with him as their model; see Breuer, *Modernity within Tradition*, 56–68, 163. The judgment seems extreme but not without truth. My own critique parallels that of Alexander Altmann, *The Meaning of Jewish Existence: The Theological Essays, 1930–1939* (Hanover, N.H.: Brandeis University

Press, 1991): Hirsch's moralizing tendency, he writes, "misses completely, in its method, the problem of meaning" (20–21). See also Katz's interesting observation that Hirsch consistently positioned himself between the forces to his Left and to his Right. Just as philosophy represented the former—hence Hirsch's criticism of Maimonides—so kabbalah represented the latter—hence Hirsch's criticism of it, carrying on a tradition of the Haskalah; see Katz, "Rabi Shimshon Refael Hirsch," 234–36.

38. Abraham Geiger, "*The Nineteen Letters on Judaism,* by Ben Uziel: A Review," *Wissenschaftliche Zeitschrift für Jüdische Theologie* 3 (1837):87.

39. On the new character of debate over the meanings of the commandments in the nineteenth century, see Isaac Heinemann, *Ta'amei ha-Mitzvot* [The reasons for the commandments in Jewish literature] (Jerusalem: Jewish Agency, 1966), 2:59.

SIX

1. Samson Raphael Hirsch, "Reflections on the Jewish Calendar Year," in *Judaism Eternal,* ed. and trans. I. Grunfeld (London: Soncino, 1956), 1:57.

2. *The Compact Edition of the Oxford English Dictionary,* s.v. "nostalgia"; *Webster's New World Dictionary of the American Language,* college ed., s.v. "nostalgia."

3. See David Lowenthal, *The Past Is a Foreign Country* (Cambridge: Cambridge University Press, 1985), 4–12. See also Richard Terdiman, *Present Past: Modernity and the Memory Crisis* (Ithaca, N.Y.: Cornell University Press, 1993); and Fred Davis, *Yearning for Yesterday* (New York: Free Press, 1979).

4. See Richard I. Cohen, "Nostalgia and 'Return to the Ghetto': a cultural phenomenon in Western and Central Europe," in *Assimilation and Community: The Jews in Nineteenth-Century Europe,* ed. Jonathan Frankel and Steven J. Zipperstein (Cambridge: Cambridge University Press, 1992), 130–40, and "Self-Image through Objects: Toward a Social History of Jewish Art Collecting and Jewish Museums," in *The Uses of Tradition: Jewish Continuity in the Modern Era,* ed. Jack Wertheimer (New York: Jewish Theological Seminary of America, 1992), 212. See also Paula Hyman, "Traditionalism and Village Jews in Nineteenth-Century Western and Central Europe: Local Persistence and Urban Nostalgia," in *Uses of Tradition,* 197–201.

5. Daniel Stauben, *Scènes de la vie juive en Alsace* (Paris: Michel Lévy Frères, 1860), iv–v; my translation, here and throughout, unless noted otherwise.

6. Léon Cahun, *La Vie juive,* with illustrations by Alphonse Lévy (Paris: Monnier de Brunhoff, 1886), 15–18; my translation, here and throughout, unless noted otherwise. Another gallery of Lévy's drawings, published in 1902, includes *Le Poisson du Samedi:* an old man, his hand on his beard, his face beaming, his glasses perched on his forehead, sits with his wife just behind him and the Sabbath fish in front; see Lévy, *Scènes familiales juives* (Paris: Félix Juven, 1902), fig. 2.

7. Cahun, *La Vie juive,* 26–27, 77, 98. Fully half of Lévy's illustrations in *Scènes familiales* are devoted to the subject.

8. See Monika Richarz, *Jewish Life in Germany: Memoirs,* from *Three Centuries,* trans. Stella P. Rosenfeld and Sidney Rosenfeld (Bloomington: Indiana University Press, 1991), 87, 104. Sabbath observance was for this reason retained, though of course modified, in the home of Ahad Ha'am; see Steven J. Zipperstein, *Elusive Prophet* (Berkeley and Los Angeles: University of California Press, 1993), 285–86, 290, 302.

9. Stauben, *Scènes de la vie juive,* 27, 31.

10. Ibid., 126; see also 83, 149.

11. Ibid., 96.

12. Ibid., 101, 108.

13. Lévy, *Scènes familiales,* fig. 6.

14. Cahun, *La Vie juive,* 35–36.

15. Stauben, *Scènes de la vie juive,* 110–13.

16. Ibid., 128.

17. Ibid., 148.

18. Ibid., 159.

19. Ibid., 161.

20. Cahun, *La Vie juive,* 96–98.

21. Ibid., 44–48, 53.

22. Robert L. Herbert, *Impressionism: Art, Leisure, and Parisian Society* (New Haven, Conn.: Yale University Press, 1988), 19, iv, 3, 19–20, 45–47.

23. See Peter Gay, *The Bourgeois Experience: Victoria to Freud,* vol. 1, *Education of the Senses* (New York: Oxford University Press, 1984), 9, 17.

24. See Colin Campbell, *The Romantic Ethic and the Spirit of Modern Consumerism* (Oxford: Basil Blackwell, 1987), 59.

25. Herbert, *Impressionism,* 198, 155.

26. See ibid., 61–65.

27. Ibid., 63–64.

28. Ibid.

29. See Linda Nochlin, "Gustave Courbet's *Meeting:* A Portrait of the Artist as a Wandering Jew," *Art Bulletin* 34, no. 3 (September 1967): 213–17. For more on the image, see George Anderson, *The Legend of the Wandering Jew* (Providence, R.I.: Brown University Press, 1965).

30. Cahun, *La Vie juive,* 57, 84. See also Russell Berman, "Citizenship, Conversion, and Representation: Moritz Oppenheim's *Return of the Volunteer,*" in *Cultural Studies in Modern Germany: History, Representation, and Nationhood* (Madison: University of Wisconsin Press, 1993), 48.

31. Richarz, *Jewish Life in Germany,* 203–5, 209–10, 235, 249–52, 256–57.

32. *Univers* (1851): 5; my translation, here and throughout, unless noted otherwise.

33. *Archives israélites de France* 4 (1843): 138; my translation, here and through-

out, unless noted otherwise. See also another, earlier piece where Cahen complained that "to write today about Jewish religion is to expose oneself to hostile criticism from some, and to mocking laughter from others" (*Archives* 3 [1842]:581).

34. *Univers* 1 (1844):33–34.

35. See the *Jewish Chronicle* (London), 31 August 1860, 2; 5 March 1880, 11–12; 13 April 1883, 5–6; and 12 March 1886, 8. On the paper's editors, see David Cesarani, *The "Jewish Chronicle" and Anglo-Jewry, 1841–1991* (Cambridge: Cambridge University Press, 1994), 32–33, 71–75.

36. *Archives* 18 (1857): 620–21.

37. *Univers* 17 (1861): 58–59.

38. *Univers* 19 (1863): 114.

39. *Univers* 24 (1869): 296–98, 315–20, 353–58.

40. *Archives* 35 (1874): 584.

41. See the Jewish *Chronicle,* 16 July 1880, 3; 20 April 1883, 8–9.

42. *Univers* 1 (1844): 120.

43. *Archives* 14 (1853): 1, 65–68.

44. *Archives* 14 (1853): 253; 16 (1855): 137, and see 135–37.

45. Abraham Benisch, the editor of the *Jewish Chronicle,* seemed, for his part, to despair of leadership from the chief rabbi of England—but for the opposite reason. That authority, whom he discreetly excoriated in his role as tribune of the people, was too steeped in books, too rigid, too removed from realities that demanded adjustment: a standard Enlightenment critique that, in turn, self-consciously drew on the venerable precedent of prophetic critiquing of priesthood. See the prolonged discussion of proposed ritual reforms in the *Jewish Chronicle,* 5 March 1880, 11–12; 12 March 1880, 9; 19 March 1880, 9–10; 18 June 1880, 12–13; 25 June 1880, 9–10; and 2 July 1880, 9–10.

46. Ibid., 2 March 1860, 7–8.

47. *Archives* 24 (1869):259.

48. *Univers* 13 (1858):541.

49. Ibid., 19 (1863):112.

50. Ibid., 24 (1869):353.

51. See, for example, *Jewish Chronicle,* 8 September 1887, 8–9.

52. Ibid., 26 March 1880, 19; 16 April 1886, 11; 16 July 1880, 3.

53. See, for example, Raphael Blum, "Rare Exemple de piété filiale: épisode de 1793," *Univers* 13 (1858):551–59; and Benoit Lévy, "Joker Dai," *Archives* 18 (1863): 476–82, 614–20, 665–71, 710–15, 755–59, 805–10, 845–52, 887–92.

54. *Univers* 18 (1863):408–10.

55. See the *Jewish Chronicle,* 4 May 1883, 10; 11 May 1883, 5.

56. Ibid., 9 March 1860, 3; 16 March 1860, 2; 1 January 1886, 9; 8 January 1886, 8, 10–11; 15 January 1886, 10–11; 26 March 1886, 7–12; and 2 April 1886, 9–10.

57. Ibid., 20 April 1883, 8–9.

58. Ibid., 23 April 1886, 5; 30 April 1886, 9. See also coverage of the exhibition and its opening ceremonies in the issues of 1 April 1887, 8–12; and supplements of 8 April 1887 and 15 April 1887.

59. Ibid., 24 June 1887, 11; 22 July 1887, 6; 29 July 1887, 8–9.

60. Ibid., 24 June 1887, 18; cf. Cohen, "Self-Image through Objects," 219.

61. Cf. David Feldman, *Englishmen and Jews: Social Relations and Political Culture, 1840–1914* (New Haven, Conn.: Yale University Press, 1994), 120.

62. Even Bloch praised the celebration of Shavuot in Mulhouse in a sanctuary decorated magnificently with flowers, the chants executed with great perfection—so much so that the faithful happily remained for four hours at a service satisfying to eyes and ears as well as to heart and spirit; see *Univers* 7 (1852): 468. The president of the Lyon temple urged all French synagogues to follow its example in instituting a divine service of "the most perfect order. . . . No one speaks. One prays with contemplation in low voice. The service is done with dignity. The chant of the choir, accompanied by the organ, ravishes the ear and rejoices the heart" (*Univers* 8 [1852]:67). Numerous accounts of rabbinic installations and synagogue dedications dwelt with similar affection on ceremonies which began punctually, were conducted without disruption, were attended by Gentile as well as Jewish dignitaries, and featured music by military bands and professional choirs; see *Archives* 18 (1863): 639–41; and *Univers* 9 (1853):60; 13 (1858):540; 18 (1862):85–88; 20 (1864):83–86; 24 (1869):285–93. The ritual reforms endorsed by the *Jewish Chronicle* in 1880 focused entirely on the aesthetics of the synagogue service—and the desire for beauty and dignity of observance was shared by the chief rabbi; see *Jewish Chronicle,* 28 September 1883, 5; 22 April 1887, 9. See also note 45, above.

63. Cahun, *La Vie juive,* 13, 64. And see Chapter 4; and Ismar Schorsch, "The Myth of Sephardic Supremacy," *Year Book of the Leo Baeck Institute* 34 (1989).

64. Abraham Geiger, "A History of Spiritual Achievement," in *Ideas of Jewish History,* ed. Michael Meyer (New York: Behrman, 1974), 168–70. I have discussed Geiger's essay in somewhat more detail elsewhere; see Arnold M. Eisen, "Constructing the Usable Past: The Idea of 'Tradition' in Twentieth-Century Judaism," in *The Uses of Tradition,* 431–33 (see note 4, above).

65. See, for example, the memories recounted in Richarz, *Jewish Life in Germany,* 92, 252; and the eastern European Jewish memoir cited in Eli Lederhendler, *Jewish Responses to Modernity* (New York: New York University Press, 1994), 674–65.

66. *Archives* 31 (1870): 451.

67. *Univers* 26 (1870): 46–49.

68. Cahun, *La Vie juive,* 55.

69. Ibid., 31.

70. Ibid., 92.

71. *Archives* 31 (1870):552–54.

72. Cf. Friedrich Nietzsche, *The Birth of Tragedy,* trans. Walter Kaufmann (New York: Vintage, 1967), sec. 3: "Thus do the gods justify the life of man: They themselves live it—the only satisfactory theodicy."

73. Cahun, *La Vie juive,* 31–32, 48–50.

74. Ibid., 98.

75. See Sigmund Freud, *Totem and Taboo,* trans. James Strachey (New York: W. W. Norton, 1989), 21–27, 30.

76. Ibid., 50–51. Note that Freud qualifies his claim about the unintelligibility of taboo behavior immediately after making it: "In some cases taboos have an intelligible meaning[,] . . . the purpose of some of the prohibitions is immediately obvious" (21).

77. See ibid., 49, 67–74, 126–32.

78. Ibid., 21.

79. See Cahun, *La Vie juive,* 108–11. This is one of many cases in which, as Terdiman points out, "although memory sustains hegemony, it also subverts it through its capacity to recollect and to restore the alternative discourses the dominant would simply bleach out and forget"—the "dominant" or "hegemonic" here being the Jewish adjustment to modernity that banishes the past to the past. "Memory, then, is inherently contestatory" (Terdiman, *Present Past,* 20).

80. See Max Weber, "Science as a Vocation," in *From Max Weber: Essays in Sociology,* trans. and ed. Hans H. Gerth and C. Wright Mills (New York: Oxford University Press, 1969), 140.

81. See Alan Mintz, *Banished from Their Father's Table* (Bloomington: Indiana University Press, 1989). The Talmudic passage on which the title is based is found at *Berakhot* 3a.

82. Renato Rosaldo, *Culture and Truth* (Boston: Beacon Press, 1989), 70.

83. Freud, *Totem and Taboo,* 144–45. The latest of these, as Philip Rieff put it trenchantly, has been the transformation of once powerful gods into ineffectual fathers—the onset of what he calls the Parent Question—in tandem with diminished obedience to the divine parent; see Rieff, *The Feeling Intellect: Selected Writings,* ed. Jonathan B. Imber (Chicago: University of Chicago Press, 1990), 341, 347.

84. Cf. Nancy B. Jay, *Throughout Your Generations Forever: Sacrifice, Religion, and Paternity* (Chicago: University of Chicago Press, 1992), 37; and Emile Durkheim, *The Elementary Forms of the Religious Life,* trans. Joseph Ward Swain (New York: Free Press, 1915), 414–16, 471. Werner Cahnman's survey of rural village life in Germany concludes that "religion and the family are closely connected at all times because the core of religion is ancestor worship," the "tie that binds us to those that came before us"—hence the special focus of village life on the cemetery (Cahnman, "Village and Small-Town Jews in Germany: A Typological Study," *Year Book of the Leo Baeck Institute* 19 [1974]: 121).

85. Personal conversation with Joseph Reimer, spring 1994.

86. Cf. Ana-Maria Rizzuto, *The Birth of the Living God: A Psychoanalytic Study* (Chicago: University of Chicago Press, 1979).

87. Martin Buber, *Hasidism and Modern Man* (New York: Harper Torchbooks, 1966), 21–22. Even when Buber, with hindsight, admitted decades later that there had been flaws in the earlier presentation of Hasidism inspired by that "something," flaws which he attributed in part to his wish to counter the relegation of the movement to "wild superstition," he still recognized no problem with his elision of "would, or rather should." To the last, he stood by his highlighting of the "kernel of this life" that is "capable of working on men even today," its overcoming of the gap between sacred and profane, which especially afflicted modern Western culture; see Buber, *Hasidism,* 28–38. See also Steven Kepnes, *The Text as Thou* (Bloomington: Indiana University Press, 1992), 149.

88. Buber, *Hasidism,* 41–42.

89. See Jack Kugelmass, "The Rites of the Tribe: American Jewish Tourism in Poland," in *Museums and Communities: The Politics of Public Culture,* ed. Ivan Karp, Christine Mullen Kreamer, and Steven D. Lavine (Washington, D.C.: Smithsonian Institution Press, 1992), 382–427; see also his "Why We Go to Poland: Holocaust Tourism as Secular Ritual," in *The Art of Memory: Holocaust Memorials in History,* ed. James E. Young (New York: Prestel, 1994), 175–83.

90. See Kugelmass, "Green Bagels: An Essay on Food, Nostalgia, and the Carnivalesque, *YIVO Annual* (1990): 57–80.

91. See Cahun, *La Vie juive,* 112.

SEVEN

1. Franz Rosenzweig, "Teaching and Law" (originally published in "The Builders"), in *Franz Rosenzweig: His Life and Thought,* ed. Nahum Glatzer (New York: Schocken Books, 1976), 237.

2. Martin Buber to Franz Rosenzweig, 3 June 1925, in *The Letters of Martin Buber: A Life of Dialogue,* ed. Nahum N. Glatzer and Paul Mendes-Flohr, trans. Richard and Clara Winston and Harry Zohn (New York: Schocken Books, 1991), 327.

3. Rosenzweig to Buber, 16 July 1924, in *Letters of Martin Buber,* 319.

4. Rosenzweig, *Life and Thought,* 91.

5. Buber, "Judaism and the Jews," in *On Judaism,* ed. Nahum N. Glatzer (New York: Schocken Books, 1967), 11, 14 (for the German original, see Buber, *Reden über das Judentum* [Berlin: Schocken, 1932], 6–7). Should one call oneself Jewish "only out of inherited custom—because our fathers did so?" Buber asks at the outset. "Or out of our own reality?" (11).

6. Ibid., 17.

7. Buber, "Judaism and Mankind," and "Renewal of Judaism," in *On Judaism,* 29, 30, 46, 48; and see 26, 40, and 44–48.

8. Buber, *The Tales of Rabbi Nachman,* trans. Maurice Friedman (Bloomington: Indiana University Press, 1962), 15, 34.

9. Buber, *The Legend of the Baal-Shem,* trans. Maurice Friedman (New York: Schocken, 1969), 25; and see 13, 17, 23–25, and 41.

10. Buber, *Hasidism and Modern Man* (New York: Harper Torchbooks, 1966), 22. See also Buber, *Baal-Shem,* 7.

11. Buber, "Jewish Religiosity," in *On Judaism,* 79–81, 90–92.

12. Buber, *On Judaism,* "Herut: On Youth and Religion," in 129–31, 160–69.

13. Buber, *I and Thou,* trans. Walter Kaufmann (New York: Scribner's, 1970), 128.

14. Ibid., 130–31, 131; and see 128–31.

15. Ibid., 158, 159–60.

16. Paul R. Mendes-Flohr, "Law and Sacrament: Ritual Observance in Twentieth-Century Jewish Thought," in *Divided Passions* (Detroit: Wayne State University Press, 1991), 352. Cf. Steven Katz, *Post-Holocaust Dialogues* (New York: New York University Press, 1983), 1–51.

17. Buber, "Dialogue," in *Between Man and Man,* trans. Ronald Gregor Smith (New York: Macmillan, 1965), 12, 16.

18. Buber, "The Question to the Single One," in *Between Man and Man,* 65–69.

19. Buber, "What Is Man?" in *Between Man and Man,* 134, 157–58, 175.

20. That is why the occasions for real human conversation enumerated by Buber in "Dialogue" and "What Is Man?"—a meeting on a train, an encounter in an air-raid shelter, attendance at a concert of Mozart—do not include the space of shared ritual performance; see Buber, *Between Man and Man,* 1–5, 203–5.

21. See also Buber, *Pointing the Way: Collected Essays,* ed. and trans. Maurice S. Friedman (New York: Harper Torchbooks, 1963), 113, 158, and *The Knowledge of Man* (New York: Harper Torchbooks, 1965), 72, 84.

22. Buber, *Moses: The Revelation and the Covenant* (New York: Harper Torchbooks, 1958), 103–4.

23. Buber, *The Prophetic Faith* (New York: Harper Torchbooks, 1949).

24. Buber, *Moses,* 71, 115, 128–30.

25. Ibid., 104.

26. See Buber, *Paths in Utopia* (Boston: Beacon Press, 1958).

27. Buber, *Two Types of Faith* (New York: Harper Torchbooks, 1961), 7, 55–57, 91. And see R. J. Zwi Werblowsky, "Reflections on Martin Buber's *Two Types of Faith,*" *Journal of Jewish Studies* 39, no. 1 (spring 1988): 92–101.

28. See Michael Wyschogrod, "Buber's Evaluation of Christianity: A Jewish Perspective," in *Martin Buber: A Centenary Volume,* ed. Haim Gordon and Jochanan Bloch (New York: Ktav, 1984), 466–70.

29. Buber, *I and Thou,* 168.

30. See Buber, *Two Types of Faith,* 170–74.

31. See Mendes-Flohr, "Law and Sacrament"; and "Rosenzweig and Kant: Two Views of Ritual and Religion," and "Franz Rosenzweig and the Crisis of Historicism," in *Divided Passions,* 283–337; and Nathan Rotenstreich, "Rosenzweig's Notion of Metaethics," in *The Philosophy of Franz Rosenzweig,* ed. Mendes-Flohr (Hanover, N.H.: University Press of New England, 1988), 69–88.

32. See Rosenzweig, "[Letter of] 20 September 1917, to His Parents," in *Life and Thought,* 58–61; and Rosenzweig, "Teaching and Law," 237.

33. Rosenzweig, *The Star of Redemption,* trans. William W. Hallo (Boston: Beacon Press, 1972), 3; and see 3–5. See also Rosenzweig, "The New Thinking," in *Life and Thought,* 190–91; and the lucid exposition in Stéphane Mosès, *System and Revelation,* trans. Catherine Tihanyi (Detroit: Wayne State University Press, 1992).

34. Rosenzweig, *Star of Redemption,* 104. For an exposition of the *Star's* logic that pays special attention to Rosenzweig's philosophy of "speech-thinking," see Yudit Kornberg Greenberg, "The Hermeneutic Turn in Franz Rosenzweig's Theory of Revelation," in *Interpreting Judaism in a Postmodern Age,* ed. Steven Kepnes (New York: New York University Press, 1996), 281–98.

35. "Experience, no matter how deeply it probes, will find only the human in man, the worldly in the world, and the godly in God. This very point, where philosophy comes to the end of its way of thinking, is the beginning of philosophy based on experience" (Rosenzweig, "New Thinking," 192).

36. Rosenzweig, *Star of Redemption,* 298; and see v–vi (table of contents), 336, and 348–49. Islam is the perennial foil of Judaism and Christianity in the book: closest of any tradition other than these to the best statement of the truth, but ever so far from truth, indeed, at times a parody of the real thing; see, for example, 116–18, 122–24, 164–66, 171–73, and especially 215–17.

37. See Rosenzweig, *Star of Redemption,* 173–88, 198–204, 213–15.

38. Mendes-Flohr, "Rosenzweig and Kant," 295.

39. For a concise statement of the conceptual architecture underlying the three parts of the book, see Rosenzweig, *Star of Redemption,* 294. A lucid critique of Rosenzweig's position on the issues examined here can be found in Gillian Rose, "Franz Rosenzweig—From Hegel to Yom Kippur," in *Judaism and Modernity: Philosophical Essays* (Oxford: Blackwell, 1993), 127–54.

40. Rosenzweig, *Star of Redemption,* 292–93; Mendes-Flohr, "Law and Sacrament," 354.

41. Mendes-Flohr, "Rosenzweig and Kant," 297; Rosenzweig, *Star of Redemption,* 302, 304; and see 298–305.

42. Rosenzweig, *Star of Redemption,* 308–10.

43. Ibid., 315–21.

44. Ibid., 321–28, 424.

45. This is so, perhaps, because of the debt to kabbalah that the two modern thinkers share; see Moshe Idel, "Franz Rosenzweig and the Kabbalah," in Mendes-Flohr, *Philosophy of Rosenzweig,* 162–71.

46. Mendes-Flohr, "Rosenzweig and Kant," 298, and "Law and Sacrament," 354. Rosenzweig's words echo Judah Halevi, whose poetry he would soon translate.

47. See the critique on this point in Robert Gibbs, *Correlations in Rosenzweig and Lévinas* (Princeton, N.J.: Princeton University Press, 1992), 96.

48. Amos Funkenstein, *Perceptions of Jewish History* (Berkeley and Los Angeles: University of California Press, 1993), 269–71; see Gibbs, *Correlations,* 120; and Mosès, *System and Revelation,* 174–217. Cf. Rosenzweig on these points with Hans-Georg Gadamer: "For the essence of the festival its historical connections are secondary. As a festival is not an identity, in the manner of an historical event[,] . . . its own original essence is always to be something different. . . . A festival exists only in being celebrated," that is, in being performed differently on each occasion (*Truth and Method,* trans. and ed. Garrett Barden and John Cumming [New York: Crossroad, 1984], 110).

49. See, for example, Rosenzweig, *Star of Redemption,* 405–8.

50. Ibid., 337–79.

51. Funkenstein, *Perceptions of Jewish History,* 292.

52. Cf. Rosenzweig, "Teaching and Law," 240–41; for the original, see Rosenzweig, "Die Bauleute," in *Kleinere Schriften* (Berlin: Schocken, 1937), 106–21.

53. Rosenzweig, *Life and Thought,* 91, 100. My view of their debate differs considerably from that of Howard A. Simon; see his "Martin Buber and the Law," *Journal of the Central Conference of American Rabbis* 2 (1971): 40–44.

54. Rosenzweig, *Star of Redemption,* 164; Rosenzweig to Buber, 4 July 1924, in *Letters of Martin Buber,* 316.

55. Buber to Rosenzweig, 4 July 1924, in *Letters of Martin Buber,* 317. Hence Malcolm Diamond's complaint in a letter to Buber, "I do genuinely believe that your approach is too individuated and that, for all the dangers of sterile observance, the *halakhah* must be corporately developed" (Diamond to Buber, 19 August 1959, in *Letters of Martin Buber,* 628; in English). Diamond's practice was characteristically in advance of his theology. "If I wait to be thus addressed [as a Thou by God], I shall never make any move in that direction. So in one sense, by starting with *tefillin* and Friday services, I shall be doing so in Rosenzweig's spirit, but not with his inclusiveness" (Diamond to Buber, 26 August 1959, in *Letters of Martin Buber,* 629: in English).

56. See Buber, *I and Thou,* 124.

57. Buber to Rosenzweig, 13 July 1924, in *Letters of Martin Buber,* 318.

58. Cf. Bernhard Casper, "Franz Rosenzweig's Critique of Buber's *I and Thou,*" in *Buber Centenary Volume,* 157–59.

59. Buber to Rosenzweig, 13 July 1924, in *Letters of Martin Buber,* 318.

60. Rosenzweig to Buber, 16 July 1924, and Buber to Rosenzweig, 3 June 1925, in *Letters to Martin Buber* 319, 327.

61. According to Maurice Friedman, Buber's biographer and frequent translator, "Nahum Glatzer once remarked that in 'The Builders' Rosenzweig was more Buber than he actually was himself—that he was leaning over backwards to find a common ground of discourse in order to communicate his own position on the Law and persuade Buber to come close to it" (Friedman, *Martin Buber's Life and Work: The Middle Years, 1923–1945* [New York: E. P. Dutton, 1983], 47–48).

62. Luigi Pirandello, *Six Characters in Search of an Author,* in *Three Plays* (New York: E. P. Dutton, 1922), 7.

63. Cf. Gordon and Bloch, *Buber Centenary Volume,* xvi.

64. Pirandello, *Six Characters,* 10.

65. Mendes-Flohr, "Law and Sacrament," 345–49.

66. See my "Re-reading Heschel on the Commandments," *Modern Judaism* 9, no. 1 (February 1989):1–33.

67. Pirandello, *Six Characters,* 18.

68. Rosenzweig, "Teaching and Law," 238.

69. On the Lehrhaus, see, most recently, Michael Brenner, *The Renaissance of Jewish Culture in Weimar Germany* (New Haven, Conn.: Yale University Press, 1996), 69–99.

EIGHT

1. See the extended meditation on this theme by Edward Shils in *Tradition* (Chicago: University of Chicago Press, 1981), particularly the introduction and chaps. 1, 9, and 10. On contemporary traditional architecture, see Carol Vogel, "Clustered for Leisure: The Changing Home," *New York Times Magazine,* 28 June 1987, 16, 125. In the course of writing this chapter, I encountered literally hundreds of vague Jewish appeals to "carry on the tradition."

2. Mordecai M. Kaplan, *Judaism as a Civilization: Towards a Reconstruction of American-Jewish Life* (New York: Macmillan, 1934); see, for example, the usages on 38, 164, 182, 197, 313, 327, and 351–52. I have treated Kaplan's thought at some length in my book *The Chosen People in America: A Study in Jewish Religious Ideology* (Bloomington: Indiana University Press, 1983), 73–98.

3. Kaplan, *Judaism as a Civilization,* 383; and see 350–84.

4. Ibid., 384. See also the passage in another one of his works where Kaplan first notes the ancestors' delusion in locating the center of gravity of their lives in a nonexistent world to come and then forgives their error on the grounds that immense suffering had created a "psychic need" for that belief (*The Meaning of God in Modern Jewish Religion* [New York: Reconstructionist Press, 1962], 50–51).

5. Ibid., *Judaism as a Civilization,* 385.

6. Ibid., 386.

7. Ibid., 388.

8. See ibid., 91–169.

9. Solomon Schechter, "The Seminary as a Witness," in *Seminary Addresses and Other Papers* (New York: Burning Bush Press, 1959), 51.

10. Kaplan, *Judaism as a Civilization,* 389; see also, for example, 336.

11. Ibid., 390.

12. Ibid., 393–415.

13. Kaplan claimed to derive the term "folkways" from the use of *minhag* in "the traditional literature" to denote ritual practices not sanctioned with the full weight of halakhah. William Graham Sumner, undoubtedly Kaplan's actual source for the term (and the conception), was mentioned elsewhere in Kaplan's *Judaism as a Civilization* but not here. Apparently, Kaplan was alert to the need to clothe modern Jewish conceptions in traditional Jewish language, a step that the method of functional revaluation not only legitimated but compelled; see Kaplan, *Judaism as a Civilization,* 431. Kaplan reported that his definition of "civilization" was "a paraphrase of the definition of ethos" (*Judaism,* 535 n. 2) offered in Sumner's book *Folkways* ([Boston, Ginn, 1906], 36). He did not report, however, that Sumner had derived positive law from folk custom—the conception undergirding Kaplan's crucial translation of "mitzvot" as "folkways." Sumner also appears in connection with Kaplan's critique of the chosen people idea; see *Judaism,* chap. 19, 539 n. 4. Other non-Jewish sources, such as Dewey and Durkheim, appear in the body of Kaplan's text and not only in the footnotes. In *The Religion of Ethical Nationhood* (New York: Macmillan, 1970), Kaplan wrote that "the ideas here associated with the term 'civilization' stem from the book *Our Social Heritage* by Graham Wallas, published . . . in 1921" (13). This reference does not appear in *Judaism as a Civilization.*

14. Kaplan, *Judaism as a Civilization,* 433–459.

15. See ibid., 189. I am grateful to my colleague Steven Zipperstein for pointing out the importance of Kaplan's near silence when it came to eastern European Jewry.

16. See Arthur Goren, *New York Jews and the Quest for Community* (New York: Columbia University Press, 1970), 237–48.

17. Kaplan, *Judaism as a Civilization,* 177.

18. Ibid., 182.

19. Kaplan, *Meaning of God,* 2–8.

20. See ibid., 40–43.

21. Ibid., 57–103.

22. See Kaplan, J. Paul Williams, and Eugene Kohn, *The Faith of America* (New York: Schuman, 1951). I discuss this effort in my book *The Chosen People,* 87.

23. Kaplan, *Meaning of God,* 38.

24. Ibid., 134–35, 210, 310.

25. Ibid., 92; cf. *Judaism as a Civilization,* 273, 291.

26. Kaplan, *Meaning of God,* 99.

27. Ibid., 96–98; for the ancestors' errors and Kaplan's explanation and for-giveness, see, for example, 50 and 55.

28. See Mel Scult, *Judaism Faces the Twentieth Century: A Biography of Mordecai M. Kaplan* (Detroit: Wayne State University Press, 1993), 19–33.

29. Charles Liebman, "Reconstructionism in American Jewish Life," *American Jewish Yearbook* (1970): 3–99.

30. Cf. Jenna Weissman Joselit, *The Wonders of America: Reinventing Jewish Culture, 1880–1950* (New York: Hill and Wang, 1994).

31. Judith Plaskow, *Standing Again at Sinai: Judaism from a Feminist Perspective* (San Francisco: Harper and Row, 1990), ix–xviii; a briefer statement, "Standing Again at Sinai: Jewish Memory from a Feminist Perspective," appeared in *Tikkun* 1, no. 2 (1986): 28–34.

32. Plaskow, *Sinai,* 35, 53; and see 1–74; for explicit linkage to the rabbis, see 35 and 53.

33. Ibid., 121.

34. Ibid., 122, 19, 21.

35. See Elliot Dorff, *Conservative Judaism: Our Ancestors to Our Descendants* (New York: United Synagogue of America, 1977).

36. See *Emet Ve-Emunah: Statement of Principles of Conservative Judaism* (New York: Jewish Theological Seminary, Rabbinical Assembly, and United Syna-gogue, 1988), 7–16; see also the foreword, by Kassel Abelson, 1–4. My argu-ment in the remainder of this chapter is drawn from my earlier essay, "American Judaism: Changing Patterns in Denominational Self-Definition, *Studies in Con-temporary Jewry* 8 (1992): 21–49. The Conservative movement has in effect con-ceded the prophets to Reform and the Shulhan Arukh to Orthodoxy, while claiming for itself the broader canvas of history, belief, and practice bequeathed by the sages and known, in the parlance common to the elites of all four con-temporary movements, as "the tradition."

37. Dorff, *Conservative Judaism,* 59–60, 103. The word "tradition" itself looms large in second-generation writings only among Conservative Jews.

38. See Gershom Scholem, "Revelation and Tradition as Religious Catego-ries in Judaism," in *The Messianic Idea in Judaism* (New York: Schocken, 1971), 282–303.

39. See Dorff, *Conservative Judaism,* 79–157, and "Towards a Legal Theory of the Conservative Movement," *Conservative Judaism* 27, no. 3 (summer 1973): 65.

40. Dorff, "Legal Theory," 75–76.

41. Dorff, *Conservative Judaism,* 115.

42. Dorff, "Legal Theory," 76–77.

43. It will not do to say, as Dorff does, that "discovering the psychological

reasons as to why we take the position that we do is far beyond the scope of this paper" ("Legal Theory," 77).

44. Dorff, "Legal Theory," 77.

45. Cf. W. Gunther Plaut, "Reform Judaism—Past, Present, and Future," *Journal of Reform Judaism* (summer 1980): 8. Plaut was referring to *A Shabbat Manual* (New York: Central Conference of American Rabbis, 1972).

46. Plaut, foreword to *Gates of Mitzvah: A Guide to the Jewish Life Cycle,* ed. Simeon J. Maslin (New York: Central Conference of American Rabbis, 1979), ix. For an earlier guide, similar in content and rationale, see Frederic A. Doppelt and David Polish, *A Guide for Reform Jews,* rev. ed. (New York: Ktav, 1957); especially 3–47. For examples of Reform responsa, see Solomon Freehof, *Reform Jewish Practice* (New York: Ktav, 1976), vols. 1–2; the earliest material in these volumes dates to 1944. Freehof is careful to state that his purpose is not to issue "a modern Shulhan Arukh" but "to describe present-day Reform Jewish practices and the traditional rabbinic laws from which they are derived" (15). Thus, "branches of traditional law" widely ignored among Reform Jews, such as Sabbath and dietary laws, are not treated.

47. Maslin, ed., *Gates of Mitzvah,* 3.

48. The 1976 *Statement of Principles* is available in Eugene Borowitz, *Reform Judaism Today* (New York: Behrman House, 1978), 1:xix–xxv.

49. Maslin, ed., *Gates of Mitzvah,* 4; for a different reading of it, see Doppelt and Polish, *Guide for Reform Jews,* 6.

50. Maslin, *Gates of Mitzvah,* 11–16, 30, 37–40, 51, 54–62.

51. Ibid., 100–110. The authors are, respectively, Rabbi Herman Schaalman, Rabbi David Polish, and Rabbi Roland Gittelsohn.

52. Peter S. Knobel, ed., *Gates of the Seasons* (New York: Central Conference of American Rabbis, 1983), 21.

53. See, for example, Leon I. Feuer, "Some Reflections on the State of Reform Judaism," *Reform Judaism Today* (summer 1980): 22–31. Debates on the merits of "reform halakhah" have filled the papers of the *Yearbook* and journals of the Central Conference of American Rabbis in the past two decades.

54. See *Gates of Prayer: The New Union Prayerbook,* ed. Chaim Stern (New York: Central Conference of American Rabbis, 1975); see also the explanatory volume, *Gates of Understanding,* ed. Lawrence Hoffman (New York: Central Conference of American Rabbis, 1977). For more on the reform of Reform liturgy, see my essay "American Judaism: Changing Patterns," 25–30, and the references cited in n. 22, above.

55. Plaut, "Reform Judaism," 7.

56. Scholem, "Revelation and Tradition," 282.

57. Hans-Georg Gadamer, *Truth and Method,* trans. and ed. Garrett Barden and John Cumming (New York: Crossroad, 1975), 241–42; and see 241–74.

58. b. Baba Metzia 59b; b. Menahot 29b.

59. Nicholas de Lange, *Judaism* (Oxford: Oxford University Press, 1987), 1–8; see also the table of contents.

60. Michael Fishbane, *Judaism: Revelation and Tradition* (San Francisco: Harper and Row, 1987), 11–24.

61. Fishbane, *Judaism,* 23.

62. Walter Benjamin, "The Work of Art in the Age of Mechanical Reproduction," in *Illuminations,* ed. Hannah Arendt, trans. Harry Zohn (London: Fontana, 1973), 219–27.

63. See Samuel C. Heilman, *The People of the Book: Drama, Fellowship, and Religion* (Chicago: University of Chicago Press, 1983), 62–65.

CONCLUSION

1. Gershom G. Scholem, *Major Trends in Jewish Mysticism* (New York: Schocken Books, 1954), 349–50.

2. Haym Soloveitchik, "Rupture and Reconstruction: The Transformation of Contemporary Orthodoxy," *Tradition* 28, no. 4 (1994): 74; see also his "Migration, Acculturation, and the New Role of Texts in the Haredi World," in *Accounting for Fundamentalisms,* ed. Martin Marty and R. Scott Appleby (Chicago: University of Chicago Press, 1994).

3. Cf. Debra Orenstein, ed., *Lifecycles: Jewish Women on Life Passages and Personal Milestones* (Woodstock, Vt.: Jewish Lights Publishing, 1994), xxi.

4. I first became acquainted with the genre of feminist Haggadot through the archive of my friend Carol Winograd and by reading Tamara Ruth Cohen, Sue Levi Elwell, and Ronnie M. Horn, eds., "Journey to Freedom" (New York: Ma'yan, The Jewish Women's Project of the Jewish Community Center on the Upper West Side, 1995). I am grateful to the National Council of Jewish Women for making its collections of feminist Haggadot in New York City available to me for purposes of this research, as well as to Tamara Cohen and the other leaders of Ma'yan for sharing their Haggadot with me and directing me to the NCJW archive; all unpublished sources cited in this chapter are available there. For a cogent reflection on the place of feminist seders in larger patterns of feminist and American ritual innovation, see Elaine Moise and Rebecca Schwartz, "The Dancing with Miriam Haggadah" (Palo Alto, Calif., 1995), viii–xv.

5. Menachem Friedman, "Life Traditions and Book Traditions in the Development of Ultra-Orthodox Judaism," in *Judaism Viewed from Within and from Without,* ed. Harvey Goldberg (Albany: State University of New York Press, 1987), 237.

6. Friedman, "The Lost Kiddush Cup: Changes in Ashkenazic Haredi Culture—A Tradition in Crisis," in *The Uses of Tradition: Jewish Continuity in the Modern Era,* ed. Jack Wertheimer, (New York: Jewish Theological Seminary of America, 1992), 178.

7. Soloveitchik, "Rupture and Reconstruction," 68.

8. Samuel C. Heilman and Steven M. Cohen, *Cosmopolitans and Parochials: Modern Orthodoxy in America* (Chicago: University of Chicago Press, 1989), 208. Heilman and Cohen note that "centrist modern Orthodox Jews repeat this pattern of using social acceptance criteria similar to those once used by Jews first emerging from the ghetto" (69).

9. "Plain living and high thinking" are preached, writes Soloveitchik. "Purity, as ever, is the goal," but "the thousand year struggle of the soul with the flesh has finally come to a close. The legitimacy of physical instinct is the end product of Orthodoxy's encounter with modernity," reflecting the "slow but steady infiltration of the this-worldly orientation of the surrounding society" ("Rupture and Reconstruction," 75; and see 81). See also Freidman, "Life Traditions," 249.

10. Recent data show two-thirds of American Jews reporting that they fast on Yom Kippur, four-fifths lighting Hanukkah candles, and almost 90 percent participating in a Passover seder; see Charles S. Liebman and Steven M. Cohen, *Two Worlds of Judaism: The Israeli and American Experience* (New Haven, Conn.: Yale University Press, 1990), 123. For Haggadot in wide use among American Jews, see Herbert Bronstein, ed., *A Passover Haggadah* (New York: Central Conference of American Rabbis, 1974); Chaim Stern, ed., *Gates of Freedom: A Passover Haggadah* (New York: Behrman House, 1982); and Rachel Anne Rabinowitz, ed., *Passover Haggadah: The Feast of Freedom* (New York: Rabbinical Assembly, 1982). The texts by Bronstein and Stern are issued by the Reform movement, that of Rabinowitz by the Conservative movement.

11. See Marshall Sklare and Joseph Greenblum, *Jewish Identity on the Suburban Frontier: A Study of Group Survival in the Open Society,* 2d ed. (Chicago: University of Chicago Press, 1979), 57; cf. Heilman and Cohen, *Cosmopolitans and Parochials,* 69.

12. For the quintessential articulation of this theme, see Michael Walzer, *Exodus and Revolution* (New York: Basic Books, 1985).

13. The issue of identity and inclusiveness surfaces again in the readings chosen by the authors of the Haggadot and in the ancestors they recall. Compare the Jewish choices in Tamara Cohen et al., eds., "From Slavery to Freedom, from Darkness to Light" (New York: Ma'yan, the Jewish Women's Project, 1994), with the citations from Kate Millett, Virginia Woolf, and others in Sherry Flashperson [*sic*] and Margaret Fuller Sablove, "Feminist Seder" (Amherst, Mass., 1973).

14. On the distinction between these two stages of feminist achievement, see Susannah Heschel, *On Being a Jewish Feminist: A Reader* (New York: Schocken Books, 1983), 3–11; and Sylvia Barack Fishman, *A Breath of Life: Feminism in the American Jewish Community* (New York: Free Press, 1993).

15. The realizations achieved by the "wise daughter" and eluding the other three in the paragraph of the four sons/children are generally the truths held to

be self-evident by the Enlightenment. "We will be slaves to no nation and before no man" (E. M. Broner, *The Telling* [San Francisco: Harper, 1994], 197). The shank bone on the seder plate in one text represents the paradox of women's lives: saved, by the denial of full participation in the world, from much of the destruction visited by and upon men. The roasted egg represents the artificial confinement of women to the biological role of childbearer; see Sherry Flashman and Margaret Fuller Sablove, "The Feminist Seder" (Amherst, Mass., 1976), 2. One humorous commentator on an early feminist text got the point exactly right when she wrote that it made her wonder whether God is an Equal Opportunity Employer; see Eleanor Lester, "New Haggadah Designed for Women Family Heads Shuns Some Masculinisms," *Jewish Week–American Examiner*, 8 April 1979, 8.

16. Exception is taken in the feminist texts to the Kantian paradigm at only one point: the postmodern and feminist rejection of "totalizing discourse." The Haggadot evince the same tension on this point as do feminist theoreticians who, while suspicious of absolutist claims, are uncomfortable with the postmodern distrust of ethical imperatives. "Postmodernism, in its infinitely skeptical and subversive attitude toward normative claims, institutional justice, and political struggles, is certainly refreshing," writes Seila Benhabib; "Yet, it is also debilitating" (*Situating the Self* [New York: Routledge, 1992], 15; see also 203–30). For the normative claims made in women's haggadot constitute (or at least function as) absolutes. The ethics they expound are not merely the preferences of persons or communities: oppression of women is held to be fact and not only value. The enemies enumerated in the course of the seder are held to be evil and not merely proponents of legitimate opposing points of view. However, respect is routinely demanded for a multitude of voices associated with divergent genders, classes, and cultures. "Hearing women's voices" is standard operating procedure, with women regarded as but one example of the many voices suppressed by "totalizing" notions of the truth.

17. Yael Zerubavel, *Recovered Roots: Collective Memory and the Making of Israeli National Tradition* (Chicago: University of Chicago Press, 1995); xiv; see also 218–20.

18. See Charles Liebman and Eliezer Don-Yehiya, *Civil Religion in Israel* (Berkeley and Los Angeles: University of California Press, 1983). The connection made in the Israeli calendar between Passover, Holocaust Remembrance Day, and Independence Day is analyzed in Don Handelman, *Models and Mirrors: Towards an Anthropology of Public Events* (Cambridge: Cambridge University Press, 1990), 194–200. For a theological articulation of the linkage, see Eliezer Schweid, *Sefer Mahazor ha-zemanim: Mashma 'utam shel hagei Yisra'el* [The cycle of appointed times: the meaning of Jewish holidays] (Tel Aviv: Am Oved Publishers, 1984), in which Independence Day receives the primacy awarded in the American Jewish calendar to Passover.

19. *Haggada Shel Pesach: Seder Pesach Ba-kibbutz* [Passover Haggadah: The Passover seder on kibbutz] (Tel Aviv: Ha-kibbutz Ha-me'uḥad, 1995), 12–13, 22, 52–55, 62–63.

20. The Haggadah has throughout the ages stimulated an outpouring of artistic creativity not matched by any other Jewish ritual or text; see Yosef Hayim Yerushalmi, *Haggadah and History* (Philadelphia: Jewish Publication Society, 1975).

21. Cohen, "From Slavery to Freedom," 1; "Seder of the Shechina" (Tallahassee, 1990), 4; the phrase "because wherever you live, it is probably Egypt" comes from Walzer, *Exodus and Revolution*.

22. Cf. Laila Gal Berner, ed., "Her Seder: A Celebration of Struggle and Survival" (New York: American Jewish Congress, 1993), 7.

23. The text at the extreme of this continuum, "Pesach with the Goddess," blesses the Asherah at kiddush, "queen mother of the universe, who createst the fruit of the vine"—this, while urging that the four questions be recited in Hebrew if at all possible and while using the Hebrew form of the holiday's name in the title; see "Pesach with the Goddess, Planned by Three Witches" (Oakland, Calif., n.d.). In another text, the matzah featured in the four questions means only the "plain and simple truth" about women's lives, bitter herbs connote "our connection to our fury," dipping twice indicates the abundance of women's resources, and reclining symbolizes that women are "connected to sensuality and proud of it"—none of them Jewish meanings; see Anna Rubin, ed., "Women's Passover Seder" (Los Angeles, 1977). Others borrow on traditional symbols in order to critique the messages which normally accompany them. "Why do we dip into the wine of history?" asks one popular (and especially acerbic) text, given that the answer to "What still plagues us?" is "The pestilence of tradition, the affliction of customs, the calamity of rabbinic decree" (Broner, *The Telling*, 194). See also Fayla Schwartz, Susie Coliver, and Elaine Ayela, "Pesach Hagadah: A Statement of Joyous Liberation" (Berkeley, Calif., 1973), 4.

24. One unpublished text from 1973 cites women's exclusion from the arts, universities, and leadership of labor unions; see Schwartz, Coliver, and Ayela, "Pesach Haggadah: A Statement of Joyous Liberation." "The Feminist Seder" of 1976 lists secretarial and editorial work, waitressing, elementary school teaching, nursing, and the like, as well as sexual relations with men, marriage, and childbirth; see Flashman and Sablove, "The Feminist Seder," 11. An Indiana University student text of 1978 lists menstruation, childbirth and bringing up children, and waiting on husbands. "The San Diego Women's Haggadah" (San Diego, 1990), lists the consistently male image of God and the lack of recognition for female rabbis and scholars, "the prison created by the rigid traditional views of men and women. From these plagues, Judaism and women must be freed" (41–42). Finally, several of the most recent texts seem to betoken a return

from anger to inclusiveness, expressed in a renewed universalization and personalization (though not Judaization) of import. "From Slavery to Freedom" speaks of "the blood shed by handguns, . . . the countless babies who die each year from drug addiction, AIDS, violence and war" (12). The dipping in saltwater, "Journey to Freedom" instructs us, should be "personal and intimate, a momentary submersion like the first step into the Red Sea. Like entering a mikvah. We will not partake of our seder feast until we undergo this symbolic purification. Because our freedom was bought with the suffering of others" (14). Clearly, symbolization remains a predominant strategy in ascribing meaning to ritual practice.

25. Mordecai Kaplan's Haggadah is an obvious case in point; see Mordecai M. Kaplan, Eugene Kohn, and Ira Eisenstein, *The New Haggadah for the Pesah Seder* (New York: Behrman House, 1942); and see also Arthur Waskow, ed., *The Shalom Seders* (New York: Adama Books, 1984).

26. Soloveitchik, "Rupture and Reconstruction," 71; Friedman, "Life Traditions," 240.

27. "And I cooked," prompts one text in the section devoted to the four daughters. "Twenty pounds of gefilte fish. Chicken soup with dill. Knaidlach. Flanken and tsimmes on the stove, a turkey in the oven. Four desserts." That Haggadah proceeds, characteristically, to express (and so to solicit, legitimate, and elevate) sentiments that in nonfeminist texts are normally left to the participants' own invention. "Mom left me her Passover pots and dishes, and every year, when I unpack the boxes, it's as if she's there, working with me" (Cohen, "From Slavery to Freedom," 10).

28. Schwartz, "Pesach Haggadah," 4; Broner and Naomi Nimrod, "The Stolen Legacy: A Women's Haggadah" (n.p., n.d.), 3. The Broner and the San Diego Haggadot both include a wicked daughter who demands to know what women could possibly have to say to or learn from one another; see *San Diego Haggadah,* 20; and Broner, *The Telling,* 195. See also Twin Cities Women's Minyan, "Women's Passover Seder" (Minneapolis–Saint Paul, 1981), 8.

29. Moses' natural and adoptive mothers also receive attention, as do the midwives who defied Pharaoh's decree to destroy all Israelite baby boys. The covenant made with Abraham, Isaac, and Jacob is extended to include Sarah, Rebecca, Rachel, and Leah. And the foremothers, in turn, clear a path for stories of other Jewish women over the centuries, including a few—such as Gluckel and Emma Goldman—who appear almost as regularly as the paradigmatic ancestors; see Cohen, "From Slavery to Freedom," 19, and "Journey to Freedom," 25.

30. For typical examples of the dynamics of nostalgia that I have described, see "San Diego Women's Haggadah," 18; and Cohen, "Journey to Freedom," 1. The power of these sections in women's seders approaches, though it cannot equal, the power in a seder of holocaust survivors, the text of which is inter-

spersed with personal stories of liberation from the camps; see "The Telling: Child Survivors' Passover Haggadah" (Los Angeles, 1982). In some texts, particularly those of the student groups, one suspects that "issues" with absent mothers are not far from consciousness. The tables to which one has not gone home at Passover are places of struggles as yet unresolved. Singing hymns "to our mothers" may, in that case, express desires more immediate than ancestral veneration, at the same time providing a level of comfort unavailable when real mothers are actually in the room; see, for example, the "Oberlin Women's Haggadah," (Oberlin, Ohio, 1984), 29.

31. Cf. "San Diego Women's Haggadah," 68–73.

32. In one text, it is the vaguest of promises, rather than God, which "has supported our foremothers and forefathers, and ourselves." The traditional claim that "the Holy One saved us from their hands" at once dissolves in the statement, recognizably truer in the authors' minds, that "in every generation there have arisen against us those who would destroy us and we have not yet been delivered from their hand." There is no *hallel* prayer of praise to God in Broner's seder, or in many others', and no redemption at its conclusion. The closest one gets is "under the wings of the Shekhinah, we fly homeward to Zion in song" (Broner, *The Telling*, 195, 202–3, 216). Finally, the message of God's noninvolvement is reinforced when one opens the door to Miriam after the meal instead of to Elijah, traditional herald of divine, messianic redemption. Miriam "soon will come to us with timbrel and song. Miriam our prophet, will dance with us"—the change points dramatically to the absence in almost every feminist Haggadah of a God who redeems (Broner, *The Telling*, 216).

33. Cf. Flashman and Sablove, "Feminist Seder," 7.

34. Cohen, "From Slavery to Freedom," 21, 23, 30. Marcia Falk's work is also used in "Seder of the Shechina"; in Marisa Brett, Jocellyn Krupp, and Holly Lowy, "A Feminist Haggadah" (Williams College, 1992); and in "Passover Haggadah" (White Plains, N.Y., 1993). For a statement of her rationale, see Marcia Falk, "New Blessings: Towards a Feminist-Jewish Reconstruction of Prayer," *Reconstructionist* 53, no. 3 (December 1987): 10–15, 22. The blessings are developed in full in Marcia Falk, *The Book of Blessings* (San Francisco: Harper, 1996).

35. Soloveitchik, "Rupture and Reconstruction," 98–102.

36. Judith Hauptman, "Death and Mourning: A Time for Weeping, a Time for Healing," in *Celebration and Renewal: Rites of Passage in Judaism,* ed. Rela M. Geffen (Philadelphia: Jewish Publication Society, 1993), 228–29.

37. See Kaplan, *The New Haggadah for the Pesah Seder;* see also n. 25, above.

38. Cohen, *Journey to Freedom,* 30–31.

39. "Symbols of a Desert Exile Bloom in Jews' Backyards," *New York Times,* 14 October 1995, 21.

40. Dean R. Hoge, Benton Johnson, and Donald A. Luidens, *Vanishing*

Boundaries: The Religion of Mainline Protestant Baby-Boomers (Louisville: John Knox Press, 1994), 12, 131, 181–82. On recent trends in Protestant and yuppie religion, see also Wade Clark Roof, *A Generation of Seekers* (San Francisco: Harper, 1993); Roof and William McKinney, *American Mainline Religion* (New Brunswick, N.J.: Rutgers University Press, 1987); and Robert N. Bellah, Richard Madsen, William M. Sullivan, Ann Swidler, and Steven M. Tipton, *Habits of the Heart: Individualism and Commitment in American Life* (New York: Harper and Row, 1986).

41. Recital of prayers for the sick have recently taken on a new importance in Conservative synagogues—arguably, at the initiative of women.

42. On American Jews' universalism, see Liebman and Cohen, *Two Worlds of Judaism,* 27–32, 96–122.

43. Gerson Cohen, "The Framework of Religious Vitality," *Conservative Judaism* 39, no. 3 (January–February 1981): 8.

44. See Jack Kugelmass, "Green Bagels: An Essay on Food, Nostalgia, and the Carnivalesque," *YIVO Annual* (1990): 57–80.

45. Cf. Arnold Eisen, *Taking Hold of Torah: Jewish Commitment and Community in America* (Bloomington: Indiana University Press, 1997).